Negotiating Difference
in French Louisiana Music

AMERICAN MADE MUSIC SERIES
Advisory Board

David Evans, General Editor
Barry Jean Ancelet
Edward A. Berlin
Joyce J. Bolden
Rob Bowman
Susan C. Cook
Curtis Ellison
William Ferris
John Edward Hasse
Kip Lornell
Bill Malone
Eddie S. Meadows
Manuel H. Peña
Wayne D. Shirley
Robert Walser

Negotiating Difference in French Louisiana Music

CATEGORIES, STEREOTYPES, AND IDENTIFICATIONS

SARA LE MENESTREL

UNIVERSITY PRESS OF MISSISSIPPI • JACKSON

www.upress.state.ms.us

The University Press of Mississippi is a member of the Association of American University Presses.

Designed by Peter D. Halverson

All photos taken by the author unless otherwise noted

Copyright © 2015 by University Press of Mississippi
All rights reserved
Manufactured in the United States of America

∞

Library of Congress Cataloging-in-Publication Data

Le Menestrel, Sara, author.
Negotiating difference in French Louisiana music : categories, stereotypes, and identifications / Sara Le Menestrel.
        pages cm
Includes bibliographical references and index.
ISBN 978-1-62846-145-9 (cloth : alk. paper) — ISBN 978-1-62846-146-6 (ebook) 1. Difference (Philosophy) in music. 2. Cajun music—Louisiana—History and criticism. 3. Folk music—Louisiana—History and criticism. 4. Zydeco music—Louisiana—History and criticism. 5. Popular music—Social aspects—Louisiana—History. 6. Cajuns—Louisiana—Social life and customs. I. Title.
    ML3560.C25L4 2015
781.62'410763—dc23   2014024114

British Library Cataloging-in-Publication Data available

To sharing music,

the source of one of the most intense and demanding pleasures in my life.

Contents

Acknowledgments ix

Introduction 3

1. The Early Twentieth Century
A Diverse Musical Landscape 35

2. Inside and Outside the Box 75

3. The Color of Music 147

4. Homegrown and Lowdown 203

5. Choosing French Louisiana 265

Conclusion 317

Notes 322

Sources 355

Index 373

Acknowledgments

Along the sinuous path of writing this book, I had the privilege of meeting a number of people whose presence and support made my work not only possible but more joyous and worthwhile.

My deepest gratitude goes to the many people who so generously gave their time through the interviews and conversations that have shaped this manuscript. I have made every possible effort to approach sensitive issues with discernment and to emphasize their intricacy. My sincere hope is that I was able to meet this challenge.

Throughout the years, my many musician friends have been crucial to my understanding of French Louisiana music and have generously shared their experience and expertise, as well as their hospitality, while nurturing me with their music. Christine Balfa and Dirk Powell guided me through my early steps, as did Rose and Earl Broussard and Jane and the late Wilson Gaspard; Sam Broussard very patiently explained and shared his extended knowledge in music theory throughout the writing process despite the distance between us; David Greely readily discussed, and Mitch Reed never counted the time we spent at his shop chatting, playing, teaching me new tunes, drinking fresh coffee, and discovering French cheese; Ben Sandmel shared his numerous contacts, greatly facilitated some interviews, showed empathy when I needed it, and has made himself available for me throughout the years; Joel Breaux and Lisa Bourque inspired me to include transplants and helped me in my difficult quest for informants about the musical landscape of the early twentieth century, as did Lisa Trahan. Linda Castle, Lori Henderson and her husband Tom Pierce, Missy Maloney, and Andrea Rubinstein embraced my presence, welcomed my son, opened a whole new circle for me, and greatly enriched my analysis through their itineraries, as did many other jammers too numerous to name. Dominick Cross and Nicole Boudreau made themselves available to transcribe some of my interviews. In France, Sarah Savoy helped me understand some musical theory, as did Vincent Blin, and her friendship and presence in Montreuil kept me connected with South Louisiana tastes and sounds.

Other friends have also been extremely helpful in sharing their experience and memories, helping me think things through, connecting me with helpful contacts, escorting me to music clubs, and opening their homes year after year. Warm thanks to Tim Anderson and his sister Jackie, Nicole Boudreau, Dana David, Herman Fuselier, Jacques and Pascale Henry, Shane and Angelique Hernandez, Susan Mouton, Shannon Neveaux and Kevin LeMaire, Heddy and Philip Nunez, Glen Pitre and Michelle Benoit, and Corey Porche for their precious friendship. I am especially and forever indebted to the entire Baudoin clan (Cynthia, Ray, Danielle, Adrian, Phyllis, Gina, and their families) for tolerating my extended presence in their homes over the past twenty years and treating me like one of their own. In New Orleans, my sincere thanks to Neti Vaan, who opened her home to me for extended periods of time and supported my work, and to Joel Dinerstein and Garnette Cadogan for first guiding me through the city's many dives, clubs, and restaurants. For graciously allowing me to use photographs, I am very grateful to Joseph A. Rosen, Bruce Raeburn, Ben Sandmel, and Lafayette Parish Clerk of Court Louis J. Perret. Many thanks to Francis Pavy for his soulful *Mystic Fiddler Suite*, a fabulous piece with multiple layers of meanings that fit this book perfectly.

A number of other Louisiana friends and colleagues have been generous with their critical feedback and helpful support. I owe a deep debt of gratitude to Bruce Raeburn at the Hogan Archive for his crucial expertise and guidance with the unexplored musical interactions between New Orleans and Acadiana, for his perspicacious comments on the first chapter, and for his enduring friendship. Thanks to Jacques Henry for teamwork and support throughout the years; to Carl Brasseaux for his encouragement at the beginning of this project and for his helpful contacts and ideas; to Kevin Fontenot for suggesting sources; and to Nick Spitzer for his interest.

The ideas developed in this book have been presented over the years in conferences and lectures at universities in the United States, in Quebec, and in Paris at the Center for North American Studies of the Ecole des hautes études en science sociales, where I have found continuous collegial support and stimulating exchanges throughout the years. Special thanks to Cécile Vidal for her stimulating feedback and ideas on common topics of interest.

Among my colleagues in France, the Musmond research team that I coordinated was invaluable in testing my hypotheses, refining my ideas, and helping my research strive for a more global perspective. Christophe Apprill, Kali Argyriadis, Julien Mallet, Nicolas Puig, Guillaume Samson, and Gabriel Segré helped foster an environment that combined camaraderie and intense work sessions. Special thanks to Christian Rinaudo and Guillaume Samson, who gave graciously of their time to share insightful comments on this manuscript and to Thomas Grillot for his careful reading of the introduction. For their financial support, my particular thanks to the International Research Fellowship of the Deep South Regional Humanities Center at Tulane University (New Orleans), to the Agence nationale de la recherche (ANR Musmond), and to Mondes Américains, my research laboratory in Paris. I would also like to express my appreciation to Craig Gill from the University Press of Mississippi for his support and patience throughout the editing process, to the anonymous reader for his insightful comments and suggestions, and to copyeditor Will Rigby for his meticulous work. Many thanks to Philippe Bucamp and Florent Chambaret for helping with the digitizing of the illustrations.

John Angell's encouragement and interest were priceless throughout the laborious writing process and he gave me the time and space to complete this project. Knowing that he would be my editorial assistant gave me confidence in my ability to write in English, and his familiarity with the field reassured me about his own understanding of my manuscript. Our son Victor greatly enriched my experience in the field through his high spirits and contagious enthusiasm, and I hope this book will nurture his sense of connectedness to Louisiana, and help him understand mine.

Negotiating Difference
in French Louisiana Music

Introduction

Descending onto the tarmac from the small regional jet in Lafayette, Louisiana, the first sensory impression is of hitting a wall of moist, fragrant air with a palpable weight bearing the smoky note of Spanish moss mixed with diesel fumes and asphalt. A small southern American city, Lafayette sprawls outward in a landscape as flat as a table from a renovated downtown district toward a web of suburbs that are gradually engulfing nearby small towns.

As in other cities of its size, the major thoroughfares are lined with shopping centers, some clearly thriving while others reveal bare shop fronts and acres of empty parking lots.

The luxuriant vegetation is striking, both in the semi-tropical environment that reaches into the suburban grid and the plantings that line the streets and surround the tidy lawns and houses. Depending on the season, the lush green is tinged with color: in spring, azaleas of every hue, and later, gardenias and magnolia trees perfume the air, with the spicier, more elusive fragrance of sweet olive with the approach of fall. Among the many trees are live oaks, the most ancient spreading their arching branches over broad areas where nothing else prospers.

Their shade provides some relief from the often unrelenting heat, but in the height of summer even their dense foliage offers little respite from the oppressive humidity. Driving away from the city in almost every direction, the suburbs gradually give way to fields and woods, punctuated by swamps and lazy, sinuous bayous that flow almost imperceptibly toward the Gulf of Mexico. Sugarcane fields sometimes dominate the view from the highways, reaching seven or eight feet in height in the summer months, interspersed with fields of soybeans and other row crops.

Water defines the region as much as land, and in lower areas, flooded paddies alternate seasons between rice and crawfish; during the cooler months, these watery fields are dotted with the brightly-colored collars of crawfish traps, as great blue herons compete with farmers for these valued crustaceans. The image of the region is inseparable from water and from the wetlands and bald cypress swamps that were long exploited for seemingly inexhaustible timber. Travelers heading West on I-10 toward Lafayette traverse mile after mile of swampland and forest before emerging onto a long, elevated stretch of highway over the silvery expanse of Henderson Swamp and its thousands of stumps. Occasional groves of larger cypresses, their feathery foliage and tapering trunks reflected in the tea-colored water, provide a glimpse of the original swamp forests of the vast Atchafalaya Basin. Once a natural part of the floodplain of the Mississippi River, the basin is now tamed by a system of dikes and floodgates, part of an extensive system of flood control.

The region's swamps, bayous, and lakes are home to a range of mammals (including legions of raccoons and nutria and an endangered black bear sub-species), birds (egrets, roseate spoonbills, herons, and other waterfowl), reptiles (alligators, water moccasins), and myriad other creatures. An evening by Lake Martin or nearly any wetland area is an experience for all the senses, with bull alligators and roosting birds joining the whine of mosquitoes and other insects and the rollicking frog section in a sometimes deafening tropical orchestra. The frequent clatter and hoot of trains provide a reminder of the busy rail line that crisscrosses the region on its way between the East and the great West and Pacific regions, rhythm for the evening's concert.

On a warm April evening in 2008 not too distant from this natural symphony, local musician Cedric Watson celebrated the release of his first CD at the Blue Moon Saloon in downtown Lafayette. The parking lot was full of cars and pickups parked at every angle, and music wafted into the garden surrounding the saloon's covered porches. Sharply turned out in a straw hat and striped shirt, Cedric's beaming face was framed by a neat, narrow beard. Accompanied by Chris Stafford on guitar, Zydeco Mike in his Rasta cap on tambourine and *frottoir* (washboard), Jermaine Prejean on drums, and Thomas David on bass, Cedric played his way through the album along with others of his favorites, among them the instrumental "Two-step de Bouki,"[1] an original, with Chris stepping in at times for a guitar solo and Cedric displaying his distinctive solo style. The playlist continued with the fiddle tune "Blues à bébé," from the late Creole fiddler Bébé Carriere; "Dambala," in tribute to the late Zydeco player Beau Jocque and accompanied by a washboard solo; "Ma Chère Grand-Mère," recorded in honor of his grandmother; "I Just Wanna Be Your Lovin' Man," recorded by the late John Delafose; "Dog Hill," punctuated by the simulated barking of dogs, a tribute to the late zydeco pioneer Boozoo Chavis. After honoring the zydeco pantheon, Cedric switched from accordion to fiddle: "Here is some Creole zydeco, whatever you wanna call it." He followed with "Chère Joues Roses," "Colinda," and "Y en a des 'Tites Brunes," songs usually labeled as Cajun classics, followed by "Bluerunner," known as a Creole classic.

The intricate interplay between sounds and smells continues in the fall as the cooling breezes bear the faintly sweet molasses aroma of burning chaff in the region's sugarcane fields. Cooler weather introduces other notes, both outdoors—a ride south of Lafayette brings the powerful aroma of marinating tabasco peppers near Avery Island—and in friends' kitchens, where chicory-laced coffee mingles with simmering gumbo in a black cast-iron pot. The dark, browned roux of the season's first chicken-and-sausage gumbo—a powerful bass note—will later be served over rice in a steaming bowl with potato salad on the side. On other days, the same kitchen might be perfumed by jambalaya or boiled shrimp, ready to peel and eat. Best of all, the shrimp are simmered with the holy trinity (the core of many regional dishes—finely chopped onions, celery, and bell peppers) and tomatoes and other secret ingredients in a rich *etouffee*. For sustenance in between convivial meals of these substantial, highly spiced dishes, a quick snack from the corner filling station might involve spicy, hot boudin sucked from its skin with one hand while the other balances a cold Miller Lite or Abita beer.

The alliance of the gustatory and the musical is perfectly embodied by Linzay Young, the leader of the Red Stick Ramblers and a celebrated cook, who never travels without his large cast-iron pot. Linzay and his band founded a festival called the South Louisiana Black Pot Festival and Cookoff that is held each year at the Acadian Village, a historic park on the outskirts of Lafayette. I spent the weekend of October 29–30, 2010, at the Black Pot, and on the program on Friday night were Les Malfecteurs, with lead fiddler Blake Miller and second fiddle Daniel Coolick, originally from Georgia, who performed dressed like the Blues Brothers in white shirts, black pants, and dark glasses. Later, Horace Trahan, who had recently returned to the music scene, drove the crowd wild with numbers from his then new CD, *Keep Walking*. With his customary confident air, he and his band pounded out innovative sounds that blended regional and R&B accents into a seductive, rhythmic groove. The interplay of saxophone and washboard (played by his father-in-law) seemed to compel dancing, while his wife sat in front of the stage in a corner, selling CDs. The Pine Leaf Boys came later in the evening lineup with a new mix of songs, some of them in English, and a rock-and-roll demeanor in their stage presence. A separate stage in the nearby chapel featured vocalist and fiddler Suzy Thompson, one of the first musicians from California to migrate to south Louisiana to learn to play local music. Her eclectic playlist included Dennis McGee tunes, Bessie Smith blues numbers like "Easy Come, Easy Go," and Appalachian old-time songs.

Jams formed almost organically, as clusters of musicians and spectators gathered here and there among the park's ponds and outbuildings. One larger cluster of about forty people centered around Ginny Hawker and Tracy Schwartz, two pillars of the old-time music scene, on the porch of one of the park's historic Cajun houses. Jams also spread among the tents and RVs competing for space in the adjacent campground. Offerings at the festival's food concessions contrast with the traditional cuisine of the cook-off and the fare offered at most other local festivals in catering to out-of-staters, including Appalachian old-time music fans. Along with the familiar smells of seafood and gumbo, the air carries whiffs of vegetarian cabbage rolls and soups that will be washed down with non-alcoholic beverages and even hot chocolate along with the more typical Abita beer.

Because it coincides with Halloween, the festival has an additional parodic overtone. On Saturday, a costume contest satirized local subjects and news events—one group was costumed as Chilean coal miners (reflecting the happy ending of a crisis in Chile); there was also a pair of pseudo-aerobics performers, a woman in a skirt composed of sponges (in reference to the Save-the-Gulf movement and the BP oil spill). Tony, an Irish musician and longtime transplant, was disguised as a baby on a woman's back. The weekend festival culminated in their signature performance before a wildly enthusiastic crowd.

The Black Pot Festival is one of many events that reflect the impressive concentration of cultural offerings, which is disproportionate relative to similar-sized cities. This is particularly true of the local music scene: On nearly any day of the week, there is a choice of jams and workshops, and weeknights offer a range of choices for music fans that is even greater on weekends. The visual arts have grown in popularity, accommodated by the Acadiana Center for the Arts, whose newly constructed theater has dramatically increased the profile of the performing arts as well. This startling cosmopolitanism in a small southern city is immediately striking, even to the casual visitor.

The town of Lafayette has grown considerably during the more than ten years in which this project has evolved. There has been a noticeable trend for cafés and restaurants to cater to outsiders, their patios often full, a change also mirrored in the increasing availability of fresh, organic produce at a farmers' market and even an upmarket grocery store, Fresh Market. The downtown strip has flourished and expanded outwards toward other streets and neighborhoods, with new music venues and bars as well as galleries and shops. The population (approximately 120,000 in 2010) has grown considerably, increasing by over 18 percent between 2000 and 2012.[2]

Identifications and Musical Categorizations[3]

THE CREOLE STATE

The various music categories explored in this book must be situated within a complex history of multiple legacies and identifications. Louisiana is sometimes referred to in academic publications or tourist brochures as the "Creole State." The state lays claim to Creoleness in part to distinguish itself from the rest of North America and to underscore its singularity and originality, which are attributed to its French and Spanish colonial heritage, numerous migratory waves (both voluntary and forced), and the ongoing influence of significant numbers of free people of color during the time of slavery. These claims to a Creole character arise from a culture defined by mixing, but the term is used in specific but highly variable ways in references to the region's cuisine, architecture, language, music, and individuals as well as groups. The multiple meanings of the term *Creole* are the result of a complex history that involves successive re-appropriations. The term first appeared during the sixteenth century and is typically traced to its Portuguese origins in the word *crioulo*, which literally meant "bred" or "brought up." It appears to have first been used in the slave trade to apply to the children of African slaves who were born in America to distinguish them from those who were captured in Africa. It later came to apply to Spanish settlers born in the colonies. Eventually, it encompassed anyone—or any product—of local origin, in other words, that originated in America. But these meanings are nevertheless highly variable and are used depending on historical and geographical contexts. Although the use of the term *creole* in Louisiana under the French colonial administration (1699–1763) was stripped of its racial dimension, French historian Cécile Vidal has noted a distinction between external and internal uses of the term.[4] "Creole" was in fact used by metropolitan French to refer to colonials as an indicator of difference, whereas in the interior of the colony, the term was apparently seldom used by French settlers with reference to themselves. Some sources indicate that slaves, to whom the term was applied, may have appropriated the term within the context of a conflictual relationship between Creole (i.e., American-born) and African slaves. Only after the Louisiana Purchase by the United States in 1803 did the designation become generalized to all inhabitants who were born in Louisiana, regardless of their origins. A distinction was nevertheless maintained between the plural form "Creoles," used to describe the former population settled since French and later Spanish colonization, and the new francophone residents who moved to Louisiana from Saint Domingue (arriving in 1809–10) or metropolitan France, who were described as Foreign French.

The massive in-migration of "*Américains*" and their takeover of the territory situated claims of a Creole identity within a relationship of domination. Francophones became increasingly marginalized. Dominated by the Anglo-Americans who coopted their economic and social power, who suspected that they even shared the blood of their colored local residents, the white Creoles felt threatened with becoming confused with black Creoles. They were prompted to develop a Creole mythology around a strictly white definition of pure bloodlines.

Following the Civil War, the emancipation of slaves eliminated the legal distinction between free people of color and newly freed slaves. The advent of Jim Crow segregation laws in the 1890s dispossessed Creoles of color of their "in-between" status and property. In 1900, for the first time, the census used the label "black" to apply to all blacks or descendants of blacks, no matter what fraction, by eliminating the "mulatto" category. Creoles of color's persistent class consciousness expressed itself through strategies of distinction, such as enduring endogamous alliances and the creation of distinct communities throughout the prairies. In fact, the sociologist Frances Woods describes a process of enclavement in the late nineteenth and early twentieth century. By 1910, however, the most economically successful French-speaking freedmen had begun to intermarry with less affluent Creoles of color. Creoles of color also assumed leadership roles during the struggles against segregation and discrimination against the black population as a whole, and later in the civil rights movement. Scholarly works on Louisiana Creoles have emphasized a lasting and ongoing ambivalence among Creoles toward black activism not necessarily incompatible with the claim of a distinct identity, an ambivalence that this book will explore throughout the music field and that I have regularly encountered during the twenty years I have been familiar with the field.[5]

According to the historian Carl Brasseaux, residents who currently identify themselves as Creoles are generally not descendants of free people of color but of French-speaking slaves emancipated after the end of slavery, a point of view somewhat mitigated through subsequent intermarriage across the generations.[6] In any case, self-description as Creole regardless of ancestry is hardly surprising considering that the term evoked a status that set such groups apart from the English-speaking protestant majority of African Americans. This may explain why the designation "black Creole" arose in the 1980s as a more inclusive identification as both African American and Creole. The new category also enabled a distinction to be maintained relative to other Creoles groups in the area, particularly those from the Cane River community and New Orleans who claim a distinct identity as neither whites nor African Americans. The color specification has since dwindled down, however, and Creole is now the preferred designation in southwest Louisiana, thus only perpetuating the multiple meanings and ambiguities surrounding the term.

This ambiguity is noticeable in the different perceptions of Creole identity in present-day Louisiana and is particularly evident in the discourses and practices of French Louisiana music. Depending on interactional settings and social factors as well as the specific region, Creoles can currently define themselves simultaneously as African American and Creole or as exclusively Creole. In the latter case, they do not claim to have been descended from slaves, and this inheritance can even be distorted in favor of mixing, which is perceived as superior to its European, African, or Native American components.[7]

1.2. "CAJUN COUNTRY"

In tandem with the development of a Creole identity in south Louisiana during the twentieth century, a regional "Cajun" identity has become a much-prized generic term used to describe everything that comes from Acadiana, including people, products, and businesses. The term *Cajun* is a derivative of *Acadian*, a reference to the history of the Acadians that is inseparable from the regional collective memory and is widely present in the region's official narrative. The original Acadians were French colonists in the New World who established a trading post in Port Royal in present-day Nova Scotia in 1604.[8] After repeated failed settlements, the colony was revived in 1632, and by 1654 the Acadian population counted three hundred people. According to historian Carl Brasseaux, at least 55 percent of Acadia's seventeenth-century immigrants were natives of provinces of west-central France.[9] They shared a common socio-economic background as *laboureurs*, a term that described the most prosperous group of peasant farmers.

Following repeated changes in the governance of the colony, Acadia was finally acquired by the British in the Treaty of Utrecht in 1713 that ended the War of the Spanish Succession. Outnumbered by their Acadian subjects, the British were anxious to extract an oath of allegiance. Negotiations were concluded only in 1730, with verbal assurances that the Acadians—who had refused the military draft—could retain neutral status in future Anglo-French conflicts. Growing tensions between the French and British North-American empires embroiled Acadians in a power struggle with the colonial government, however. The new governor, Charles Lawrence, advocated deportation, an old plan that had been rejected for lack of funding and troops. But the novelty was to expel them toward other British colonies as part of a plan for linguistic and religious assimilation.[10] Lawrence demanded an unconditional oath of allegiance from the Acadians, whose refusal served as a pretext for the execution of his plan. On July 31, 1755, the deportation of the Acadian population was ordered, and it continued on a smaller scale throughout subsequent years. Among the 12,000 Acadians, approximately 6,000 were separated from their spouses, detained and sent into exile, while their property was confiscated and their houses and crops burned. They were dispersed among the English colonies to the south along the Atlantic seaboard (the Carolinas, Georgia, Massachusetts, Connecticut, Pennsylvania, and New York), as well as England. For many Acadians, these expulsions began a long period of wandering. Transported on overcrowded vessels and suffering from malnutrition and disease, at least half of the Acadian population perished during the *Le Grand Dérangement* (the great upheaval), forging the collective memory of the Acadian population and the notion of an Acadian diaspora.

Numerous survivors of this forced exile, as well as those who were able to escape deportation, formed an Acadian resistance movement that was centered in the province of New Brunswick. As a result of British harassment, they were reduced to starvation before finally being allowed to resettle in Nova Scotia in 1763 following the Treaty of Paris that ended the Seven Years' War. Because of the colonial government's refusal to grant the Acadians permanent status in Nova Scotia, 193 Halifax Acadians led by Joseph Broussard (a.k.a. BeauSoleil) sailed to Saint Domingue before reaching New Orleans in late February 1765.

Although Louisiana was ceded to Spain in 1763, the French colonial administration continued to operate in New Orleans because of the refusal of the Spanish governor to take official possession of the colony. As a result, the French administration funded the Acadian settlement until early 1767. The Spanish crown allowed the Acadians to settle along Bayou Teche in the Attakapas prairies, encouraging other exiles from the Mid-Atlantic colonies and in France to join them. The final wave of 1,596 Acadians arrived from France in 1785, where survivors who had deported to England had made their way twenty years earlier. With his highly successful poem *Evangeline: A Tale of Acadia*, published in 1847, Henry Wadsworth Longfellow immortalized the tragedy of the *Grand Dérangement* through the separation of Evangeline and Gabriel and their vain attempt to reunite, these saintly characters embodying tenacity, timeless constancy, and restoration of a lost world. In his book *The Acadian Diaspora* (2012), Christopher Hodson offers a new take on their history, contextualized in postwar imperialism. These realities generated a superheated demand for labor. European statesmen and entrepreneurs had grown suspicious of both the enslaved and their masters in time of crisis. "Acadians witnessed the rise and fall of a new imperial era, all as their own lives flowed inexorably away. Their response was not an uncomplicated turn inward to the memory of their Bay of Fundy villages dismantled in 1755. When refugees such as Charles White [who became a successful businessman and landlord in Pennsylvania] did look to the past, it was a garbled mess. So they rebuilt in the ever-changing present, using the materials at hand. The results, like their destinations, were nothing if not diverse."[11]

Adopted as an ethnonym at the turn of the twentieth century, *cadien* originated in early Acadian speech and was codified and popularized in English as *Cajun* in the 1880s.[12] It eventually became an umbrella term to describe the francophone populations of distinct origins (poor Acadians, poor white Creoles also called prairie Creoles, descendants of colonists, and Foreign French) but who shared an inferior social status and were stigmatized as white trash. The distinction between Cajuns and Acadians reflects the social stratifications at stake in the eighteenth century following the expulsion of the Acadians from Nova Scotia by the English in 1755.

As noted by Marc David, Acadian historiography paradoxically focused on these fractures while affirming "the continuous existence of a unified, collective subject through the use of formulations like "Acadian society," "Acadian culture," or "Acadian community," "subsisting across time and space."[13] It describes the emergence of class divisions in antebellum Louisiana between an educated and influential minority who modeled their existence upon that of the white Creole planter class and a large majority of small-scale farmers, ranchers or *petits habitants* (yeoman farmers) who "preferred the less ostentatious existence of their forebears."[14] The heterogeneity of social positions was further complicated by the increase of farmers who abandoned their agricultural occupation to become workers in the sugar industry. C. Brasseaux explains that, after the Civil War, the political turbulence of Reconstruction combined with social and economic changes accelerated class distinctions, and frames them within a binary opposition between the acculturated Acadian educated elite and indigenous Louisiana Cajuns abandoned by their antebellum leadership and reduced to tenantry and poverty by the end of the nineteenth century.

The "Cajun" and "Acadian" labels are thus situated within a narrative of social stratification that has shaped the current registers of identification. Banned from classrooms by the Louisiana State Board of Education in 1916 and later in the state constitution of 1921, the French language increasingly became the object of deprecation. During the 1950s, calling a white person a "Cajun" was perceived as a similar category of insult as calling a black person "nigger," according to many accounts. This image endured until the rebirth of Cajun identity during the 1970s under the influence of a movement inspired by a political and intellectual elite that led to the creation of a state agency to promote the teaching of French, the Council for the Development of French in Louisiana (CODOFIL). This concrete step began the process of transformation of Cajun identity from a pejorative label into an identity to be heralded and proclaimed.[15]

The francophone renaissance gradually took on a new dimension by becoming part of touristic promotion. The oil crisis of the early 1970s struck a devastating blow to the region's economy, inciting Louisiana to diversify its economy and turn to other sources of revenue. An entire series of official designations honored Cajun/Acadian identity by focusing on Acadian heritage, which had the effect of marginalizing the Creoles within the French Louisiana landscape.[16] The Cajun/Acadian labels were used to create an official name for the region—Acadiana—and later, the application of a touristic denomination, Cajun Country. These changes also encompassed the creation of a second name for the state university in Lafayette—*l'Université des Acadiens*—and its athletic teams (Ragin' Cajuns) and civic center (Cajundome).

CURRENT MUSICAL CATEGORIES

This quick overview of Cajun and Creole identifications significantly informs current music categories. French Louisiana music has benefited enormously from the regional touristic policy, which has involved regional academic and cultural institutions through the efforts of regionally and nationally recognized folklorists. These efforts have led to the elevation of the status of French Louisiana from dissonant and old-fashioned—and from the derogatory label "chanky-chank"—to that of a folk music tradition meriting preservation.

Prior to the 1960s, the terms applied to French Louisiana music covered a range of styles without associating it with a specific identification. The terms in use in the first half of the twentieth century were either *musique française* or French music. By contrast, musical categories currently in use make distinctions between Cajun music, Creole music, and zydeco. Although some underline the blurred boundaries between them, the use of these categories has achieved a certain degree of consensus among Louisiana musicians, folklorists, experts, and fans and are encoded in the discourse of touristic and academic publications.

The term *musique cadienne* describes the music of the Cajuns, understood as white and of francophone culture, whereas Creole and Zydeco music refer to Creoles who are understood to be black francophones. Music labeled as Creole is presented as representing the traditional repertoire of the Creole people and as the ancestor of zydeco. During the first half of the twentieth century, these musics were also referred to as "lala" or "French lala." The coexistence of these two distinct categories, which dates from early in the twentieth century, seems to act as historical proof that justifies the distinctions currently in use between these various styles. Rather than speaking about *musique française* in reference to the style of the early pioneers, some prefer to use the expressions "old-time Cajun music" and "old-time Creole music," depending on the origins of the musicians in question. This logic of musical genealogy based on African descent is often invoked to explain the existence of a unique "Creole sound" that is distinct from Cajun music and is defined in particular by its syncopated rhythms.

Zydeco as a musical category became popular in 1964 following the release of Clifton Chenier's first album on the Arhoolie label. According to most writers, the term comes from *les haricots* (snapbeans) in the regional French etymology.[17] *"Les haricots sont pas salés"* (the snapbeans are not salty) is a proverbial expression referring to hard times—in reference to the lack of salt pork when salt was used to preserve meat.[18] The expression is found in several Creole songs from the 1934 Lomax collection, and eventually became the name of Chenier's signature song.[19] The genealogy of the term (see ch. 4) is revealing of the combined role of researchers, record producers, the media, and official institutions in the creation and diffusion of new music labels. The meaning of the term expanded to designate the music, the dance, and the social gathering. The music is most often described as "based on the rhythms of Afro-Caribbean, blues, and Cajun music." It is sometimes characterized as the "cousin" of Cajun music by journalists and musical experts, both from Louisiana and outsiders. The way in which these categories are defined instantly reveals a persistent paradox, in which Creole and zydeco styles are positioned in a symmetrical relationship with respect to another so-called white style by associating their resemblances and even their kinship within a biological register. At the same time, their differences are forcefully accentuated with reference to the African origins of Creole and zydeco musics. Current musical nomenclature thus clearly reveals an immediately perceptible tension between creolization and the racial imaginary.

Approaching the Subject

An exhaustive portrait of French Louisiana music is beyond the scope of this project, and my objective is neither to trace the history of local music styles nor to cover the entire French Louisiana music scene. Numerous publications and documentaries have documented the music played by Cajuns and Creoles, in particular publications by such figures as Barry J. Ancelet, Shane Bernard, Ryan A. Brasseaux, John Broven, Mark DeWitt, Kevin S. Fontenot, Mark Mattern, John Minton, Ben Sandmel, Ann Savoy, Rocky Sexton, Nick Spitzer, Michael Tisserand, and Roger Wood.[20]

I propose to study how social hierarchies and stereotypes based on the notions of race, class, and region shape, and in turn are shaped by, tastes, representations, and musical practices within French Louisiana music. The fundamental questions that propelled this study are: How do people delineate this music? When and for whom do they choose the various categories in use? How does the vision of music as framed by racial, ethnic, and regional identifications guide categorizations by social actors, from individuals to institutions, the music industry, and academia?

Several authors have approached the topic of racial hierarchies and segregation within music in various works (mostly published by the late nineties) exploring issues of racial tensions, claims of ownership, and unequal power relations between Cajuns and Creoles.[21] While significantly contributing to a discussion on racial stereotypes, few of these authors combine those stereotypes with others related to class and region in the realm of music, and therefore to broader processes of differentiation; furthermore, their reflections on racial hierarchies and on the limits of creolization do not lead them into a discussion on music categories, or to situate this music outside of any ethnic and racial identification, even when they readily admit blurred boundaries.

I argue for the importance of desegregating the understanding of French Louisiana music by situating it beyond ethnic or racial identifications, bringing to light the other identifications and factors at stake in the perception and practice of French Louisiana music and the complexity of the musical landscape. This book explores the role of music in constructing, asserting, erasing, managing, and negotiating difference. The logics at play combine questions of power relations, competing claims to authenticity and ownership, and processes of differentiation and hierarchization, all of which are questions that span several levels, including local, national, and global, and are also influenced by market-related strategies.

My ultimate goal is to show how the construction of the French Louisiana repertoire results from constant negotiation—rather than a contradiction—between the effacement and the reiteration of social divisions. This study seeks to contribute to a reconsideration of certain oppositions and correlations regarding the social uses of music and dance, which are typically situated within polar divisions: rural versus urban, center versus periphery, tradition versus *métissage*, local or national versus global. These negotiations reflect symbolic as well as social and economic factors through access to the music market. Rather than functioning as polar opposites, I intend to demonstrate how these social spaces interact with and complement each other.

An additional objective is to examine taken-for-granted music categories and representations. Instead of using vernacular categories as analytical tools, I consider them to be themselves objects of analysis by exploring commonsense understandings. This analytical approach has been inspired and reinforced by previous scholarship that explores the segmentation of music along racial lines, including studies by Peter Wade, Ronald Radano, Philip Tagg, and Karl H. Miller.

My purpose, then, is to interrogate the music categories that are in use, including Cajun, Creole, zydeco (and their various qualification as "old time," "traditional," "progressive," "nouveau," among others), LaLa, French, French blues, swamp pop, as well as black, white, folk, roots, vernacular, and indigenous music. These categories will be discussed as they are applied to music in order to reveal the conditions and contexts in which they are used and the meanings, values, and worldview with which they are invested. Interrogating these categories does not imply by any means that I consider them invalid. Instead, I attempt to contribute to French Louisiana music scholarship by offering a different angle of analysis and by pushing further the observation that boundaries between these music categories are blurred.

Rather than strictly using the music categories commonly associated with the French heritage of southwestern Louisiana, I made the choice for this book to include the various styles under the broad umbrella "French Louisiana music." This choice was first driven by my intention to situate this music outside of any ethnic and racial identification and to focus instead on regional identification. By contrast with the scholarly approach adopted in previous work, this choice also emphasizes the commonality of these styles beyond musicological distinctions. My point is obviously not to negate differences within French Louisiana music, nor to musically categorize the old-timey style labeled French music alongside the "new" zydeco or Cajun sound; there can be no question that these styles are musically miles apart. Instead, the purpose is to situate them along a continuum in which French music is assigned to one pole, and contemporary zydeco and Cajun to the opposing pole. Using a continuum helps emphasize the shared regional identification of these musics, as well as their common cultural heritage and reverence for tradition, in combination with various degrees of creative agency, and their cross-musical influences and eclectic styles, sounds, and textures. As innovative as the various French Louisiana music styles might be, each to a certain extent continues to draw on a common repertoire that is on occasion submerged while at other times ubiquitous, but which is always invested with meaning and claimed as the roots of their musical heritage.

Why talk about "French Louisiana music" rather than "Acadiana music," since both are used as a regional designation? "Acadiana" was initially used as a marketing gimmick by KATC-TV, but in 1971 the Louisiana legislature officially designated as "The Heart of Acadiana" a triangular area covering twenty-two parishes with "strong French Acadian cultural aspects" whose base runs along the Gulf Coast. The choice of parishes was somewhat arbitrary and its function was further clouded by the inclusion of parishes "of similar cultural environment" (House Concurrent Resolution No. 496, June 6, 1971).[22] This name is now widely used by businesses, public services, the media, and cultural institutions (i.e., the Acadiana Open Channel, the *Times of Acadiana*, the Acadiana Center for the Arts, KRVS 88.7 Radio Acadie). The adoption of an official Acadiana flag in 1974 added additional symbolic power to the designation, which was grafted onto the touristic term "Cajun Country" also adopted by local trade and organizations, which also occasionally alternates with the label "Bayou Country."

These regional designations did not seem appropriate to me in the particular framework of this research, however, because they placed the emphasis on a single ethnic identification—Cajuns with a focus on Acadian ancestry—rather than embracing the multiple origins of the French Louisiana population. Since its emergence in the mid-nineteenth century, the ethnonym *Cajun* has been used to cover diverse francophone origins as well as other immigrant groups that settled in Louisiana, including Spanish, Irish, Scottish, and German.[23] The regional terms in use today are etymologically focused on Cajuns and Acadians, although *Acadiana* is now used as an inclusive term. I could also have chosen to talk about "southwest Louisiana music," which is strictly regional, but that would have restricted the various styles in presence to this region to the exclusion of southeast Louisiana. While I focus in this book on the southwest because it clearly established itself as the heart of French Louisiana music and played an undeniable leading role in the development and circulation of this music, there is a need to include the largely ignored southeast Louisiana musical dynamics in further scholarly discussion.

The designation "French Louisiana music" seemed much more appropriate for the purpose of this book. *French Louisiana* is a historical term that is not restricted to Louisiana's French colonial heritage (1699–1763) and that encompasses the different waves of francophone immigrants who settled in Louisiana. In addition to French settlers who counted among their numbers voluntary and forced immigrants and French military personnel, Acadian exiles, and refugees from the Haitian revolution, this historical category applies to refugees from the French Revolution and from the Bonapartist coup d'état, Christian Lebanese immigrants, Vietnamese,

Laotian, and Cambodian refugees, and French, Belgian, Swiss, and Quebecois immigrants, who are all part of twentieth-century French Louisiana. Indeed, historian Carl Brasseaux has listed at least eighteen distinct French-speaking groups for whom Louisiana became home.[24] The term thus involves a range of historical periods, heritages, and populations that tends to blur its meaning but does not entirely erode its symbolic power among Louisianans.[25]

Ultimately, I chose "French Louisiana music" because I believed it was important to include the term "French" for the simple reason that, regardless of the style considered, all musicians and music fans attach meaning to it, even if these meanings in terms of French heritage are highly variable. As this book will abundantly demonstrate, this does not mean limiting French Louisiana music to its French heritage or to exclude American popular music influences. Indeed, "French music" is used in this book as a vernacular term that was in use during the first half of the twentieth century and is also found today, primarily in reference to an old-timey style.

My reflection on social stereotypes and processes of differentiation was fueled by a concomitant effort to interrogate categories of identifications such as race, ethnicity, and community and to reveal the multiple dimensions involved in how, when, and by whom they are used. They continue to exert enormous impact within the social imaginary of the region due to their emotional and political associations. Although as intellectual tools they enable us to reflect on the social world, these categories can also be used to maintain the social order. Multiple actors participate in the circulation and diffusion of these notions, including international organizations, activists, intellectual and artistic elites, and researchers themselves who, like it or not, feed their reconduction into the common language and their legitimation.[26] Unlike France, where the term *race* is widely avoided and is not referred to in official documents, the ubiquity and institutionalization of the term in the United States is such that its use is taken for granted. The notion that race is a social construction has long been accepted within the social sciences, to the extent that its eminently ideological, political, and arbitrary character has become a commonplace.[27] While social analysts refuse the reification and legitimation of the term, they also readily acknowledge its intensity and utility as an analytical category in the fight against racism, discrimination, and inequality.

The insightful work of sociologist Rogers Brubaker has provided important inspiration for my efforts to come to grips with this paradox and to problematize the question of race as well as other categories of differentiation. I discovered his work rather late in this project, but his theoretical view expresses with startling clarity the framework within which I sought to situate my work.

Instead of employing the language of bounded groups as entities, Brubaker calls for an analysis of how, when, and why people interpret social experience in racial, ethnic, or national terms. "Instead of speaking routinely of racial, ethnic, or national 'groups,' for example . . . which biases the discussion by *presuming* the relevance of a racial, ethnic, or national frame or self-understanding, a cognitive perspective suggests speaking of *groupness* as a variable."[28] He shifts the analytical focus from the overdetermined, ambiguous notion of "identity" to the active, processual term "identification," inviting us to "specify the agents that do the identifying."[29] Other alternative terms include self-understanding (situated subjectivity), commonality (the sharing of some common attribute), connectedness (the relational ties that link people), and groupness (the sense of belonging to a distinctive, bounded, solidary group).[30] This framework, Brubaker insists, does not imply that vernacular categories and people's understandings are not taken seriously. Nor is it intended either as a way to deprive anyone of identity as a political and economic tool or to question the legitimacy of identity claims. However, it draws an important distinction between vernacular and analytical categories by suggesting that the former constitute "categories *for doing*": "By invoking groups, they seek to evoke them, summon them, call them into being."[31] This approach has informed my critical analysis regarding the categorizations and identifications at work within the field of French Louisiana music. "Cajun" and "Creole," for example, are not understood as groups but as categories of identification, and I will focus on how they are used, at what period, in what situations, and for what purpose, as part of an attempt to historicize and contextualize them.

My understanding of categories and taste was further enriched by the notion of musical legitimacy and, in particular, the approach of French sociologist Bernard Lahire, who repositions the individual at the center of the understanding of the social world. His notion of inter- and intra-individual behavioral variations refers to the plurality of taste within a single social group but also within a particular individual, without calling into question the existence of social inequalities regarding the most legitimate forms of culture.[32]

Lahire thus invites us to focus not strictly on the music scene (in this instance) but on the individual himself, as a field of struggle, an internal division, "which can give rise in certain cases to *battles of self against self*."[33]

This perspective is particularly appropriate for the understanding of the multiple positions held by single individuals within the French Louisiana scene, embracing various aesthetic judgments, musical identifications, and modalities of recognition that can at first appear contradictory but that ultimately attest to the fact that the individual is a site of struggle.[34] The legitimist strain within the theory of cultural legitimacy has been widely criticized by French sociologists, among them Lahire, Claude Grignon, Jean-Claude Passeron, and Nathalie Heinich.[35] The approach taken by these scholars takes the diversity of cultural influences and their hierarchies into account, thus critically re-evaluating previous analyses that have privileged a monolithic system of legitimization. As Heinich argues, these earlier studies have not adequately addressed how legitimization systems operate on multiple levels that alternate and interact with each other. Taking the plurality of these systems of valorization or justification into account leads us to handle notions inherited from Bourdieu such as "legitimacy," "distinction," and "domination," as well as the polarization that they produce, with considerable caution: "Certain positions can be, depending on situations and points of view, legitimate *and* illegitimate, just as those who occupy them can find themselves in positions of dominating or being dominated."[36] What researchers have tended to perceive as contradictions and even inconsistencies arise instead from the multiple registers among which social actors pragmatically know how to navigate.

Within music scholarship, American sociologist Richard Peterson suggested that patterns of musical taste are not so much structured around an opposition between the elite and the mass, but rather between eclectic and specific taste, what he called the omnivore-univore distinction.[37] Omnivorousness is understood as a measure of the breadth of taste and cultural consumption. French sociologist Hervé Glevarec questions the notion of legitimacy in its common understanding; according to his view, individuals no longer establish hierarchies between music genres but within a single genre (within rock, jazz, or classical music, for example).[38] Instead of arguing in favor of the plurality of "orders of cultural legitimacy," Glevarec thus asserts their heterogeneization, emphasizing the variety of authorities involved in the construction of legitimacy, a notion that is exceptionally well exemplified in the case of Louisiana.

Musical legitimacy is understood here in its broadest sense, as a social judgment that induces classification, valorization, and disqualification, in other words as a marker of status and hierarchy. Who has authority on music taste, judgments, and categories? Who defines and dictates the musical canon and its criteria? How is this authority contested, what kinds of conflicts does it generate, and on what grounds are they centered? The processes of legitimation also involve the factors at play in the ways in which musicians are deemed to be legitimate interpreters of the various French Louisiana music styles. Several themes are explored in this perspective. This study focuses to a significant extent on the logics of classification and categorization, on their social, economic, and political dimensions, and on how they are instrumentalized by various actors (artists, cultural institutions, music industry, media, researchers). Musical legitimacy also involves the construction of a musical genealogy and the claims of a specific cultural heritage. In the case of music anchored in a "tradition" like French Louisiana music, legitimacy is attained by situating oneself within the legacy of musical pioneers and musical dynasties, whereas musics tied to religious practices are rooted in ancestors, initiations, or ritual lineages. In reality, the process of musical transmission proceeds via a variety of channels that include elders, ancestors, rituals, peers, jams, folkloric groups, recordings, videos, media, performances, workshops, activists, or musical archives.[39] Finally, the quest for legitimacy involves the social stereotypes in which musical tastes and categories are rooted, as well as the conflicts of authenticity and power struggles that arise from them. Debates often center on the adequacy between a specific musical style and the identification—whether ethnic, racial, social, or regional—of its performer. This work attempts to untangle these many divisions and the imaginaries on which they draw, while bringing to light relationships of symbolic domination through processes of differentiation and of hierarchization.

Conceptualizing Creolization

A further component of this critical project involves interrogating the paradigm of cultural interactions. Social scientists have deployed a variety of notions in order to conceptualize what they consider to be cultural interactions, including *métissage*, hybridity, and creolization. These notions have been the subject of a number of controversies among researchers whose positions on their theoretical relevance and field of application are sometimes divergent. Each of these notions in turn depends on other constructs that extend them in a kind of game of nesting Chinese boxes. This study does not seek to catalogue these concepts, nor to retrace their origins and development,[40] but instead to field-test them in Louisiana by revealing the ways in which their use is negotiated, circumscribed, and appropriated on the local level.

Created as a "model for" society in the 1980s by the Martinican literary and political movement called *créolité*,[41] creolization is currently used as an analytical concept by anthropologists and historians and as mechanism in identity claims within so-called Creole societies. Rather than restricting its use to these plantation societies, Ulf Hannerz has broadened its application within a macro-anthropological approach to the relations between center and periphery that structure contemporary cultural globalization.

Eminent anthropologist of the Caribbean, Sidney W. Mintz, however, has criticized this theoretical use beyond historically specific contexts. Other thinkers have acknowledged the specific features that characterize creolization in the Caribbean while also advocating contemporary uses of the notion to describe the aegis of global capitalism beyond a limited set of examples.[42] Folklorists and cultural anthropologists continue to remain divided on its use, as the special issue on creolization in the *Journal of American Folklore* (2003) amply illustrates, as does the forum in the *American Ethnologist* (2006) and *The Creolization Reader*, edited by Robin Cohen and Paola Toninato (2010).[43] These sources reveal that universal application of the concept is not unanimously advocated. The specific intentions of the editors of the *JAF* special issue arise from a desire to rehabilitate Creole cultures and to oppose negative understandings of the construct: "Creolists see creolization as creative disorder, as a poetic chaos, thereby challenging simplistic and static notions of center and periphery. The cultural and critical lens of creolization allows us to see not simply 'hybrids' of limited fluidity, but *new cultures in the making*."[44] Considered an outcome of this culture-making process, "Creole cultural forms" are associated with those who have no voice, and they are thus restricted according to this view, if not geographically at least socially, to functioning as a political tool in the fight against oppression and cultural hegemony. Although in this case the authors make their understanding of the political connotation of the concept explicit, creolization is in fact inseparable from this ideological operation, a fact that is not uniformly foregrounded by those who use it.

For several North American and European researchers who have reflected on creolization, the concept, like all the metaphors for cross-cultural mixing (such as hybridity, and *métissage*), bears within it the myth of origins and of racial purity and is therefore inseparable from strategies of exclusion, as reflected by my field in Louisiana. Anthropologist Charles Stewart stresses the tension revealed by the etymology of the word "creole," which intersects with the meanings attributed to the term creolization: "*Crioulo* comes from the past participle of Portuguese *criar*, 'to give birth to, to raise.' *Criar* derives from Latin *creare*, the first sense of which was reproductive: 'to procreate, to give birth to.' The 'create' in creole is thus both biological and cultural. A tension between cultural context and physical nature has been present in the word from its inception [Arrom 172; Perl; Mintz; Palmié, 'Out of Place']."[45] Stewart thus calls attention to the fact that the early senses of the word "creole" were stamped by an imperial history that established a connection between New World birth and deculturation. He reveals "the inequities of power that allowed European colonizers to discursively legislate the importance of 'race,' culture, and environment in determining where one fit along a chain of being that placed the Old World homeland and its subjects at the pinnacle."[46] Furthermore, Stewart adds, "the ideas of creolization as continuum and as a synonym for mixture may well have run their various courses," affirming the need to contextualize and historicize a notion that cannot be restricted to a single, monolithic definition.[47] Stephan Palmié has noted that the term creole is rooted in the highly specific geo-historical context of the Caribbean. "Notionally highlighting endemic divisions rather than suggesting their transcendence even in its 'native habitat,' as a designator of Caribbean 'identities,' the term creole would thus appear to create but illusory contrasts to the seemingly more rigidly exclusionary fork typologies of human kinds and communities observed elsewhere."[48] By focusing our attention on the ground and on daily practice, as suggested by Khan, we can distance ourselves from these concepts and reveal the multiple stakes involved in creolization and in the process of hierarchization with which it is associated.[49]

Other metaphors of cultural mixing can confront similar obstacles. The capacity of *métissage* to frame the analysis of cultural interactions, for example, is impeded by the paradoxes inherent in it. The notion ultimately fuels an essentialist, biological reading of societies. In *Branchements. Anthropologie de l'universalité des cultures*, French anthropologist Jean-Loup Amselle explains why one should

> exercise the greatest caution with respect to the idea of the *métissage* of the world or creolization in ways that some have argued, including Ulf Hannerz with his concept of "global ecumene[.]" . . .

> It is in departing from the postulate of the existence of discrete culture entities called "cultures" that one arrives at a conception of a post-colonial world or a post–Cold War world that is perceived as a hybrid. In order to escape from this idea of mixing through homogenization or hybridization, one must postulate on the contrary that every society is *metisse*, and hence that *métissage* is the product of entities that are already blended, thus extending to infinity the idea of an original purity.[50]

Once the process to which the concept of *métissage* refers is assumed from the start to be inherent in a society, using it as an analytical category becomes problematic.

To further complicate this discussion, the rhetoric of "world music" has ever since the 1990s involved the simultaneous valorization of the notion of hybridity in popular music studies and the concealment of racial imagination. Ronald Radano and Philip Bohlman argue that "the transnational mix has not erased race from music, but rather it has recontextualized it," strenuously objecting to the invisibility of race in the music field, "for it is in music that the racial resonates most vividly with greatest affect and power."[51] They define racial imagination "as the shifting matrix of ideological constructions of difference associated with body type and color that have emerged as part of the discourse network of modernity."[52] Further, they refuse to restrict the intersection of music with the racial imaginary to the United States, applying this interaction to Europe and arguing that it is relevant globally. The association between a particular music and a given group or place is indeed widely shared. Claims of ownership and authenticity are embedded within the racial imagination and the rhetoric of origins. According to Simon Frith, scholars in popular music studies have tended to define the notion of hybridity as a new form of authenticity, a creativity that is characteristic of the transnationalization of contemporary musics and of their syncretic nature.[53] Frith is not interested in finding clues to understanding the postmodern condition in "world music." Instead, he suggests replacing the concept of globalization by an understanding of networks—bottom-up globalization—and on how vernacular and academic discourses intertwine in how transnational musics are described and understood.

All these paradigms (creolization, hybridity, métissage) can find themselves at the crossroads of scientific, ideological, and aesthetic issues within academic research. The case of Louisiana illustrates particularly well how discourses emanating from different spheres interact, whether they be scholars, activists, musicians, music producers, music fans, journalists, or cultural institutions, while also illustrating how the same individuals circulate among spheres and hence switch from one register to another. The eminent specialist on Cajuns and Creoles Barry Ancelet, for example, shifts among an array of hats as a scholar, teacher, activist, cultural broker, poet, and author involved in cultural programs such as the *Rendez-Vous des Cajuns* radio and television show broadcast from the Liberty Theater in Eunice. Ancelet has also long been involved in touristic projects, festival programming, CD production, and the composition of liner notes, and is also frequently consulted by musicians for collaborations and translations between English and French. The presence of the Center for Cultural and Eco-Tourism at the University of Louisiana at Lafayette, which houses a research center and the Archives of Cajun and Creole Folklore and is actively engaged in community outreach, provides an excellent illustration of this overlap and multi-layered circulation. The activities and status of the center enables specialists like Ancelet and historian Carl Brasseaux to be solicited by a number of towns as consultants for a wide range of projects.

Cultural mixing in Louisiana is emphasized, often drawing on a culinary metaphor, *gumbo*, a regional specialty some of whose ingredients—in particular *roux*, okra, and *filé* (powdered sassafras leaves)—are cited to illustrate the European, African, and Native American origins of this "unique culture." Since the early 1990s, musicians and music commentators have underscored the musical exchanges and borrowings between Cajuns and Creoles. Several popular Cajun bands have increasingly incorporated old-time Creole and zydeco tunes in their repertoires and performed with Creole musicians. Interviews, publications, and CD liner notes represent significant opportunities to affirm this will to inclusivity. Researchers working on the region echo this unifying discourse by apply the notion of creolization to the field of music. Associated with adaptability, creativity, and cultural interaction, creolization has been used within certain limits. More specifically, it has not incorporated the appropriation of mass culture and the process of Americanization of the music, nor the divisions between Cajuns and Creoles and the resonance of the color line. Rather, the valorization of the notion of creolization is combined with a rhetoric of origins, which perpetuates the racialization of French Louisiana music. A constant oscillation takes place between the metaphor of cultural mixing and creativity on one end, and the naturalization of difference on the other.

Indeed, creolization tends to be used by regional scholars to point to the local culture's "uncanny adaptability," and it is also widely promoted by the tourism industry as an example of the effectiveness of the "melting pot" or a "cultural cornucopia." This argument is found even in the most recent critical scholarship by local researchers. Ryan Brasseaux contends that there is a "French North American survival scheme rooted in pragmatism and openness to change,"[54] a perspective mirrored according to him in Cajun music. This approach attributes a unique capacity to Cajuns and francophones as opposed to illustrating a general cultural process.[55] The tendency among scholars working on south Louisiana to emphasize the assimilation by the Cajuns of cultural traits from other groups is often paired with praise for their capacity for innovation and their exceptional ability to adapt—to the environment, to historical circumstances, to modernity. This ennobling narrative is part of efforts to rehabilitate a group that experienced long periods of stigmatization, as well as an expression of the refutation of recurrent predictions of the culture's imminent extinction.

This propensity to adopt a harmonious, uncritical representation of creolization is highly present in historiography and other work on the musics of French Louisiana. Adaptation is represented as a choice instead of a survival strategy, which has the effect of obscuring the physical violence and power struggles that are inherent to the actual local context. In their book *Blues for New Orleans*, which was published as a tribute after Katrina and the failures of the federal levee system, Roger D. Abrahams, Nick Spitzer, John F. Szwed, and Robert Farris Thompson described creolization as a "comprehensive and dynamic phenomenon of cultural give and take, invention and reinvention, of dialogue and disagreement."[56] More than "disagreement", I would argue that a troubling array of tensions, divisions, and power struggles are involved in the process. Creolization serves as a frame for these writers' discourses, revealing a pattern of cultural salvage and rescue rooted in vernacular creativity and improvisation.[57]

In Louisiana, as in other research terrains, the close proximity between academic research in social science, activism, and institutions involved in defending or promoting local culture can lead to the production of discourses in which factual description overlaps with identity claims.[58] One of the consequences of this situation is the idealization of mixing as a constitutive process in shaping a necessarily open, dynamic, and to a certain extent, exemplary identity.[59]

In this book, I have preferred to distance myself as explicitly as possible from the ideological and identity-based claims embedded in the notion of creolization by adopting a critical approach. This position does not imply that I subscribe to a strict distinction between social actors and researchers and between civic engagement and ethnographic involvement, or "knowledge for knowledge and knowledge for action" (to borrow the expression of the anthropologist Daniel Cefaï).[60] From my perspective, activism and political involvement are unquestionably not antithetical to the anthropological enterprise. My theoretical choice does not question our engagement as ethnographers, but instead focuses on the terminology that is most appropriate to my anthropological project and to what I have observed in the field. The debates around creolization in the Caribbean world and globally further nourished this preference. Instead of serving as an analytical category, my purpose is to explore the multiple meanings this vernacular category takes on through its appropriations by a range of actors and contexts, and the multifaceted dynamics it embraces. This has led me to establish a distinction between the narrative of creolization in use among scholars and experts and the features of the musics of the region that reflect processes of transformation, adaptation, creation, and reinterpretation. Although I do not offer a musicological analysis of these adjustments, I have provided some musical material to illustrate the functioning of this transformative process by emphasizing certain shared features among the region's musics, repertoires, and representations beyond the diversity of French Louisiana music styles.

Instead of interpreting the parallel emphasis on cultural mixing and difference as a contradiction, I have approached them within dialogic interaction. I have found inspiration for this approach in Peter Wade's work on music from the Caribbean coastal region of Colombia. According to Wade, the identification of certain styles, techniques, and instruments with a specific origin only reinforces the metaphor of cultural mixing: "I am arguing that *mestizaje* has both difference and sameness, homogeneity and heterogeneity, inclusion and exclusion as constitutive elements." He expands on this argument by asserting that "[t]he difference between ideas of mixture as seen from above and below in the racial hierarchy is not the difference between seeing it as a fusion and as a mosaic, but rather the role played by hierarchy and power in the ordering of the elements of the mosaic. . . . [*mestizaje*] is a site of struggle to see what and who is going to be included and excluded, and in what way; to see to what extent existing value hierarchies can be disrupted."[61]

The How

Discussions of research methods and field experiences have now become an integral part of anthropology, if not a full-fledged branch of the discipline through what has been named reflexive ethnography.[62] As Cefaï expresses it, "the principal *medium* of the study is the embodied experience of the ethnographer," and "its primary material results from situations of activities, of actions and of interactions."[63] Calling attention to our positionality and experience appears inevitable when considered in this way, on the condition that extended self-centered considerations are avoided and that the overall purpose of deepening anthropological understandings are kept firmly in view.

For these reasons, I have deliberately included reflections concerning my experiences and feelings and also about the kinds of relationships in which I was engaged. I consider this introspective element (which was the subject of *Working the Field*, a book I co-edited with anthropologist Jacques Henry) to be essential, particularly for an anthropologist of music, which is considered to be a collective sensory experience.[64] Subjectivity can be a delicate matter in a field in which aesthetic judgments often blur analysis. I was especially careful to use my practice of music and involvement in the local music scene while also keeping in mind in which capacity—researcher, musician, fan, or friend—I was expressing myself.[65] As strong and genuine as my love of and involvement in French Louisiana music are, I was attentive to the question of my own potential aesthetic and ideological biases and to maintaining a critical insight that I earnestly hope will not be misunderstood by my friends and colleagues in whose lives, like in mine, this music plays a significant role. Being an anthropologist requires a decentered posture that attempts to combine a deeply intimate and emotional relationship with places and people and a critical analysis of the social life that we participate in. This book is certainly not intended to either correct or affirm particular "truths" about the people who represent and contribute to this music through their practice and lived experience. Instead, it is my own tale, an anthropological narrative that is intended to offer a fresh perspective on French Louisiana music.

This project is the product of a variety of ethnographic techniques. The methodology used for this book involved extensive ethnographic fieldwork between 2001 and 2008 situated within a twenty-year relationship with south Louisiana. Previous projects have including repeated and often extended fieldwork regarding the anthropology of tourism and music, and since 2005, of disasters. In fact, I had planned to conclude this project much earlier, but just as I began writing, Hurricane Katrina and the levee failures, quickly followed by Hurricane Rita, disrupted the lives of the residents of New Orleans and the coastal parishes of southwest Louisiana. Watching the devastation caused by the flooding, the forced exile of evacuees, and the ineptitude of the government's response, and initially unable to contact any of my friends in Louisiana, my feelings of helplessness, anger, obligation, and stinging pain compelled me to become involved in efforts to understand these catastrophic events and led me into the field of disaster research.

I should add that the scope of these disasters has affected every aspect of social and cultural life in south Louisiana, and as a symbol of New Orleans, music has consistently served to support calls for resistance and action. This led me to become involved in a new field and to conduct intense and challenging fieldwork, participate in conferences, and publish about post-Katrina and post-Rita Louisiana. This work delayed my return to the French Louisiana music field that is the subject of this book.[66] This fateful digression unquestionably has enriched my perspectives and provided opportunities for further fieldwork and for a new comparative perspective with the New Orleans music scene, however. Perhaps more importantly, it also fundamentally altered the initial project, which became broader in scope and analytical depth, in particular because of the influence of transplants on the region's music scene and the importance of the notion of sense of place.

During the periods covered by this project, I lived in the southern and northern parts of Lafayette: the Saint Streets neighborhood near campus, and later on Saint Charles Street in a mixed neighborhood across the Evangeline Thruway. I conducted and recorded fifty-two semi-directive interviews—some with the same individuals—that involved a variety of actors in the music field, including practitioners of music and dance, music and dance teachers, studio owners, record producers, musical events organizers, club owners, and radio program producers.[67] Interviewees also included cultural activists, music fans, and simple residents. I also recorded several music workshops that I attended at the Dewey Balfa Cajun and Creole Heritage Week (DBCCHW) at Chicot State Park outside of Lafayette. Additional informal, unrecorded exchanges involved music writers, music lovers, and exhibit curators.

My participant observation of the music scene encompassed clubs, festivals, concerts, and jams (regular and informal, public and private), and a few recording sessions in several places in Acadiana. I also attended and participated in music camps in Louisiana and in New York State (Ashokan) as a fiddler, a singer, or a dancer. Over the years, I have had the opportunity and indeed the privilege of often being a participant, student, or performer during public as well as private cultural and musical events, thus experiencing firsthand the different situations and positions described in the book. The project evolved even after it went into the writing phase, and several return trips to Louisiana since September 2008 have enabled me to update my observations concerning festivals and gigs, and even to conduct an additional interview. I have also engaged in continued email correspondence on specific aspects of my research and remain current about the music scene through mailing lists and websites.

Another methodology used in this book and described in greater depth in *Des vies en musique*, was the construction of the itineraries of several transplants.[68] Instead of merely reporting the words of actors based on one or several interviews, this approach involves composing one or more life itineraries using a wide range of field techniques. The construction of an individual itinerary entails collecting multiple discourses surrounding the individual, including those of other persons involved in his narrative. The itinerary process offers the possibility of linking the musical universes of musicians to other spheres of their social lives, helping us understand these actors in their entirety, without restricting them to specific roles or contexts. In this way, such dimensions as readjustments over time can be observed, and we are able to follow individuals as they take different paths, distinguishing the variety of their "social roles" as they navigate the different flows of their lives. Beyond the illustration it provides, the itinerary accounts for a specific experience while revealing the refraction of the social in the trajectory of an individual.

The fact that I first met Cajun music performers and played the fiddle, an instrument rarely used by contemporary zydeco musicians, circumscribed my experience as a musician. Because of this fact as well as the absence of regular public jams among zydeco players, I was not able to approach zydeco with the same depth of perspective and knowledge as other styles.

Early in my research, some of my interlocutors, among them Creoles, proved to be more challenging to approach and sometimes less inclined to meet me for an interview. Months might go by before I was actually able to set a firm appointment, and in in a few cases, my motivation was tested during the interview. Persistent efforts to establish trust and my preference for informal conversations bore fruit, however, and were routinely acknowledged by the very individuals who had resisted my efforts to approach them. People generally became persuaded that I was not a journalist and that I was more open to addressing and trying to understand sensitive subjects such as the color line.

For many older French-speaking informants, learning that I was French served as a remarkable icebreaker that in many cases immediately dissolved any suspicion or reluctance to talk to me. Being fluent in English occasionally blurred my origins, and it was often useful to switch to French to engage them in conversation. People often assumed that I spoke "standard" French and concluded that this ostensibly prestige variety of French was not accessible to them, a belief that I made a point of contradicting by mentioning the variety of French dialects within France. This apprehension is the result of a long history of stigmatization of Louisiana regional French. Because I attempted to speak clearly and to adjust my pace, syntax, and vocabulary, switching back and forth between English and French was nearly always a source of relief and complicity. The fact that I come from France also created expectations among some musicians regarding my knowledge about French "folk" music. I was ironically unable to inform them, because my involvement in folk circles in France was limited to French Louisiana music fans. I knew nothing about the music of the Poitou and other regions, by contrast with an earlier generation of French musicians involved in the folk music revival and knowledgeable about French regional music traditions.

Approaching working musicians proved challenging at times.[69] Although most Louisiana musicians are very accessible to the public compared to other music fields, their hectic schedules (for those who travel outside of Louisiana) and evening schedules, as well as the flood of media requests that they receive, make it difficult to meet them outside of gigs or to maintain contact in other ways. They are frequently on tour and often extend their gigs with jam sessions that last until the wee hours, surrounded by fans and hangers-on, and most popular musicians have little time for themselves. When they return home, they do not particularly relish the prospect of recounting their life histories to visiting scholars. For this reason, it is not always easy to engage in in-depth conversations outside of an interview. Even when I was able to set an appointment, I was sometimes torn between my eagerness to interview the artist immediately before he slipped away and my inclination to go slowly in order to build trust and develop a relationship.

Participant observation and informal discussions are the only techniques that can be used in dancehalls and at jams, but they represent significant challenges of their own, requiring memorization for detailed descriptions of locations, decor, how people are dressed and their dance and music-styles, their use of space, the interactions among dancers or musicians and with the public, the repertoire, and the ebb and flow of multiple stories and gossip that increases as the evening wears on and the number of drinks consumed grows. I could not conceivably take field notes openly in such settings. Alternative methods of note-taking crossed my mind, but I soon realized that they were inadequate: repeatedly sneaking to the bathroom with a hidden notebook could arouse suspicion, and I was afraid people would think I either stayed too long or went too often.

My investigation of the early-twentieth-century music scene led me to search for people who had witnessed that period and were informed about it, a challenge that after a long, tortuous process resulted in interviews with relatives or other people who were familiar with musicians—the "jazzmen" of the period as well as Cajun and Creole musicians active during that era. Oral histories drawing on the collections of the Hogan Jazz Archive at Tulane University (New Orleans), with generous assistance from its director, Bruce Raeburn, complemented these interviews. Further interviews and recordings were provided by the collections of oral history and recorded music contained in the Archive of Cajun and Creole Folklore (ACCF) at the Center for Cultural and Eco-Tourism of the University of Louisiana at Lafayette (ULL). My search for sources on the circulation of musicians between New Orleans and southwest Louisiana also led me to the New Iberia Public Library, which dedicated a whole room to jazz trumpet player Bunk Johnson, a resident of the town since 1920.[70]

The microfilm collection of the Dupré Library at ULL enabled me to search five daily regional newspapers from the late 1920s through the late 1930s, a period during which the music scene was eclectic and flourishing and that saw the first Cajun recording in 1928. Articles on music were very informative concerning the perceptions of the time, and I collected announcements of festivals, contests, and recordings. Advertisements for dancehalls and bands were useful stimulus during interviews. Collections of photographs were equally helpful in prompting interlocutors, one of which, the Martin Collection, is located at the Iberia Parish Library and covers a period of ninety years between 1895 and 1981 by local photographers I. A. Martin and his son Carroll. Another important private collection of photographs is located in the Lafayette Parish Courthouse and collected by clerk of court "Dan" Guillot.

Other bibliographical research was conducted in the Louisiana Room of the Dupré Library (ULL), where I was able to consult the Sandra Himel collection of Cajun and Creole commercial music collection, including instructional videos for learning instruments; at Middleton Library at Louisiana State University in Baton Rouge; and at the Howard-Tilton Memorial Library (Hogan Jazz Archive and Louisiana Research Collection), as well as at the Amistad African-American Research Center, at Tulane University in New Orleans.

Chapter 1 provides historical insights on French Louisiana music. It explores the music categories in use in the first half of the twentieth century and depicts the eclectic musical landscape of southwestern Louisiana at the time, including what would now be identified as jazz ensembles that have been largely neglected by scholars. The chapter reviews evidence of the versatility of the early recording musicians who are today considered emblematic of French Louisiana music. This interchange of musical styles, repertoire, and instrumentation also reveals the significance of stereotyped perceptions and hierarchies.

Chapter 2 explores the politics of cultural authenticity. Under whose authority are criteria shaped to define a legitimate, "authentic" French Louisiana repertoire? What power struggles underlie the assertion of musical legitimacy? What aesthetic differences are claimed, and on the basis of what imagery? This chapter also shows how musicians negotiate with the national and regional music market as well as how the notion of tradition is combined with new musical experimentations in the French Louisiana music scene. Finally, the politics of musical authenticity is considered in light of the involvement of governmental agencies and state-funded institutions in the promotion of a "cultural economy."

Chapter 3 seeks to demonstrate how music categories, tastes, and representations are ingrained in the racial imagination. It situates musical forms and conventions across the color line and reveals the ideological basis of ethnic and racial categories within French Louisiana music. The distinctions drawn between Cajun and Creole styles over the commonality of the label "French music" encapsulate the complex narrative of French Louisiana music. In fact, Louisiana actors know how to navigate between musical sameness and difference. Finally, the representations of zydeco show the ambivalence of blackness and the relationship between eroticism and the transgression of the color line.

Chapter 4 investigates the meanings involved in the valorization of a rural heritage. Characterized as simple, plain, and unpolished, the attributes of the region's music are integral to the ways in which it is technically described, practiced, lived, staged live or displayed on CDs, taught, and recorded. The alleged technical simplicity of this music can be deceptive, however, and presents its own particular set of challenges. The insistence on fun and an approach that presents this music as a way of life combine to constitute a set of codes, rules, and expectations. The representation of the "new" zydeco sound encapsulates the oppositions between rural and urban and black and white that zydeco musicians seek to reconcile in order to achieve respectability through their music. Finally, this chapter examines how French Louisiana music is grounded in a profound attachment to place, and more broadly to regional identification with south Louisiana.

Chapter 5 illustrates the decisive role of outsider interest and mobility in the development, evolution, and reconfiguration of French Louisiana music. Beginning with professionals, collectors, and fans in the 1960s and 1970s, particularly in Northern California, the chapter describes how the development of a network of fans eventually laid the foundations for a migratory wave of transplants to Louisiana that began in earnest in the early 2000s. By examining the intersecting itineraries of some of these "transplants," the chapter portrays the changes in status and new hierarchies created within the music and among musicians. It also describes relational networks and the ways in which they overlap and extend. The process by which the mobility of French Louisiana music contributes to its reconfiguration is the focus of this chapter.

The Early Twentieth Century

A DIVERSE MUSICAL LANDSCAPE

We may all like fried chicken but we don't like it every day.
GENO DELAFOSE, APRIL 22, 2004[1]

While researching French Louisiana music and exploring the music available in the early twentieth century and the categories in use at the time, I came across a book by Creole clarinetist Austin Sonnier entitled *Second Linin': Jazzmen of Southwest Louisiana, 1900–1950*. It was ironic that I had discovered the book, which is published by the University of Louisiana at Lafayette, not in Lafayette, where I had conducted much of my fieldwork and bibliographical research, but at the Hogan Jazz Archive of Tulane University in New Orleans, whose director is Bruce Boyd Raeburn. The regional collective memory and official narrative so powerfully enshrine Cajun, Creole, and zydeco music that an investigation outside of these categories seemed incongruous, if not irrelevant. While I was researching traces of "rural jazz" and the circulation of New Orleans and southwest Louisiana musicians at the Hogan Archive, I had the opportunity to run into Chris Strachwitz, a central figure in the revival of French Louisiana music in the 1960s through his recordings and the record company he founded, Arhoolie.[2] When I explained the direction I was exploring, he expressed skepticism, because in his view, jazz was associated with a higher class than Cajun or zydeco. Indeed, New Orleans and southwest Louisiana are often viewed and promoted as two separate entities associated with distinct music genres and influences. The dearth of recordings of regional bands from that era other than French music greatly contributed to their sinking into oblivion, an official amnesia that is mirrored in the accounts of the population itself. Indeed, never in my fieldwork in southwest Louisiana have jazz or popular music been mentioned by my informants unless I brought it up. Although swamp pop musician Johnnie Allan lists "big bands/Dixieland/jazz musicians" in his 1995 *Memories: A Pictorial History of South Louisiana Music, 1910–1990*,[3] and fiddler Michael Doucet personally investigated that topic and music style,[4] the only publications about regional jazz bands and musicians were authored by Sonnier.[5] In the introduction of *Second Linin'*, however, his view of what he calls "rural jazz" explicitly reinforces its status as a musical genre that is distinct from French music.[6] Still, his research intrigued me and inspired an investigation of the southwest Louisiana musical landscape in the early twentieth century in all its diversity and a desire to understand the mobility of musicians between New Orleans and French Louisiana and the circulation of music in and out of Louisiana.

A number of writers representing a variety of perspectives have contributed to the literature dedicated to French Louisiana music. Academics, music critics, and producers, and passionate collectors have all shared their knowledge through diverse publications and an ever-increasing number of websites. Considered as a whole, these sources comprise an encyclopedic database concerning the history and evolution of this singular repertoire, some of them supported by original and sometimes rare recordings. For the most part, these writings and compilations label their object "Cajun music," despite the fact that they inevitably encompass the multiple legacies of French Louisiana music.

Among the early writers to expressly characterize French Louisiana music as a distinct regional repertoire was John Broven, a British music writer who published an extensive study in 1983. Broven relates in his preface that "it was dawning on me that it was wrong to think of Cajun, zydeco and the Louisiana brands of hillbilly, blues, and rock 'n' roll as separate, incompatible entities. There was a unifying factor, a special South Louisiana 'feel' that won me over completely."[7] The intrinsic heterogeneity of French Louisiana music, however, has rarely led scholars and commentators to re-examine how these categories are used and their implications.[8]

The approach I adopt here seeks to call into question how these designations have come to define French Louisiana and to contextualize its transition into the commercial era through a broader portrait of the musical landscape. Notwithstanding the categories most often associated with contemporary French Louisiana music—Cajun, Creole, zydeco, and swamp pop—a diversity of styles and influences began shaping the region's musical identity well before the commercial era. The neglect of this early period by most scholars has perpetuated assumptions that have in turn generated misleading information about the roots and contemporary character of these musics. In fact, until historian Ryan Brasseaux published *Cajun Breakdown* in 2009, there was no significant published effort to explore the history of French Louisiana music, with the notable exception of French musician Gérard Dôle's research, which spanned the colonial period between the settlement of Acadia to the Louisiana Purchase in 1803 in search of the sources of the singularity and continuity of "the old Acadian music from Louisiana."[9]

Musical data about the nineteenth and early twentieth centuries are consequently limited to references in travelogues and extrapolation from historical accounts. Beyond the regional imagery of a homogeneous southwest Louisiana music, the French Louisiana repertoire never constituted a formal category, and its evolution has entailed the convergence of multiple musical streams. French Louisiana musicians typically reinterpreted the latest trends in American popular music such as rags, jazz, hillbilly, and western swing, which in turn shaped the early French repertoire. In fact, during the first half of the twentieth century, especially when radio became the major medium for music in the 1930s, local bands had to be able to play popular music—the radio hits of the time—in order to meet audience expectations.

Rather than an exhaustive historical panorama, the discussion that follows is based on particular examples and contextual data from the first half of the twentieth century. It focuses on the diversity of musical styles, repertoire, and instrumentation that contributed to the construction of French Louisiana music during its early development, and on the versatility of early recording musicians who have now attained iconic status as pioneers. The mutual interchange and the profusion of musical styles and repertoires, however, did not prevent the propagation of stereotyped perceptions and hierarchies among the musicians. Evidence of these competing music statuses is the very sporadic if not nonexistent attention that has been paid to southwest Louisiana ensembles that did not identify with French music but whose members shared common hometowns and sometimes venues with French music bands.

From Duets to Big Bands

The Palace on Second Street of Eunice, where my parents went when they were kids, it was the big Cajun dancehall, what they don't know is that there were Cajun bands there only one night a month. The other three Saturday nights of the month, it was Kid Ory, Louis Armstrong played the Evangeline Club in Ville Plate. For my dad generation, New Orleans jazz was the rock 'n roll of that period, everybody wanted to hear and dance to it, even Cajuns. . . . You know, these people have this idea there is a time in the history of Eunice where there was no other music heard, except some Acadian music, pure music from France or Canada. It was never like that here! There was always plenty of music from other parts of Louisiana, from New Orleans. . . . My dad told me when he was a kid [in the 1920s], everybody used to play and sing in French, and this old New Orleans song that the Meters recorded, most people think they wrote the song in the seventies, "They All Ask For You." My dad said in the twenties, all the jazz bands that came here played that song, and all the French musicians heard it and started play it, cause they loved it.

ETIENNE VIATOR, EUNICE, MAY 1, 2001

Rural areas were exposed to music through a variety of traveling performers from out of state, like the minstrel shows, medicine shows, carnivals, and circuses that made entertainment accessible to everybody. In his autobiography, Baton Rouge clarinetist Joe Darensbourg (1906–1985) mentions two dozen minstrel shows in the early twenties that traveled through Opelousas and came from New Orleans and as far away as Florida and Georgia.[10] Darensbourg played saxophone with Doc Moon's medicine show, which he describes as one of the biggest such shows touring the country.[11] In Lafayette, the Jefferson Theater and the Royal Theater provided exotic high-class entertainment. In January 1918, the latter announced the coming of Hockwald and Pughe's native Hawaiian singers and players.[12]

An examination of southwest Louisiana newspapers in the late twenties, when French music truly began soaring in popularity through hit records, provides a vivid portrait of the diversity of the musical landscape in Depression-era rural Louisiana. For example, in relatively urbanized Lafayette, in June 1929 the Jefferson Theater presented *The Broadway Melody* from New York, also proudly announced on showboats.

The many dancehalls of the southwest[13] took pride in regularly scheduling out-of-town orchestras and used their radio performances, recordings, and tours throughout the country as promotional tools. On May 30, 1929, the Elk's Club of Opelousas featured "America's famous orchestra—Pep!

1.1. Ad for "The Broadway Melody." *Daily Advertiser*, June 11, 1929, p. 3. Source: Microforms Room, Dupré Library, ULL.

Personality Plus! Clayton Hunt and his Golden Gate Orchestra, Los Angeles, Ca. Broadcasting over K.F.I, K.H.J., K.F.W.B., Hollywood. WBAP, Fort Worth, WMC, Memphis, WSMB, and Edison recordings artists, Vocal Trio and entertaining specialties." In the same vein, on April 1, 1933, The Levert Gym in St. Martinville announced "music by the famous Allen and his Rhythm Playboys. Formerly the Paul D. Barnes Orchestra, which broadcasted from stations, KFDM Beaumont, WGCM Gulfport and WWL New O. This dance will be the best dance in Stw La on Easter Sunday." Many bands were invited to tour throughout Acadiana, whether they were from Baton Rouge, like Victor's Orchestra, the Original Toots Johnson, and the Deluxe Harmony Orchestra, or New Orleans, like the popular Papa Celestin and his Tuxedo Band, and Pat and Bob Decuir's Louisiana Ramblers. The leader of the Xavier University orchestra, Clyde Kerr, visited southwest Louisiana regularly and was known for performing

1.2. Warren Lacoste Orchestra, 1924–1928. Photograph courtesy of Lafayette Parisht Clerk of Court Louis J. Perret.

and arranging the latest songs shortly after their release.[14] Warren Lacoste also gave a series of performances in Lafayette with New Orleans's notorious clarinetist and songwriter Sidney Arodin, known for co-writing the pop standard "Lazy River."

In addition to live access provided by dance clubs, records and phonographs were available in drug stores, jewelry and furniture shops, and music stores. Although these music machines were often unaffordable for working-class Cajuns, music was made accessible for free through regular events organized by storeowners.[15] In Opelousas in 1923, Dietlein's sold records by Bill Murray, the notorious pianist and composer Clarence Williams, and other blues artists for 75 cents, restocking their shelves every other week.[16] In 1925 a music store opened in Crowley that carried a variety of instruments that included violins, mandolins, banjos, guitars, and ukuleles, as well as sheet music for popular songs that included "Love Has a Way," "Memory Lane," "June Night," "Sally," "Washington and Lee," "Dreamer of Dreams," and "Where Is My Sweetie Hiding."[17] In Opelousas the New Drug Store, which also sold records, announced a free weekly concert every Monday night in a circular on January 30, 1930.[18] In 1938 Mat LaVail opened a music store in New Iberia that sold popular sheet music and boasted a music conservatory offering instruction in piano, violin, organ, piano, accordion, and voice. For the store's opening on December 10, he directed the seventeen-piece Jeanerette community band as they played pieces like "Alexander's Ragtime Band," "A Tisket, A Tasket" (an Ella Fitzgerald hit recorded earlier that year), "What Goes On Here," and "Bells of St Mary."[19] According to country musician Al Terry, whose grandfather led a 1920s brass band, the Old Folks Band, in Vermilion Parish, other song titles of the period may have included "Under the Double Eagle," "The Westphalia Waltz," as well as some of the more popular songs of that day, such as "Bird in a Gilded Cage," "Shine On Harvest Moon," "Put On Your Old Gray Bonnet" and "After the Ball," one of the biggest songs of its time, first published by Charles K. Harris in 1892.[20] The presence of this Tin Pan Alley sentimental ballad in the 1920s underscores the importance of a nostalgic repertoire that coexisted with a variety of styles popular in that era, including minstrel songs, Broadway hits, ballads, blues, and ragtime.

As these examples suggest, throughout the Depression era, southwest Louisiana offered a wealth of American popular music, eagerly participating in the multifaceted and variegated market during the so-called Jazz Age. These songs were widely circulated among local music venues, music stores, and radio stations, thus making bands, records, and sheet music from across the country accessible to the local audience. Darensbourg notes that "in those days all the music publishers had a list of bands and active nightclubs, and they'd send you a lead sheet or little orchestration free 'cause they wanted their tunes played."[21] As the oil industry began to boom in the 1930s in Louisiana and East Texas, job opportunities in the oilfields offered an alternative to struggling Cajun farmers and significantly increased their incomes, further enhancing working-class access to records, phonographs, and radio sets.[22]

Technological issues also played a significant role in this musical diversity, including the boom in the phonograph recording industry through the 1920s. Radio essentially replaced phonograph records as the medium for disseminating popular music circa 1928–34, and radio corporations acquired the top record companies by the end of the 1930s. The radio effectively contributed to the breakdown of regional musical barriers. It also helped establish a new trend from smaller-piece groups to big bands of more than ten pieces—opening the way for Benny Goodman, Count Basie, Duke Ellington, etc.—relying on written arrangements and giving less room for improvisation.[23]

As the Etienne Viator quote in the epigraph above underscores, various bands from both out of state and major Louisiana cities performed frequently in southwest Louisiana, enriching the existing offerings of a highly active circle of jazz ensembles in rural towns. A range of musical combinations and styles thus interacted together, from two- to nine-piece bands that could manage collective improvisation to ten-member and even larger bands that might substitute one clarinet with five or six saxophones

Graph 1. A Sample of Music Venues and Bands in Southwest Louisiana, 1920s–1930s

This selection is based on advertisements collected in regional newspapers (see sources). It gives a snapshot of the variety of music venues and music styles of that period, of the eclectic social landscape of the regional music field, and of the circulation of bands within the South.

Towns	Dates	Music Venue	Band(s)
Lafayette / Carencro / Scott	1918	Scott Theatre	Vic Girard's Orchestra
		Guilbeau's Hall, Carencro	Martel's Band of Opelousas
	1929	Parent's Hall, Youngsville	Banner Orchestra
		Foreman's Hall, Scott	Warren J. Lacoste and His Orchestra (Sid Arodin on clarinet)
		Martin's Hall	Louisiana Six of Loreauville / Landry's Hot Six orchestra / Bill Landry and His Orchestra
		Evangeline club, Lafayette	Warren Lacoste and His Orchestra
		Antoine Duhon's Dance hall (3 miles south of Scott)	Jack Tanner and His Orchestra
		Guilbeau Hall, Carencro	Landry Orchestra
		Suburban Gardens Amusement Club	
		Breaux's Pavilion, Carencro	Franck Mutz Orchestra / Victor's Orchestra
		Arceneaux's Hall, Carencro	Joe Falcon / Banner Orchestra
		Esta Herbert's (near Vatican)	Martel Orchestra
	1931	Romero Hall, Veazey addition	Black Swan Orchestra
		Robin's Dance Hall	Lafayette, Dixieland Cotton Pickers
		Andrew Hernandez Hall	Landry's Jazz Orchestra
		Evangeline Hotel Ballroom	Jack Tanner's Radio Orchestra / Evangeline Band (Lomax rec., St. Martinville 1934)
		Edgewater Club (later the Hilltop), near present-day Pinhook Bridge	Louisiana Six
St. Martinville	1932 to 1937	Levert Gym	Pat & Bob Decuir's Louisiana Ramblers (NO) / Monk Hoggart's 12 Joy Spreaders of NO / Allen and His Rhythm Playboys / T.H. Chrone / Amos Searcy and His 10-piece Orchestra, featuring "Steady Nelson" / Original Toots Johnson, 11-piece Orch (BR) / Victor's Orch (BR) / Al Wentzell / Tony Martino and His Southerners, "from the 'Oasis' club, Corpus Christi" / Alex White / Celestin and His Tuxedo Orchestra

Location	Year	Venue	Bands
		Durand's (Main & Bridge): dancehall upstairs, grocery downstairs	Monk Hoggart's 12 Joy Spreaders of New Orleans (before 1932) / Harry Walker and His All State Orchestra / Pinky's WWL Staff Orchestra
Crowley / Rayne	1925	Hollywood Club, Rayne	Louisiana Six
		Abner Roussell Hall	Yelping Hounds Jazz Band / Cosey's Red Cap(s?) / Iowa Rhythm Kings
Opelousas	1929	Elks Club	Deluxe Harmony Orchestra (BR) / Franck Mutz and His Orchestra / Clayton Hunt and His Golden Gate Orchestra, Los Angeles / Victor's orchestra / Kid Dime's orchestra
		Cedar Lane Club	Louisiana Six / Martel Orchestra
		Music by Victor's Orchestra Dance at Washington: series of dance every 2 weeks given Tues by Callis Shexnayder near Southern Pacific Station. Also Joe Falcon	Opelousas Brass Band, 20 members
New Iberia	1938	Attakappa Night Club, New Year's Eve (in 1937, Attakappa Dinner Club)	Clyde Kerr and His Sensational 14-piece Orchestra / Celestin's Tuxedo Orchestra of New Orleans
		Acadian Club	Don Felton and His Ten Pals / Segura Brothers (Lomax rec., White Oaks 1934)
		Jungle Club (owner: Eloi Doré)	Louisiana Six
		Club Louisiane	(big bands) / Louisiana Six
		Club Casablanca	Louisiana Six
		Teche Club (Hwy 90)	Filo Gonzales / black bands
		(Mat LaVail music store; voice, piano, piano acc, violin instructor: Elizabeth Fullerton)	
Abbeville / Maurice / Delcambre / (also based on interviews)	1929 to 1940s	Belvedere, Delcambre	Louisiana Six / Bill Landry & Al Terry
		Silver Star (Abbeville/Maurice)	Louisiana Six
		Maurice Hall	The Yelping Hounds of Crowley / Louisiana Six
		River Oaks Club	Filo Gonzales, Mexican (1940s)

1.3. The Banner Orchestra. L–R: Gus Fontenette, Bunk Johnson, Evan Thomas, Robert Stafford, William Burner, Ed Reedom, John Sanders (standing), Tom Edwards, Lawrence Duhé, Clossie Roy. At Iberia Parish Training School, New Iberia, ca. late 1920s (where Bunk Johnson would later teach music for a WPA project, 1940–41). Courtesy of I. A. and Carroll Martin Photo Collection at Iberia Parish Library in New Iberia, LA, #11,000.

(with some doubling on clarinet), three or four trumpets, and two or three trombones, in addition to a rhythm section—a standard big band lineup requiring an arranger to rationalize the sections and place the solos properly.[24] These regional ensembles included the Jeanerette community band but also some better-known bands. These bands have received little attention, and their influence is absent from the official narrative concerning French music, contributing to its reputation as an isolated and discrete musical genre that at one time dominated the region.

The silence about these bands is all the more striking given that more than fifteen of them performed several times a week in clubs and at church fairs, in lodges and social clubs, during parades, and even at picnics and excursions across southwest Louisiana. These ensembles and orchestras had an important turnover among musicians, and they were organized around the constant circulation of musicians, some with long-term engagements and others temporary, between New Orleans and rural Louisiana. The Banner Orchestra of New Iberia was known as the best big ensemble in the area.[25] Founded in 1908 by native cornet player and barber Gustave Fontenette, the orchestra remained popular for the next forty years. As many as thirty-five musicians at times played with the band, which traveled as far west as Port Arthur and Beaumont, Texas. In Louisiana, they toured most southern towns, sweeping from west to east. Fontenette "had no trouble to have musicians come from the New Orleans area to play with his band," and the orchestra counted eminent musicians such as clarinetist George Lewis, Lawrence Duhé, and Bunk Johnson among its members.

Willie Geary "Bunk" Johnson (1879–1949) moved to New Iberia from New Orleans in 1920 after playing with Jelly Roll Morton, Joe "King" Oliver, and Buddy Bolden. Johnson earned his living at the local rice mills and taught music through the WPA program in the New Iberia public school system. Orres Leblanc grew up in New Iberia and graduated in 1945. A retired parish clerk, he was not aware of Bunk's teaching assignment but recalls meeting him when he was about fourteen years old:

> Bunk used to hang around my father's service station a great deal. He had an old jalopy that my father helped him keep going. My father would give him free gasoline. He was quite a softspoken man. He never showed a pretentiousness or anything like that. What he would do, when he was down and out, he would take the horn out and play at the service station and the people would come and pass the hat and put in . . . very little money. And then he'd go back across the street and work on the grounds at the Shadows [of the Teche, a plantation house]. He was virtually a pauper then. In retrospect I think how terrible it must have been, because in his world travels later on or before that, he was quite a significant figure in the jazz world. And nobody paid attention to him in this locale.[26]

Credited by musicians and friends with teaching Louis Armstrong, he eventually attracted the attention of the jazz critics Frederic Ramsey Jr., Charles E. Smith, and William Russell, who encouraged him to return to performing by booking him for concerts and recording sessions in the New Orleans area and on the East and West Coasts. In 2001 the Iberia Parish Public Library opened an entire room devoted to Johnson, with extensive archives collected by the late jazz fan Harold Drob. The collection includes more than 500 books, 175 photographs, periodicals, correspondence, video interviews and recordings. A close friend of Johnson's, Drob booked for him a series of New York dance concert appearances, and helped him record on the Columbia label with musicians of his own

1.4. Bunk Johnson, May 1945, 638 Franklin Street, New Iberia, Louisiana, photographed by William Russell, OPH000811. Courtesy of William Ransom Hogan Jazz Archive, Tulane University.

choosing at Carnegie Hall in New York in 1947. To this day, New Iberia sponsors an annual Bunk Johnson Festival. Despite his prestigious career, Johnson has remained largely absent from the official narrative about regional music, except in his adopted hometown.

Another widely celebrated musician, Evan Thomas, had a reputation as the region's greatest trumpet player. Originally from Crowley, he founded a very popular band, the Black Eagle Band, around the mid-1910s. George Lewis played his first job with him, and Bunk Johnson played second trumpet as well as tuba. Although there is little data about Thomas, we do know that he was celebrated for his powerful sound and wide register. He would advertise a dance for his own band or the Banner Band, in which he also played, by blowing his horn out the window of a store or a hall earlier in the afternoon.[27] His ill-fated life came to an abrupt end in 1931 while he was playing in a dancehall in Rayne and was murdered by the

1.5. Louis Armstrong at Cedar Lane Club, Opelousas, date unknown, H155. Photograph courtesy of Lafayette Parish Clerk of Court Louis J. Perret.

husband of his mistress. Johnson got his front teeth broken in the battle, interrupting his career for ten years.[28] Herman James, a retired schoolteacher who learned the snare drum under Bunk Johnson in high school during the forties, attests that legendary figures such as Louis Armstrong, Ella Fitzgerald, Count Basie, and Cab Calloway were among the musicians who played in the New Iberia public school gymnasium.[29] Black musicians would stay at the Robinson, a café and hotel in town that accommodated blacks. North of Lafayette, around Opelousas, Arnold DePass, a trumpet player who moved there from New Orleans in the late forties, recalls a popular club that scheduled Glenn Miller, Les Brown, and Harry James. Duke Ellington, Count Basie, and Lucky Millinder were also known to have played a black club called Bradford's.

Another popular band at the time was the Martel Orchestra, a Creole of color family band led by Albert, the father. The band was apparently successful throughout the South, travelling as far as Mississippi and Arkansas.[30] It included trumpet, trombone, banjo, violin, bass, and sometimes piano and drums. Joe Darensbourg, who joined the band in 1923 for about a year, confirms its popularity when he mentions that he earned a good living with them for the time, making twenty-five dollars a week.[31] Darensbourg dated Hillary Martel, who played in the band, and married her after getting her pregnant, but their relationship did not last long. Earlier that year, New Orleans multi-instrumentalist Manuel Manetta

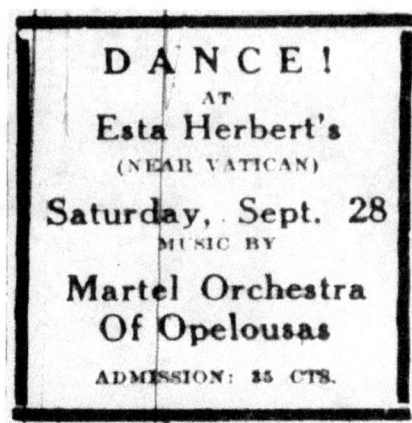

1.6. Ad for Martel Orchestra at Esta Herbert's, Lafayette. *Daily Advertiser*, September 27, 1929. Source: Microforms Room, Dupré Library, ULL.

and drummer Alex Bigard played in the band for three months. In fact, historian Bruce Raeburn notes that Manetta, a Creole of color musician in high demand, was hired as a leader to teach the Martels "about New Orleans tempos," which at that time would have meant jazz dance tempos, illustrating the apprenticeship involved in the interactions between New Orleans and southwest Louisiana musicians.[32] In the interview with Alex Bigard providing this data, Bigard adds that "the band played the same things and in the same way as New Orleans bands." He did not really remember what Manetta specifically taught, except that he would demonstrate how to perform particularly difficult parts in the music.[33]

Although Sonnier wrote exclusively about black jazz ensembles, there were also numerous white bands playing the regional circuit. A recurrent band name is the Louisiana Six, who began as a family band. Delma Hebert was a violinist who played polkas, mazurkas, quadrilles and other dance tunes.[34] As they were growing up, the taste for these musical styles was already fading, and the Hebert siblings started a band more in tune with the popular musical landscape of the time. They are mentioned in the *Daily Advertiser* as early as 1918, in reference to a dance at the Martin Dance Hall in Scott, apparently a "classy" club. Led by Sidney "Cap" Hebert on trumpet, the band included Leo Girouard, Alief "Coosoon" Girouard, Noah Hebert, Wilson Hebert, and Viola Hebert Landry. Eventually growing to comprise a nine-piece band, it was in high demand and toured throughout Louisiana and Texas. They were able to afford a Model T,

1.7. Cover of the LP *Cap Hebert & His Louisianians* (Mil Records 101).

followed by numerous cars in which they toured for twenty years until disbanding during World War II. After the war, the band was reconfigured and consisted of three sets of brothers, Noah and Wilton Hebert, Lucien and Bill Landry, and Aaron and "Dub" Domingue. They went under the name of their new leader, the Bill Landry Band, until his death in 1979.[35] Among all of these bands, the Louisiana Six is apparently the only band whose music was commercially recorded, on a single LP. The album, entitled *Cap Hebert and His Louisianians: Remember When . . . Those Were the Good Old Days*, was recorded after the band disbanded, on an independent label (#101) and probably dates back to the early to mid-fifties.[36] The selection of songs reflects the standard Tin Pan Alley tunes popular in the early twentieth century. This *a posteriori* recording reveals an intriguing blend of the plain style of the 1920s with a more Glenn Miller–like, standard big-band sound.

Like the French music bands of the period, most of these bands played a variety of rhythms—schottisches, quadrilles, waltzes, fox trots, rags, blues, polkas, mazurkas, and the Charleston. They shared common instruments such as clarinet, piano, and violin. Hypolite Charles, a cornet player from Parks, east of Lafayette, maintains that he always had a violin in his band.[37] The Banner Orchestra's original membership and the Martel family band also included violin players. Charles provides a list of violin players whom

1.8. The Louisiana Six, no date. Courtesy of I. A. and Carroll Martin Photo Collection at Iberia Parish Library in New Iberia, LA, #11,013.

he considers to have been outstanding, such as Peter Bocage, A. J. Piron, John Robichaux, McNeal, and Jimmy Palao (leader of the Imperial).

According to available documents regarding instrumentation after the arrival of the Acadians, the violin appears to have been the dominant instrument well into the early decades of the nineteenth century.[38] The evidence of the presence of clarinets, even though too slim to testify to its longevity or prominence, contrasts with the instrumentation typically associated with French music. Similarly, the harmonica became important in the musical landscape as early as the Civil War, prefiguring the sound of the diatonic accordion, which is intimately linked to French Louisiana music, to such an extent that it is now designated as the "Cajun accordion," although it is neither restricted to the Cajun style nor to French Louisiana music.[39]

The introduction of the accordion in Louisiana has been attributed to German settlers and German-American migrants arriving from the Midwest in the 1870s,[40] but there is scant evidence to support this assertion.[41] It appears likely that the accordion was in wide use by the latter half of the nineteenth century, but the time of its incorporation into French music

1.9. Hypolite Charles and his band, 1920s. H 112. Sonnier mentions that in 1919 Charles organized his own orchestra and started working at the Moulin Rouge in New Orleans. His group was composed of Sonny Henry, trombone; Joe Welch, drums; Sam Dutrey, clarinet; Emile Bigard, violin; and Camille Todd, piano. This photograph does not include all of them but testifies of the presence of a violinist. Photograph courtesy of Lafayette Parish Clerk of Court Louis J. Perret.

remains the subject of debates. However, despite extensive historical research, Sexton found little reference to the use of the accordion by Cajuns or Creoles until the early twentieth century.[42] The importation of accordions that were compatible with the fiddle (C and D) undoubtedly contributed to its widespread adoption by the 1920s, when it was occasionally accompanied by a guitar and/or a *'tit fer* (triangle), or simply by a fiddle.

Despite scarce evidence of the use of the accordion in jazz ensemble, the name and instrumentation of the Accordiana Band, as early as 1894, suggests the inclusion of the accordion in dance orchestras. The Accordiana Band was led by Henry Peyton on accordion, and also featured Alphonse Picou on clarinet, Punkie Valentin on cornet, and Bouboul Valentin on valve trombone.[43] Trombonist and bandleader Edward "Kid" Ory remembers hearing Henry Peyton's band while growing up in LaPlace.[44]

In *La Nouvelle-Orléans, capitale du jazz*, Robert Goffin makes three references to Buddy Bolden, a key figure of jazz, playing the accordion.[45] Quoting Emmanuel Perez, he mentions: "At this time [1895–96], Buddy Bolden did not exist. He came in three or for years later. He was first an accordion player and worked as a barber assistant."[46] In a chapter titled "Buddy Bolden," Goffin writes: "While he played accordion in public, it seems like Buddy Bolden, in love with ragtime and full of imagination, looked for a more complete form of expression and bought a cornet that he kept like a jewel."[47]

At this time [1895] Gregson was a kid who sold newspapers at Roman and Third Street and he played some harmonica. He met a blind little boy who handed down schedules, Emile Stalebread Lacombe or Lacoume, of creole origin, and they progressively built a core of young men who worked during daytime and went singing in front of restaurants and honky-tonks at night. There was Willy Bussey, Bourbon's barman, who pinched the guitar on a box he had fixed. Bolden caressed the accordion.[48]

Charley Gallaway [sic] is also listed as playing accordion in his family band circa mid-1890s.[49]

The role of Mexican musicians in the presence of the accordion is a further unexplored aspect of the history of the region's music. At the 1884–85 World Industrial and Cotton Centennial Exposition in New Orleans performed the Eight Cavalry Mexican Band led by Encarnacion Payen, more commonly known as the Mexican Band. This performance is often cited as the beginning of Mexican influence on the early development of jazz and on the New Orleans sound. In fact, Historian Jack Stewart maintains that there was more than one Mexican band, as the Mexican government was one of the largest sponsors of the World's Fair.[50] Payen's band returned several times, and other groups continued to tour in the early twentieth century, like the hundred-member Mexican National Band. Some Mexican musicians decided to remain in the city, and gained influence as notable music instructors. Bunk Johnson's early teacher was a Mexican named Wallace Cutchey. Florencio Ramos (1861–1931), from Nueva Leon, is said to have taught piano and accordion. It is possible that the oft-cited Tio family also established a link with the accordion on returning from Mexico at the end of the Civil War. Mexican music was promoted through the efforts of music publisher Junius Hart, who started a Mexican Series, and published "Over the Waves" ("Sobre Las Olas"). Inextricably linked to New Orleans jazz, the song has also been incorporated into the French repertoire, where it was popularized in the 1940s and continued to be requested by audience members of that generation into the 1980s in Acadiana dance halls.[51]

It is not difficult to imagine that Mexican musicians toured or stayed in southwest Louisiana in the early twentieth century, although the subject would require further research. Many residents of Vermilion and Iberia parishes recall a band from the 1940s led by Filo Gonzales, whom they identify as Mexican. He apparently used to perform at the River Oaks Club in Abbeville, as well as the Teche Club on Highway 90, and was known for simultaneously playing the maracas and the bass with his right hand.[52] Fiddler Adner Ortego further reported to Etienne Viator that he heard a mariachi band in Vidrine in 1932, and that he learned several of their songs.

These musical interactions and exchanges traversed the Gulf of Mexico in both directions. "La Cucaracha" was played up until the late 1970s by Creole musicians Bois Sec Ardoin and Canray Fontenot. In 1931 Boudreaux's Electric Piano Shop in Lafayette advertised "Mama Ines,"[53] a rumba popularized by Cuban pianist and songwriter Bola de Nieve in 1927. Cajun accordion player Nathan Abshire adapted it in the early 1950s under the name "Mama Rosin," assuring its entry into the French repertoire. In the process, the self-derision of blacks gave way to consensual lyrics. "Ay Maman Iné, todo los negros tomar un café" ("all niggers to drink coffee") is in its Cajun reinterpretation turned into a song about dancing and having a good time.[54] The adaptation and appropriation of diverse musical styles within popular music from the Unites States, extending to Mexico and Cuba, has been an ongoing and profoundly influential dimension of French Louisiana music.

"Whatever the Public Wants"

A lot of the guys would say, it wasn't so much about keeping the tradition alive, or keeping the style alive, it was just that there were fiddlers and they wanted to play what was popular at the time. What was popular was Texas music, people didn't want to dance those old mazurkas and polkas and old time stuff. So it was more about playing what was popular. And that style of fiddling stuck around for a long time. Doc Guidry, Rufus Thibodeaux. That really stuck around up 'til the seventies. It wasn't until maybe the eighties that Michael Doucet brought back the style he heard from Canray and Dennis, and young people started catching on to that.
MITCH REED, SCOTT, JUNE 25, 2008

It is in this bubbling musical landscape, constantly adjusting to the latest trends in American popular music, that French music evolved and began to gain recognition. Despite the implosion of the record market around

1928–34 phonograph companies maintained their predominance in the foreign record business. They promoted their product as a scientific and educational tool, associating themselves with anthropology and folklore. By recording "native bands" throughout the world, they claimed to preserve national "folk" musics—a concept that differed from its use in the social sciences in isolation from the commercial market—becoming a catchall marketing term to denote difference from the norms of Western "art" music. As demonstrated by Karl H. Miller, the paradigm of local music that came to dominate the U.S. talking machine business after World War I was based on the idea that immigrants would purchase music that represented their own identity.[55]

The first commercial recordings of French music took place in this context.[56] Record companies followed the lead of Ralph Peer with the OKeh label, launching field-recording expeditions in the South. During this period, A&R men like Peer realized that ethnic music provided a sea of untapped potential royalties, particularly considering that an important part of it could be claimed as "traditional" and therefore converted to the benefit of the finder. From 1923 to 1936, a number of national record companies organized regular sessions in different southern cities to collect the music of hillbilly, blues, Mexican, and French bands, forging an image of southern music as distinct from mass-produced music. French music bands became trendy and came to share the same music venues as jazz ensembles in southwest Louisiana. For example, Arceneaux's Hall in Carencro featured accordion player Joe Falcon on September 13, 1929, then on December 12 presented the Louisiana Six. On January 17, 1929, a dance announcement proudly promoted Falcon as "the Victor's artist" (mistakenly, instead of Columbia). Fiddler Varise Conner, who grew up during that era, explains that "when old Joe Falcon made the first records, then anybody that could play a little bit on the accordion, that was the style, they started playing the accordion."[57]

Joe Falcon (1900–1965), celebrated as the first Cajun musician to make a commercial recording, was sponsored by George Burrow, a local politician and jewelry store owner from Rayne, to go to New Orleans in 1928 to make records that Burrow agreed to sell in his store.[58] Contacted by Burrow, the recording studio set up in New Orleans by Columbia ultimately gave a lukewarm welcome to the musicians, apparently because they were seeking orchestras. After hearing Falcon on the accordion and his wife Cleoma Breaux on guitar, however, the manager allegedly shouted out: "Lord, but that's more music out of two instruments than we ever heard in our lives."⁵⁹ As a consequence, "Lafayette" (generally referred to as "Allons à Lafayette") and "The Waltz That Carried Me to My Grave" were the first French songs ever to be recorded, inaugurating a niche market for French music and ensuring its profitability.

Like many other musicians of the time, however, Joe Falcon was not exclusively dedicated to French music. String bands were gaining ground in the 1930s, and it is said that the advent of amplification contributed to the prevalence of string instruments, whose sound was previously overwhelmed in acoustic performance by more powerful instruments like the accordion. In the later 1930s, Falcon led the Silver Bell String Band of Rayne, picking up his accordion occasionally and at other times turning to his drums.⁶⁰ In an interview with folklorist Ralph Rinzler in 1965, Falcon is clear. Rinzler asks: "Did you prefer Cajun music to other types?" "I like my hillbilly," answers Falcon.

Fiddler Leo Soileau, also interviewed by Rinzler, claimed Bob Wills, the icon of Western swing, as his favorite.⁶¹ The raw sound of Soileau's early recordings, as Savoy notes, did not foreshadow the smooth style he would later develop.⁶² But in an interview with Michael Doucet in the early 1980s,⁶³ Soileau said that he expanded his repertoire and broadened his style thanks to the teaching of a Creole fiddler from New Orleans, Bradford Gordon, in turn influenced by Sam Morgan's musical style. Through the mediation of a sponsor and jewelry store owner from Opelousas, Franck J. Dietlein, Victor, a rival of the Columbia label, hastened to record Soileau in Atlanta with the accordionist Mayeuse (also spelled Maius) Lafleur, scooping Columbia by releasing the record first. That very same year, in 1929, the commercial success of these early recordings encouraged other major record labels—Paramount, Brunswick/Vocalion, and OKeh—to record French Louisiana musicians like Amédé Ardoin, the Breaux Brothers, Angela Lejeune, and Dennis McGee.

Accordion contests were another means by which recording studios recruited talented musicians. Winners would play the dance that night, and the prize for the largest events was a recording session. A statewide contest in Opelousas on September 27–28, 1929, sponsored by the *Opelousas Herald* and leading local businessmen, attracted more than 2,000 people from the region and was attended by representatives of four major record companies, Columbia, Victor, Brunswick, and OKeh.⁶⁴ Dennis McGee and Lavergne from Evangeline Parish took the grand prize at this event, which included 400 dollars. Soon after this contest McGee recorded with the Creole accordion player Amédé Ardoin, on December 9, 1929. Although many publications establish Amédé Ardoin as the first Creole musician to record, that distinction actually goes to Douglas Bellard, who released a song with Kirby Riley two months earlier on the Brunswick label, in October 1929. Still, Ardoin (1896–1941) is noteworthy as one of the figures of early French Louisiana music to achieve the most recognition both among his contemporaries and subsequent generations. Ardoin continues to be cited by both Creoles and Cajuns as one of the fathers of the repertoire. He formed a successful and legendary duo with Cajun fiddler Dennis McGee (1893–1989). Both tenant farmers on the same farm, they collaborated for twenty years, playing in dancehalls and house dances throughout the region.[65] Emar Lejeune, a Cajun farmer, owned a dancehall in Swords where Ardoin played weekly for two years. Lejeune's son, Vincent, recalls that "he played it all. He'd play a waltz, he'd play a two-step, he'd play a one-step. He played for people that used to do Charleston. And he'd play the old New Orleans blues."[66]

Canray Fontenot, another major figure, was a cousin of Douglas Bellard and first learned to play behind Ardoin as a triangle player, only later learning to play fiddle. There are few documented sources concerning the eclecticism of Creole musicians' repertoire; most focus on the French and blues genres, a tendency that appears to be strongly shaped by the representation of "black music," a question discussed in detail in chapter 3. We do know, however, that what was catalogued as "hillbilly" and later designated country music was an integral part of Creole musicians' repertoire and taste.

Fontenot also formed a string band in the thirties. Musicians mentored by Fontenot, such as Michael Doucet, testify that he played a variety of rags. Fiddler Doucet accompanied Fontenot during a recording session in the eighties, with Arhoolie director Chris Strachwitz, and heard him play rags that he had never heard before.[67] "Fi-Do," "Shoo, Black," and "Canray's Breakdown" (which fiddler D'Jalma Garnier identifies with the jazz standard "Salty Dog") constitute some recorded examples.[68] Creole fiddler Bébé Carrière relates that he played the blues standard "Baby Please Don't Go" as well as Bill Monroe's "Kentucky Waltz." "I liked that very much," he says, "and poor Jimmie Rodgers's song, I could play 'I'm Going to California Where They Sleep Out Every Night.'"[69]

Following in the footsteps of Soileau and drawing inspiration from Bob Wills, Jimmie Rodgers, and Bessie Smith, the Hackberry Ramblers became the most popular band in the mid-thirties and one of the most influential of the swing era. The leader of the band, Luderin Darbone, explained that he never went to Cajun dances when he started playing, and when he played with fellow musician Edwin Duhon at house dances, they "played popular and hillbilly tunes, not Cajun."[70] Ben Sandmel, who played with and managed the band after their comeback in the late 1980s until the late 2000s, contextualizes the band's choices, shaped by their taste for modern sounds and the need to make a living during the Great Depression: "Unabashedly commercial, with nary a thought of folkloric legacy, the Ramblers wanted to record hits."[71] They were also given to reinterpreting hits, like the New Orleans standard "High Society," which they reworked to create "Vinton's High Society," "an instrumental spin-off of Johnny Dodds's famous clarinet solo from the King Oliver recording."[72] They even recorded a Hawaiian novelty song, "A Little Rendezvous with Honolulu" (1936), at the suggestion of their label Bluebird. Along the same line, eager to enhance their performances and take advantage of modern developments, they were the first southwest Louisiana band to use amplification in the mid-1930s. By the mid-1940s the band had evolved into a nine-piece Western swing orchestra with horns, piano, drums, and electric and steel guitar. "Whatever the public wants, Darbone says, whatever they enjoy dancing to, that's what we give them. We always have," reports Sandmel.[73] Using an approach perfectly consistent with that adopted by other bands of the region, French music bands were following popular music trends. Like all musicians, they considered meeting public expectations their priority.

According to historian Ryan Brasseaux, what has come to be called the Cajun swing era can be considered (stylistically, instrumentally, or technically) the most innovative commercial period in the history of the genre. This era is closely linked with the name of Harry Choates (1922–1951), to the extent that Arhoolie released a compilation album titled *The Fiddle King of Cajun Swing* in 1982. It is during that period that the most successful and influential hit of the French repertoire, "Jole Blon," was also produced. First recorded by Leo Soileau, Choates's 1946 recording by Gold Star in Houston crossed the threshold of one million sales and propelled French music to the top of the charts, for the first time transcending regional boundaries and inspiring numerous nationally acclaimed musicians to offer their own adaptations of the tune.[74]

It is commonly asserted that the accordion declined in the 1930s and 1940s in favor of string bands, although historian Kevin Fontenot questions this view.[75] Accordions nonetheless did fall into disfavor among most record companies. After a gap of about four years during the Depression, major companies like Decca and Victor started signing musicians including Leo Soileau, who is said to have "prided himself on being able to draw from such diverse traditions as polkas, Mexican music, and square dances."[76] With the Four Aces, Leo Soileau met many Texas band musicians, at the Dallas recording sessions where up to forty bands would attend, and mostly recorded current hillbilly and pop translated into French, joining other offerings in the Decca label's Cajun series.[77]

Instrumentation also varied from one band to another, even from one song to the other, including instruments not typically associated with French Louisiana music. Soileau and his band, rechristened the Rhythm Boys in 1937, diversified their instrumentation with electric mandolin, saxophone, and piano. "You Belong to Me" from Artelus Mistric is a vocal and harmonica solo;[78] the western swing–styled "The Crawfish in the Pond" (1938) by Happy Fats and The Rayne-Bo Ramblers features a piano solo, and their "Veuves de la Coulee" from 1940 is accompanied by piano. Arhoolie's subsequent album *Cajun Honky-Tonk*, which reissued recordings cut by the Khoury label in the 1950s, includes piano solos such as "Lawtell 2-step." Although harmonies are more associated with post–World War II bands, the Hackberry Ramblers sang harmony on 1938 "Je va t'aimer quand même," the Rayne-Bo Ramblers use them on "Les Tete Fille Lafayette" and "La Veuve de la Coulee" in 1940, as did Octa Clark on his covers of Jimmie Rodgers.

Studies of French Louisiana music universally signal examples of popular blues, country, and hillbilly songs that were translated into French, arguing that these translations demonstrate the various influences of American popular music and its habitual appropriation by French musicians. Among many other examples, standouts include "Birmingham Jail," "My Brown Eyed Texas Rose," "Little Dutch Hill," "My Wild Irish Rose," "Red River Valley," "Bonnie Blue Eyes," Bob Wills's "Maidens' Prayer," and the Hawaiian song "Aloha." Some renditions are associated with specific musicians: "Wonderin'" by the Hackberry/Riverside Ramblers was made a country music standard by Webb Pierce in 1952; "What's the Matter Now" by Lawrence Walker;[79] Jimmie Davis's "Nobody's Darlin' But Mine," released as "Personne N'aime Pas" by the Rhythm Boys; William Warren and Arlie Carter's "The Wild Side of Life" entitled "Le côté farouche de la vie" by Marie Falcon and Shuk Richard.[80] Cleoma Breaux, Joe Falcon's wife, rendered French versions of country and western songs like "Pin Solitaire" (Lonesome Pine) and "L'amour indifférent" (Careless Love) as well as popular Harlem jazz numbers such as "Lulu's Back in Town."[81]

For many bands of the period, Jimmie Rodgers, whose influence would extend well beyond country music, was a perennial source of inspiration. Joe Falcon in 1936 recorded "Raise Your Window," which incorporates verses from Rodgers songs.[82] Leo Soileau's band recorded a version of "Frankie and Johnnie." Leroy "Happy Fats" Leblanc states that his "guitar style was based on Jimmie Rodgers." Claiming to be similarly influenced by Bradley Kincaid and Bob Wills, Leblanc avows that "during those years [he] more or less copied them."[83] With his string band the Rayne-Bo Ramblers, he incorporated Rodgers's motif into their 1937 recording of "Bosco Blues." Similarly, "La valse de la prison" by the Hackberry Ramblers is a takeoff on "Birmingham Jail." Roy Gonzales's translations of Jimmie Rodgers songs like "Waiting for a Train," "Lonely and Blue," and "T for Texas" recorded in 1929 are other remarkable examples.[84] Historian Barry Mazor notes that accordion player Iry Lejeune drew the connection with Rodgers even closer in "Grand Bosco" and its variation "Bosco," where the similarity with the lyrics about walking down the railroad track and the motif of "Anniversary Blue Yodel" are unmistakable.[85]

Many songs were translated or directly composed in English as well, even among those strongly associated with French-lyric tunes. Cleoma Breaux recorded "Hand Me Down My Walking Cane" in a style imitating southeastern mountain music.[86] Lawrence Walker, who along with Iry Lejeune and Nathan Abshire helped revitalize the accordion after World War II, in 1935 made a version of "Corinne, Corinna" named "Alberta," sung in English. That same year, the Dixie Ramblers recorded the folksong "Saint James Infirmary"—made famous by Louis Armstrong in 1928—as "Barroom Blues," followed by a dozen titles of popular hillbilly tunes.[87] Lawrence Walker recorded "Lena Mae" and "Let's Rock and Roll Tonight" in English along with Cajun classics.[88]

This flow between languages, styles, and musicians continued throughout the 1950s. Some influences are not apparent, as was the case with translated versions of the same song into French or English. Songs were substantially rearranged and did not necessarily share the original melody. Luderin Darbone learned standard New Orleans tunes like "Eh La-Bas" from African American trumpeter Ike Jenkins, who led an orchestra based in Crowley. His version is nonetheless quite different in terms of lyrics and melody from its original release by jazz musician Kid Ory in 1946, as well as from other interpretations by eminent New Orleans musicians like Papa Celestin (1947), Dede Pierce (1962), or Paul Barbarin. For Darbone, finding his own arrangement is essential to make it attractive: "To go record we'd have to have new material."[89] Also based on "Eh La-Bas," "Chanson de Limonade," which seems to have been first recorded by Leroy Broussard in 1956, was popularized by Nathan Abshire. Although the melody is again dissimilar from "Eh La-Bas," the lyrics are comparable.[90] In both cases, the character in the song delights in eating good food and drinking good wine. In his collection of *Creole Songs of the Deep South* from 1946, Henri Wehrmann gives the words of another song named *La maison Denise*, which is also based on the celebration of overindulgence.[91] Darensbourg indicates that "Eh La-bas" was itself a version of "Over There" by Irving Berlin that Ory reinterpreted in French.[92]

As shown through the circulation of bands and musicians between New Orleans and southwest Louisiana mentioned above, rural areas were exposed to the influence of New Orleans not only through musicians but also workers who divided their lives between the city and the country. This was the case of Paul Verdun, a farmer who in the late 1940s earned extra income as a barber in New Orleans for five years while his family stayed in Grand Marais, a small Creole of color community near Jeanerette. There, he hung out in clubs, listened to a lot of jukebox music, and saw Fats Domino perform. His daughter, Melva Patton, reports: "When he would come back here, everybody would say, 'OK, Let's throw a dance, let's get a platform.' Because Ti Paul was coming back home. And daddy and his first cousin would play together. One of them was a violin player and a guitar player, another was an upright bass player, dad played guitar and bass and harmonica and violin."[93] He sang in both French and English, from "Jolie blonde" to "You Are My Sunshine," "Mathilda," and "You're Cheating My Heart."

This diversity of styles and influences was then encompassed into what the record labels termed as "French" or "Cajun" recordings that targeted marginalized ethnics. After World War II, the decentralization of the recording industry led to the proliferation of independent small-town record companies across the country.[94] Their interest in the diversity of regional traditions gave musicians greater freedom for musical experimentation and translated into a more targeted marketing strategy, contributing to the partition of French Louisiana music into distinct musical categories. Among the most successful local producers were Eddie Shuler from Lake Charles, J. D. "Jay" Miller from Crowley, and Floyd Soileau from Ville Platte, all of whom operated recording studios in their hometowns.

All sources concur that French music was much in demand among the local public. Miller was first to produce a 78 record in 1946 featuring

Cajun musicians Happy Fats and Doc Guidry with the Boys at Cosimo Matassa's studio in New Orleans.[95] A controversial figure among musicians who worked with him because of his remuneration practices, E. Shuler had been part of the Hackberry Ramblers in the early 1940s. It was on his label, Goldband Records, that accordion player Iry Lejeune (1928–1955) achieved his popularity. Credited for reviving the accordion after the war, Lejeune never restricted himself to Cajun music: "Luderin Darbone recalls that [Lejeune] came by the Silver Star on numerous occasions to listen to the Hackberry Ramblers style of music." His collection of 78s included albums by Jimmie Rodgers, Gene Autry, Bob Wills, and the Carter Family, to name a few, and he recorded Jimmie Rogers songs in 1954.[96] Like Miller, Shuler embraced country, rhythm and blues, and rock 'n roll artists, producing some of the most prolific performers. He is particularly well known for releasing the first record identified as zydeco, Boozoo Chavis's "Paper in My Shoe," in 1954.

Both Miller and Soileau, who started his own studio in 1958, issued a number of labels, categorizing French Louisiana music into different styles to better target audiences and reach a wider public. Using the same strategy as the Hackberry Ramblers who, as early as 1936, started playing and recording under the name the Riverside Ramblers for English numbers, Soileau started distinguishing his French recordings (Swallow) from those of swamp pop musicians (Jin), explaining that "at that time Cajun was not cool."[97] Another key figure in the evolution of labels was J. D. Miller, who founded Fais Do-Do, later replaced by Feature, for which he released a number of hillbilly hits. These included such numbers as Bill Hutto's "Some of These Days," Lou Millet's "That's Me Without You," and Al Terry's "God Was So Good."[98] In a letter to John Broven, Miller makes no secret of the important role played by hillbilly: "I started recording French Cajun records, that is the type of music that is quite popular here in Southwest Louisiana. From that I went into hillbilly music; that, I must confess, is my favourite type of music."[99] He achieved success with country-oriented Cajun musicians like Jimmie C. Newman and Al Terry and helped break into the national scene by his Nashville connections. Other labels were dedicated to rock and roll (Rocko) and a variety of musical styles (Zynn, Showtime). Miller is best known for his recording of emblematic blues musicians (Lazy Lester, Lightnin' Slim, and Slim Harpo) for the Excello label of Nashville.

"From the Other Side of the Fence"

A guy asked me one time: where would you learn to play the washboard? I said, you sure wouldn't go to Julliard [giggles]. See, you would never go to school to learn how to play zydeco. That's strictly a folk music.

Born in 1929, Arnold "Pap" DePass Jr. was still working as a deliveryman for Bodemuller print shop in Opelousas at age seventy-five, in 2004. His father was an eminent Creole drummer in New Orleans and the founder of The Olympia Brass Band who was known for giving musicians their first chance in his band, such as King Oliver, and, like many musicians of the period, he regularly played in Storyville, the city's red light district until 1917. His French-speaking family lived in Tremé, and Pap learned the trumpet, flugelhorn, and cornet, surrounded by prominent musicians. In the early 1950s, he enrolled in the Army band. At one of their performances, while on tour in southwest Louisiana, he met his wife in a club that she describes as "one of the exclusive nightclubs" of Opelousas called the White Eagle Club. His wife was herself from Pot Cove, a rural Creole enclave near Mallet that she both claims and rejects, through insistent references to her exclusive education while defining herself first and foremost as a human being who embraces all skin tones.

DePass's profile helps illustrate the social hierarchies linked to Louisiana musical tastes and musical status in the first half of the twentieth century. Free people of color in antebellum Louisiana were inserted into a tripartite society that gave them the opportunity to own goods and property, including slaves, and to will them to the succeeding generation. The legal distinction between freedmen and Creoles of color was challenged after Emancipation. In 1900, for the first time, the census merged blacks and people of black ancestry under the "Black" category, eliminating the category "Mulatto." This confusion of status led them to identify as Creoles of color after the Civil War, in order to distinguish themselves from freedmen, with whom they became associated during segregation.[100] Endogamous marriages were combined with other differentiation strategies based on family, language, light skin color, and moral values.[101] Benevolent societies were particularly instrumental in maintaining a distinctive social status. They provided Creoles of color with entertainment, camaraderie, and mutual aid such as assistance with burial and healthcare. Jeunes Amis and Francs Amis were among the most prominent of these societies in south Louisiana.

The history of Good Hope Hall in the "Freetown" neighborhood of Lafayette is especially intriguing. Freetown was originally part of Governor Alexandre Mouton's plantation and was inhabited by people of color prior to the Civil War. The True Friend Association, chartered in 1883, worked during Reconstruction as a society for mutual defense against racist military organizations such as the White League and the Knights of the White Camelia. In the 1880s it evolved into a public welfare society.[102] In 1902 the Good Hope Society built Good Hope Hall, located on the corner of Gordon and Stewart streets, which served as a meeting hall, a Catholic church, and a dance hall. This lively location provided a venue for local popular bands, New Orleans groups like Fats Pichon from the Absinthe House, and touring bands from out of state like the New York City Band of Walter Bond and McKinney's Cotton Pickers out of Detroit. Evan Thomas and the Black Eagle Band often played there as well, but these concerts ended with the beginning of World War II.

It is in the benevolent societies of New Orleans that the reputation of another important Creole figure of the period, Hypolite Charles, was formed. Born in the hamlet of Parks in 1891, he was the son of a schoolteacher who played horn in the Parks Brass Band, which Charles himself joined as a child. In 1908, at the age of seventeen, he moved to New Orleans, where he studied with Manuel Perez, first playing with the Silver Leaf Band before joining "Papa" Celestin's Tuxedo Brass for years, and by 1919 the Maple Leaf Band. Charles played for high society, recalling that at the country club where he performed frequently, "people attending the [afternoon] teas were quiet, old, and rich."[103] He eventually formed his own band before retiring from music in 1925 to sell life insurance. Following an accident, he moved back to Parks in 1940.

Whether descendants of Creoles of color or of Anglophone Protestants, black musicians interacted with the local Creoles of color. The experiences that they relate in oral histories serve to illustrate the class consciousness at work in the regional music scene. Some musicians emphasized the importance of the color line and were discriminated against as being dark-skinned. Georges Lewis relates an incident that occurred when he was playing with Arnold DePass Sr. on Villere Street in New Orleans. A lady at the hall, mistakenly thinking Lewis would not understand, asked in Creole, "'Where is Mr. Picou [who had been playing with them]?'" According to Lewis, Arnold replied, "'He don't play with me no more.'

"And she says," continues Lewis, "she didn't say him, she say, 'Why did you get that?'" Then when they are finished with their drinks, the lady comes to pick up the glasses and tells Lewis to keep his. He got mad:

They was Negroes just like I was; she could have picked up mine, but I had to keep mine, so nobody else would use mine, because they were light skinned people, you see. I just come and didn't play nothing, you see, because I was hurt, and I know they were colored people.

John Joseph relates a similar experience in Lafayette: "I was playing with Evan Thomas. They wouldn't hire us because we were too dark to play for them. They got a band and they all looked like whites themselves." He mentions that only light-skinned musicians could play at Jeunes Amis and Francs Amis, an assertion contradicted, however, by the fact that the dark-skinned Thomas played at Good Hope Hall. In fact, skin tone was not the only factor involved, but was combined with others like language and social background, together forging Creole distinctive social status. "We used to go to Francs Amis Hall, but I couldn't get in until he [a Creole friend] would talk to those fellows at the door in Creole. Inside, the girls wouldn't dance with me until he's tell them in Creole, 'Dance with him,' and would tell them I was from uptown and a nice boy."[104]

Whether anglophone Protestants, francophone Creoles, or Cajuns, and whatever their skin tone, the social background of jazz musicians in southwest Louisiana enabled them to afford formal music education or at least to be encouraged to pursue it. When they were not full-time musicians, they—or their parents—were either craftsmen of various trades (barbers, carpenters, shoemakers, etc.), teachers, or held music-related jobs (like the Hebert family of the Louisiana Six, who were piano-tuners and radio technicians). Unlike Cajun and Creole families, which in the past tended to devalue the accomplishments of family members who developed an interest in music and associated them with drunkenness, the families of these musicians valued musical studies and formal education in music theory and practice. This education was available in several regional music schools, which were staffed by accomplished instructors. As a consequence, jazz musicians typically were able to read musical scores, whereas most French music players were musically unschooled.

Wilson Hebert, of the Louisiana Six, started by taking twenty-seven saxophone lessons for fifty cents a piece and was a sight reader for saxophone and clarinet.[105] In his native town, on Iberia Street, a music store and conservatory of music called the New Drug Store opened in late 1938.[106] Its manager, a local politician named Mat LaVail, offered lessons in piano and violin and also served as the director of numerous high school and college bands throughout the South. The New Drug Store boasted as an instructor Elizabeth Fullerton, whose musical education and experiences were advertised in detail and included having taught in Venezuela.

The question of formal training in music is a recurrent theme linked to the stratification of the region's music world. Although "Pap" DePass does not report believing that reading was a prerequisite to being an accomplished musician, he confirms the importance of this skill in shaping a musician's reputation when he was growing up in New Orleans:

> When I was a kid, if you couldn't read, oh, man, the word would get out on you! That wasn't good. [Whispering] "He's all right but he can't see too good," or "He got dust in his eyes." Or either "He's all right, he can't read too much, but he can spell pretty good." Which means: you take music and you can spell it out before you play. It's like in English, you have to break it down. But in my time all the bands could read. You didn't have to be an expert, but . . . Plus, it was also bad to be able to read and not be able to play by ear! See? So you had to balance it out.[107]

The son of Harold Potier and Mercedes Fontenette, who played in the Banner Band, John Potier explains how his parents, although from different social origins, shared a similar concern for musical education:

> Mom was not a Frenchman, Mom was not a Creole. She was a Black woman that spoke English. My dad was a Creole. . . . My [maternal] grandfather's people were from New Orleans, and he moved down here. At that time, grandpa on my Momma side played down the river road. His sister used to play upright piano, Aunt Sissy, she was a trip. It was a big family, and a close family, and a musical family, and an educated family. My father, although he went to school till the second grade, I can talk to him until I would die. Couldn't even write his name! He worked for the railroad for thirty-five years.[108]

Although non-literate, Harold Potier received a high-quality music education at the hands of Professor Oger from Crowley, a graduate of the

1.10. The Banner Band. No date. Alan Pratt (leader), Robert Stafford (drummer), Donald Marsh, Carlton Wilson, Gus Fontenette, John Sanders and three unidentified members. The band poses here with dark pants, white long sleeve shirts, and dark ties as they focus on sheet music, combining markers of respectability as properly dressed and musically educated. Courtesy of I. A. and Carroll Martin Photo Collection at Iberia Parish Library in New Iberia, LA, #11,001.

Mozart Conservatory of Music in Paris, who started a music school with living quarters after he retired.[109] Oger had toured throughout Europe and North Africa in the 1900s with the Paris Symphony. Potier started attending his school at the age of twelve, studying, clarinet, trumpet, saxophone, and theory for five years and receiving a "Certificate of Excellence in Trumpet and Saxophone." His father, a founding member of the Banner Band and a member of the Hypolite Charles marching band from Parks, dreamed of having his son join the Banner Band as well. Fulfilling his father's wish, Harold joined the band.

Potier's wife, Mercedes, whose father had founded the Banner band, graduated from Xavier University in New Orleans. She was classically trained, along with her sister, with whom she performed on riverboats. John remembers how demanding she was about his practicing: "They were very strict when it came to the music part. Moma was a great teacher for me too. I use to like to take short cuts on the piano. [she would tap on his fingers] That's how serious she was 'bout that. I still cheat a little bit.

Moma was just almost like a nun, a married nun. With discipline. Moma's favourite singer was Billie Holliday. Moma sang everything song by her." When I asked John whether his parents ever played French music, he responded: "No, because it was from the other side of the fence. You had your French music, and your jazz. And French music really wasn't the educated musician. It was just a cultural gig. The jazz was the people that were taught to read music. That's the only difference. But it's still the same culture."

The uncle of the successful young zydeco musician Corey "Little Pop" Ledet, whom he supports and encourages, Potier does not deliberately devalue French music. His father, on the contrary, did not seem to hold French music in high esteem, according to an interview from 1998, shortly before his death. Talking about John, who established his musical legacy as a keyboard player, he mentions succinctly: "He ain't playing no zydeco," clear evidence of his irritation with the popularity of this music style.[110]

"Pap" DePass was somewhat reluctant to talk about his opinion of zydeco, a music he perceives as lacking harmonic structure. He contends that zydeco is too primitive because it does not use the pentatonic scale. To be sure, what came to be categorized as jazz was considered higher on the social ladder in the first half of the twentieth century, and the fact that musicians from that period never bring up French music in interviews, or expressed discomfort regarding that question, is telling; jazz music was more readily associated with elite status. Austin Sonnier related that musicians were more explicit off-record, admitting that they found French music unchallenging.[111] One such case was the pianist Mercedes, John Potier's mother. When asked if there were many requests for French music and zydeco in New Iberia in the 1930s and throughout the 1950s, when she was part of the Banner Orchestra, she answered: "I don't really know. In fact I can't think of ever hearing that kind of music around here. You found a lot of that around Opelousas where the mulattoes live. Most of the musicians I knew played jazz. I'm not saying that they didn't have zydeco here, I just wasn't interested."[112]

This elitist perception of jazz might suggest that its primary audience shared the same views. We know that bands playing popular music from that era were appreciated by whites and by members of Creole benevolent societies. Blacks of English-speaking and Protestant heritage who migrated to southwest Louisiana after the Civil War may also have been part of their public. All of these audiences were likely to look down upon French music, although for different reasons that involved both race and class stratification. The link that Mercedes drew between French music and "mulattoes," which in southwest Louisiana are associated with free people of color, suggests that she distinguishes herself from mulattoes and denies them a specific status. Her perception remains ambiguous, since she apparently had a light-skinned complexion, was married to a Creole, and received a Catholic education while appearing to claim a distinct identity as an Anglophone. Stereotypes probably went both ways, as some French music players held their own value judgments about big band music. A zydeco fan once told me, "Big Creoles like jazz, small Creoles like zydeco"—"Big Creoles" not only referring to urban Creoles but also to the landed elite.

Many Creoles of color in south Louisiana belonged to a Catholic fraternal organization named the Knights of Peter Claver. The largest African American Catholic organization in the United States, it was founded in 1909 in Mobile, Alabama, and is now headquartered in New Orleans. The organization was founded by the Josephites, an African American Catholic order, born out of prejudice in the Knights of Columbus that caused concern among the Josephites about losing African American members to other organizations, such as the Elks and the Masons, through their black lodges. The Knights of Peter Claver is organized like the Knights of Columbus, with degrees and division into councils. Herman James, from New Iberia, shared the same lodge as Morris Dauphine and Gus Fontenette from the Banner Band, who performed for the fraternity's annual ball. He remembers naming the Banner Band "the Catholic church band," because of the time they would donate for the church, besides performing for high school graduations and proms. Trumpet player Harold Potier was also a member of the 3rd degree of the Knights of Peter Claver. It is thus likely that membership in the organization created a sense of belonging and consequent social stratification among Creoles.

The disdain for French music was as virulent among musicians from Cajun ancestry, as demonstrated by Helen, the daughter of Wilton Hebert from the Louisiana Six: "Dad used to say [about French music], it's so ugly it's pretty" [giggles]. The relatives of the Hebert family unanimously confirm the contempt of the previous generation for French music and dances, which had the reputation of being a hotbed of fighters and alcoholics.[113] Denise, the daughter of Noah Hebert, wrote a piece on the history of her father's band.[114] She narrates the musical talent of her grandfather Delma Hebert, a violinist of several generations who played old-time dances as well as classical and popular tunes like "O Sole Mio," "Blue Danube," and

"Mockingbird Waltz." Interestingly, she views old-time music and the big band era that followed as part of a musical continuum inscribed in the Acadian heritage. This vision contrasts with French Louisiana music scholarship, which has mostly ignored or at best overshadowed brass band and big band music as an integral part of the French heritage. In fact, they seem to perfectly conform to the respectable image associated with the aesthetic of upper-class Acadians, sometimes designated in the academic literature as "genteel Acadians."

This aesthetic was anchored since the mid-nineteenth century in the character of Evangeline, constructed by Henry Wadsworth Longfellow in his epic poem *Evangeline* (1847). Through its romanticized narrative of Acadians' forced exile, the heroine became emblematic of the middle-class Acadians who, while promoting their upward mobility and identifying with the white Creole elite and later the Anglo-Americans, maintained a link to a pastoral vision of the past and distinguished themselves from lower-class Cajuns. Numerous writers up until the middle of the twentieth century have perpetuated the stereotype of a noble, pious, and isolated population untouched by the vices associated with modern, urban society.[115]

In June 6, 1929, the New Drug Store in Opelousas booked a full-page ad in the *Clarion News* to advertise the recordings of "Acadian Records" by OKeh.[116] The manager of the store, who took the group of six musicians to Atlanta, Georgia, used rhetoric explicitly based on the Evangeline myth. The numbers included on the album were presented as "real Acadian selections which our Acadians in the days of Evangeline spent their leisure hours entertaining friends on the shore of Bayou Teche." The song "Evangeline," interpreted on vocal and piano, further establishes her as the quintessential romantic figure of Acadian history, and "By the Light of the Moon" enhances a musical legacy rooted in France. The banjo player, Patrick "Dak" Pellerin, is presented as a "student at Southwest Louisiana College," his education validating the authenticity and the weight of his selections and promoting Acadian social status.[117] Congruent with the same imagined construction of "Acadian music," the Evangeline Dancers and Band from Saint Martinville performed at the 1936 Texas Centennial National Folk Festival dressed in "traditional" Evangeline costumes with long skirts of dull blue, white waists, black bodices, and sheer white caps.[118] Incidentally, the New Drug Store did not see any marketing inconsistency in promoting old-time "Acadian music" while actively and mostly advertising what they called jazz. A few months later, the store switched to a snappier tone: "Red hot dance hits that'll gitcha! Here is some mighty tight

1.11. The Evangeline Dancers and Band, Texas Centennial, June 14–21, 1936. *Weekly Messenger*, June 13, 1936, front page. Source: Microforms Room, Dupré Library, ULL.

tunes that'll sure put your dogs into motion. Sizzlin' fox trot, slow drags, full of snap, pep and originality, all turned out by syncopatin' papas who know their jazz. Come here and hear the New Brunswick records today."[119]

Working-class Cajun musicians, on the other hand, sought to escape stigmatization linked to both their ethnic background and their trades by developing a respectable image, somewhat offset by the figure of the rambler that they appropriated.[120] Brasseaux argues that Cajun swing musicians adopted an urbane façade as a strategy to gain respectability. Soileau's Four Aces, the Hackberry Ramblers, and the Rayne-Bo Ramblers all placed their polished appearance and efforts to achieve economic independence at the service of this move towards social acceptability.

To be sure, attendance at dance halls was selective and depended on social background. Bands playing an eclectic repertoire of popular hits were more prominent in railroad towns like Opelousas, Crowley, New Iberia, and Erath. But within each town, there was also a variety of clubs designed to accommodate every taste and audience. While the Bijou Dance Hall in the small town of Erath catered to a stylish public, providing music from the Banner Band, the Melody Girls, and Filo Gonzales, two other dance halls were "coarse and ruggedly built with facades that had a barn-like look, but provided large dance floors," with the Louisiana Six providing the music.¹²¹ While French music seems to have been prevalent in Loreauville, a hamlet located about six miles away from New Iberia, it was also present at Palumbo's in industrial Abbeville, a stopover for steamboats that also housed the State Rice Mill. Herman James recalls that "there was a group of black people, with an accordion player, washboard, a bass fiddle, a guitar." In Martin's Hall in Scott, where the Louisiana Six performed regularly, pop, gum, and cigarettes were sold. "The men wore coat and ties. They would come in cars but most of the people rode in a buggy."¹²² Some clubs can be socially identified through the reputation of the bands that they hired, the frequency of the dances, and the number of musicians involved, which increased the cost for club owners. The Levert Gym in Saint Martinville, for example, hosted gigs for ensembles coming from Baton Rouge and New Orleans several days a week, with special guests and high-end musicians. The Attakappa Night Club in New Iberia celebrated the 1938 New Year's Eve with no fewer than two famous New Orleans bands competing for the title of "The South's Best Band": Clyde Kerr and his sensational fourteen-piece orchestra and Celestin's Tuxedo Orchestra. In Opelousas, the Cedar Lane, where Arnold DePass met his wife, was also a classy joint. The Louisiana Six and the Martel Orchestra were their regular bands.

The social landscape of the regional music field was far from homogeneous, as different clubs catered to socially diversified audiences within rural as well as industrial areas. The complexity of this social context and the many layers of social hierarchies invalidate simple correlations between performers and audiences or geographic distribution that have been associated with big band music on one side and French music on the other. The stigmatization of French music was based on social stereotypes and class consciousness that did not reflect the reality of the exchanges and circulation among music styles within southwest Louisiana, and between it and the broader world of American popular music. It would be restrictive to simply associate "old time" music and big band music with an upscale audience and an urban environment while ascribing appreciation of French music primarily to rural, working-class French Louisianans. This binary schema does not adequately reflect the richness of the sources of southwest Louisiana's musics, its musical eclecticism, nor the musicians' versatility and sharp awareness of popular trends, whether these musicians were Creoles, members of the Acadian elite, or working-class Cajuns. It also fails to take into account the aspirations of working-class

1.12. Ad for Clyde Kerr and Celestin Battle of the Bands, Attakapa Nite Club, New Iberia. *Weekly Iberian*, December 30, 1937. Source: Microforms Room, Dupré Library, ULL.

Cajuns to benefit from the region's booming industrial economy and to appropriate a modern, urbane style far from the stereotype of a backward, improper French music.

The existence of music statuses also needs to be related to the broader context of the emergence of cultural hierarchies in the country at the end of the nineteenth century. Lawrence Levine shows that "in the nineteenth century, especially in the first half, Americans, in addition to whatever specific cultures they were part of, shared a public culture less hierarchically organized, less fragmented into relatively rigid adjectival boxes than their descendants were to experience a century later."[123] While Shakespearian drama and opera were then simultaneously popular and elite art forms, the notion of entertainment was progressively replaced by erudition, leading to a class-bound definition of culture where categories were more sharply defined.[124] This context probably contributed to positioning southwest Louisiana music styles on a social ladder.

The circulation of music styles between city and countryside and between local and mass culture clearly emerges though the numerous exchanges, reinterpretations, and appropriations of American popular trends within French Louisiana music. Although its multiple influences and borrowings have been mentioned by most French Louisiana music scholarship since the Lomaxes, they primarily have been viewed as part of a process of "cajunization," which echoes the valorization of creolization and the ability to adapt that has been deemed idiosyncratic to Cajun culture. Through this neologism, a particular heritage is elevated instead of reflecting on the repertoire as a process of regional creation that continually integrates exogenous influences. The translation of American standards into Cajun French further reinforces the presentation of "Cajun music" as incorporating outside influences into its repertoire and turning it into its own.[125] Adaptability, however, is understood as a positive process as long as it does not threaten distinctive French roots. By contrast, when western swing influence predominated, or rock in the 1950s, the influences and exchanges with American popular music were perceived as loss, as a period during which tradition was adrift and fading. In this regard, the comeback of accordion music after World War II looks like a relieving rebirth, and gives evidence of the resilience of a "traditional" sound and culture as a whole in the face of mainstream America. Instead of viewing the process of Americanization as unfortunate or inevitable, Ryan Brasseaux fully embraces it and argues that American popular music is inseparable from Cajun music, depicted as "a distinctive American-made expression": ". . . Cajuns were proactive participants who shaped their own culture by engaging and ultimately appropriating the mass culture information disseminated within the United States."[126] As a result, Brasseaux argues against the myth of an isolated culture and music, disconnected from American trends.

In many studies of French Louisiana music, however, not every influence is deemed legitimate. Whereas African American influences are acknowledged and valorized—although this book will show that this process is ambivalent—some local researchers still view the influences of Anglo-American music and mass culture less favorably. Hybridity is thus circumscribed to a particular perception of the French Louisiana repertoire, and appears beneficial—as long as it "stays within the tradition," a tradition that in fact holds multiple interpretations.

2

Inside and Outside the Box

When I was beginning my fieldwork in southwestern Louisiana in the fall of 1992, I attended one of Barry Ancelet's course at ULL and befriended Christine Balfa, without knowing much about her musical legacy. Her father Dewey Balfa, a prominent musician and major figure in the French Louisiana musical revival of the 1970s, had passed away several months before, and she and her future husband, Dirk Powell, were in the process of forming the band Balfa Toujours. I ended up staying with them for a couple of months, surrounded by the Balfa legacy and spirit, and developed a strong relationship with my hosts that profoundly shaped my introduction to the music of the region. I became immersed in the French Louisiana music scene initially as a listener and dancer, and only later as a musician, adapting my classical violin training to playing the fiddle. The sounds of the Balfa Brothers provided the soundtrack to my early steps into French music, and I benefited from the direction of Dewey's most prized student, Peter Schwarz, through a cassette he had recorded to teach Christine the fiddle, as well as assistance from Dirk, who patiently showed me the basics of a few tunes in front of a camcorder. Although my ignorance of the local repertoire at the time meant that I lacked any preconceived notions, my increasing attachment to the music took root in this specific environment, at the virtual side of an icon of "traditional" French Louisiana music. Like earlier folklorists and anthropologists who have exercised a degree of control as assessors of authenticity, and still ignorant of Dewey's own broad view of the music, I was at first tempted to see certain styles as more faithful to the "tradition" that I was witnessing. Once I began playing and working on songs, selecting what I liked in each recording I listened to and appropriating it, however, the boundaries that I had set became far more fluid, and my vision became correspondingly less restrictive. I became better able to understand some musicians' desire to incorporate new elements—rhythms, chord progressions, structure, instruments, textures, styles—and to stretch the aesthetic conventions of the genre without having the impression that they were betraying or distorting it. Despite a personal preference for old-time twin-fiddle tunes, my own practice helped me develop a less clear-cut perspective on the genre, opening my understanding to new horizons and innovative techniques and musical influences. My work greatly benefited from my musical involvement at a number of levels, one of which was unquestionably my understanding of musicians' influences, choices, and itineraries, regardless of the style they embraced and whether I was personally drawn to it or not.

To further question French Louisiana music styles as natural or organic musical categories, this chapter will consider them as a site of contestation. The controversies surrounding the idea of tradition enable us not only to point out its unstable and constantly negotiated nature but, more importantly within the framework of my research project, to emphasize the factors at stake in these very conflicts, including the interplay of a variety of domains of power and social divisions. In fact, musical traditions are constantly redefined and reconfigured, a process widely acknowledged and documented by cultural anthropologists and folklorists. My interest here is to explore the politics of cultural authenticity and the intricacies of the elements that frame these competing ideas. Under whose authority are criteria shaped to define a legitimate, "authentic" French Louisiana repertoire? What power struggles underlie the assertion of musical legitimacy? What aesthetic differences are claimed, and on the basis of what imagery? This chapter will also show how musicians negotiate with national and regional music markets, as well as how the notion of tradition is combined with new musical experimentations in the French Louisiana music scene. Finally, the politics of musical authenticity will be considered in light of the involvement of governmental agencies and state-funded institutions in the promotion of a "cultural economy."

The Formation of a Regional Folk Canon

> Cajun music is not pure. It never has been. That's why it is Cajun music. If it was pure, it would sound like . . . [He picks up his fiddle and plays a tune he learned in Poitou, in Western France, where many Acadians originated.]
>
> DAVID GREELY, BREAUX BRIDGE, JANUARY 14, 2003

> The accordion was primarily a German instrument that Cajuns appropriated because it suited their needs or wants. Authenticity was not, obviously, an issue to them, because the accordion is Here. The steel guitar of Country and Swing is Here. Bass guitars and drums are Here. The list goes on of what is Here that wasn't previously Here. Was it authentic or inauthentic, all that borrowing? It doesn't fucking matter.
>
> SAM BROUSSARD, EMAIL CORRESPONDENCE, JULY 14, 2013

As Regina Bendix has argued, the idea of authenticity in the discipline of folklore pervades the core concepts and canon of the field. "Folklorists for a long time located authenticity within the anonymity of entire social groups, or the 'folk,'" who were viewed as the repository of a pure, unaffected state of being.[1] She demonstrates that a longing for authenticity remains deeply embedded in scholarly approaches to cultural analysis. In examining this view as it has been applied to southern music, Karl Hagstrom Miller explores the idea of "folk music" as a paradigm: "I do not understand the term 'folk music' to refer to a kind of music or a kind of music culture that exists out in the field prior to its discovery. Rather, I think that the preponderance of commercial music in the South before, during, and after the great wave of southern song collecting by folklorists suggest that 'folk music' was a framework placed on an existing, complex musical culture, a model that did little to describe the musical complexity on the ground."[2]

In southwest Louisiana, the idea of "creating within the tradition" is often emphasized by local publications on music, liner notes, and interviews with musicians who proclaim a "traditional" style or legacy. The notion appears frequently in the work of folklorist Barry Ancelet, where it serves to legitimize certain trends within contemporary French Louisiana music as valid expressions of the Louisiana French heritage while also framing the boundaries within which these trends operate in his view.[3] The resulting framework, however, is not necessarily a matter of consensus; in reality, opinions among dancers, musicians, producers, cultural brokers and institutions about what "fits within the tradition" vary widely, and the question of legitimacy with respect to tradition is the subject of frequent controversy and long, heated conversations among south Louisiana music lovers.[4]

Debates over the authenticity of south Louisiana's music styles have in fact been a regional leitmotiv since the early twentieth century. Nostalgia for old-time music placed the agrarian lifestyle, perceived as "real" and "honest-to-goodness," in opposition to "artificial" and "sophisticated moderns." These terms appear in the 1932 *Rayne Tribune*, where they support expressions of regret concerning the disappearance of old-time fiddlers in favor of what the newspaper refers to as jazz orchestras in an article entitled "Days of Old Square Dance, Alas! Seem Gone Forever More."[5] As was often the case with the introduction of new dance and music styles, jazz immediately became the center of controversy. Novelty in dance has often been perceived as a threat to middle-class values and morality—waltzes and other ballroom dances from central Europe that became fashionable in the nineteenth century were initially seen as shockingly libertine, as were tightly-garbed tango dancers, or the shimmying posteriors associated with the fox-trot and the Charleston after World War I.[6] A hygienic discourse objected to the detrimental effects of modern dance and to the fast-paced lifestyle that was considered to be associated with it. The *Opelousas News* in 1928 quoted national public health experts as having confirmed that "physical breakdown threatens the modern American girl because of her intensive pace in the whirl of the present jazz age."[7]

Jazz historian Bruce Raeburn argues that the initial wave of jazz recording activity prior to 1926, "changing fashion, the rise of the radio, and the implosion of the phonograph record market in advance of the Depression acted to remove most of the New Orleans artists (except Armstrong) from record companies' rosters by 1931."[8] The same trend that was marginalizing New Orleans artists like King Oliver, Jerry Roll Morton, and even Sydney Bechet was simultaneously eradicating local "old-time" fiddle music.[9] A wave of nostalgia began to spread, as illustrated by advertisements in southwestern newspapers for old-time dances: polka, military music, mazurka, Scottish, gallop, *variétés parisiennes, lancier, valse à deux temps*, two-step, and waltz. In Saint Martinville, the Levert Gym, which was primarily known for big band music, announced old-time dances during the summer of 1934, including "Polka, Mazurka, Two Step, Tee Pigeon Roti, Casey Jones and Old Time Waltz."[10] Music for these events was provided by the Evangeline Band, which included a clarinet, two trombones, two cornets, and a baritone. The dances roughly coincided with the Lomaxes' recording of the band on June 13, part of their quest for authentic regional music.[11] Two weeks later, the Lomaxes again recorded the Evangeline Band leader, Henry DeCuir, in New Iberia on June 29, when he performed two songs on the clarinet with Delma Hebert on the violin, accompanied by Delma's children. They were described as "descendants of the original Acadian settlers of south Louisiana specialized in old colonial music of Louisiana," which included a waltz, "said to be the first one introduced in Louisiana under the French Dominion."[12] Attempting to meet the Lomaxes' expectations of authentic southwest Louisiana music, the duo selected numbers based on their ancient origins and Old World style, leaving their mark on the most prominent institution in "folk" music, the Archive of Folk Songs at the Library of Congress.

Academic folklore and the music industry combined to shape the idea of the distinctiveness of southern music, an idea that excluded mass-produced pop music. Within this context, folklorists involved in collecting French Louisiana music were the early shapers of the implications of this approach on the French legacy. Under the auspices of the Archive of Folk Songs, John and Alan Lomax began their folk song–collecting tour across the South during that same year of 1934, laying the foundation for the revival of American folk music.[13] The interest in folksongs was situated at the convergence of three streams: the older work of various collector/lecturer/author types, the then-new political left, and growing academic interest in American culture.[14] John Lomax expressed his interest in collecting the region's music in a letter to the editor of the Donaldsonville newspaper from Austin, Texas, in 1912 in which he requested assistance in collecting "the songs of the negro. His 'yells,' his spirituals, his play songs. I ask your aid in bringing together the words and music of the most distinctive Negro ballads precisely as he has sung them and in many places continues to sing them. . . . Possibly the music of the Negro will turn out to be his most important contribution to American culture."[15] Determined to promote indigenous music without restricting it to the Anglo-dominated musical canon, the Lomaxes considered the long-overshadowed music of African Americans to be the most distinctive representation of American folk music.[16] Their depiction of the tradition was rooted in a certain primitivism and in a "cult of authenticity." During their field-journeys in Louisiana, they were aided by Irène Thérèse Whitfield, whose landmark 1935 thesis was dedicated to "Louisiana French Folk Songs." Their numerous recordings in New Iberia, Lafayette, Avery Island, Lake Arthur, Crowley, and Delcambre in 1934 include a striking variety of musical styles and instrumentation, ranging from English ballads and cowboy songs to klezmer music and from obscure fiddle tunes to popular American songs. This diversity reflected the influence of Anglo-American genres, amplified by the impact of mass media, transportation, and compulsory English-only education in the state of Louisiana beginning in 1921.[17] However, their publication *Our Singing Country* only mentions ballad singers as direct conduits for what was perceived to have survived of European music.[18] Despite the wide range of genres in their recordings, French Louisiana music was seen solely through the lens of the French legacy, to the exclusion of a number of other influences.

This same one-sided tendency can be observed in the work of the Louisiana cultural geographer Lauren Chester Post, a faculty member at Louisiana State University in Baton Rouge. Through his choice of performers and tunes for the 1936 National Folk Festival in Dallas, Texas (the first national festival to include French Louisiana music), Post helped validate popular trends in commercial-era French music. His selections featured commercial songs such as "J'ai passé devant ta porte," "Hip et Taïau," and "Lafayette," and included the recording artist and bandleader Lawrence Walker, thus acknowledging modern musical trends. At the same time, the "old-time" style was well represented by the Evangeline Band and Dancers. The troupe corresponded well to the conception of folk music that defined the festival, which was dedicated to American populations considered marginal and primitive, thus supporting the myth of the "noble savage." As much as he perpetuated the image of a timeless music and people, Post also opened the door to a new perception of French Louisiana music that was not solely based on the ballad tradition and that incorporated contemporary trends. Following in his footsteps, the musicologist and founder of the Louisiana Folklore Society Harry Oster, also from Louisiana State University, conducted field recordings in the 1950s that reflected the influence of blues, jazz, and country-and-western music. The most popular release from his recordings, however, was a tribute to the *Folksongs of the Acadians*, the title of an album, recorded between 1956 and 1959, that emphasizes the opposition between the French influence and a process of acculturation that he lamented was "rapidly approaching the point where the music of the Cajun country will be indistinguishable from the popular hits disseminated by the mass media of entertainment."[19]

This recurring duality is still perceptible in present-day writings on French Louisiana music. For some, the process of appropriation of American popular musical trends is sometimes perceived as inevitable but not always desirable, while on the other hand, the French tradition is deemed necessary for this music to remain faithful to its roots. In his discussion of folklorists of the past, historian Ryan Brasseaux demonstrates how they combine the isolation myth—which supports the fetishization of the purity of French music—with the acknowledgment of a process of adaptation and change. Oddly enough, his criticism of present-day scholars and music writers for perpetuating the isolation myth ignores their argument concerning the "creolization" of the music. In the wake of New Deal–era folklorists,[20] modern-day music promoters do not perceive these two processes as mutually exclusive, instead construing them in terms of continuity and compatibility. Historian Benjamin Filene clearly demonstrates a shift away from the demands for standards of folk purity that dominated folklore studies until the late 1930s and toward a new fascination with adaptability. New Deal folklorists, beginning with Alan Lomax, originally conceived of their work as the study of "living lore" that simultaneously reinterpreted the old while incorporating the new. His ambition was also politically driven in that he sought to re-frame folk music as a powerful democratizing influence on the nation's culture.[21]

This trend is naturally inseparable from the political, social, and economic context of the region in the first half of the twentieth century. The first decade saw a period of economic change triggered by the discovery of oil in the eastern part of the state in 1901 and the industrialization of East Texas. The improvement of living standards in the still-remote region was accelerated by the extensions of the highway network under the celebrated—and notorious—Louisiana governor Huey P. Long during the 1930s, and by the electrification campaigns of the 1940s. World War II brought young GIs from the region into contact with nationalism and the American way of life and contributed to changes in their aspirations. It is in this context that English, which was associated with economic power, gradually displaced French, which became seen as a stigma before being forbidden in schools by a state law passed in 1921.

This combination of factors fueled the industrialization of Louisiana's economy and the emergence of a service economy. Whereas in the 1920s, a majority of Louisianans was classified as farmers or fishers, by the end of the century the number of skilled craftspeople had increased. Louisianans turned into service and office workers. Cajuns became oil workers, founders of small businesses, and salespeople, forming what Henry and Bankston called "a blue-collar working class."[22] This socio-economic transformation also helped create the conditions for the ethnic mobilization of the Cajuns, whose upward social mobility ensured their socio-cultural rehabilitation. The newfound value of the Cajun identity enabled them to promote themselves and to proclaim their difference and uniqueness. Migrations, particularly stemming from employment in the oil industry, a newfound openness to the external world brought on by education (and the concomitant spread of English), and the proliferation of audio-visual media, as well as increased tourism in the region also helped the Cajuns become aware of their membership in the broader global francophone community while developing an appreciation for the specificity of their own culture.

The "French Renaissance" emerged from this newfound collective consciousness, as the quest for a common identity experienced profound cultural, economic, and social transformation. Many contemporary folklorists and music writers who specialize in southwest Louisiana belong to the generation of activists who dedicated themselves to the resurgence of French Louisiana music in the 1970s as part of a Cajun activist movement that was inspired by the legacy of the "folk revival" in the late 1950s. In more recent years, the term revival has generated some debate among scholars.[23] Thomas Turino, for example, questions the adequacy of the term "folk revival," which he argues represented "more of a transference than a revival," in other words the adoption of musical influences and styles from rural and working-class Southerners by suburban, middle-class Americans.[24] In the case of Louisiana, the interaction between cultural outsiders and insiders established the conditions for a local revivalism based on populist ideology that advocated "art in the hands of the people."[25]

In this book, insiders and outsiders and native and non-natives are not distinguished in terms of legitimacy. In fact, like Ray Allen argued in the context of American folk revivalism, I contend that non-natives have played a decisive role in the development, evolution, and validation of French Louisiana music throughout the twentieth century and have continued to be crucial to its reconfiguration in recent years.

Under the auspices of national cultural institutions, key figures in the mid-century folk movement exerted a particularly strong influence on the revival of French Louisiana music. One important example was Ralph Rinzler, who famously invited the fiddler Dewey Balfa to perform at the 1964 Newport Folk Festival in Rhode Island. Because it brought the French Louisiana music repertoire before an outsider audience, this event is hailed by scholars as a turning point in the revitalization of French Louisiana music. The politics of culture at the time determined the subsequent ramifications of this landmark event. Rinzler, the founding director of the Smithsonian Folklife Festival in 1967, also brought Cajun music to the National Mall in Washington in July 1976. Ray Baudoin, a resident of Maurice, Louisiana, born in 1937, recalls that hearing the music on the Mall brought him back to the "accordion music" of his youth. Visiting the D.C. area for the bicentenary of the funding of the United States, Baudoin and his family "were on [their] way to the Smithsonian's Air and Space Museum. . . . When I heard the music, rather than going to the museum, we spent the whole day with Dewey Balfa, Bois Sec Ardoin, Lionel Leleux, Don Montoucet. . . . When musicians would leave the stage, everybody followed Cajun musicians! That's when I really started to listen to French music, with Allen Fontenot."[26]

Rinzler was similarly instrumental in creating a new audience for bluegrass music, successfully kindling interest in a sound that might have disappeared without his collaboration with Bill Monroe. Along with a group of young, urban, middle-class, folk-oriented performers and musicologists, he saw bluegrass as the only authentic form of country music.[27]

Fondness for folk music among young middle-class New Yorkers was a "passionate avocation" in which it was held in contrast with commercial music. Among them were the members of the New Lost City Ramblers, all from New York City and raised in the suburbs. The Ramblers were pioneers in introducing what they believed was "authentic" southern mountain music (also called "old-time string band music" by music preservationists) to urban northern audiences. Tracy Schwartz, the fiddler of the trio, met Dewey Balfa at the Newport Folk Festival, an encounter that led to the Ramblers' recording of "Parlez nous à boire" in 1966, a recording that played a major role in disseminating Cajun music and the Balfa Brothers' style among folk revival audiences.[28] Schwartz further contributed to this process, subsequently recording three Folkways albums with Balfa in the late 1970s and early 1980s. The Ramblers were never comfortable being labeled folk revivalists, however, because they perceived it as a pejorative term that perpetuates misconceptions about an urban folk revival associated with commercial folk groups. Allen, who chronicled the lives and music of the Ramblers, observed that they continue to resent comparisons with the commercial folk groups of the 1960s such as the Kingston Trio or the Limeliters, whom they viewed as the "real imposters."[29]

The issue of authenticity thus pervades the earliest phases of the Cajun music revival and helped perpetuate a dichotomy between commercial, urban popular musicians and rural, traditional artists. This distinction is nested inside the further problem of legitimacy, which is bestowed on traditional musicians on the basis of native, insider status. Because they could not lay claim to being natives, the Ramblers were never seen as legitimate candidates for funding by entities such as the National Endowment for the Arts Folk Arts Program.

A similar process can be observed in other music revival movements. The Mexican *jarocho son*, in which the distinction between "traditional" (i.e., rural, simple, and "authentic") and "commercial" (urban and touristic), provides an excellent illustration. The musicians who initiated the *jarocho son* revival are often of rural origins, later moving to the city where they created the conditions for the revival to become transferred to the urban environment, particularly among university students. "Traditional," "campesino" (rural) *jarocho son* thrives today as a result of these young activists combining different status (student, musician, musicologist, cultural promoter) in Veracruz and even more so in Xalapa (Veracruz State), Mexico City, and Los Angeles.[30]

Cultural institutions have been fundamental influences on the definition of the musical canon. The New Lost City Ramblers, for example, never received either a National Heritage Fellowship, given to outstanding practitioners of the traditional arts, nor the annual Bess Lomax Hawes Award for teaching and preserving "traditional" art.[31] The community-based criteria for eligibility for such awards clearly gives priority to insiders or natives, based on a definition rooted in the "assumed isomorphism of space, place and culture." Akhil Gupta and James Ferguson have called for a reevaluation of the assumptions underlying these criteria in favor of an approach to the notion of place grounded in the realities of a world of diasporas, transnational cultural circulations, and ever-increasing mobility.[32]

After several unsuccessful applications, the NEA eventually awarded Dewey Balfa a folk-artist-in-the-schools grant in 1977, an award sponsored by the Southern Folk Revival Project based in Atlanta. Along with a dozen artists from around the country, he later was awarded the newly minted National Heritage Fellowship in Washington in 1982. Two years later, he was followed by Clifton Chenier, and in 1986 by Canray Fontenot and Bois Sec Ardoin, both icons of the "old-time" Creole style, who also received National Heritage fellowships. Since its inception, a total of ten Cajun and Creole musicians have been awarded the grant, establishing French

Louisiana music as a significant presence within the national culture but also confirming selection criteria that consider native artists as the sole bearers of authentic traditions. Other grants from the same agency, such as the Folk Arts Apprenticeship, encouraged the young Michael Doucet to study "old-time" fiddle styles with Dennis McGee. These awards and other grants have institutionalized a "traditional" style centered around particular iconic figures, thus contributing to the creation of an orthodoxy that systematically enshrines native-ness and is in stark contrast with other popular trends like swing or country and western music. This policy mirrors the broader cultural politics within the country, which brought an end to the stigmatization of "folk art," "rural art," and "primitive art" and renegotiated their relationship with "high culture": "The hierarchy between 'elitist' arts and popular culture have been shaken, the criteria have evolved, and the definition of what does or does not constitute 'art' has changed. The elite that relied on the 'arts' to defend its social status has become a minority."[33]

It is clear that the determining influence of cultural institutions and middlemen on the diffusion, legitimation, and success of music styles should not be viewed as univocal, but instead as a compromise between the intentions of producers and artists and the sometimes divergent appreciations of the public. The negotiations at work in this process are well exemplified by the first Tribute to Cajun Music in Lafayette in 1974. The turnout at this event was the largest ever for a rally held by the emergent French Renaissance movement and represents another milestone in accounts of how French music was revitalized in southwest Louisiana. Barry Ancelet relates that Rinzler cautioned against including "crooners" on the program, voicing his "preference for clear, high-pitched vocals and unadorned instrumental styles of earlier Cajun music."[34] Interestingly, the unanticipated success of the event, which drew nearly twelve thousand people, was inseparable from the presence on the program of the Cajun country star Jimmy C. Newman; Balfa saw his participation as a way of hooking the audience for a lineup otherwise devoted to the "traditional" style.

Music producers also orchestrated the revival of French Louisiana music as a plain, raw music style that adhered to its French roots. In the wake of mid-century blues revivalists and their idealized perception of African American culture, which led them to depict bluesmen as "the embodiments of an anti-modern ethos,"[35] the founder of Arhoolie and producer Chris Strachwitz was fascinated when he discovered the Creole accordion player Clifton Chenier. Strachwitz had been introduced to Chenier by Lightnin' Hopkins, his cousin by marriage, in Houston in 1964 and was captivated by Chenier's minimalist approach to performance, accompanied only by a drummer. He encouraged Chenier to promote his understated, "old-time" French style, which differed from the musician's conviction that an English-speaking rhythm-and-blues full band would gain him greater success.[36] The first single record that they produced happened to constitute a compromise, and Chenier became Arhoolie's highest-selling artist, ironically becoming a commercial success against Strachwitz's will.

Strachwitz's choices were less clear-cut in the anthology of *Louisiana Cajun Music* that he produced in the 1970s, an example of the recurring duality among "traditional" French music advocates. In including the Hawaiian influence popularized by "Prenez Courage" and the English-lyric song "Hand Me Down My Walking Cane," Strachwitz was expressing his understanding of the diversity of the French Louisiana repertoire, even quoting Catherine Blanchet in celebrating Cajun adaptability: "There is probably not one song or piece of music on this record which belongs entirely to the Acadian tradition. They say that Cajuns are Chinese, they survive by absorbing the conquerors."[37] Other influences were nevertheless considered atypical: "La Valse du Mariage" from the Guidry Brothers is presented as "apart from most Cajun songs for several reasons. The theme, the yodeling, and the use of future tense." Yodeling was typical of the 1930s, however, and was incorporated into the French singing style. Strachwitz's selection shows that he is both aware and interested in the multiple influences and development of Cajun music, and he referred to "never-ending evolutionary changes,"[38] but his comments seem to frame them as intriguing but exceptional oddities that were therefore outside of the tradition he strove to support. Cajun Paul Tate, a music activist and lawyer, made this perception still more explicit by stating: "the discovery in Cajun music of borrowings or assimilations from other musical traditions, while interesting and significant from musicological and sociological standpoints, in no way detracts from the existential fact of a distinctly Cajun music tradition."[39]

French Louisiana music scholarship tends to circumscribe musical "creolization" by its French roots, which nevertheless remain ill defined; it is never fully clear whether the term refers to language, instruments, song structure, rhythm, or melody. Creolization was long held at arm's length relative to Americanization in the process of defining an "authentic" repertoire whose singularity was being celebrated. More recently, however, a notable shift has been observable among young scholars working on French Louisiana music.[40] When viewed as a process, Americanization becomes the object of legitimate analysis instead of being viewed as an assimilationist movement with inevitably damaging consequences. This newer generation of researchers demonstrates that this process is an integral part of the construction of the French Louisiana repertoire. They thus legitimize styles such as swamp pop that were previously contested and the influence of country and rock musics, which proceeds from reinterpretations or adaptations of popular American music, mainstream culture, and mass consumerism, without losing its integrity.[41] In his retracing of the itinerary of the song "Jole Blon" (Jolie blonde), Ryan Brasseaux demonstrates the commercial success of the song and its unrivalled impact throughout the history of Cajun music. Recorded by Harry Choates in 1946 (Gold Star 1314), the song was catapulted to the top of the Top 100 songs and reinterpreted by major figures in popular American music ranging from country start Roy Acuff to Bruce Springsteen, thus crossing local and regional borders to become part of the popular canon.

While Ryan Brasseaux embraces the process of Americanization in its analysis of Cajun music, he erects the notion of adaptation into a unique cultural attribute, adhering to the exceptionalist tendencies of his predecessors. What he defines as "a Cajun musical ethos" therefore appears as a typically Cajun mechanism for adaptation that is anchored in improvisation, enabling Brasseaux to operate on both the cultural and musical registers.[42]

Since the 1960s and 1970s, however, the vision of music projected by French Louisiana music revivalists has nevertheless evolved. This change is not necessarily made explicit in their publications, but is observable through their involvement in recordings and other documents; and it reveals a growing understanding of French Louisiana music as less restrictive than it first appears. The two volumes of *Cajun and Creole Music: The Lomax Recordings*, first released by Swallow in 1987 (and later re-released in a wider compilation under Rounder in 1999 by Barry Ancelet), focus on the French-speaking a cappella songs contained in the Lomax recordings. In this sense, they do not reflect the extent of the repertoire that was played and recorded by the Lomaxes in French Louisiana, as demonstrated recently by writer and musician Joshua C. Caffery.[43]

Other endeavors, however, such as the recordings of fiddler Varise Conner in 1975–77, illustrate Ancelet's early awareness of the eclecticism of the regional repertoire. But more than twenty-five years passed before he helped producing a CD based on his recordings with Conner. Despite the variety of his repertoire—which, as Ancelet himself observes, went well beyond French Louisiana music (from *valse à deux temps* and mazurkas to old-timey mountain and Irish tunes, rags, and swing)—Conner was still identified as a Cajun fiddler, a definition that Michael Doucet did not embrace in the same liner notes.[44] This example reflects the political agenda of the French Renaissance as well as a romantic vision of French Louisiana music that prevailed until recently and that prioritized its French legacy, acknowledging the legitimacy of other influences more readily when they were associated with veterans such as Conner.

In a similar vein, the musician and music writer Ann Savoy has dedicated considerable time and effort in her publications to the notions of French roots and an unaltered sound. *The Early Recordings of Dennis McGee*, which she produced in 1994, introduces McGee as the unique heir of a timeless heritage who plays "tunes from a hundred years before his ninety-nine years, tunes he learned from a hundred-year-old man."[45] This focus on an unvarnished legacy did not prevent her from covering the swing era in her anthology, *Cajun Music: A Reflection of a People*, a repertoire she began to explore with her own band, Ann Savoy and Her Sleepless Knights. Her efforts have in turn inspired other bands to embrace this style, including the young Red Stick Ramblers, who describe their music as "a unique hybrid of Cajun, country, string band, and swing influences." Radio stations have also contributed to this ambivalence between the focus on French legacy and the inclusion of a variety of influences, at times contributing to real contradictions, as illustrated by KBON in Eunice. Rumor has it that this station, which prides itself on promoting Louisiana artists and showcasing an unrestricted and "unique variety of music with a Louisiana flavor; Cajun, Swamp Pop, Zydeco, Country, Classic Country, Oldies, Blues, and more," would have nevertheless refused to air the Feufollet 2010 album *En couleurs*, based on the contention that it sounds too Canadian, despite the fact that its members are from Louisiana. The French legacy in this instance is confined within the borders of French Louisiana.

The definition of a traditional repertoire is the product of the dialectical relationship throughout the twentieth century between a singular, unaltered heritage and the valorization of eclectic influences by folklorists and music promoters. The romanticized view of the French legacy framed by folklorists, collectors, and music producers throughout the twentieth century has joined a range of apparently divergent choices that, combined together, give a more complex picture of the perception of past and present folklorists alike. In the late nineteenth century, a national revival of interest in the South helped create a national market for southern writing tinged with "local color," as evidenced by the success of Washington Cable and Lafcadio Hearn's essays.[46] This trend also prompted the foundation of the Louisiana Folklore Society, a branch of the American Folklore Society. The myth of the South as "a world of pure and authentic traditions" and "as the backbone of the nation's folk culture" continued throughout the twentieth century and has only served to reinforce the representation of an unadulterated French Louisiana repertoire, further legitimizing in the process its inclusion in the category of "folk" and later "roots" music traditions.[47] The French musical legacy has been constructed through resistance to the discourses of modernity and the ideology of the melting pot. It has offered an alternative that is undergirded by the maintenance of a strong collective identity in the face of incursions from the mainstream. As a result, the commercial dimension naturally becomes an object of controversy and is at odds with the idea of an authentic "folk."

Tradition within Borders

The one [musician] who is not concerned with whether or not it's marketable is the one I call a traditional musician.
MARK SAVOY IN ANCELET AND MORGAN 1999: 138

Whatever music genre is considered, its commercial face has often been subjected to criticism as a perversion of a "pure" tradition. The myth of a folk musical tradition corrupted by consumer society and bastardized by mass media only furthers the gap between genres. Conflating industrial culture, mass media, and mass culture nourishes a negative perception of mainstream mass-produced music among folk music fans, leading some of them to believe that "mass culture laminates art, relegated to an object of production."[48] More broadly, the emerging distinction between high and low culture in the late nineteenth century, meticulously demonstrated by Lawrence W. Levine, was based partly on the perception of a difference between unique and mass-produced objects. Accessibility became a key to cultural categorization. "Anything that produced a group atmosphere, a mass ethos, was culturally suspect." In fact, this mindset led to the assault on brass band music, causing one of the nation's most popular forms of music to be labeled as "impure art, pseudo-culture, and disorder."[49]

The commercial dimension continues to this day to provide support for negative accusations regarding an array of music genres, establishing the authenticity of certain styles while labeling others as spurious. Aesthetic judgments oppose the purity of the former to the simplification and taintedness of the latter (cf. antagonistic musical binarisms such as hot versus straight jazz, folk versus commercial blues, and alternative versus commercial country). The French Louisiana repertoire is no exception to this trend, and several influences have frequently been singled out as detracting from its authenticity, among them the "Nashville sound" that divides musicians and music fans.

By the late 1940s country music exerted a powerful influence on French Louisiana music. What came to be called "the Nashville sound" was used at that time to describe the rock- and pop-influenced country music. Bill Malone asserts that the emergence of this style was the result of an attempt by music industry leaders to create a sound that would preserve a rural flavor within an urban style, thus expanding the appeal of country music to urban, middle-class listeners in a era when the success of rock and roll was threatening other styles:

> Banjos, steel guitars and the honky-tonk sound were replaced by string sections, brass instruments and vocal choruses, and the studios built up a group of backing musicians who performed with a variety of soloists. The repertory emphasized melodic ballads and novelty songs over more traditional country material. Among the earliest performers influenced by this trend were Eddy Arnold, Patsy Cline and Jim Reeves. From the 1970s the term gained broader usage, describing any kind of popular or traditional music produced in Nashville.[50]

The new Nashville sound came to be defined by "its smooth character, conditioned by strings; a subdued rhythmic feeling; influences from pop jazz in harmony and arrangement; and finally the overall impression of professional craft and high-quality studio sound."[51]

In country music, like in French Louisiana music, these elements contrasted with the nasal, high-pitched vocals and lack of polish of the old-time sound. In fact, late fiddler Lionel Leleux, who began playing in the late 1920s with accordion players like Nathan Abshire before switching to swing in 1932, drew a clear distinction between the "old-time" style of Amédé Ardoin, "*qui jouait par escousse un tas*" (who played choppily), and the "smoother" modern style represented by Lawrence Walker, one of his favorite accordion players.[52]

Doug Kershaw, Jimmy C. Newman, and Rufus Thibodeaux are typical examples of musicians who thrived during the 1960s in the mainstream country world while proclaiming their Cajun heritage. Newman's biggest hit "A Fallen Star" reached number 4 in the *Billboard* country charts before crossing over to rise to the number 42 position in the pop chart.[53] Thibodeaux played with Newman at the Grand Ole Opry, went on tour, and recorded the first song in Cajun French to become a gold record, "Lache Pas la Patate" (1970), leading a successful country career while also comfortably incorporating western swing as well as blues and rock into his repertoire.[54]

The stigmatization of country music and the Nashville sound are frequently described as emblematic of the "selling out" of French Louisiana music in the accounts of folklorists and music producers. Ancelet's choice of words is explicit when he describes the Cajun icons of this style as having "strayed from traditional sources and veered toward popular or country music styles en route to the west coast and Nashville. To remain a legitimate expression of Louisiana French society, Cajun music would need to return to its roots."[55] This definition of the local canon unambiguously differentiates country influences from traditional Cajun music. Furthermore, the musical choices of those who "strayed," according to their detractors, appear to constitute a strategy for gaining access to the market and reaping the benefits. In the *American Folk Music Occasional* edited by Chris Strachwitz in 1970, Paul Tate laments on what he perceived as the degeneration of Cajun music. "[Traditional Acadian music] lay captive, isolated and dying, hedged in by a sub-tradition of mediocre imitation of country-and-western or popular music," both assimilated to a "new noise."[56]

In the same way, swamp pop has long been denied credibility by cultural activists both in and out of French Louisiana. A regional musical style developed by Cajuns and Creoles, it combines New Orleans–style rhythm and blues and country and western with French Louisiana music influences. Historian Shane Bernard, the son of one of the most popular swamp pop musicians, Rod Bernard, dedicated a book to this style and advocates its recognition as an integral part of south Louisiana musical heritage. In Bernard's view, the appeal of swamp pop among Europeans further reinforces the argument for elevating its status. He describes "this small, ill-defined, but well-entrenched faction [that] regards swamp pop artists as apostates—Cajuns and black Creoles who turned their backs on their heritage in exchange for a greater chance at national fame and commercial success—and so deny swamp pop music and artists the benefit of the preservation and promotional efforts afforded to traditional Cajun and black Creole music."[57]

Within French Louisiana music, criticism of certain influences and debates over their authenticity also tend to ignore the evolution of taste over time, sometimes leading them to deliver what appear to be anachronistic judgments and to forget that today's tradition was perhaps considered avant-garde in the past.

According to Ben Sandmel, manager and drummer of the Hackberry Ramblers, "[s]o many of the musicians we now revere as traditional were quite avant-garde in their day—such as the [Hackberry] Ramblers, who introduced amplification to southwest Louisiana and profoundly changed the music. If ProTools had existed then, Luderin would have been all over it."[58] Sandmel toured with and promoted the band, beginning with its stage comeback in the late 1980s and until the leader, Luderin Darbone, passed away in 2008. Already in their late sixties when they returned to the stage, their profile contrasted with Sandmel's, then in his early forties and an "outsider" from Ohio. In fact, on several occasions he was pointedly excluded from requests for photos of the band. The Hackberry Ramblers' current image as traditional, fueled by their unmatched longevity as a band, tends to efface the novelty of their sound when they first started playing in the early 1930s. Similarly, whereas Dennis McGee or Canray Fontenot have become icons of "traditional" fiddling within French Louisiana music, that position was held until the late 1970s and early 1980s by fiddlers with a very different swing style like Doc Guidry and Rufus Thibodeaux. The boundaries of authenticity inevitably drift over time, as illustrated by country music, in which country boogie, tragedy songs, heart songs, and a cappella ballads, which were perceived as authentic when they emerged, are no longer considered elements of the country canon.[59]

Among the indisputable icons of "traditional" Cajun music and considered by Ancelet to have given new life to the "root" sound,[60] the Balfa Brothers have embodied that style for generations of dancers, musicians, and folklorists. Few people today point to the novelty of their sound when they first began playing in the 1960s, or their important role in rendering

French Louisiana music more accessible to outsiders. Chas Justus, the guitar player of the Red Stick Ramblers, laughingly expanding on this point, asserts:

> A lot of what the Balfa Brothers did was to go to different bluegrass festivals and play with Bill Monroe, and adapt that music to their music. I don't know if people think about it, how they changed the face of Cajun music, as far as taking it out of Louisiana, changing it to suit audiences and even sit-down audiences, who didn't have any context of the dancehall, where people don't applaud, they don't really pay attention to the band. They just dance, do their thing. It's not the same thing as going to the Newport Folk Festival and playing for these people. A Cajun band would end with a two-step because it would get everybody pumped up at the end. And the Balfas started singing vocal harmonies, like bluegrass bands and country bands. They made it smoother and more listenable and less out of tune and a lot more palatable to the average listener. . . . I heard Dewey made a tofu gumbo [at an out-of-state camp]![61]

Chas underscores the already boundless efforts made by Dewey Balfa to adapt to an outsider, folk-loving audience nourished even by vegetarian food, a completely foreign idea at the time in Louisiana, where animal protein was—and is—king.

Like the Hackberry Ramblers, whose principal goal was pleasing the public and adjusting to their expectations, through the determination of Dewey Balfa, the Balfa Brothers were committed to promoting Cajun music and transforming its status following their success in Rhode Island. They even began to perform for seated audiences, a novel practice for music typically played for an audience of dancers. The anthropologist Thomas Turino does not conceive of music as a series of different genres or styles, but rather as four distinct fields of music making. Two fields pertain to making recorded music, and the others relate to real-time performance.[62] The latter category includes "presentational performance," which refers to situations in which artists provide music for audiences who do not participate in making the music or dancing, while "participatory performance" is primarily concerned with making people dance.

This shift from participatory to presentational performance reflected the Balfa Brothers' advocacy for reaching out to different audiences and realizing the full potential of every performance context. The same strategy led Dewey Balfa to suggest a sit-down concert format for the first Tribute to Cajun Music in 1974, reasoning that if the local audience were prevented from dancing, they might listen to the music differently.[63] The musicians were greeted with wild applause, in fact, and the event changed the image of French Louisiana music on its home turf. The following year, however, the police providing security prevented people from spontaneously dancing, eventually leading the organizers to modify the format by declaring the event a festival, thereby adjusting to the local requirements of participatory performance.

By contrast with those who managed to retain their label as "traditional" musicians, the repudiation of certain musicians in the late 1960s reflected the political context of the time.[64] Embracing the counterculture that blossomed throughout the nation while also reclaiming their French heritage, a small minority of Cajun youths were regarded as subversive hippies by the Acadian establishment and by ordinary Cajuns as well. Among these alleged Cajun hippies was Benny Graeff, who founded the Rufus Jagneaux Band, which combined rhythm and blues and country and western with rock and folk music. In 1973, they recorded "Opelousas Sostan" with Swallow. The single sold over 30,000 copies during the first month following its release, but no radio station agreed to air it.[65] Differentiating themselves from a conventional perception of Cajun music, partly engaged in a caricature of the older generation, they nevertheless embraced the rehabilitation of regional music, which was becoming known outside of Louisiana at the time, as "traditional."[66] According to Graeff, Rufus's regional hit, however, was rejected by a faction of local cultural activists who considered the band an affront to respectable values, and their career was impeded when they were blackballed by local festivals.

A major figure in French Louisiana music, Zachary Richard's itinerary and local reception were also strongly affected by this era. Among the few Cajun students to express opposition to the war in Vietnam by temporarily leaving the country, Richard began to advocate for a new militancy through music and poetry devoted to preserving French culture. His political claims were well received in Quebec, and he was awarded the Prix de la Jeune Chanson by France in 1980. In Louisiana, however, Richard's connections with francophone activists in Canada and overseas and his radical public statements against the establishment and its Anglo-conformism incurred the wrath of Jimmy Domengeaux, the upper-class preservationist and founder of CODOFIL. An influential lawyer from Lafayette, former state congressman (1941–48), and an accomplished politician, in 1968 Domengeaux persuaded the Louisiana legislature to fund a public agency dedicated "to further the development, utilization and preservation of the French language and culture of Louisiana . . . for the cultural, economic and touristic benefit of the state." Based on the teaching of French in elementary schools, the cultural policy of CODO-FIL quickly drew protests from a variety of actors that included local administrators jealous of their independence, frustrated parents whose children could not converse in Louisiana regional French, and activists who clamored for greater integration of French Louisiana cultures and Acadian history into the curriculum.

Zachary Richard's activism and ideological position inclined Domengeaux to ban him from local cultural events.[67] His evolution toward rock excluded him even further from the local music scene. Although an icon of Cajun music in Quebec and France, he has spent decades on the margins of the French Louisiana music scene. These examples, which have had long-lived consequences, serve as illustrations of the ways in which the construct of "tradition" has been deployed to counter particular ideological views and musical choices.

The "commercial" argument is sometimes attached to any style deemed too "urban" or too "mainstream" by traditionalists. According to this logic, songs in which exogenous forms are too visible become the focus of dissent.[68] But others hold a different representation of commercialism. Today, the commercial dimension is acknowledged as a necessity for young bands that seek to play music as a full-time occupation. What is considered tasteless refers to the choice of commercial success over what is perceived as quality and soulfulness. Mark Savoy refers to crass commercialism in several interviews, one of which was published in the Lafayette weekly *Times of Acadiana*. His argument for artistic integrity is based on a moral judgment about sellouts: "I'm a firm believer . . . that there's always going to be a market for quality. If you sell a cheap version of the culture, if you sell a watered-down snake pit Hollywood-Nashville style of your culture—that's the people that you're going to get to come over."[69] The commitment to fame and fortune seems to be associated with an inability to be in touch with "real" people.

His son, Wilson, further explores this argument. In 2008 the young leader of the popular band the Pine Leaf Boys felt some hits were detrimental to the music: "There is much good music. And there is much bad music too. And these people hurt the reputation of Cajun and Zydeco, they mess it up, they're doing this ridiculous . . . they sing everything

English, singing about vibrators, and they call it Cajun and Zydeco, they're doing more harm to the music. Even though it's popular . . . I don't wanna be known for Lâche Pas la Patate, I think it's the cheesiest thing in the world. . . ."[70] In 2014 he acknowledged that he "had grown to learn that just because I don't like something, doesn't necessarily mean it's a bad thing."

But in Savoy's view, both "Lâche Pas la Patate" (1970) and Travis Matte's regional hit "Vibrator" (2005)—a song that evokes the movements of a large dancing woman's posterior— still exemplify tackiness through their lyrics, independently of the artists' talent and their tremendous success in the region. "I believe music can evolve and inspire without resorting to singing about nasty lyrics. Lack of soul needs to be compensated by dirty lyrics for audiences in Louisiana or else the band will never make it."

The deployment of a "folk" ideology is also based on the context of performance. According to Joel Savoy:

> Any time I play music I'm not playing for people. If I feel like I'm playing for the audience then I quit. I don't have any interest in playing for you or playing for anybody. If anything I want to play music with my friends, or play by myself, or play somewhere for myself. But I don't want to play for an audience and that's not what roots music is. Roots music, or folk music, is music made by people for amusement, to me. And that's what I do. Anytime I play music, I'm playing because I feel like playing. It's social music especially here. I've never had a party at my house that didn't involve music. Never. It's just what we do. It just happens, you know?[71]

Joel Savoy also acknowledges that what appealed to him as one of the founding members of the Red Stick Ramblers in Baton Rouge related as much to the music as to the performance aspect. When he first began playing with Josh Caffery and Richard Burgess, he was several years younger and was fascinated by the whole scene and the excitement over their music at a moment when roots music was becoming increasingly popular. The status of performer and consequently the role of the audience was far from incidental: "It was a college town and I'd go play with their band and it was just—you know, there were beautiful young girls and everybody was just partying and drinking and they were real popular and it was an amazing experience. And for me to see that . . . , to see them being a success and having so much fun. . . ." Recognition and fame were therefore an integral part of what encouraged him to start a musical career.

A depiction of a "natural, approachable, honest" music is also associated with the view of music "by the people for the people." Defenders of this view emphasize a circle of connoisseurs, experts, and fans as opposed to mass audiences often not deemed as a legitimate audience. A former editor of *Folk Roots* magazine, Ian Anderson, defined folk music as "non-commercial music," consumed by "people who aren't willing to be spoon-fed something that the music business has concocted as a commodity; dare I say it . . . a more intelligent audience who will pick up on the integrity of music that comes straight from the heart."[72] For Corey Porche, a music lover and musician from Lafayette, old-time music and Cajun music are both real expressions of people. "It's people's music. It touches your soul," he says. Realness and emotional qualities seem to be antithetic with music commodities and commercial value. This notion of music "that comes from the heart," a music situated above technique in the realm of feelings, shared experience, and emotions, is shared by natives and transplants alike. Within debates concerning authenticity, this argument widens the gap between "roots" and "mainstream" music, paradoxically situating French Louisiana music as the product of "people" while defining people in a restrictive manner and validating some choices and not others. In this vision, some have access to the emotional intensity associated with this music while others do not.

An additional factor that frames discussions of authenticity is the urban corollary and its artifices (see ch. 4), particularly when it is expressed by those for whom zydeco is not considered music, whether in its "old school" or "new" form. The number of detractors has increased during the course of the rise of zydeco. Veterans of the Creole style, defined as the "true" or "traditional" music of Creole people, have made a point of dissociating themselves from zydeco by issuing disdainful remarks: "There never had no such thing as zydeco music. That's bullcorn. If you was black, you played Creole, if you was white, you played Cajun,"[73] claimed Canray Fontenot, who continued to relate how the C.C. Chenier song "Les Zaricots Sont Pas Salés" was the result of speeding up a *juré*. By the early 1990s, amateurs of old-school zydeco that pursued the legacy of Clifton Chenier began objecting to what was commonly designated as "nouveau zydeco," a label applied by journalists more often than by musicians and now rarely used.[74] Its major characteristics, as described by music writers Roger Wood and Ben Sandmel, include beat-dominant elements of hip-hop fused with repetitive accordion riffs and washboard rhythms, with booming bass lines locked in with a prevalent drum beat called "double kick," along with the staccato and declamatory vocals of rap. Instrumental soloing in the "new" zydeco sound is uncommon and certain common forms in old-school zydeco (and more broadly in French Louisiana music like blues and waltzes) are nonexistent.[75]

In fact, these stylistic changes inside zydeco also took place in the New Orleans brass band tradition. Inspired by the Dirty Dozen Brass Band in the late 1970s, a new generation of brass bands started emerging in the mid-1980s that incorporated elements of funk, R&B, and hip hop, reinvigorating a brass band tradition previously associated with jazz. Since then, brass bands such as Treme, the Soul Rebels, Rebirth, and Hot Eight have flourished and have attracted the sponsorship of large corporations like Red Bull. Like many contemporary zydeco bands, they cultivate "hip hop" personas in a quest for higher status and aspire to access to the American mainstream popular music market.[76]

As for many others from the older generation, William Hamilton, owner of the Hamilton's zydeco club in Lafayette (now closed), believed when he was still running the club that "The music has changed a lot. It's more fast records, chachas, it's not zydeco. Zydeco is slow, it's not fast fast." (*La musique a changé un tas. C'est plus des fast records, des chachas, c'est pas zydeco. Zydeco c'est doucement, c'est pas vite vite.*) Staying true to a single style is another argument in the debate concerning what constitutes "real" music, as opposed to imitative, artificial, and contrived music that absorbs influences and changes.[77]

There are exceptions, of course, and the idea that commercial success is a curse or incurs the risk of being labeled a sellout is far from unanimous. These arguments against success peeve Ted Fox, the music producer of the successful Stanley Dural, a.k.a. Buckwheat Zydeco, since the late 1980s. "Chris Strachwitz made a lot of cool records with Clifton Chenier. But Chris is completely anti-commercial in any way, shape, or form. And I've had a problem with these people, because these musicians got to make a living. Clifton Chenier should have been sitting like B.B. King is now."[78] Buckwheat was among the first to adopt a full-fledged commercial strategy with the assistance of Fox, leading to unrivaled success. Buckwheat played for the closing ceremony of the 1996 Olympics in Atlanta, and for Bill Clinton's presidential inauguration. He recorded with celebrities of American popular music such as Eric Clapton, Keith Richards, and Willie Nelson, and performed covers of major rock hits, including "Beast of Burden" by the Rolling Stones and "On a Night Like This" by Bob Dylan. On the strength of five Grammy awards, he was the first to record advertisements for globally distributed merchandise from such brands as Isuzu, Budweiser, Coca-Cola, and Cheerios. According to Fox, "that doesn't fit into the discography-ethnomusicology-blah-blah-blah.... But to me, that's the real story of zydeco over the last ten years."[79]

Other musicians with Cajun heritage like Travis Matte and Jamie Bergeron concur with Buckwheat in not viewing commercial aspirations and techniques as insincere or necessarily a cultural sellout. Matte, for example, expresses pride in "giving his audience what they ask for." Among the top party acts in the region, Matte excels at marketing his music, along with a variety of merchandise and a large selection of ringtones, while Bergeron offers beverage coozies, mouse pads, spices, and hats. In the eyes of these artists, such marketing choices seem to be an inherent feature of their strategies for appealing to a broad audience.

The differences between old-time French music and the smoother sound influenced by country and Texas swing mirror the perceived antagonism between bluegrass and "Appalachian old-time music," a category that emerged in the 1920s. The Appalachian style is the most renowned among a variety of regional distinctions. Similar points to those made in the Louisiana context are advanced to legitimize the relative authenticity of these styles: While old-time music is considered more raw and emotional, bluegrass tends toward a smoother sound. In fact, the two styles are often confused and share the same instrumentation. The banjo, however, is played more gently in old-time, with the fingernails, whereas in bluegrass, the banjo is played with picks. The virtuosic solos of bluegrass are another difference, whereas old-time musicians typically play together when formed into a band. As a result, some bluegrass fans look at old-time as boring and amateurish, whereas old-time practitioners tend to contend that the high level of musicianship and complicated musical arrangements in bluegrass are overly polished and lacking in emotion. The commercial aspect of bluegrass, which is featured on television shows and in popular movies, also fuels conflicts concerning authenticity, although old-time music, too, has reached the big screen.[80] In this case, rival aesthetic perspectives once again reflect different musical goals, values, and practices that, according to Turino, should be considered separate art forms with different potentials that are "equally authentic, or true to the people who practice and enjoy them; they are simply distinct traditions."[81]

Regardless of their taste, music lovers in southwest Louisiana have clear ideas about what "traditional" music should be and are quick to express disapproval of a style that fails to meet their expectations. Until recent years, this condemnation could be virulent when a band introduced musical innovations that sounded too distinct from the repertoire with which it was first associated. The album *Bayou Ruler*, released in 1998 by Steve Riley and the Mamou Playboys, featured zydeco, swamp pop tunes, and a rock style combined with some English-lyric or bilingual songs. The album was greeted with harsh, caustic feedback from many of their fans. Other songs on different albums have also attracted criticism for musical innovations considered too drastic at the time, like unusual harmonic structures, changing the order in which instruments usually come in, or simply using an instrument not considered "traditional." David Greely explains:

> Everybody in the audience feels qualified to come up and tell me what they think about the music we're playing. There will be people coming: "That stuff y'all used to do, I really liked that, but that new stuff you do, that's garbage"; "I asked you to play the Kaplan waltz three songs ago and you never played it!"; or "Don't play that saxophone until the old folks go home." Literally. To your face! . . . It used to upset me. But I came to realize the conservatism of the audience is a very important aspect of our culture. If these people were not so resistant to change, we would have lost our language a long time ago. We would have lost our identity a long time ago. I'm just a function of society here. I'm not really an artist in Louisiana.[82]

Dancers, whose criticism is typically exclusively based on "danceability," play a powerful role in establishing a music canon. Exposure at local country dance clubs is essential to the popularity of local bands, but it also requires a certain degree of compromise between musical choices and the expectations of dancers, who "vote with their feet . . . on the dance floor or out of the door," as Greely eloquently phrased it, continuing, on another occasion:

> Often a new song will empty the dance floor. Tchoo! Floor is empty. We're like, oh no, they hate it, what's gonna happen now . . . Some of the songs that used to empty the dance floor, the floor is full now. Sometimes it takes a year or two for them to get used to this new sound. "J'm'en fous pas mal" used to clear the floor . . .
>
> When *Happy Town* came out we played the Mardi Gras ball in Rhode Island, somebody said, some of the stuff they do is undanceable. Which is not true, I made sure it was danceable, they just didn't

recognize it. Normally a Cajun song will start really hard and loud, accordion and drummer going, wap! wap! on the snare drums, everybody is clear about what the beat is. ["Les vigilantes"] starts with acoustic guitar with a 'tit fer. And they didn't know what to do.

Such blunt statements and unvarnished reactions from local and out-of-state dancers indicate that the public clearly asserts itself as a referee on matters of taste and preference. On the zydeco dance scene, young musicians eager for a faster tempo or a loud beat find themselves criticized by the older generation for not playing enough waltzes. In fact, dancers are often a priority for musicians, and their dissatisfaction deeply affects them. Michael Tisserand recalls one of Beau Jocque's gigs at the House of Blues in New Orleans, where most of the audience, although applauding and visibly thrilled, was just standing in place, maybe in part because they did not know how to zydeco dance. "I got them cranked up, but they just looked at me," he said with concern in his voice.[83] His wife had filmed the stage and the dancers and they intended to study what had happened. Terrence Simien, who has stayed on the margins of the local zydeco scene and explored varied music while focusing on delving into rock, funk, reggae and New Orleans R&B, is aware of the vagaries of local reception: "Those people at home are your biggest critics. If they like you, they'll let you know, but if they don't, they tell you that, too, and they're not always very nice about it."[84]

On the French Louisiana music scene, the local public generally feels entitled to demand certain songs from musicians or to offer snap judgments about their music, due to the lack of an artist-audience distinction that is consistent with Turino's "participatory performance" category. In Cajun and zydeco venues, as for any other dance venues—whether dancehalls, ceremonies, or ritual gatherings—there are only participants and potential participants performing different roles. As Turino describes it, "[a]rtistic freedom and experimentation in these core roles are restricted by the responsibility of providing the musical foundation that allows others to participate comfortably. . . . The success of the performance is more importantly judged by the degree and intensity of participation than by some abstracted assessment of the musical sound quality."[85] Within the context of this particular music-making field, the aesthetic judgments referred to by Turino assume their full meaning. If dancers do not feel that musicians have fulfilled the terms of their "contract," in other words, if they cannot recognize and dance to the music, the band may be disavowed and even vilified. The feeling of social unity and belonging—what Turino refers to as "social synchrony"—predominates in participatory performances, although, as will be argued later, this consensual feeling does not efface social divisions and discrimination. What is really at stake in the criticism of certain styles within a participatory performance is the ability of musicians to create this level of synchrony in the audiences' view, which in turn serves as one means of establishing the degree of "authenticity" of French Louisiana music.

Greely has come to accept the constraints of playing for dancers and, until he had to quit the band in 2010, managed to retain his reputation as the talented fiddler of the Mamou Playboys intact while simultaneously exploring new musical directions. He introduced sit-down performances based on old-timey and original twin fiddle tunes at local clubs and events, targeting a new audience whose aesthetic is less concentrated on the criterion of the music's adequacy for dancing.

Multiple Musical Identifications

The master fiddler and teacher Mitch Reed offered the following views on the questions of status and taste:

> What happened was you started having all these college kids hanging out, and it was like a French thing too, because a lot of kids from Quebec and Montreal and Nova Scotia found this little cool place [The Blue Moon, a popular dancehall and guesthouse in downtown Lafayette]. The local kids who were Cajun and proud that played a little bit of music started hanging out with them, merged. And the next thing you know, they're having a little jam. But the tunes they're picking are the old-time tunes. The Dennis McGee stuff, the old stuff. And they're kind of excluding the modern stuff that's coming in. And you have other kids that come in and see it and go wow, that's cool. Local Cajun people. So when they pick up the fiddle or the accordion they want to listen to Amédée Ardoin or Dennis McGee.... Even in my shop [Louisiana Heritage and Gifts, closed in 2008]. I can see it. I sell so much of the old remastered 78 stuff that's put on the CD.... It's more the educated crowd, the kids who are going to school and interested in history and anthropology and their culture. They probably come from a better upbringing. More

educated, grew up on the south side of town. They're proud to be Cajun for the first time. And it's hip, it's really cool. Those are the kids who are digging up the old stuff. But you find maybe more of the kids that grew up in the country, they're maybe more into Jamie Bergeron, the kind of slick new Cajun music, the zydecajun. That attracts more of a beer-drinking crowd that just wants to . . . young people get together, dance, have fun. Meet other people. Which is a cool thing too . . .[86]

These remarks invoke the social stratification that is sometimes perceived as a reflection of musical styles. Since the late 1990s, there has been a renewed interest in the "old-time" style among francophone youth; in fact, the most successful bands in French Louisiana music since the first decade of the twenty-first century include a new generation of Cajuns in their twenties who have been highly influenced by musicians involved in the French music revival of the 1970s. Some of these young musicians are direct descendants of musical families, including Wilson and Joel Savoy and Louis and Henri Michot. Whether or not they are related to an earlier generation of activist musicians, many studied in public school French immersion programs or made the effort to learn French on their own, including members of Feufollet, Louis Michot, and Cedric Watson. The success of the two annual French immersion programs at the Université Sainte Anne in Nova Scotia has also fostered a network of relationships between young Louisiana Cajuns wanting to learn French and Acadians from Nova Scotia, creating regular travel and exchanges in both directions. Cultural activism in favor of French and a renewed emphasis on the French language, to which French immersion programs in some Louisiana public schools have contributed, have thus played a role in increased interest in the "traditional" style, part of efforts to assert the distinctiveness of French heritage.

According to Ryan Brasseaux and Kevin Fontenot, three distinctive musical aesthetics are at work, forming a continuum along which Louisiana bands evolve depending on the circumstances. At one end, music is conceived as constituting support for an ideology based on French cultural activism; at the other, primacy is given to the entertainment function of music through dance.[87] These divergent goals tend to correspond to specific social groups: a group of middle-class activists with working-class roots who prefer the old-time style, the legacy of the pioneers, and French-language songs; and a group of working-class Cajuns who favor the eclectic sounds of swamp pop, zydeco, and modern country and popular music, without considering English-language songs to represent a betrayal or deficiency. A third aesthetic promoted, by the Cajun French Music Association, is positioned between these two poles. The association is a blue-collar group that does not identify with the French movement but embraces a French cultural agenda.[88] This perception is in fact not restricted to the CFMA and is common among middle-aged and elderly Cajuns in small towns and rural areas.

In my view, however, establishing different aesthetics on the basis of fundamentally different perceptions of the function of music seems highly misleading.[89] French Louisiana music participants, beyond a handful of critics, researchers, and other music professionals, adopt the view that music is something to be experienced rather than talked about. The entertainment function is not restricted to one faction, but functions instead as a common denominator. This is a crucial point for all of the local music bands, including those who promote a particular cultural agenda. Fun is constantly invoked on stage, in liner notes, and on bands' web sites. Whether they choose to present themselves as "party bands" or to highlight heartfelt, "raw," "gutsy" music, bands uniformly define themselves by the infectious energy with which their music is infused. Their principal goal is to pass this energy on to the public, with the promise of an intense physical experience through frenetic dancing and late-night fun and sociability. It is precisely this achievement that lies at the heart of their claims to authenticity.

Instead of presenting them as a continuum, Brasseaux and Fontenot organize the definitions of these aesthetics according to a hierarchy. While they advocate for the development of studies of the "blue-collar aesthetic," this aesthetic is associated with "working-class Cajuns who spend their hard-earned dollars for entertainment value.... If the music is performed well and danceable, it is good—better if cold beer is being served."[90] Such a superficial vision of musical tastes contributes significantly to the cultural caricaturing of particular social groups. As French sociologist Bernard Lahire has methodically demonstrated, the model of cultural consumption founded on individual taste relies on the reductive image of the individual solely as the official representative of a class, of a fraction within a class, or of a social group.[91] Lahire argues that in fact, the individual is exposed to heterogeneous socializing influences that result from upward (sometimes downward) mobility at the social, educational, and professional levels, as well as from different cultural preferences within conjugal relationships and peer groups.⁹² From these multiple and diverse experiences emerges the notion of "intra-individual variations," which suggests the internal differences found within the range of behaviors and tastes of each individual. These various—and occasionally contradictory—influences can coexist within the same person and can manifest themselves in different ways and at different times depending on situations and personal itineraries.⁹³

Esthetic differences are not constrained by social backgrounds or education, nor are they restricted to one specific genre. Moreover, in practice these aesthetics cross the different music styles—Cajun, Creole, zydeco—and the process can be said to encompass all French Louisiana music. At first glance, it seems easy to assign college-educated Cajun musicians who claim inspiration from an old-time style and advocate for the French language and heritage to a single homogeneous category. They are eager to emphasize their rural, working-class roots as the descendants of farmers, cowboys, and workers; they often work as full-time musicians, in combination with other activities related to music (producing, studio management, instrument-making, teaching private or group classes, or music camps) and sometimes, for the latest generation, with higher education (often in French or Folklore studies).

Those who are categorized in the blue-collar aesthetic, however, such as Travis Matte who is into GPS electronics, or Jamie Bergeron, an emergency medical technician with a regional ambulance service, deploy a linguistic and social register based on regional slang and southern working-class accents in their song or album titles (i.e., "Dis ain'tcha momma's Zodico" from Travis Matte). These musicians' web sites and liner notes focus on their acclaim on radio stations and among sport fans and players, and they proudly display their commercial sponsors (Budweiser, Chevrolet) and successful marketing efforts (like Buckwheat Zydeco or Jamie Bergeron). The notion of a blue-collar aesthetic actually also refers to an older generation with very different tastes. The annual Cajun and Zydeco Festival in Branson, Missouri, attracts retired country blue-collar workers. Local attendees from rural Vermilion Parish, where I did fieldwork, filled nine buses for the first edition of this festival in 2001 organized by Cedric Benoit, a native of the area.

The idea of a blue-collar aesthetic that is primarily focused on entertainment evokes Bourdieu's definition of a popular *art de vivre*, in which the ability to party and play is considered a specificity of the working-class and a sign of spontaneity and the absence of taboos. Some Louisiana dance clubs provide excellent examples of this aesthetic, such as Whiskey River

Landing. On a Sunday afternoon in May 15, 2001, the club was packed with a frantic crowd for Jamie Bergeron's gig. Honoring a club tradition in which the waitresses dance on the bar at some point, five women climbed up. An older woman threw a very-large-size bra into the crowd that was picked up by a man and swirled above his head. Another man joined them and facetiously pretended to try it on.

More than a reflection of spontaneity and uninhibited entertainment practices, working-class aesthetics are based on particular norms that allow recognition among peers rather than distinction. The fact that some Cajun and zydeco players aspire to a position in the mainstream music market, develop complex commercial strategies, and choose a specific linguistic register for their lyrics and representation reveals an aesthetic that is unarguably as highly codified as any other. Furthermore, the choice of a working-class aesthetic does not keep these musicians from emphasizing their education and social position. Zydeco accordion player Keith Frank provides an example of this when he calls attention on his website to the college and music degrees possessed by the band's members and his own skills in electronics. "Lil Nate"—Nathan Williams Jr.—presents his bachelor's degree in music and jazz studies as a professional qualification.

In fact, the distinction between blue-collar and middle-class French activists' aesthetics tacitly refers to a category of identification that for the most part has been carefully avoided in local scholarship and among French activists, which relates to the tendentious self-ascription "coonass." Considered by the local elite a strictly derogatory meaning applied by Anglo-Americans that borrows from ethnic slurs applied to blacks ("coon") and reveals the process of blackening working-class Cajuns, the term has been officially rejected in 1974 by the Louisiana legislature as inappropriate for use in public spaces and on products, theoretically a definitive denial of the term as a legitimate identification.[94] However, those who continue to self-identify as "coonass" proclaim their desire to distinguish themselves from "Cajun" (or not be to limited by this appellation), and by extension to sustain and publicize a connection to rurality, a self-sustaining lifestyle, and a working-class background. By rejecting the negative connotations of the label Cajun, they proclaim the authenticity of their lifestyle. "Coonass" thus positions an individual in opposition to the commodification of the French heritage and the Cajun label, as well as to middle-class revivalists. Shanna Walton argues that the Cajun revival movement has propelled a submerged class struggle to the forefront that is expressed in the controversy over labels, causing some to choose this self-ascription to denote authenticity and clear racial alignment ("coonass" as opposed to "niggers") that could be perceived as being blurred by the regional use of the term "Cajun" (a perspective worthy of further exploration).[95] "Coonass" occupies a parallel space to "redneck" and indicates reference to white rurality and poverty. She suggests considering it a "category of southern whiteness," a process of differentiation in which the notions of race and class prevail.[96] By contrast, those who reject the label "coonass" are advertising their understanding of French-ness in language and lineage (on how the racial aspect of this latter issue expresses itself through issues of musical ownership, see ch. 3). Rocky Sexton also explored this multifaceted process of ethnic labelization and presents complex patterns of utilization linked to class, gender, context, and involvement in ethnic organizations, although he notes that there is no consensus of opinion within any particular group. Considering the ambiguity and controversy over the meaning and use of this label, "coonass can be viewed as simultaneously helping to construct a contemporary Cajun community while also dividing it with dissent over the label that articulates diversity within the group."[97]

Rather than reflecting distinct aesthetics, social stratifications echo different self-understandings, conflicted perceptions of regional identifications, and different expressions of "racial" difference. Musical preferences are far from uniform and are not strictly conditioned by social determinants. They result from the intricate interaction of eclectic influences through various encounters that are revealed by musicians' choices and itineraries.

A celebrity inside and outside of Louisiana, highly praised by lovers of old-time French music, Mitch Reed inevitably evokes the musical sounds of his late hero Denis McGee as well as an inimitable bluesy, rhythmic fiddle style. Jovial, friendly, and welcoming, Mitch's engaging personality is imbued with a solid sense of humor and a talent for turning the most insignificant detail of everyday life into an entertaining, sometimes hilarious tale, a narrative gift traditionally associated with the people from the Mamou Prairie where he was raised. In fact, before meeting his former wife Lisa Trahan, Mitch spent hours playing video games and collecting *Star Wars* and *Lord of the Rings* figurines. He is fascinated by fantasy films and characters, an attraction that traverses his stories. His father played harmonica, piano, and accordion with the Mamou Prairie Band and with Tit Mamou with Al Berard. His first major source of inspiration, however, was very distant from the sounds of southwest Louisiana, as he recalls on the radio show "Quoi Y A" on Lafayette public station KRVS:[98] "I had a neighbor down the road, it was the Gutierrez family, his father made electric guitars. They played heavy metal, Led Zeppelin. . . . I'd go in the summer, they'd smoke cigarettes, drinking black coffee, playing heavy metal. I was 7, my buddy was 9. . . . I borrowed one electric guitar, got an amp, and my buddy showed me how to play the chords. . . . And I start listening to Black Sabbath, Iron Maiden." He continues to describe the leap from heavy metal to learning the cello:

> The cello, I listened to Kate Bush, the Hounds of Love, and that record totally changed my life forever. . . . Amazing producer, she's hired great musician, had a cello player. I went to a conservatory and started taking lessons, she used a lot of Irish fiddle. I got into that and realized how close it was to Cajun fiddle. I'd listened to fiddle music all my life, Cajun, bluegrass, but Irish music kind of reintroduced me to Cajun music again and made it cool. I ordered a video tape, "How to Play Irish Music."

His encounter with Michael Doucet left an indelible mark on him, and he likes to remind any audience—here at Balfa Camp in 2008—about the moment that caused him to immerse himself in Cajun music:

> When I was about fourteen, I went to Mulate's [restaurant and dancehall] with my mom and dad to have gumbo, and BeauSoleil was playing. I played rock 'n roll, electric guitar, and then I saw Michael Doucet on the fiddle, the whole band, I was like blown away. My dad played the accordion, he wanted me to get into Cajun music, and I always appreciated it, but when I heard BeauSoleil, I thought, man, this is really cool, this is not a bunch of old guys, crying [laughs] . . . Then I wanted a fiddle, but I ended up getting a mandolin, but started listening to BeauSoleil and it really helped me, because to me those were the guys who connected the old music with a new approach, or new sound to it, some kind of modernization.

In a personal interview, Mitch describes the process that drew him to "old-time" French music:

> When I started getting into Mike's tune, understanding where he was coming from, it was the Dennis tunes that really drew me.

That's when I started going to Mark Savoy's shop [where, since the 1980s, a jam has been held every Saturday morning] and met Corey McCauley, Randy. Corey really helped me a lot. He said—I'm going to the library, I'm going to get you some field recordings. And he brought me back two tapes. And that's when I started sitting down and learning directly from Dennis.[99]

He eventually formed the band McCauley-Reed-Vidrine, which launched his musical career, after dropping out of college. He met a variety of musicians through his connections and through the Louisiana Heritage and Gift Shop, which he and his wife at the time managed in the northern Lafayette area and which became a focal point for both local and outsider musicians. Through his friendship with Eric Martin, who was among the first to bring Cajun music to France after Gerard Dole, he learned about the French folk tradition as interpreted by bands such as Malicorne, who were popular in France in the 1980s, and the fiddler Jean-François Vrod. He started playing with the band Celjun, a blend of Irish and Cajun music started by Tony Davoren, an Irish transplant who moved to Louisiana in the early 1990s. 2007 marked his accomplishment as a fiddler when he was invited to join the band of his first hero, Michael Doucet. From heavy metal to Irish fiddle, Mitch's musical itinerary was strewn with different milestones that eventually brought him to view French Louisiana music in a different light and to decide to embrace the cause.

Echoing the itineraries of performers from earlier in the century, other musicians illustrate the wide degree of eclecticism in tastes and itineraries, with the influences of American and European popular music leading them to discover folk music before settling on French Louisiana music. Depending on their generation, heavy metal, country, R&B, boogie-woogie, rock, bluegrass, western swing, jazz, gospel, hip hop, or reggae comprise the formative musical experiences of most if not all contemporary French Louisiana musicians. Memorable live gigs and recordings function as turning points that triggered their interest and prompted them to take a new direction, while local music veterans supported their discovery and developing abilities through apprenticeships (as was the case for Mitch, who apprenticed with Adner Ortego, and for David Greely, who learned his craft from Dewey Balfa).

Like Mitch, although fifteen years earlier, David Greely was a fan of Black Sabbath, the Beatles, and the Rolling Stones, unexpectedly opening the way for his attraction to folk:

When I was seventeen, I went to see Black Sabbath at the Warehouse in New Orleans. They had three bands that night. The second band was Seatrain, and the fiddler was Richard Greene, playing electric fiddle. My mind was blown, I barely remember Black Sabbath. Folk rock band. Next day I went to the pawnshop and bought a fiddle. I was making up songs the first day, the easiest thing I had ever tried. Got into folksy. I went from Black Sabbath to Flatt and Scruggs in one day. My neighbor was in a bluegrass band, I went to a bluegrass festival with him, felt hard, felt deep, felt forever.[100]

As he describes it in his bio on his website, David went out the very next day and bought a Japanese plywood fiddle and two brand-new $35 bows in a Baton Rouge pawnshop a couple of blocks from where he was born.[101]

David Greely's decisive encounter with folk music paved the way for a career into Cajun music. In 1974 he started playing in a bluegrass and western swing band called Corn Bread "with a punk attitude." Later, while living in San Antonio, he started creating gigs: "I pretended I knew Cajun music and played in a restaurant. It was a lie, I knew a few songs in phonetic French, some Doug Kershaw tunes." Raised in Livingston Parish near Baton Rouge, Greely grew up with neither French nor Cajun music. He eventually decided to learn Cajun music from Balfa Brothers records recommended to him by Jo-El Sonnier, who was beginning his solo performances in Louisiana, California, and Nashville that blended his Cajun roots with country, rock, and pop influences.

Among aspiring Cajun musicians, the Savoy's jam has often helped connect young musicians, initiating relationships and sowing the seeds of new bands. Just to mention a few of the more celebrated examples of such encounters, it was there that David Greely met then eighteen-year-old Steve Riley, leading to the creation of the Mamou Playboys; Mitch Reed met Randy Vidrine and has played with him ever since in different bands; and Linzay Young met Joel Savoy, which led to the formation of the Red Stick Ramblers.

Georgina Born and David Hesmondhalgh concur with Lahire in arguing for heightened awareness of the "multiple musical identifications or subject positions to which individuals are susceptible as producers or consumers. This conception allows for an understanding of mobile, conflicting and changing musical identifications."[102] Whether they are musicians or dancers, participants in French Louisiana music are likely to integrate multiple practices into their lives that are sometimes in conflict with each other, essentially creating divisions that instead of being between different social groups are within a single individual, between self and self. Individuals learn how to operate in these different registers depending on the context and on the stage of their careers, without undermining the sincerity of their choices and practices.

A Sound of Their Own

> VARISE CONNOR: I'd say the Cajuns, and the Mexicans, their music is more lively than anybody else. But them Cajuns they break all the rules! They play one tune, but then they take apart that tune with another tune and make a new one, you know that Michael?
> MICHAEL DOUCET (chuckling): Yeah, that's liberty.
> —INTERVIEW WITH VARISE CONNOR, ERIC BENOIT, AND MICHAEL DOUCET, MAY 26, 1977, LAKE ARTHUR ANCELET COLLECTION, AN1.005, ACCF

The diversity and distinctiveness of how an individual plays music not only is recurrent in musicians' discourses and performances but also is considered a fundamental prerequisite for learning to play French Louisiana music well. In his instructional video on Cajun accordion, Dirk Powell explains to intermediate and advanced students that the "most important thing in Louisiana is to have your own style."[103] Other music instructors also insist on this point at music camps, including Mitch Reed, who often tells his students about the multiple scenarios and possible variations available to a musician playing a particular song. At the 2008 Balfa Camp at Chicot State Park, Michael Doucet rattled a reverent audience during a twin fiddle class:

> There is no such thing, [he pauses] as Cajun music. It's a fallacy. There is no such thing as Cajun. It doesn't exist. [Everybody is very quiet.] I don't know why y'all are here. [Laughs of the audience.] You can't say, that is one thing and it's not another thing. . . . Basically it's sung in French, it's a certain French based fiddle style playing, but it's all individual. . . . Cajun is a vast, vast thing. And I would say right now, if it's an umbrella then it's open, so whatever YOU play, and you put in the music, becomes whatever it is. In other words, there is no wrong way to play this. . . . So, the basic part of that is, listen to what you like, be attracted to what moves you.

The setting for this thought-provoking statement—at the only Cajun and Creole music camp held within Louisiana, which draws dedicated fans from all over the country—provides even more weight to Doucet's argument. His intention was clearly to ensure that his students did not feel constrained by their reverence for their instructors and that freedom of choice and taste became integral parts of the learning process. In fact, most Louisiana instructors and instructional videos incessantly repeat that students should listen to as many versions as possible of different songs in order to find their own voice, and that the way in which songs are taught represent but one approach among many. In public lectures during music camps or other events, David Greely also has conveyed the idea that musicians have been faced with musical choices throughout the history of Cajun music, adding that the advent of modern times and technological advances have made this truer than ever.[104] "The only thing you can say about rules in Cajun and Creole music is that they're lonely," synthesizes Sam Broussard.[105] In a similar vein, folklorist Ralph Rinzler started his foreword to Barry Ancelet and Elemore Morgan's *The Makers of Cajun Music* with the assertion that "the style is the artist."[106]

Musicians can use different techniques to create a style of their own. Choosing instruments is one fundamental choice. The first chapter of this book made it apparent that the "traditional" instrumental basis of French Louisiana music—accordion, fiddle, guitar, *tee fer* or *frottoir*—has changed over time and was in fact historically far more diverse. Some contemporary bands pursue this more open instrumental legacy with instruments such as the mandolin, dobro, saxophone, and Hammond B-3 organ. Among Cajun bands, most use a button accordion also known as the melodeon, which has one row of ten buttons for primary notes in a major scale for the right hand, and three buttons for bass for the left hand. Zydeco exhibits greater variety in terms of accordions, from the one-row to double or triple-row and occasionally the piano accordion. Only a handful of zydeco musicians—including C.J. Chenier and Buckwheat Zydeco—restrict themselves to what is also called the "big accordion." The customization of instruments is another way of personalizing one's sound: Examples include Beau Jocque's bass player's five-string bass, the extra reeds and reed stops for the right hand on Wayne Toups's accordion, Jo-El Sonnier's MIDI retrofit, and Travis Matte's accordion, which he can switch from wet to dry tuning.

A common musical structure found in the French Louisiana repertoire, AABB or AABA, incorporates a first melody (A) and a distinct second melody (B) called the "turn" or the "bridge" in French Louisiana music—although some songs do not include a B part.[107] A range of musical embellishments is offered for each lead instrument. Fiddle players, for example, can use different techniques with their left hand (such as sliding notes, rolling notes, among others); they can play octaves on the melody; the bowing can be more rhythmic (like Dennis McGee), or smoother (like Dewey Balfa); the seconding can be based on chords or on playing the same melody an octave apart; another technique is tuning in less common keys, called "low" tuning (FCGD) or standard (GDAE) (for more on musical techniques, see ch. 4). For their part, button-accordion players, other than playing octave or double (meaning playing two-note combinations with the right hand), can squeeze notes in between octaves, incorporate triplets, slurs, and rolling licks, anticipate the bellow change to add an extra kick to the turn, or hammer the melody to create a staccato effect.[108] Among numerous other techniques, such embellishments and their appropriation by musicians contribute to the creation of a distinctive sound.

More recently, Cajun bands have also reevaluated the roles assigned to the basic instruments. Unlike bluegrass, swing, or jazz, for example, the guitar has often functioned as a rhythmic instrument. Guitarists who play lead guitar are still few in number; well-known examples include Sam Broussard of the Mamou Playboys, David Doucet of BeauSoleil, Josh Caffery and Chris Stafford of Feufollet, and Chas Justus of the Red Stick Ramblers and the Malfecteurs. Chas explains that it took him several years to develop confidence to play lead and not feel out of place as "the wanker guitar-player in a Cajun band," his reservations about playing lead perhaps augmented by his identity as a non-native. Exploring the potential of playing lead guitar has stimulated his creativity and attracted praise for his innovations. Not only does the guitar play solos, it also can collaborate with the accordion or fiddle, playing in unison or harmonizing on the turn. The (re)introduction of wind instruments as an integral part of the basic formation like the clarinet and saxophone has also become increasingly common among young bands like Cedric Watson and Bijou Creole, Horace Trahan and Ossun Express, and the Malfecteurs.

Some young bands identified with "traditional" style have also evolved from producing exclusively French-language albums to introducing English into their repertoire. The inclusion of songs in both languages by the Pine Leaf Boys, for example, appears to have been influenced by the success of other bands like Steve Riley and the Mamou Playboys. Discussing the 2010 album *Back Home*, Wilson Savoy offered the view that "times have changed, and with time, the music changed. We have worked extraordinarily hard to preserve Cajun French in our music, but at the same time, we remember that we live our day-to-day lives in English and hear records of the legends of Cajun music, from Lawrence Walker's 'Allons Rock 'n Roll' to various blues and one-steps. We are not too proud to sing a few songs in English."[109]

In addition to such choices and variations, contemporary musicians have experimented with highly eclectic music styles, sounds, and textures. Michael Doucet was a pioneer in the 1970s, exploring rock, bebop changes, Haitian syncopation, and Cuban clave.[110] In the late 1980s, a few other bands like the Bluerunners revisited French Louisiana music, blending Cajun and zydeco with rockabilly, punk rock, and acoustic folk, earning a place in the national limelight. In spite of this recognition, innovations tended to be somewhat marginalized, constrained by the powerful framework of tradition, especially among bands that adopt the Cajun label.

Since 2010 a fresh breeze has heralded a new trend and challenged the boundaries of these traditions. Whether they refer to their new sounds as "experimenting," "pushing the envelope," or playing "outside the box," more bands share a need for stepping out of traditional arrangements and sounds without being afraid of "taking chances." Music journalists and producers have taken note of these changes, emphasizing this daunting task in a musical world in which traditionalists do not hesitate to send hate messages when their expectations are not met. There have been articles in praise of this new wave described as redefining the present and infusing "traditional" music with new energy, shaking off what has been characterized as a dusty, hidebound style. The journalist Geoffrey Himes, for example, drew a comparison with punk rock in his description of the Pine Leaf Boys' performance at the 2011 Jazz Fest: "Savoy stood center stage with his legs dramatically spread apart like Billy Zoom from the punk band X, but instead of an electric guitar, Savoy held a handmade button accordion, its bellows stretching and collapsing with the propulsive beat."[111] The common ground between old-time string bands, best illustrated by the collaboration among Joel Savoy, veteran Jesse Lége, and the Oregon-based Foghorn Stringband on the deliberately entitled album *The Right Combination*, opens up the potential for appealing to a wider audience.

Among Cajun bands, Feufollet, a band founded in the late 1990s by a group of French immersion students in their early teens, embodies this new generation. *Cow Island Hop* began to experiment with new sounds with the addition of a Mellotron, an early electronic keyboard, and the full use of every track that ProTools could offer, including the sound of a trash can. In 2010 their album *En Couleurs* extended this fusion by including indie- and roots-rock influences in six original songs that were sung in French. The songs explored new textures, like a distorted guitar from a tiny Pignose amp playing power chords and the use of brief interludes, often in stark contrast to the feeling of the songs. A friend of the band and the album's co-producer, Ivan Klisanin, stimulated their imagination by making unusual instruments available in his studio, including a 1980s digital autoharp, a toy piano, and a glockenspiel. In fact, for local musician and producer C. C. Adcock, who produced Steve Riley and the Mamou Playboys' 2011 album *Grand Isle*, original songs have become the best approach to adopt: "There's not even much need to record old, obscure Cajun covers anymore. It's all been well documented now and is really accessible. That ain't a card to play anymore. You got to write your own tunes and come up with new stuff, because everyone knows the old songs."[112] He encouraged the band to experiment with drum loops, which are commonly used in modern pop. Experimentations on the album include playing a waltz to a drum machine, using a sample of submarine sonar pinging as part of the rhythm track, and collaborating with New Orleans underground musician Quintron on the song "Chatterbox." This search for a new sound also led the band to diversify their equipment by recording in as many as nine different studios in Lafayette, New Orleans, and Austin for this one album.

Horace Trahan firmly situates his band as south Louisianan, and his return to the music scene in 2010 with his album *Keep Walking* revealed a wide variety of musical influences. The album contains echoes of such icons of the Cajun style as Iry LeJeune, Aldus Roger, and Lawrence Walker, as well as country (Hank Williams, Hank Williams Jr., and George Jones), zydeco (Wayne Toups, John Delafose, Boozoo Chavis, Beau Jocque, and Clifton Chenier), reggae (Bob Marley), and folk rock (Bob Dylan). From French songs to soulful and funky numbers like "HDTV" with channel surfing, a firm beat, humming, and rapping, his album encompasses every possible source of Trahan's inspiration, ultimately bridging the gap between Cajun and zydeco.

This kind of experimentation in fact began over a decade earlier among contemporary bands that fused zydeco with an eclectic blend of R&B, soul, reggae, funk, gospel, and hip hop beats and vocals. Novelty defines the identity of some bands, a tendency exemplified by names like J. Paul Jr. and the Zydeco Newbreeds and Chris Ardoin and NuStep. Seeking a new sound is a matter of pride and a mark of high musicianship, regardless of the influences that serve as inspiration, from veterans of zydeco music to rappers and the theme songs of popular television sitcoms. During his short-lived career in the 1990s, Beau Jocque (Andrus Espré) combined ZZ Top and War influences with rap, from his "Cisco Kid" cover to his hip-hop mix "Make It Stank." His biggest hit, "Give Him Cornbread," was a reinterpretation of a Willis Prudhomme song combined with a rap song by FM, "Gimme What You Got (For a Pork Chop)," that added a contemporary double-kick. Along the same lines, Keith Frank's early hit "What's His Name" reflected the imprint of the celebrated rapper Snoop Doggy Dogg, and his big hit "Moving On Up" was based on the theme song of the television show *The Jeffersons*. "His lyrics," according to Michael Tisserand, "are a hip-hop style pastiche of popular cultural references. During a zydeco festival, he played his local hit 'Get on Boy' with added accordion licks from 'The Star Spangled Banner' and the themes to 'The Woody Woodpecker Show,' 'The Andy Griffith Show,' and the Clint Eastwood film 'The Good, the Bad and the Ugly.'"[113] In a different vein, Geno Delafose has followed in the footsteps of his father John, who as early as the 1980s found a middle ground between the two major branches of zydeco then represented by Clifton Chenier and Boozoo Chavis. Retaining the francophone songs blended with the strains of country music and the piano accordion, he inspired his son to borrow from blues, country, and swing and to integrate renditions of such R&B classics as "Sweet Soul Music" or "Sugar Pie, Honey Bunch" into his set lists.

In addition to these musical choices, many bands play on different registers, adapting to their audience (locals/outsiders; urban/rural) by selecting the kinds of songs they perform for a particular gig. The popularity of the Mamou Playboys, which is as strong locally as it is internationally, results partly from their ability to relate to different crowds and to meet their expectations. Since they began performing in the mid-1980s, they have made a point of playing in eclectic settings, from honky-tonks and country dance clubs like Gilton's, Nick's in Eunice, the Red Rose in Lake Arthur, or Pat's in Henderson to Lafayette dancehalls and out-of-state festivals, judging successfully the settings in which novelty sounds will be well received. In general, there is an evident concern with pleasing the average Louisianan as much as an out-of-state audience, and the band adjusts its repertoire to meet these sometimes divergent goals.

Some musicians fulfill the diversity of their tastes in French Louisiana music through involvement in different bands. During the early phase of his career, Michael Doucet chose to honor old-time French music while also experimenting with a modern rock sound. His band Coteau, which was highly influential during the 1970s, turned young people on to French music by blending influences from country, rock, and old-time French music. The band performed every Sunday night at Boo Boo's on the Breaux Bridge highway on the outskirts of Lafayette. At the same time, greatly influenced by a trip to France with his cousin Zachary Richard, where he met French folk musicians, Doucet began the all-acoustic band BeauSoleil, which "would emerge as the traditionalist antiquarian concert-touring counterpoint to Coteau's more rock-pop avant-garde Louisiana dancehall orientation—with various members going between the band depending upon the gigs," as noted by Nick Spitzer. Coteau disbanded in 1977, and Doucet concentrated his efforts on BeauSoleil, which has since become one of the most successful and nationally recognized Cajun bands.

As a fiddler in two very distinct all-woman Cajun bands, Anya Burgess demonstrates the variety of her musical identifications: the Magnolia Sisters focus on ancient ballads and little-known old-time songs, whereas Chère Catin exhibits an upbeat, honky-tonk style focused on dance. Embracing contrasting styles and imaginaries within French Louisiana music, Anya also occasionally plays Appalachian old-time music, her first love.

While some musicians diversify their styles by exploring different directions within the same band or in different bands, others change their style over the course of their careers, a riskier path that can be greeted with displeasure by their original fans. Travis Matte is one example. In the early 2000s, he switched from being a hired musician in traditional Cajun and zydeco bands to playing in his own band what he eventually termed "hip-hop-zyderock," successfully attracting audiences among the region's college students. In 2004 Chris Ardoin, who used to play with his brother Sean and his father in Double Clutchin', broke with them and eventually founded a new band with a contemporary R&B sound.

Many other musicians combine their careers as French Louisiana music performers with other bands or solo performances in which they play different music styles and instruments. Whereas their main band helps ensure them a livelihood, these artists diversify their skills by playing with other bands. Kevin Wimmer, for example, in addition to being the fiddler for the Red Stick Ramblers before he replaced David Greely with the Mamou Playboys in 2010, also plays with the Sleepless Knights, Preston Frank, and Balfa Toujours, adjusting his sought-after fiddle playing to the Cajun or Creole style, to swing or to jazz. Other examples of this switch-hitting trend include the Revelers, formed in 2011 by founding members of the Pine Leaf Boys and the Red Stick Ramblers, and Lisa Trahan, who likes to switch from playing bass with the Magnolia Sisters to the accordion in her own band, Lisa Trahan and L'Esprit Cajun. Still others like to give free rein to their inspiration as songwriters, although interestingly, zydeco musicians do not appear to ever follow this path. This is the case of Chas Justus, the guitar player for the Red Stick Ramblers, who recorded a CD of original rock songs with Chris Segura and Chris Stafford (of the band Feufollet) in the band Hungry Hungry. Chas stripped himself of his instrumentalist cloak to take the lead on vocals and songwriting: "It's like organ and keyboards and guitars like sixties pop or something kind of sounds, rock and that kind of stuff. The Beatles or Rolling Stones, or John Prine; wordy, brooding songs. . . . Some of the songs have a harp on it. It's just a completely different sound [than the Red Stick Ramblers]." This different sound results as much from musical influences as from a different approach to making music that is not focused on dancers: "Chris Segura listens to tons of indie rock and all the Beatles albums. And Chris Stafford is into the Kinks and the Beatles and bands that were really into recording, not just performing, but really into recording as a medium in itself."[114]

In recent years, some musicians have released solo recordings that are distinct from their involvement in full-time bands. Examples include Sam Broussard of the Mamou Playboys with his albums *Geeks* (2000) and *Veins* in (2010), and Yvette Landry from Bonsoir Catin and the Lafayette Rhythm Devils, with her self-produced debut solo honky-tonk album *Should Have Known*. Taking center stage, they switch from being accompanying instrumentalists (as guitar player and bass player, respectively) to the role of singer/songwriter, demonstrating their talent as lyricists and their desire to display their creativity as single artists.

As Chas, a somewhat discreet figure when performing on stage with the Red Stick Ramblers, but a humorous, articulate, even loquacious one-on-one conversationalist confides in a particularly honest moment: "I can appreciate the folk side—but also, I've got to admit, I'm a performer. That's what I try to do with my life. I've spent hours and hours and hours listening to other performers and learning from records and things like that so that I could, one day, you know, show off . . ."

In fact, by recording or performing original songs in their own styles, and more broadly in displaying their versatility, performers of French Louisiana music reveal themselves among their peers as accomplished musicians capable of navigating between different types of music. This ability is also prized and cited as evidence of professionalism among New Orleans musicians.[115] The dynamics appear to be different within the zydeco scene, in which musicians tend to be more focused on their own bands and display creativity and eclecticism within that context instead of engaging in different bands or as solo artists.

Although music genres are impossible to define through a definitive set of rules, aesthetic conventions do exist, and they serve to regulate creative practices.[116] Musicians experience authority differently, depending on who exerts it. The risk of having some of their choices disapproved of by dancers is a possibility to which musicians are highly sensitive and that they are prepared to confront. Whether musicians choose to target dancers or stretch their repertoire to include presentational music that reaches a sit-down audience, the public is considered a legitimate arbiter, even if their opinion can also on occasion be ignored.

The authority of folklorists, on the other hand, can at times be vehemently rejected.[117] One illustration is the virulent debate that erupted following the publication of an article by Ryan Brasseaux in his anthology on music scholarship. In his paper, Brasseaux discussed the "authenticity" of the music of the Mamou Playboys, whom he portrayed as the "poster children" of the French movement. Attempting to point out the ambiguities of the notion of authenticity as defined by French activists, he argued that their music, mostly written in French at the time like in numerous other bands, was not representative of south Louisiana's mainstream linguistic landscape.[118] Naturally, the band took serious issue with this value judgment concerning their art, as well as the confusing fashion of the argument, a confusion probably due to the fact that the article was actually intended more to settle scores with French activists, their views of authenticity, and their hegemony over the field than to analyze the uses and meanings of the notion of authenticity among participants in the French Louisiana music scene. The real stakes involved in this controversy ultimately revealed a power struggle over the perception of "authentic" music between two different generations of Louisiana scholars.

Among the motives for the resentment that the article stimulated, more acute because of Brasseaux's status both as a non-musician and as an academic from the prestigious institution of Yale, was the major role it attributed to Barry Ancelet in the group's musical choices. In fact, organizers—among them Ancelet—of festivals such as Festivals Acadiens et Créoles set parameters through which they exercise a certain degree of control over the music being played. The context of these events needs to be differentiated, however, from the broader musical evolution of bands throughout their career. Both David Greely and Sam Broussard were adamant about the Playboys' musical independence with respect to cultural middlemen such as Ancelet. Broussard's public response to the article on his personal website is quite explicit:[119]

> As a member of the Playboys, I can state that we willfully play whatever we want—within the bounds of our respect for the tradition—to the delight or dismay of both our audience and CM [cultural middlemen] agents. As to the CMs, I've known Dr. Barry Ancelet since the first grade, and the previous longtime president of the Council for the Development of French in Louisiana is my brother-in-law, and I can categorically state that the issue of our authenticity has never come up in conversation—why would it?—and neither has there been an effort to guide us. That last sentence arrives with a soundtrack: the sound of a door slamming. It is the final word on the subject.

The allegation that they were under Ancelet's control seemed particularly infuriating to them probably in part because they felt it damaged their reputation by questioning their autonomy, and hence their creative agency.[120] Their fierce defense of artistic freedom does not mean that they are unaware of the impact of folklorists on the development of their style. Greely frequently acknowledges that he learned much of what he knows of "old-time" French music from field recordings at the Archive of Cajun and Creole Folklore, where Ancelet led him by the arm one day. This acquiescence, however, does not diminish his conception of his right to appropriate this music on his own terms.

Musicians frequently stress the uniqueness of their sound and reference differences from French music veterans in a clear effort to differentiate themselves, even as they acknowledge and praise the veterans' legacy. In 2004 Cedric Watson, a Creole and native Texan, was a recent arrival on the French Louisiana music scene. The scarcity of young Creole fiddlers earned him the reputation of being a reincarnation of the late Creole fiddler Canray Fontenot and he was perceived as a blessing on the local scene. One fall evening after the weekly jam at the Blue Moon had just wrapped up, accordion player Joe Hall began a conversation with Watson in the parking lot. At some point, he moved to face the fiddler, and solemnly said: "Have I ever told you anything wrong?" After generously complimenting Watson and predicting a brilliant career, he added: "You play with a swing, though. Canray didn't play with a swing." To which Cedric answered on the spot: "I am not Canray! It ain't what I wanna be! What I play is *my* Creole style." He has subsequently continued to develop his own style, playing classic zydeco songs including Clifton Chenier's, original material, and traditional Creole pieces. The following year, I went with Joe Hall to visit "Bois Sec" Ardoin, and, as Joe discussed the different fiddle styles of Douglas Bellard compared to Canray Fontenot, Bois Sec summed up in a few words what seemed obvious to him: "Just like me and you. You play you, I play mine."

Remaining perfectly faithful to a role model is perceived as offering a pale imitation that undermines musicianship. As late Zydeco Joe put it: "Me, I'm a creator, not an imitator. A lot of bands all do the same thing. But me, it's different" (*"Moi c'est un creator, pas imitator. Un tas de band asteur tout fait le même affaire. Mais moi c'est different"*). For Beau Jocque, there is actually no alternative in order to be successful: "Clifton was very popular because he did Clifton's music. And Boozoo did things his way. But now I'm doing it my way, and I figure if I do that, I'll always have a road to travel on."[121] Chris Ardoin's decision to name two of his albums *M.V.P.* ("most valuable player," typically used in sports) and Keith Franck nickname "the Zydeco Boss" follow the same competitive logic.[122] For David Greely, self-confidence among musicians contributes to the process: "Everybody thinks he's the best!" he affirms, amused and impressed by musicians' pride regardless of their ability, unlike other music such as bluegrass in which technical skills are prized above originality or self-assuredness. Billy McGee, Dennis's son, testifies concerning his feisty father's self-confidence: "He said there was only one kind of music, and that was his music! [laughs],"[123] while Wilson Savoy and Corey Ledet wittily approach competitiveness in the *Corey Ledet Instructional Triple Accordion* DVD:

> "I'm going to play 'Jolie blonde.' You don't have to play it like me, everybody has different styles," says Corey Ledet, grabbing his piano accordion.
> "What if I wanna play it exactly like you?" asks Wilson Savoy.
> "Then I'll have to kill you!"[124]

Some young musicians justify the novelty of their sound as a means of self-emancipation from any role model or tradition. After sixteen years as a fiddler for traditional Cajun, zydeco, and country bands, Travis Matte decided to switch to the accordion and to form a new band, originally named the Zydeco Kingpins, that explored into rock and hip-hop. In 2008 the band decided to drop zydeco from their name as a way of proclaiming their unique style. This new direction, which also involved risqué songs, sparked sharp criticism among his fans, and left Matte with a bitter aftertaste:

> If you're singing a Belton Richard song, or an old Aldus song, you're likely to sing like the record. Or, if you're playing a Balfa song, you want to hear the "Valse de Balfa" played similar to Dewey and sung similar to Dewey. And I don't want to do that anymore, I did that for sixteen years, I want to play my own songs, you know. . . . We just try to do it in our style as best as we can without trying to copy. I don't like that. . . . Cajun music, they don't want to see no kind of evolution in it. You play like Aldus and Dewey Balfa and that's it. They don't want to see any changes in it and they're not open to any changes in it.

Eager to defend his choice against the controversies surrounding his explicit sexual references ("Vibrator," "Let's Get Nasty," "I'd Tap Dat," "Slap That A—," "Wam Bam Thank You Mam"), he portrays Cajun music lovers as "obsessed with tradition," pursuing his argument to the point of discrediting the "traditional" style altogether, which he associates with mere imitation. In fact, his bitterness in the context of our interview is not fully reflected in his musical choices, and several of his CDs have contained reinterpretations of Cajun standards, some of them translated into English, like "Sugar Daddy" ("Eunice Two-Step") and "Your Daddy Don't Want Me Around" (Canray Fontenot's "Tes parents veulent plus me voir"). Even his 2006 album *Booty Zydeco* uses the melody of "Scott Playboys Special" for his song "Cheech and Chong," while "Without You I'm Not Me" echoes the sound of "Bonsoir Moreau."[125]

The accusation or suspicion of imitation is a serious matter that has sometimes taken a cruel twist on the zydeco scene, as Corey Ledet drily acknowledges in the above quote. Controversy over the rightful claim to the title of "King of Zydeco" began during Clifton Chenier's lifetime, between him and his former keyboard player Buckwheat Zydeco. His death precipitated proclamations of kingship for Rockin' Dopsie, followed by other figures who also aspired to the zydeco crown. In *The Kingdom of Zydeco*, filmmaker Robert Mugge uses a "battle of the bands" shot in 1993 to illustrate the power struggles between Boozoo Chavis and Beau

Jocque. Each musician uses different arguments to assert the legitimacy of his claim to the crown. As Chavis irritably argues in the film: "I got 300 songs. I'm coming from way back, not from yesterday. Beau Jocque is just coming to this. I feel I don't have to prove. There is no battle, no comparison." Against this claim of seniority and affiliation with "old-school" rural zydeco, Beau Jocque self-confidently and provocatively lays claim to the ingenuity of his progressive urban style with: "The best man might win if I do." The king title, which was never resolved—with self-proclaimed kings adding a certain piquancy—is only the most theatrical aspect of these power struggles over status.

Claims of ownership, whether related to musical techniques or songs, are a further expression of this kind of conflict. Michael Tisserand reports a conversation in which the drummer Steve Charlot, who played with Beau Jocque and the Highrollers, credits the band for major innovations: "Before I started whistling and rapping, nobody was doing that. Before Beau Jocque started going into the low keys, nobody was doing that. Before Chuck got on that five-string bass, nobody was doing that. And now they're all trying to do it. But Beau Jocque will keep doing what nobody has done before."[126]

The most belligerent feud, however, took place within modern-style zydeco, between Beau Jocque and the young Keith Frank, beginning an epic battle over the songs "Went Out Last Night" by Keith Frank and "Yesterday" by Beau Jocque, both recorded in 1993, which unfortunately were the same song claimed by both musicians. It was ultimately determined that both songs derived from "I Got Loaded" from Little Bob and the Lollipops. But nothing was resolved and the battle continued, developing an increasingly sour tone. Tisserand notes that attacks in rhyme through song lines echoed the acrimonious break up of Eric "Eazy-E" Wright with Los Angeles gangsta rap band N.W.A (Niggaz With Attitude).[127] The virulence of such disputes illustrates the far-reaching implications of questions of ownership. What is at stake in such disputes is the quest for higher status and recognition through royalties on a possible hit, which can sometimes ensure lifelong financial security for people living in precarious conditions, not only because of job insecurity but also because of a challenging social environment. The debate within zydeco parallels broader conflicts between posses in contemporary rap, based on individual, regional, or ethnic identifications.

Although these rival claims appear to take on more aggressive forms among zydeco players, they pertain to the entire French Louisiana music scene. Self-proclaimed originals sometimes result from the renaming of songs based on the style or the arrangements of the musicians who play them: McGee's "La Robe barrée" was called "Madame Etienne" on another recording with Ardoin. Similarly, McGee's "One step de Mamou" became "Lake Arthur Stomp" when played by fiddler Varise Conner. And the "One-step de Morse" by Nathan Abshire and The Rayne-Bo Ramblers was recorded by Lawrence Walker, with a different bridge, under the name "The Mamou Two-Step." The replacement of one title with another in order to make a personal contribution to an existing song is a time-honored practice. Numerous traditional songs are known under a variety of names (including "Dit Bye-bye," a.k.a. "Louisiana waltz"; or "Valse d'Oberlin," a.k.a. "Tit monde"), a practice that was undoubtedly encouraged by early commercial recordings, when musicians had to name songs (as opposed to field recordings, like the Lomaxes', which contain numerous untitled songs), and were credited as the songs' authors. This is the case with "The Guilbeau Pelican Waltz" and the "Marcantel Reel," both attributed to Dennis McGee because he was the first musician to record them.

The notion of a unique sound is sometimes tied to the term "hybrid," cited as a mark of distinctiveness. The Red Stick Ramblers present their music as "a unique hybrid of Cajun, country, string band, and swing influences." Music writer Ben Sandmel assigns this characteristic to the entire zydeco style, as if to neutralize any enduring questions about authenticity in zydeco: "These questions [of purism and authenticity] are particularly murky in the case of zydeco, which has always been a hybrid."[128] In fact, this question can be applied to the French Louisiana repertoire as a whole, including zydeco but also early twentieth-century French music. In effect, claiming to have an inimitable sound connects with the idea of creolization and the notion of adaptation and creativity that it implies. But instead of associating it with a Cajun or French Louisiana cultural process as do academics, activists, and touristic and cultural institutions, musicians tend to experience it on an individual level that reveals their musical talent and personal creativity. This difference is suggestive of a shift in scale, from the collective to the individual, depending on the social actors and the cultural, social, and ultimately aesthetic and musical processes in which they are implicated.

Self-positioning on the Music Market

> Cajun music is like a tree, that you plant and you water and you take care of it, and you want it to grow, but you don't want it to mutate, and grow arms and teeth and eat your kids!
> DAVID GREELY, IN *THE MAMOU PLAYBOYS ROCKUMENTARY*, ALMENA PICTURES, 2004

Regardless of the form in which it presents itself, creativity relies on a connection to a tradition or even a lineage. Innovation becomes possible and creativity gains credibility with reference to the position of "disciple" or "relative," which enables an artist or artwork to enter the musical canon. This affiliation with a specific style and a particular heritage thus enables musicians not to limit the spectrum of their choices or their creativity.

Nearly two decades after his death, the voice of Dewey Balfa continues to reverberate in books, liner notes, and interviews in support of the innovative nature of tradition and the delicate balance between the twin risks of discontinuity and calcification, risks that invoke the question of musical legitimacy. Some of Dewey's quotes have become catchphrases for generations of musicians who claim him as a mentor. Without doubt his most famous and oft-quoted line is: "a culture is like a whole tree. You have to water the roots to keep the tree alive, but at the same time, you can't go cutting off the branches every time it tries to grow."

Balfa's reflections on tradition captures the way in which musicians position themselves both as tradition-bearers and artists whatever style they embrace, from old-time French to the "new" zydeco and Cajun sound, whether they align themselves with Balfa or some other mentor's legacy. In addition to Balfa, a number of twentieth-century musicians have functioned as role models for generations of musicians. To name just a few of these revered figures and mentors from the French Louisiana pantheon: Amédé Ardoin, Dennis McGee, Canray Fontenot, Harry Choates, Clifton Chenier, Lawrence Walker, Iry Lejeune, Nathan Abshire, Belton Richard, Boozoo Chavis, Beau Jocque. Again, musicians who claim their legacy systematically emphasize the uniqueness of their mentor's style, as exemplified by Mitch Reed, whose attraction to Michael Doucet was precisely due to his new sound, which also explains his obsession with the distinctive, inimitable style of Dennis McGee.

Situating oneself within the heritage of these musical pioneers and the lineage of ongoing family dynasties among them (including the Ardoins,

Balfas, Franks, Delafoses, and Savoys) is a recurrent motif, both in terms of the rhetoric involved in written and spoken discourse, websites, CD liners, and interviews and in musical practices (such as interpretations and arrangements of the songs of these pillar-like figures and through explicit homages). The idea of "creating within the tradition" is appropriated and invoked in support of the individual artist's creative agency. Among the most popular contemporary musicians in the Lafayette area, the Red Stick Ramblers define themselves on their website as "at the very forefront of a new generation of Louisiana roots musicians who are reinventing their tradition while remaining deeply aware of their heritage." The rhetoric of the Pine Leaf Boys enacts a similar process: "Steeped in music since children and hailing from farms and towns in Cajun country, the Pine Leaf Boys have preserved the traditional Cajun sound, while allowing it to breathe and stretch with those who play it."[129] The Lost Bayou Ramblers, who embrace and extend their own family musical legacy (the Michot Brothers), have mixed early accordion dancehall tunes, pre-twentieth-century fiddle tunes, and Cajun swing "to form a definitive sound—capturing the 'roots' spirit of their culture's unique music while initiating a renewed cultural identity and pride among their generation."[130] More recently, the new sound represented by their album *Mammoth Waltz* (2012) did not emancipate them from the influence of their forefathers: "All of our Cajun influences are very hardcore and raunchy. Most of them are thought of as very traditional—you know, Joe Falcon, Austin Pitre and Lawrence Walker—but they're just real rock and roll–based Cajun music," says Louis Michot.[131] He describes Falcon in the 1950s and 1960s playing through "Fender twin amps" while his (second) wife played drums, as "chockin' loud, you know, and it's very raunchy and we love that," defining *chockin'* as "the one-drop rhythm of Cajun music," and raunchy as "Just loud and nasty." "Not clean, not folky, not acoustic. Just real open-minded as in very creative with their tunes." These quotes suggest that tradition is thus systematically cited in support of and integrated into nearly any music projects, even the most innovative.

Looking still further back, Wayne Toups expresses similar feelings about his relationship with tradition, although he built much of his career outside his native Louisiana. Along with Michael Doucet and Zachary Richard, he helped kindle interest among the younger generation in the 1980s, developing a rock-style that was controversial at the time with a group called Wayne Toups and Zydecajun. Citing influences as diverse as Otis Redding, Aretha Franklin, Percy Sledge, and Wilson Pickett, as well as rock bands like the Doobie Brothers, Lynyrd Skynyrd, and the Allman Brothers, he pays tribute to his roots, particularly with his album *Little Wooden Box* (2000): "I wanted to reach back, yes, but I call this creating tradition within the tradition. So we took these old songs and made them 'Wayne Toups' songs." Mixing songs in English and French versions of English songs ("Les Filles de la Ville," based on "New Orleans Ladies," and "Couillon," a version of John Wesley Ryles's "Fool" that Toups first did in 1979), he offers his rendition of French standards like "Jeunes Filles de la Campagne," "Lacassine Special," and "La Chanson de Lemonade," and Clifton Chenier's "Tous les temps en temps."

In fact, several Cajun bands have pursued a similar strategy musically by unwinding throughout a song the thread that ties them to the past. Reversing the current of time, BeauSoleil starts off with "Happy One Step," a Dennis McGee song, using a modern style before gradually returning to an old-style of fiddle playing (*Cajunization*). "Ardoin Medley" from the Mamou Playboys (*Dominos*) begins in an old-time mode, with the accordion and fiddle playing together against the beat of the 'tit-fer, before gradually slipping into a modern-style tune with the introduction of the bass and acoustic guitar, with the fiddle and accordion alternating in taking solos and other additional embellishments. In their album *En Couleurs*, which extends their French repertoire to indie rock, Feufollet makes a point of expressing an alliance between their new direction and a traditional legacy. On "Ouvre La Porte," the band transforms a 1930s Alan Lomax field recording of Elita Hoffpauir into a snazzy waltz, with bright melodies on piano and glockenspiel. The voice of the revered anthropologist also appears as a conclusion to the album in the form of a sample in which he speaks about his recordings, which dissolves into a backbeat of drums and looped guitar, as if to offer a tribute to the canon while proclaiming the right to define it in their own terms. These "musical quotes," both instrumental and vocal (through interview excerpts that start the song), function both as a form of reverence to the legacy of veterans and as an assertion of creative agency from present-day musicians. Instead of moving in a "restorative" direction like the 1950s folk revival[132] and the French Louisiana music revival of the 1970s, the emergence of this new music scene encodes its re-appropriation and ultimate transformation of their inheritance.

By contrast with these rhetorical and musical subtexts, some musicians choose not to express their musical choices in words, allowing the music to speak for itself, regardless of which style they pursue. This is the case with Dexter Ardoin, who performs the old-time French music repertoire, and Corey Ledet, who embraces a wide range of styles ranging from the old-time French repertoire to Clifton's legacy. It is also the case of Jamie Bergeron, who encourages people to see for themselves without commenting on his rock style, the heavy use of electric guitar, and the use of both French and English. One of his album's titles, however, ironically characterizes his style as *Traditionally Untraditional* (2000), a rhetorical sleight-of-hand that speaks of an attempt to position himself outside of, or at least interrogate, the question of canon.

Even within the most contemporary, urban style on the zydeco scene, the link to tradition remains undisputed. Among descendants of musical dynasties, tradition is established by blood lineage, cited by Keith Frank, Sean and Chris Ardoin, and Lil' Nate in order to define themselves as "innate" zydeco musicians, or the "royalties" of the zydeco kingdom. The young Texas-born accordionist Brian Terry, originator of a sound he calls "z-funk," also considers himself heir to a tradition: "That's in the blood of my family from Louisiana." As eager as they appear to promote the novelty of their styles, these musicians always anchor their styles in their roots, establishing and obeying the genre-based criteria for a legitimate tradition.

The production strategies of zydeco musician Keith Frank are put into stark relief in his series of double CDs. In 2007 he released *Undisputed*, followed by *Loved, Feared, Respected* (2009), and *Follow the Leader* (2012). All three double albums are based on the same concept: one CD features "the best of the contemporary zydeco sound seamlessly fusing zydeco with R&B, hip hop, reggae, and gospel," while the other is "traditional zydeco at its finest," featuring three generations of the Frank family singing in regional Louisiana French. His claim to modernity and tradition is paradoxically rendered in two separate styles conceived as a whole but tangibly separated into two distinct CDs. *Follow the Leader* and *Boot Up* are sold together as a set; the latter is supposed to trace Frank's roots to his more contemporary style. Yet *Boot Up* is far from a clear allegiance to tradition. Even "Johnny Can't Dance" or "Adam 3-Step," which is sung in French, have their own signature twists and turns, as pointed out by music journalist Dan Willging: "'Adam 3-Step' features the accordionist playing quick, infectious syncopated riffs over a tight, interlocking rhythm section.... [In] the instrumental title, Frank trading licks with guitarist Lucien Hayes sounds something like the Meters jamming on zydeco back in the day."[133] This distinction between a traditional and contemporary style appears even fuzzier through Frank's choice to include two numbers on both discs, an adaptation of the Meters' "Fire on the Bayou" and "That's Why They Call Him the Boss," which starts with a live segment from Boozoo Chavis urging the younger generation to keep zydeco alive. The juxtaposition of appearances of the old master and of guest rappers Level and DCRAVE in the same disc only reinforce the powerful significance of paying tribute to mentors and asserting a role of tradition-bearer. Despite these obvious intermingling of styles, Frank makes a point (both through marketing choices and explicit claims in his lyrics) to link his contemporary style to an overarching tradition, regardless of the musical style of his songs.

Regardless of their style, musicians on the French Louisiana music scene strive to maintain their legitimacy with respect to their fans and the music industry, shaping and being shaped by demand for cultural distinctiveness while positioning themselves in the midst of American modernity. The Lafayette area is home to hundreds of musicians, and over half of the nearly 300 Lafayette-based musicians listed in the *Offbeat Music Directory* identified themselves as playing either Cajun or zydeco music, about twice as many claiming the former over the latter.

Musicians use distinct marketing strategies to target different music markets. Bands that favor eclectic influences and echo particular styles—zydeco, Cajun, rock, rap, funk, R&B, reggae, blues, and soul, ranging from Wayne Toups to Travis Matte and from Buckwheat to J. Paul Jr.—seek to join mainstream American popular music, i.e., to attract the broadest possible audience by producing music that is disseminated via the mass media and that generates the greatest revenue.[134] They are explicitly not seeking to remain on the margins of the musical economy. Some artists such as Travis Matte achieve enormous success in the regional market, while others, like Buckwheat Zydeco and BeauSoleil, have gained national and international reputations. While proclaiming multiple influences and advocating for eclecticism and innovation, the vast majority of these musicians still ground themselves, to varying degrees, in regional and ethnic identifications as Cajuns, Creoles, and/or Louisiana roots.

If anything, Creoles go to even greater lengths to penetrate the popular music market, in all likelihood due to their position at the bottom of the Louisiana socio-economic scale and to their motivation to transcend their Creole identity and achieve status and prestige as African Americans.[135] It is probably no coincidence that zydeco musician Terrence Simien and his wife Cynthia instigated the creation of the Cajun and Zydeco Grammy Award after a seven-year-campaign. Eventually established in 2007, this new category repositioned French Louisiana artists and music as an integral part of the national market and was perceived as an upgrade from their status as a sub-category of traditional, country, blues, or folk music. In 2011, however, the Recording Academy decided to reduce the number of categories, resulting in the removal, among a number of other categories, of the Cajun and Zydeco award; French Louisiana music has since been relegated to the "Regional Roots" category.

The use of English lyrics in zydeco, with the exception of Step Rideau and occasional songs in regional French, is further evidence of a desire to belong to the American popular music market while retaining regional identification. In the 1970s zydeco was a musical niche that represented a symbolic and economic shift in status for musicians like C. C. Chenier or Rockin' Sidney, providing an alternative to the blues. After Clifton declared, "Zydeco got me the Grammy," Sidney openly acknowledged its economic power, affirming that "I still like the blues, but I go to the grocery store with zydeco. Zydeco pays the bills."[136] Since the 1990s, the influence of rap and other influences has defined the evolution of his music. Brian Terry, the leader of Lil' Brian and the Zydeco Travelers, explains his ambition to elevate zydeco to the level of rap: "Zydeco was practically a meal at my table. But, you know, I'm a young man, and I started liking Snoop Doggy Dogg rap, and Tupac [Shakur]. So I started to feel, if they can do it, why can't I do it—but just do it with zydeco music, something I was brought up with?"[137]

The hip hop industry is in fact thriving in Louisiana. The survey "Louisiana: Where Culture Is Business" reports that New Orleans–based Cash Money Records, which has released number one hits by the multi-platinum artist Juvenile and the Hot Boys, sold over fifteen million records in a four-year period. Master P, who grew up in the violence-plagued Calliope projects in New Orleans, has built an empire around his No Limit Records label, which enjoyed over $7 million in record sales in 1998.[138]

Since the early 2000s, the appeal of the newer sounds of zydeco for the younger generation has significantly altered the configuration of the zydeco music and dance scene. "Traditional" or "old-school" zydeco has gradually lost its following, causing once highly popular dancehalls in the Lafayette area to close their doors, including Hamilton's, which closed in 2005 after forty-nine years and less than a year after being hailed by the *New York Times*. El Sid O's, another zydeco club old favorite, struggles to attract dancers despite a lineup of internationally renowned artists like Buckwheat Zydeco and Nathan Williams. Bands that fill dancehalls like

Chris Ardoin and Double Clutchin' or J. Paul and the Zydeco Nubreedz are able to draw a young crowd in their teens and early twenties. On July 30, 2008, Chris Ardoin was playing at El Sid O's for a Gas Relief Party. Dressed in an elegant red T-Shirt and sunglasses and sporting earrings, Ardoin opened with a diatonic accordion before swapping to a three-row. Each song followed a similar pattern in which he introduced a funk, soul, or rock standard like "Sweet Home Alabama" before switching to a zydeco song, occasionally using electronically distorted sound effects. As the dancehall became increasingly crowded, the volume increased. Men were dressed in hip hop–style outfits, with price tags hanging from their clothes, and sported earrings, sunglasses sometimes encrusted with diamond-like rings, and chains around their necks, many of them with crosses hanging from them (including Chris). Many of the girls stood by themselves, ringing the stage, and as the crowd became denser, they perched sitting on the edge of the stage itself with their backs turned to Chris, looking at the dancers as they sipped their drinks, shaking and moving with the music. Constantly glancing at cellphones or Blackberries in the palms of their hands, some of these women eagerly checked and composed text messages, but most of them just stood around, and even those who danced were forced to stay on the dance floor after they were finished in order to avoid fighting the crowd.

By appropriating television theme songs and identifying with pop music icons (e.g., Lil Nathan's website featured a picture of "Michael Jackson R.I.P." for awhile), zydeco players reach out to a mass audience and adopt globalized black and African American symbols. The complexity of the local-global interplay is embedded within this process as the balance between claims to a specific heritage and the incorporation of those symbols is endlessly renegotiated. The strong regional market reflects the impact of territorialized musical traditions and taste.[139] R&B ballads and hip hop beats infuse zydeco shuffles and contemporary two-steps, amid an overarching reverence for zydeco forefathers or "soldiers" (i.e., "Where My Soldiers At?" from J. Paul Jr.).

Other bands position themselves within "roots music," a category that emerged in the 1980s in the United States under the influence of rock critics. Referring to music styles that are considered major sources of inspiration for twentieth-century American popular music, "roots" specifically embraces zydeco and Cajun music.[140] Bands that have branched out more or less recently into swing, Texas swing, swamp pop, country, rock, or indie rock include the Bluerunners, the Mamou Playboys, Roddie

Romero and the Hub City All-Stars, Feufollet, the Pine Leaf Boys, the Lost Bayou Ramblers, and the Red Stick Ramblers. Other groups that identify to a greater extent with Creole or with "traditional" zydeco tend to stay closer to the core of the French Louisiana repertoire (for example Dexter Ardoin and Corey "Lil Pop" Ledet), while still others have explored new connections, including Cedric Watson and Bijou Creole, who have found inspiration in Haitian kompa and merengue. All retain an aura of rootedness, however, and, along with a variety of influences, continue to incorporate French classics and old ballads or to revisit obscure old-time tunes from southwest Louisiana, Canada, or the Caribbean. These bands situate themselves with respect to a tradition, however they appropriate and reshape it, and assert their territoriality in southwest Louisiana and its French heritage.

Speaking French and being able to write songs in the language has become an increasingly appreciated asset, as French has steadily dwindled throughout recent generations despite expanding bilingual and immersion language programs in the local education system. Since the early 2000s, however, a strong tendency to embrace English has arisen among younger musicians, who do not feel that they are betraying their heritage by opting to write in English. In fact, what constitutes their primary characteristic is their regional affiliation with southwest Louisiana, a niche market within roots music. Being able to market their music to roots fans locally, nationally, and internationally is considered the key to success among musicians and producers, a view echoed by Joel Savoy, whose Valcour record label specializes in southwest Louisiana artists: "What interests me is finding new audiences for the music and putting out music that's recorded in a way and packaged in a way that will attract people who are interested in other kinds of roots music around the world. So we just decided that was going to be our focus—to market Cajun music more in the roots music category and to try to find new audiences instead of just staying local-minded."

"There's *always* going to be a market for Louisiana music," he continues, asserting the longevity and power of Louisiana's distinctiveness. The Roots Music Report, based on radio airplay and national music charts listed David Greely's *Sud du Sud* album in twenty-fourth place among its 2011 "Top 100 Folk Albums," and on its music charts by state, the 2011 Louisiana chart listed The Lost Bayou Ramblers' *Mammoth Waltz* album at number 13.

From American popular music to roots music, French Louisiana bands can thus situate themselves within different music categories and address themselves to distinct music markets, as reflected in their career strategies and choices of music styles, collaborations, venues, tours, audiences, and recordings. Beyond these distinctions and whatever their style, nearly all of the region's bands embrace to varying degrees their regional identification and French Louisiana heritage. Furthermore, positioning oneself in roots music is far from comprising an exclusive aspiration for national recognition and strategic use of the mass music market. In fact, Roddie Romero, who has been performing for over twenty years, presents his band as "Louisiana Roots-Rockers," had a Grammy-nominated double album *La Louisianne Sessions* (2007), and promotes his Louisiana style, expressed through a blend of Cajun and Creole, swamp pop, 1950s rock, and originals, as fundamentally modern. "American music *is* Roddie Romero and the Hub City All Stars—born out of the Delta dirt—rising high off the levee of traditionalism and into the future of Louisiana Music." BeauSoleil is a typical example of a band that fits firmly inside the roots market while also seizing any opportunity to reach a wider audience by exploring a variety of musical settings and fields such as movie soundtracks, advertisements, and the like. The group has accumulated the largest number of distinctions of any other band during its thirty-year career. They have been nominated eleven times for Grammy Awards and have won three times, and are regular guests on the legendary National Public Radio show *A Prairie Home Companion*. They also played at the 1997 Super Bowl and even opened for the Grateful Dead. Michael Doucet has furthermore been awarded individual national distinctions, including a United States Artists Fellowship (2007) and a National Heritage Fellowship (2005). The range of influences that BeauSoleil has explored and its national visibility have ensured the group the top ranking among the nation's Cajun groups. Although winning Grammys probably did not directly affect the band's record sales, being advertised as a Grammy-winning artist opens the door to better gigs and increases sales opportunities, along with providing maximum exposure and recognition. In fact, the impact was probably greater when Doucet was the only Grammy nominee representing southwest Louisiana against all other musicians in the Traditional Folk category than during the brief (2007–10) lifespan of the Cajun and Zydeco category.

Regarding zydeco players, because they situate themselves within global black culture while retaining regional identification, major music producers can incorporate them in the world music circuit by emphasizing their distinctiveness. Consequently, the groundbreaking album *Graceland*, produced by Paul Simon in 1986, included Rocking' Dopsie's "That

Was Your Mother" (a cover of Clifton C. Chenier's "Josephine"), for which Simon received sole songwriting credit, whereas South Africans were credited for their collaboration. As Mark DeWitt argues, French Louisiana was at the time considered marginal within the world music circle and, while distinctive and attractive, did not compare with the exoticism of music from outside U.S. borders.[141] Fifteen years later, world music label Putamayo produced the album *Zydeco* (2000), followed in 2005 by the Rough Guides album *Zydeco: Allons danser! Creole Accordions Dance*. Like the Columbian costeño music described by anthropologist Peter Wade, the successful appeal of zydeco, particularly outside of Louisiana, is tied to this ambivalence: a music played by blacks but that reinterprets both white and black popular standards (the Rolling Stones, Bob Marley, B.B. King, Sam Cooke, etc.). It is both traditional and modern, regional and national.[142]

Ironically, recognition in the national music industry and among out-of-state fans has not necessarily had a ripple effect on reception at the regional level. In fact, some of the most popular bands, both nationwide and abroad (i.e., BeauSoleil, Zachary Richard, and Buckwheat Zydeco) have not always been respected within southwest Louisiana. In 2001 music journalist Herman Fuselier was pointing out the lack of respect felt by local musicians like zydeco player Chubby Carrier, who gave testimony to the contrast between his reception locally and outside the region. "When we go on the road we're treated like kings. . . . The first thing my people here tell me is 'Hey, I heard you're back. Loan me 5$.'"[143] Don Brasseaux, an accomplished dancer in his native region, was introduced to teaching by musician friends in the late 1990s and became a well-respected dance teacher in out-of-state music camps offering a Cajun and Creole program. He explained how a good friend bluntly brought him back to reality, teaching him a lesson in humility that counterbalanced the overwhelming attention he received from out-of-state students: "One day a lady from Connecticut was mentioning how nice I was, how much of a good dancer, and I said 'See, I'm famous there.' And my friend answered, 'You may be famous there, but you're nothing here, shut up and let's go dance!'"[144]

A range of musicians express a similar gap between outside and local reception, an observation that is not restricted to southwest Louisiana but was also reported statewide by an official assessment for the Department of Culture, Recreation, and Tourism: "Among artists, there is a widespread belief that the affection falls short of respect, and too often fails to translate into meaningful economic remuneration. Artists believe that they are taken for granted, called upon to contribute when their skills are needed but disregarded when they are not."[145] In order to reverse this trend and capitalize on Louisiana's culture, state and public agencies have promoted an economic agenda based on the notion of "cultural economy."

The Development of a "Cultural Economy"

These marketing strategies and the negotiations between tradition and uniqueness, which encompasses every musician regardless of their style, take place within a specific economic context. Louisiana for decades has remained the poorest state in the country, alternating for this distinction with neighboring Mississippi. Beginning in the 1980s, the French renaissance took on a new dimension by becoming the focus of touristic promotion. The oil crisis encouraged diversification of Louisiana's economy, and French Louisiana culture thus became converted into a favored focus of the state's touristic authorities. Beginning in the 1990s, this initiative was underwritten by an action plan; the budget for developing tourism in the area was doubled, with music and gastronomy taking pride of place in promotional literature. In 1984, the World's Fair was held in New Orleans, and Cajun and Creole cultural events received extensive exposure before a large public. During the same period, the Cajun chef Paul Prudhomme, based in San Francisco, popularized blackened redfish, bringing international recognition to Cajun cuisine.[146]

Since the mid-2000s, companies, private foundations, and public cultural institutions have propounded the notion of cultural economy, defined as "the people, enterprises, and communities that transform cultural skills, knowledge, and ideas into economically productive goods, services, and places." Among the top priorities of the Department of Culture, Recreation, and Tourism (CRT)—compiled in the 2004 agenda *Roadmap for Change*—were the creation of "cultural economy" and the development of "eco-cultural and heritage tourism." Launched by the Office of the Lieutenant Governor and the Department of CRT, the Cultural Economy Initiative has since expressed its support for the development of creative industries as a viable sector of Louisiana's economy. During his service as lieutenant governor, Mitch Landrieu announced the birth of a world cultural economic forum to start on August 29, 2007, the anniversary date of Katrina. His office commissioned a group of economists to develop a strategic plan that was unveiled in July 2005 under the title "Louisiana:

EMPLOYMENT IN THE CULTURAL SECTOR

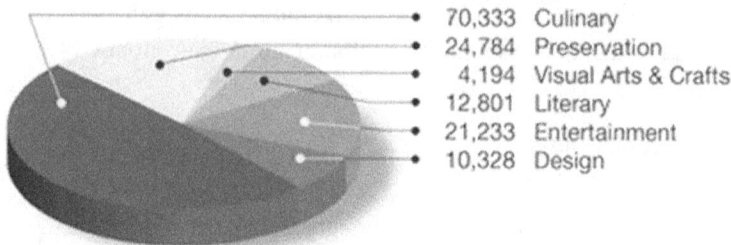

- 70,333 Culinary
- 24,784 Preservation
- 4,194 Visual Arts & Crafts
- 12,801 Literary
- 21,233 Entertainment
- 10,328 Design

Graph 2. Employment in the Cultural Sector, 2005. Source: *Louisiana: Where Culture Means Business*, prepared by Mt. Auburn Associates, July 31, 2005, funded by National Endowment for the Arts and the State of Louisiana, Office of the Lt. Governor, Department of Culture, Recreation and Tourism, Office of Cultural Development, Louisiana Division of the Arts.

Where Culture Means Business." It is important to note that the perception of culture as necessary and valuable capital predated the double blow of hurricane Katrina and Rita in 2005, which only reinforced this political strategy.

In July 2005 Louisiana's cultural enterprises were reported to provide nearly 144,000 jobs, accounting for 7.6 percent of Louisiana's employment beyond healthcare and above tourism and oil and gas (employment in the tourism sector is not included).

Cultural industries were said to grow at a faster rate than the state's economy as a whole, an evaluation likely to have been reinforced since the 2005 hurricanes and the oil spill in 2010. The slight decline in the industry reflects national trends, as well as the effects of Hurricane Katrina and Rita. In 2010 the number of jobs had reached 150,000, contributing an estimated annual $12 billion to the state's economy. There are an additional 10,000 cultural workers who do not work for cultural industries but are self-employed. Direct employment in the cultural industries provides $3.8 billion in wages and income (5 percent of the state's total wages and income).[147]

The survey by Mt. Auburn Associates points to a significant number of weaknesses, however. The researchers note a perceived lack of recognition among Louisiana artists—and among them by a majority of African Americans and Creoles—confirmed by a lack of economic opportunity to support themselves from their work: "The economic issues that we found in Louisiana are by no means unique to the state. What is striking though is the disproportionate amount of wealth generated by culture relative to what finds its way back to the originators of that culture. Too often, the community that produces Louisiana's distinctive culture fails to reap a proportional share of the economic benefit."

The survey examines Lafayette as a case study and identifies the gap between its unique musical and cultural strengths and the assessment that "musicians are one of the Lafayette's most important but least appreciated economic assets," underscoring musicians' and music establishments' precarious lives. The researchers call for the creation of proper structures (i.e., an industry association), a wider recognition of music as an industry by local economic development agencies, music industry educational and training program, management and business development services tailored to meet music entrepreneurs, strategic support from tourism agencies, and investments from municipalities, banks, private investors, and foundations.

Despite this assessment, the authors remain ambivalent, as noted by ethnomusicologist Mat Sakakeeny: "The problem, musicians and Mt. Auburn researchers agree, is that *culture* begins with culture workers who originate content but *cultural economics* ends with these same workers who are last to receive any financial return.... However valiant the efforts of the researchers to identify this economic gap, in their recommendations for rectifying the problem they continue to devalue originators of culture."[148] Sakakeeny supports this argument with the striking analogy made in the survey between the cultural and the petrochemical industries. "The oil analogy is meant to appeal to business investors and politicians who might not otherwise evaluate culture as a resource, but this only underscores the principal motive behind the plan: it is intended, above all, to spur investment, to bring a profitable return, with less regard to those on whose labor the plan is based. The work of culture workers is interchangeable; they are ultimately expendable, as long as their labor generates profit."[149] This perception and its consequences need to be taken into consideration to better grasp the gap between the situation of the music industry in southwest Louisiana and the abundance of musical practices, musicians, the various institutions dedicated to local music, and its state-, nation-, and worldwide attraction.

Hurricanes Katrina and Rita prompted an increase in the development of funding agencies and entities. In the fall of 2005, the Louisiana Cultural Economy Foundation was created as a public/private partnership to provide relief and recovery funds for Louisiana artists and cultural organizations in the aftermath of Katrina and Rita. At the same time, New Orleans

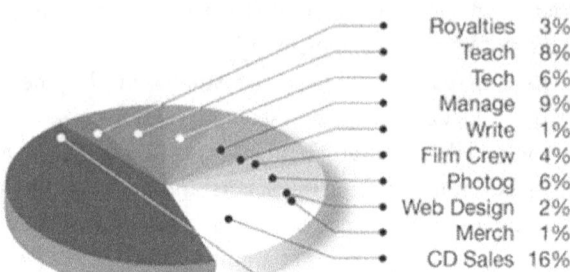

Graph 3. Tipitina's Co-Op member music/media revenue sources, 2009. Source: Tipitina's Music Office Co-Op Economic Impact Study 2010.

Musicians Clinic opened a shop in Lafayette and provides multiple assistance to musicians in southwest Louisiana, from healthcare and housing to music venues.

In 2007 the Louisiana Cultural Economy Foundation took control of the Acadiana Musicians' Clinic, saving the nonprofit from bankruptcy. Moreover, the foundation expanded its coverage to include cultural workers in film, design, literature, the culinary arts, and the performing and visual arts. The LCEF has now become proactive in encouraging and supporting cultural industries through grants. Now called the Louisiana Cultural Economy Healthcare Initiative, the Lafayette-based Acadiana clinic provides basic health care to artists.

Established in 2003, Tipitina's Co-Op—created by the non-profit Tipitina's Foundation to "support Louisiana's irreplaceable music community"[150]—played a central role after the 2005 hurricanes. It provides practical business infrastructure and a statewide network of facilities and connections for Louisiana's musicians, filmmakers, and digital media artists that included specialized media tools and workshops as well as office space and equipment. An office opened in Lafayette in 2009, and by 2010 there were more than 2,400 co-op members. These non-profit organizations have proven critical in the individual and collective recovery of these artists and in helping them cope with the challenges shared by members of the state's music industry.[151] They have also helped strengthen Louisiana's musical infrastructure, a crucial foundation for a strong industry.

Government agencies have also become more proactive in addressing the need to capitalize on Louisiana's musical talent in order to raise its profile as a "swampy backwater" to that of a creative, innovative place with a pool of skilled tradesmen and entrepreneurs. This is the view of the Louisiana's Office of Entertainment Industry Development, which since 2009 has developed a new strategic plan to develop "an indigenous entertainment industry" that will have a significant impact on the state's economy. The agency presents Louisiana as "the global leader in music/sound recording production incentives,"[152] and since 2007 has offered tax credits for investments in sound recording projects in Louisiana.[153] Other tax incentive programs have been implemented in film, the most profitable entertainment sector, as well as digital interactive and live performances. Concomitantly, since being elected mayor of New Orleans in 2010, Mitch Landrieu has shown a specific interest in developing this sector by creating the Mayor's Office of Cultural Economy, appointing Scott Hutcheson as his advisor "to both quantify the cultural economy and to steer my administration's policy in this area."[154]

Lafayette-based economic development agencies began showing an interest in the region's musical industry in the late 2000s. A local governmental agency, the Lafayette Economic Development Authority (LEDA), took the lead by creating a position specifically dedicated to that purpose. In partnership with the Acadiana Center for the Arts, LEDA launched Louisiana Crossroads—a concert series and live broadcast, as well as a record label. The program produced more than 160 live events and live radio and Internet broadcasts, providing a showcase for regional and visiting artists, with the same show performed in four different venues in the region (Lafayette, New Iberia, Lake Charles, Baton Rouge). Todd Mouton, who has directed the program at LEDA since it was created in 2001, explained at the time of his first appointment: "We propose to start making the connections, empowering the artists to have more control of their career.... This place could be Branson. But if we're driving the train, maybe we can work a better arrangement and have some of the benefit without some of the problems. The oil industry is a good example. Other people come in, they take what they want, they leave us with the trash. Had we known we had all that oil . . . We'd have golden school buses!"[155]

In 2006 Mouton was also appointed director of Louisiana Folk Roots, a cultural organization funded in 1999 by Christine Balfa that has expanded after creating the first Cajun and Creole music camp held on Louisiana soil to organizing a host of annual programming (workshops, jam, music school, children's music camp). Mouton, who feels strongly that there needs to be a clear business strategy, propelled the organization to capitalize on its indigenous status, arguing that its greatest asset was that "we celebrate Louisiana culture right at the source, right here at home," unlike other popular music camps. Attracting about a hundred full-time students to its annual spring camp, among whom 90 percent are from out of state, the camp has had a notable economic impact while contributing significantly to the growing network of dance and music fans, many of whom come to the region several times a year for different occasions. In 2008 the French consul even traveled from New Orleans to visit the camp and express his support, a powerful nod to the event's success. For local musicians hired as instructors and performers, their fee, which according to Mouton is one-third of their typical earnings, does not constitute their primary motivation for participating. The fact that none of them has ever declined an offer to work the camp reveals the significance that they seem to attach to their role as cultural ambassadors on their home turf, as opposed to out-of-state settings.

The efforts of local economic agencies to support regional music were combined with regional events like the Louisiana International Music Expo (LIME). Presented by the well-attended Festival International de Louisiane, LIME was created in 2004 to generate professional opportunities for Acadiana musicians, through interactions with presenters, agents, and music labels including Lincoln Center Music Festival (New York), World Music Institute (New York), Marabi Productions/Musiques-Metisses Festival (France), Blues Passion Festival (France), Lake Eden Arts Festival (North Carolina), Red River Revel Music Festival (Louisiana), Festivals Acadiens de Caraquet (New Brunswick), Rhythm and Roots Festival (Rhode Island), Savannah World Music Festival (Georgia), and Montreal Jazz Festival (Canada). The fact that in April 2012 Festival International was voted Best World Music Festival in the About.com Reader's Choice Awards only increased the attendance to this event and its interest for the world music network.

Despite these efforts, several reports in the mid- to late 2000s have documented that the industry's infrastructure is weak in the state, especially due to the lack of a major record company or major label to provide global exposure and profits.[156] Indeed, Lafayette's musicians typically have not behaved like members of an industry but have instead operated as individual entities. The 2011 economic report from Louisiana Economic Development shows that Louisiana maintains a low concentration of music-based employment relative to other states (California and New York being the leaders), demonstrating an enduring lack of music business infrastructure.[157]

The music industry includes a variety of occupations in the state, ranging from musicians, club owners, recording studios, record labels, musical instrument makers and retailers, photographers, concert promoters, radio stations, and DJ services. According to the *Tipitina's Music Office Co-Op Economic Impact Study 2010*, live music performances are the primary source of income for Louisiana musicians. Venue closings, a dwindling population base, declining tourism, and a global economic recession have slowed that stream. Many musicians are employed full-time in other industries to supplement their wages, and many of them actually diversify their activities by turning to teaching, recording engineering, film work, and helping other artists. Included in these strategies is also the involvement in wider marketing, the expansion of touring regions, and the cutting out of middlemen such as agents, managers, and record labels. Artists are mitigating the effects of a long-term, industry-wide decline in recorded music sales by producing and distributing their own CDs, taking advantage of Internet marketing and on-demand self-publishing, and avoiding traditional record labels. The trend toward the creation of new local record labels requires locating sponsorships as well as self-promotion and indeed complete autonomy, as these music entrepreneurs learn that they have to manage as much as they can in order to avoid contracting for expensive services. A good example is the label Valcour, founded in 2006 with help from a private donation. The small staff handles recording, mastering, photography, design, and local delivery, and its productions are distributed by the largest independent distributor, Select-O-Hits.

Across Louisiana, the pool of investors in the music industry often includes artists, independent producers, and songwriters who take a personal financial as well as aesthetic and cultural stake in their work. The availability of home-studio recording equipment and the transition to digitized distribution have encouraged and supported these startup labels.[158] An increasing number of musicians in southwest Louisiana now produce their own CDs, even the most nationally popular bands who used to record with major independent labels (Rounder, Arhoolie, etc.). Musicians who start solo albums and are still little known—like Yvette Landry at the time of her first country CD—create their own record label. For bands identified as Cajun that have ventured into new styles and sounds, this new trend also appears to provide a means of avoiding the constraints associated with "roots" labels; this appears to apply to 2010 albums produced by Horace Trahan, Feufollet, and Steve Riley and the Mamou Playboys. Instead of being forced to purchase their records back from a commercial record label, self-producing enables them to manufacture CDs at very low cost (between one and two dollars apiece), increasing their profits. It also prevents a certain degree of conflict among bands, producers, and record companies, which can develop into confrontations over royalties or distribution rights. The Pine Leaf Boys, for example, who signed with the major film production company Lionsgate in 2008, eventually lost control over the distribution of their album after failing to win the Grammy that year. Distribution changed radically with the rapid increase in digital downloads and plummeting CD sales, and many artists have increased touring to generate revenue from merchandise and CD sales at concerts, in addition to ticket sales.[159]

Despite enduring weaknesses of the regional and state music industry, several cultural organizations funded by the Louisiana Division of the Arts and based in southwest Louisiana (i.e., the Lafayette-based Cité des Arts and the Acadiana Arts Council, Nunu's Arts and Culture Collective in Arnaudville including the art school Frederick L'Ecole des Arts) provide facilities and support indigenous music through jams, concerts, festival, classes, and dances. Local cultural initiatives are often made possible by decentralized art funding like the JAMbalaya series at Tom's Fiddle and Bow shop in Arnaudville, which was able to invite popular professional musicians to come lead a monthly jam for a year, and the Music of Acadiana performance series promoting regional music through an open jam and discussion with musicians in an intimate setting. Such grants have been essential to the development of rural Arnaudville—a town of fewer than 2,000 inhabitants twenty-five miles north of Lafayette—which since the mid 2000s has become a growing arts hub under the initiative of artist George Marks, who decided to move from Baton Rouge back to his native town after his father died. Arnaudville now concentrates a great diversity of artists (visual artists, fiddle makers, craftsmen, and musicians) and facilities (art galleries, studios, and school and dance clubs). In 2008, the town's mayor Kathy Richard won a Louisiana cultural district designation from the state's Cultural Economy Initiative, which grants sales tax exemptions for original art purchases and eligibility for state historic tax credits. Since then, property values have climbed, bucking national trends. As a result, Arnaudville was among the fourteen pathbreaking case studies presented in *Creative Placemaking*, which was written for the Mayors' Institute on City Design, an initiative of the National Endowment for the Arts in partnership with the United States Conference of Mayors and American Architectural Foundation. The report confirms that "place has always been important for the emergence of new products, industries, and jobs. We find that creative places are cultural industry crucibles where people, ideas, and organizations come together, generating new products, industries, jobs, and American exports. They nurture entrepreneurs and expand the ranks of self-employed artists and designers who market their creations far afield," advocating a collaborative work across agencies, levels of government, and public/non-profit/private sector organizations.[160]

In the Lafayette area, privately owned facilities like the two local heritage and folklife parks (Acadian Village and Vermilionville) host events like the Blackpot Festival and a weekly jam. For several years the Whirlybird, a non-commercial facility located until 2011 in the countryside north of Lafayette, also periodically opened its doors to musicians with little cover or donations. In downtown Lafayette, the Blue Moon Guesthouse and Saloon has been a cornerstone of the Lafayette music scene for the past ten years. Combining an affordable guesthouse and an outdoor music club, it has grown from hosting jams in the early 2000s to what its owner describes as a honky-tonk that offers live music four or five days a week. Although it was associated with Cajun and zydeco music by many locals, drawing fans during their stay,[161] Mark Falgout, the manager, never intended to limit it to these styles. Instead, he has turned his club into a venue offering a variety of roots music (Cajun, zydeco, country, indie-pop, rock, rockabilly), as well as experimental music. Despite alarming reports in the press in 2008 warning about the decay of live music in the area, the Blue Moon is thriving and provides an example of the marketing strategies necessary to keep a live-music club in healthy operation. Well-connected to major southern music conferences (including Memphis, Austin, Nashville), Falgout remains in touch with booking agents, managers, and musicians, successfully capitalizing on his unique combination of guesthouse, music club, and meeting place, negotiating special deals that enable him to attract musicians whom he could not afford at market value.

> What we can't afford to give them in money, we can return that in hospitality and make it a good experience so where they know it's not a money-making gig, but they're going to want to come back because they really enjoyed the experience of being here. And so I'm able to put people up in the guesthouse and I'm able to give them some food, introduce them to local folks, they get out of the van they can wash their clothes, they hang out here.... I can work a deal with them: "Look, you're coming through. You want $1,500, I'll tell you what, I'll give you $500, plus lodging and if you bring in

more people, then you get some back end, because that's what I can afford to do to stay in business. Because I want to be open the next time you come back through." And they're like, "Okay." Whereas, if they don't have any relationship with me, or the club owner, they'll say, "I need $1,500, plus hotel rooms, plus whatever . . ." So you end up spending $2,000 and forty people come in, you make $400 and you're losing $1,500.[162]

Other strategies are based on inviting out-of-town bands that have never performed locally to open for of a large local act in order to assure some profit and help them build a reputation. Regardless of the reputation of the band, the deal stays the same. The band receives 80 percent of the door, while Falgout keeps 20 percent to cover the costs of the door staff and sound engineer, and he reaps the considerable bar sales. Alcohol consumption is in fact an essential factor in running a live club, and from Falgout's experience, bar sales differ depending on bands: a country honky-tonk band like Mike Dean will generate greater bar sales than Geno Delafose, for example. Consequently, diversity (of music styles, of generational profile of the audience, and of drinking habits) is the key to maintaining a successful business among local roots music clubs, which otherwise risk going out of business, like the once very popular zydeco club Hamilton's. Other uses of the Blue Moon include hosting fundraising concerts (the annual Archive Aid to benefit The ULL Archive of Cajun and Creole Folklore) and private benefits.

In recent years several regional institutions have contributed to changing the status of French Louisiana music locally and nationwide. The Acadiana Symphony Conservatory of Music offered a Cajun fiddle master class series for the first time in 2010; although the initiative did not attract enough students to be continued, it represents a noteworthy development.[163] One year later, Mark DeWitt was hired from northern California to chair the ULL's Tommy Comeaux Endowed Chair in Traditional Music and to implement a curriculum in traditional music, including a new course on traditional music ensemble that focuses on Cajun and Creole music. In the fall of 2010, a private donation enabled the Acadiana Center for the Arts to open the James Devin Moncus Theater, which seats 300 people and can now offer top-quality accommodation for theater, dance, film, and music for the first time in the region and has become a first-class venue for visiting and local artists. The new facility thus participates in the elevation of French Louisiana music within the cultural hierarchy, offering a high art venue to "folk" musicians and regional "roots" music that can complement local festivals and dance clubs. French Louisiana music is no longer exclusively performed in jams, cafes, dancehalls, and saloons and has crossed the boundary into the regional and national performing arts centers. In fact, this upward mobility has in some cases involved not only a formal art venue but also a choreographic approach to local dance styles. *Zydeco, Zaré* was the first modern dance project based on zydeco and was commissioned by the Performing Arts Society of Acadiana, whose Executive Director Jacqueline Lyle articulated the explicit goal of providing "a platform for zydeco that showcases Creole heritage as a thriving culture in quite literally a far-reaching way. We will literally export zydeco music and dance to modern dance audiences around the world and across our country." Choreographed by Elisa Monte with a musical score by local musician Jonno Frishberg, the 2008 art show featured Monte's dance company from New York City and local zydeco band Jeffery Broussard and the Creole Cowboys. The show was subsequently performed in New York City at the Joyce Theater.

Although downtown Lafayette clubs continue to function well and draw more crowds each year, the local market for French Louisiana music has declined since the 1980s, when a local band like the Bluerunners could draw 1,200 people to the Grant Street dancehall. Since that heyday, approximately three or four hundred people attend live French Louisiana music events in Lafayette on weekends, which compete with the significant hip hop DJ scene in the downtown area, a trend also reflected in the decision by Grant Street's owner to reserve Saturday nights for hip hop music. In this context, recognition of the value of French Louisiana music is all the more timely. Its institutionalization through art venues, shows, and instructional workshops and media offer high valued-added services and settings that increase its recognition and legitimacy locally, statewide, and nationally.

The different threads that weave the debates over musical authenticity within French Louisiana music mirror the multiplicity of subject positions and of interpretations of this powerful discursive trope, which lies at the heart of many other music revivals.[164] Based simultaneously (or alternatively) on a certain vision of the past in which French heritage predominated, on moral judgments ("commercial" versus "traditional," "artificial" versus "organic"), on class divisions, on creative agency, and on the legacy of or the kinship with musical dynasties, issues of authenticity continue to shape perceptions of French Louisiana music, regardless of the style or market within which it is considered to belong (American popular music or/and roots music).

Today, more Cajun bands are stepping outside the box, as zydeco bands began doing earlier, and all of them are exploring new styles and textures in an effort to create distinctive sounds. For the rest of the regional music scene that is also an integral part of southwest Louisiana music (primarily indie-rock and other forms of rock, folk, reggae, metal, and country), the notion of tradition does not seem to hold such importance as an unavoidable common reference. By contrast, for bands identified as Cajun, Creole, and zydeco, tradition continues to nourish their experimentations and enable them to assert their legitimacy as both traditional and modern, regional and national, local and global.

3

The Color of Music

In 1996 I had the opportunity to see twenty-year-old Horace Trahan perform at Festivals Acadiens for the first time. As he frowned in concentration, squeezing his accordion with his eyes closed, and the raking light illuminated beads of sweat on his face, his haunting, heartfelt voice rolled out over the audience. Many stood silently, glued to the youthful musician and taken aback by his power, while others danced furiously. Young and old appeared bewitched by his performance and his first CD, *Ossun Blues* (1996), and the same name came to mind for many of his listeners: Iry LeJeune, the ill-fated Cajun accordion player who contributed to reviving Cajun music after World War II. No one doubted that this was only the beginning of a glorious career in the legacy of "traditional" Cajun music. A strong advocate of tradition, the Cajun French Music Association formalized this status and dubbed Horace Accordionist of the Year at the 1997 Le Cajun award ceremony and labeled his album Best First CD.

When I first interviewed Horace five years later at his home in Scott, he had just begun to pursue a new direction. With his earnest gaze and imposing stature, he gave an immediate impression of being strong-willed. His lifestyle seemed typical of a young country boy from the area. Working as a carpenter for the local school board, he played with his new music partners every Wednesday afternoon in a barn that was full of tools, with a punching bag standing in the middle. That day they were sipping beer while roasting rabbit to be served with black-eyed peas and smothered potatoes. "I liked what I was doing, but I felt I was being confined to just a certain type of music and I couldn't really change it up and do different things," he confided. "I got nothing but respect for the people I played with but I just need to do my own thing. A young man, I have to go my own way. *C'était dur. Quand j'ai dit ça à Mr. Hubert pis les autres, ouh! Ça a cassé mon cœur* [It was hard. When I told Mr. Hubert (Maitre), and the others, ohh! It broke my heart]."[1]

While paying tribute to his mentors, Horace nonetheless persevered. He revamped his band with new members of different skin color tones and released two groundbreaking albums, *Get On Board* (1999) and *Reach Out and Touch a Hand* (2000). Branching out to the "new" zydeco sound, not afraid of provocative lyrics, his new sounds were met with racist hostility and dissenting voices uttered in the name of a "pure" tradition. Some bluntly called him "nigger" and "Uncle Tom." Others who were careful enough not to condemn his new musical partners deplored his wasted talent and mistaken musical choices.

Horace continued to defy his detractors in his songs[2] and to seek out club owners who would not turn him down when they discovered either that he was white or that his fellow musicians were black. *Hard Pressed, But Never Crushed*, was how he was characterized in the video that his friend Wilson Savoy made about him.[3] Eventually, the burden of his regional hit "That Butt Thing," which conflicted with his Catholic upbringing, combined with the discrimination and resentment of certain dancehall fans, drove him to quit the music scene entirely. Initially seeking refuge in the Bible and the church, he spiralled downward into alcohol and drug addiction. After a year and a half in a rehab facility, he slowly began to recapture his audience before recording *Keep Walking* (2010) with the New Ossun Express. The CD met with huge success, and his band now continues to intoxicate crowds throughout the region.

"Looking back on it now, I shouldn't have given a fuck what anybody said, but I was young at the time and I let a lot of stuff get to me. But I don't blame nobody else for it," said Horace to local journalist and musician Dege Legg, who eventually told Horace's story in the Lafayette weekly paper in 2010.[4] Horace was not the first musician to be ostracized for daring to cross the color line. By the same logic, Ed Poullard and Geno Delafose have also confirmed that they have been "accused" by black people of playing Cajun music. Travis Matte, who belongs to the same generation as Horace, also changed directions, transforming himself from a "traditional" fiddler into a zydeco and rock accordion player, a move that was also greeted with broad expressions of disapproval. But the virulent opposition that Horace endured at a young age left him in a life-threatening turmoil that reveals the potential ripple effects that categorization of music according to racial or ethnic identifications can produce.

This chapter seeks to demonstrate how music categories, tastes, and representations are ingrained in the racial imagination. Instead of being restricted to being symbolic of mixture, the notion of creolization as used in regional scholarship to define French Louisiana culture and more specifically its music implies a logic of differentiation.⁵ Following in the footsteps of music scholars such as Ronald Radano, Peter Wade, and Philip Tagg and the historians Les Back, Benjamin Filene, and more recently Karl Miller, my intention is to situate musical forms and conventions across the color line and to reveal the ideological basis and limitations of ethnic and racial categories within French Louisiana music. In fact, Louisiana actors themselves are more conscious of these limits than they might appear to be, and they find a variety of methods for working around them by positioning themselves differently depending on the interactional frame and the interests inherent in a particular context and navigating between musical sameness and difference. Although they can contribute to musical segregation, the racial and ethnic categories that local actors of the music scene invoke are more broadly situated within a quest for recognition and an effort to meet the different interests and expectations of the music industry and music fans. Because the racial imagination remains extremely powerful in the field of music, and in southwest Louisiana in particular, musical forms and conventions must be situated within particular social spheres, historical moments, and local circumstances. People's representations of music are related to a cluster of situations and interests located within personal, social, economic, and political spheres, and the Louisiana context contains highly diverse and multi-faceted discourses and practices. As social analysts, however, invoking racial or ethnic groups to justify music categories contributes to the reification of these very categories. Like Les Back and Karl Miller, who call attention to the importance of desegregating the understanding of southern culture and music, I would like to advocate in favor of a richer and more nuanced understanding of French Louisiana music that takes the complex interwoven threads of its representations and practices into account. To this end, this chapter will endeavor to unravel the various threads of the prevailing ethnic and racial framework and interrogate its underlying assumptions.

Music in Black *or* White

The connection commonly drawn between "racial" or "ethnic" identification and a specific sound has been powerfully shaped by the music industry. The associations that tie Cajun music to country and western and zydeco to rhythm and blues are situated within a reorganization of

American popular music into "race," "old-time," and "popular" music recordings. Indeed, most record companies have typically employed distinct series numbers and printed separate catalogs for each category. Earlier music catalogues, as Karl Miller has demonstrated, were compiled according to genre, based on the distinction between customers who invested in classical recordings and those who preferred everything else. By contrast, "separate catalogues suggested a correspondence between consumer identity and musical taste, one that was both holistic and exclusive. They implied that unique segments of the population were satisfied by particular kinds of records yet uninterested in others."[6]

First categorized as "blues," the secular music recorded for blacks by black performers was labeled "race music" in the 1920s, while white performers were assigned to the generic designations of "old-time music" or "hillbilly" (a category embraced by record companies in the 1930s and marketed to rural white audiences despite its negative connotation). This process was encouraged by the massive wave of migration toward urban areas following World War I, which led record labels to promote southern music among migrants by targeting circumscribed audiences defined according to "racial" criteria. After World War II, a new terminology came into use that perpetuated the distinction between what would from then on be classified as rhythm and blues and country and western. This classification was relayed by the radio, thus feeding the segmentation of listeners in order to better target the different market segments with advertising. Hugh Barker and Huval Taylor summarize this process: "Encouraged by record companies and other cultural authority figures who promoted the authenticity of 'old-time' white American music and by folk collectors and blues aficionados who promoted the authenticity of the most isolated forms of black music, the segregation of American 'folk' music—blues versus old-time country—would become enshrined and canonized."[7] Folklorists played an instrumental role in this process by connecting racial music with racial bodies. Black or white, according to historian Karl Miller, they "vigourously debated the value and meaning of black music, but on this they eagerly agreed: African American music was performed by black people."[8] To support this argument, they avoided considering the prevalence of common stock repertoires in order to maintain a distinction between black originators and white carriers.

The segregation of music was not restricted to mere classifications. Marketing strategies had direct impact on musicians themselves, who were forced to position their music within a pre-segmented market.

Companies often did not allow black artists to record pop songs or hillbilly tunes, while "old-time" musicians were discouraged from reinterpreting Broadway or Tin Pan Alley songs. White southern artists nevertheless had considerably more latitude that allowed them to record pop and blues than black artists, who were restricted to recording nothing other than blues.[9]

The music collector Harry Smith stands out as an exceptional figure in this context. A beatnik from the Pacific Northwest who had studied anthropology at the University of Washington, he was approached by Moses Asch, the head of Folkways Records, to compile a collection of "folk" music that resembled the jazz anthology that the company had produced earlier. The resulting *Anthology of American Folk Music* (1952) was a six-record series of southern commercial songs released between 1927 and 1932 and selected for their "oddity" and "exotic" value, in Smith's words. Barker and Taylor emphasize the fact that Smith had made a radical selection for his time:

> In his elaborate liner notes, he deliberately omitted any mention of the performers' race or the record companies' classification of the music. As he later said "There has been a tendency in which records were lumped into blues catalogues or hillbilly catalogues, and everybody was having blindfold tests to prove they could tell which was which. That's why there's no such indications of that sort (color/racial) in the albums." I wanted to see how well certain jazz critics did on the blindfold test. They all did horribly. It took years before anybody discovered that Mississippi John Hurt [a black Mississippi musician from the twenties] wasn't a hillbilly.[10]

The collection includes selections of south Louisiana artists Joe and Cleoma Falcon, the Breaux Brothers, Delma Lachney and Blind Uncle Gaspard, Columbus Fruge, the Hackberry Ramblers, and Didier Hebert.

In the early 1950s, what came to be called Cajun honky-tonk became labeled as a subgenre of country music and was reissued in the 1990s under that same label in CD albums. Along with hillbilly and western swing, it is thus identified as belonging to the wider group of genres of so-called "white" musics. Regional independent labels further fueled this racial categorization by creating separate labels for Cajun music and for Creole and zydeco. Floyd Soileau from Ville Platte founded his own record company in 1958 and soon decided to devote his Jin label to pop music while reserving the Swallow label for Cajun music in order to avoid the stigmatization of his recordings by consumers and promoters who disliked French Louisiana music (hence the Americanized spelling, as well as a wink at the Bluebird label from RCA). Around 1974 he founded the label Maison de Soul to promote zydeco recordings.[11]

Today, however, ethnic or racial identifications have become less common, and the repertoire tends more to arise from an artist's choice. On CD covers, independent producers and musicians themselves simply mention the names of the artist and album. Examples of this new tendency are found even in reissues of so-called "Cajun legends" such as the album Dennis McGee, *Himself* (2010 Valcour), or institutional recordings such as the Louisiana Folk Masters series produced by the Archive of Cajun and Creole Folklore at ULL.

Mitch Reed is highly aware of the impact of radio and recording industry on the coloring of sound by labeling music styles and their consequent transformation within French Louisiana music:

> Basically what happened is that when you go back to the turn of the last century, when they were doing the 78s and stuff, people were all playing the same kind of music, blacks and whites. And then what happened was that the radio stations had a huge impact. Because then the white people started listening to country music, black people started listening to blues. And R&B and that kind of stuff. So gradually, the blacks and whites started to . . . music started to change. So maybe say, by the fifties or the forties, all of a sudden if you take a black accordion player and a white accordion player, yeah, they're starting to play a little bit different. Because a guy like Lawrence Walker is going to have a little bit of country and western now in his style. And you take a guy like Bois Sec, or Eraste Carriere or someone like that, they're going to have more of that because you know the Carrieres they started listening to the radio and they started picking up Muddy Waters tunes. And they started playing those blues like "Baby Please Don't Go." . . . I think the blacks started listening to rhythm and blues and they got even blacker in a sense, and the Cajuns got whiter in a sense because they started listening to Anglo-Saxon country music.[12]

The valorization of shared French Louisiana heritage in the present imaginary of regional music silences the stormy political context of the first half of the twentieth century. Segregation, racial tensions that grew out of the civil rights movement, and the mobilization of Cajuns against integration and school desegregation are all subjects that have been tacitly ignored by most music scholars. Pioneering publications by the British scholar John Broven, the anthropologist Rocky Sexton, and the Louisiana historian Shane Bernard have not hesitated to broach the tense relationships that predominated during the 1960s in the realm of music, but they stand as exceptions in the field.

Protest songs by Leroy "Happy Fats" Leblanc and Clifford "Pee Wee" Trahan reflect the violent counterattack of the white population that traversed the country in response to the triumph of the civil rights movement in empowering blacks. Leblanc's most popular song, "Dear Mr. President" (a reference to the 1968 presidential candidacy of the segregationist George Wallace) openly relates the story of a Cajun farmer who, using animal metaphors, questions integration.[13]

In the sixties, the civil rights movement created the conditions for the emergence of a "white" ethnicity. At the very moment when black Americans obtained their rights and announced the end of segregation, the growth of the country's economy slowed, salaries plummeted, and unemployment increased considerably. Whites at the bottom of the social ladder, whose status had become equivalent to that of blacks, found themselves in direct competition with them and sought to defend the social advantages that their skin color not longer sufficed to ensure. The "white" movement contributed to the emergence of hyphenated Americans among the descendants of Italian, German, Irish, and other immigrants, awakening fears concerning the capacity of American society to assimilate the different cultures that had contributed to the celebrated melting pot.

The rise of white ethnicity and black nationalism favored claims for cultural legitimacy based on "racial" criteria. The evolution of musical categories in Louisiana appears to have constituted a negative photographic image of these social dynamics, even if this appearance does not reflect reality. Whereas during legal segregation, "French music" was referred to, a category that included different French Louisiana styles, it appears that beginning in the 1960s, in the context of the civil rights movement, the perception of this genre became increasingly influenced by super-imposed "ethnic" and "racial" boundaries.

In fact, this evolution should be situated within two distinct chronologies. The first half of the twentieth century was dominated by a process of differentiation based on French language and descent and expressed through the opposition between French-speaking people and those they called *"les Américains"* (or "rednecks"—*Cous rouge*—a designation more particularly addressed to Texans), at a time of strong waves of migration across the Sabine River due to the development of the oil industry. In the 1960s, a shift took place that gave primacy to racial identification, gradually redefining the musical repertoire into segmented categories (Cajun, Creole, zydeco) on the basis of musicians' racial identification and skin color.

In the beginning, CODOFIL fueled this perception by focusing exclusively on white *francophonie*, reinforced by the development of cultural tourism by the 1980s that long promoted a monolithic image of French Louisiana, celebrating Cajuns and excluding Creoles.[14] A series of official designations endorsed Cajun identity as being defined by Acadian ancestry, making the terms Acadian and Cajun interchangeable: "Acadiana" and "Cajun Country" (the official and touristic regional identifications); *l'Université des Acadiens* (the University of Louisiana at Lafayette); the Cajundome (the sports center). Publications also fostered an interest in genealogy, particularly Father Donald Hébert's compilations of church and civic records starting in 1974, the sixty volumes of which continue to be consulted in local libraries.

The notion of the Acadian diaspora became an increasingly prominent feature of Cajun identity with the development of the French renaissance movement, which had notable ripple effects on the population. In addition to the claim of a "blood" kinship with Acadians from the Canadian Maritime Provinces, this sense of belonging is expressed through shared historical memories of the expulsion of the Acadians by the British in 1755 (*le Grand Dérangement*). This narrative fits within a recurrent survival theme, situated in a fictive dual territory illustrated by the parallels established between Acadiana/*Acadie* or *Acadie du Sud/du Nord*. The idea of an Acadian diaspora has been reinforced and institutionalized by the World Acadian Congress that has been organized every five years since 1994 that reunites people of Acadian ancestry, and by the development of museums, monuments, exhibits, and cultural events that pay tribute to the Acadian diaspora. For example, the Saint Martinville Acadian Memorial founded by civic leaders and scholars in 1997 includes a mural depicting the arrival of Acadian exiles in Louisiana, a "wall of names" identifying the 3,000 known exiles who settled in the colony, an eternal flame in memory of the exiles of those who perished, and a research center where people can trace their Acadian ancestry.[15] The memorial and the World Congresses embody the victory of the Acadian people through their reunion, both symbolically (through the monument) and in present-day reality (through the Congresses).

The weight of the Cajun and Acadian register triggered a powerful activist backlash among the black population. As early as 1971, black students spoke out when the university in Lafayette dubbed its stadium "Cajun Field." The Un-Cajun Committee later derided the designation of the ULL sports teams as the "Ragin' Cajuns" because "ragin'" in reverse spelled "nigar," a polemic regularly reactivated by black students. According to Bernard, the committee joined the Nation of Islam in protest at the name of Lafayette's civic arena, the Cajundome.[16] Political activism also contributed to the tensions between Cajuns and Creoles. In 1980 the federal government officially recognized Cajuns as an ethnic group after the lawsuit *Roach v. Dresser*. Legislator Raymond "La La" Lalonde then attempted to pass a bill to recognize Cajuns as a minority. The bill encountered strong local resistance from black legislators who opposed sharing state affirmative action benefits with a group that could not reasonably be described as an oppressed minority, as Bernard emphasizes. However, it probably encouraged the census to incorporate them among their ancestry groups.

The founding of CREOLE Inc. in 1989 reflected the strong desire of black Creoles to be represented in the French Louisiana landscape. In tourist literature until the mid-1990s, the term "Creole" referred primarily to white Creole heritage and/or to urban, sophisticated gastronomy. The promising potential of African American tourism eventually caught the interest of the region's tourism authorities, however, and they have since actively promoted black Creole culture. A touristic guidebook devoted to "African American attractions" is now available, contributing to the rise of specifically African American tourism that encompassed both the Creole dimension and the shared African roots of all black Americans. As just one example, the African-American Museum in Saint Martinville—one of whose "twin cities" is the Senegalese island of Gorée—devotes part of its collections to the slavery connection between West Africa and the American South.

French Louisiana music scholarship and publications have contributed significantly to the segregation of music styles, while also celebrating the notion of creolization and the impact of black Creoles on Cajun music. Barry Ancelet was particularly instrumental in restoring Creoles' role in local history, folklore, and tourism. He has systematically made a point of crediting Creoles with a highly syncopated accordion style and for the blues influences on Cajun music. At the same time, Cajun music has been differentiated from Creole music and zydeco on the basis of ethnic and racial representations. *Jurés* are acknowledged as the ancestors of both Creole and zydeco music, and are presented as the incontestable reflection of African polyrhythm, a perception legitimized by the most eminent of folklorists, including Alan Lomax. From the 1930s recordings with his father to the 1987 reissue of *The Louisiana Recordings*, Lomax maintains in his notes the parallels—with numerous examples—between *jurés* and zydeco and "the musical style of West Africa and the West Indies" on the basis of a shared polyrhythmic and sung dance tradition. He also recalls a trio of young singers at a Baptist church in Jennings whose clappings and rhythmic accompaniment "at a distance sounded as though there were an African drum ensemble in the church." He describes the playful vocal style, the repetitive and unintelligible lyrics, and the syncopated rhythm of the classic "Blues de la Prison" as a "style which lies back of the blues, [and] is the only black American type that I know of that can be precisely matched in West Africa."[17]

This logic of musical genealogy based on African heritage feed claims of a unique "Creole sound" that is distinct from Cajun music and is defined in particular by a syncopated rhythm. Even the most recent anthology by Ryan Brasseaux and Kevin Fontenot refers to "parallel but independent" evolution that is often used to justify the systematic choice not to examine Cajun music and Creole and zydeco music in the same book. The similarities between Creole and zydeco are emphasized, while Cajun music is considered separately. Many authors provide summary arguments that have become classics in their genre in support of these differences: African influences, associated with a syncopated rhythm, that are considered so self-evident that they do not merit elaboration or analysis.[18] This view is inscribed more broadly in theories of African retentions that have informed contemporary musical scholarship on "black music," based on "the assumption that black music grows, like a living, organic form, from fixed, predetermined origins, an assumption that, after all, betrays the legacy of the color line," according to Ronald Radano.[19] Allusions are often made to an interview of Canray Fontenot, whose father, who played with Amédé Ardoin, told the story that Ardoin went to black dances after playing for the "whites." He apparently played a repertoire of blues and ancient African songs at the black events, adapting his playing to the public's tastes in a common process among musicians, regardless of their identification. His polyvalence has encouraged some scholars to argue that what he played for the blacks was the fruit of his own creativity whereas the music that he played with and for the Cajuns is considered as an "alteration" of his style.[20] One can wonder, however, why both styles could not be considered as equally representative of Ardoin's musical heritage and identifications. Furthermore, do we really know what Adam and then Canray Fontenot referred to when talking about "African" songs? Spitzer's analysis links Ardoin's polyvalence to the creolization process "where something new could emerge from synthesis of dual aesthetic systems understood by a performer."[21] Focusing on this synthesis enables one to emphasize the agency of the performer regardless of his/her origins and his ability to navigate from one context to the other.

Some scholars working on French Louisiana music have brought to light the salience of racial stereotypes and discrimination within French Louisiana music, pointing out enduring segregation at music venues and negative value judgments towards zydeco. Among them, Ancelet did not hesitate—despite a tricky positioning and involvement as scholar, activist, and local writer—to condemn "the racist, exclusionary standards that ran deep in the community." The discrimination against black visitors that took place in 1995 at the Eunice Mardi Gras and at the La Poussiere dancehall in Breaux Bridge led him to assert:[22] "The old time Cajun music dance hall has remained a bastion of segregation. . . . The real border of the creolization process is clearly apparent in black and white terms."[23] While authors who have approached the topic of racial discrimination in the music realm argue that these stereotypes obscure the processes of interplay among musical forms, they still situate music categories within ethnic and racial identification and more particularly within African or European origins and continuities. For example, Rocky Sexton defined the *lala* style, another designation for the Creole style, as "in many respects faster, more highly syncopated, with upbeat rhythms, highly repetitive song texts, and the use of the rubboard. The variation in musical styles of blacks and whites was due to Afro-French music retaining African melodic and rhythm styles."[24] Wood also acknowledged the similarities between the Cajun and Creole styles, while also affirming their differences (but providing no specifics), and extending the African influence of the Creole style to zydeco.[25] In *Texas Zydeco*, he discusses at length the sound of foot-tapping captured in the San Antonio recordings of Ardoin and McGee, emphasizing "the prominent role of rhythmic accents in Ardoin's cultural legacy (harking back to *juré*)" and its evolution toward the washboard.[26] Shane Bernard contrasts Cajun and zydeco music, which he characterizes as following racial lines, with swamp pop. "Unlike its Cajun and zydeco sister genre, which divide along racial lines and depend strongly on folk instrumentation and francophone lyrics, swamp pop is a biracial genre that relies primarily on English lyrics and 50's rhythm and blues instrumentation."[27] In this case Cajun and zydeco are contrasted with the hybridity embodied by swamp pop. In his dissertation on zydeco, Spitzer initiates a reflection on the variations within zydeco based on sub-regions, urban and rural environments, and generation, pointing out the commonalities between French Louisiana music styles, and suggesting that "creolized musical expression derives from wherever Black French people have been in contact with Cajuns."

The widespread conception of inherently "black" or "African American" musical traits is prevalent among many music lovers and experts. This perception is based on ideological assumptions and a deep-rooted imaginary. The musicologist Philip Tagg meticulously deconstructed these assumptions in a ground-breaking open letter published in 1989 that discussed black, African American, and European music, as well as in his 2011 film about Scotch snap.[28] While polyrhythm is in fact a characteristic of many West and central Sudanic musics, it differentiates these musics as much from other African musics as from European music. Blue notes themselves, as they are used in jazz and blues, can be found in the music of some West Sudanic groups today, but they were also common in the folk musics of Scandinavia and, more importantly, of Britain at the time of the principal colonization of the New World.

As for syncopation, which is systematically cited as a "black" cultural trait in American popular music and particularly in southwest Louisiana music, Tagg questions the relevance of the notion that "'syncopation' presupposes that only one rhythm and metre can be dominant at any one time (as in the Viennese classical music which forms the basis of old-style musicology). However, medieval, baroque, and Tudor music performance practice, with its use of tactus instead of metric conducting, shows that the fixation on symmetric monorhythm . . . is totally foreign to the music of that time." He offers further evidence of

> the inadequacy of the term "syncopation" and of the obvious popularity of birhythmic practices in Europe [which] can be found passim in the Fitzwilliam Virginal Book, compiled in the "Randgebiet" of England in the early seventeenth century. Considering the popular ("folk") origin of practically every other piece in that collection,

it would be no rash speculation to suppose that European (at least British) colonists possessed some competence in birhythmic devices when they arrived in the New World in the seventeenth and eighteenth centuries. Moreover, they brought with them the rhythmic idiosyncrasies of the English language, which, in comparison with most other European languages, favours certain "offbeat" (whose beat?) settings in music. Apart from the frequent need of triplets (as in the songs of Vaughan Williams) or of triple metre superimposed on duple or quadruple (as in madrigal settings by Byrd) it is important to mention the "Scotch snap."[29]

Tagg continues by asserting "It is unclear whether 'inverted dottings' came from what West African music or from 'Scottish folk tunes' or from the rhythmic idiosyncrasies of English language dissyllabics. . . . it is unclear whether the birhythmic character of much North American popular music should be traced back to Europe or Africa."[30] In-depth research remains to be done about the musics that Africans actually brought with them to the Americas, and about early acculturation between West African and British music traditions in Virginia and the other American colonies. Furthermore, "European music" is too often restricted to an elitist, bourgeois, and monolithic image of music from Europe, neglecting the folk musics of New World settlers. The formation of black rhythmic difference at the turn of the twentieth century is also described by Ronald Radano as part of the overarching development of modern American ideologies of race.[31] Also arguing against the view of an African-derived rhythmic impulse, Radano sheds light on the specificity of the American historical framework on which hot rhythm is grounded. Hot rhythm, although appealing, was viewed by most educated white Americans as the antithesis of civilized artistic practice, as opposed to harmony, perceiving it as potentially destructive, destabilizing, and threatening to European superiority and white hegemony. His analysis does not lead to a dismissal of African influences but instead, shows that the assertion of African influence is much more complex to demonstrate that it may appear. It stands as a critical response to the assumed salience of African influence in certain music categories identified as "black."

The history of instrumentation in southwest Louisiana music further reflects the naturalization of "black" and "white" music and the strong tendency to assert a logic of origins and ownership that supersedes acknowledged cross-influence and multiple usage. The diatonic accordion is thought to have been exported by Germany to the United States beginning in 1840 and popularized by minstrel shows. Masters are supposed to have bought them in order to be entertained by their slaves, fueling the theory that the adoption of the accordion by Cajuns came from an Afro-Creole tradition that extended back to the 1850s, and more broadly that a significant number of Mississippi-born black musicians between 1870 and 1880 played the diatonic button accordion.[32] Available illustrations show accordions in the hands of black musicians, corroborating this view, although Milton suggests the possibility that it was also in use among Cajuns.[33]

In the nineteenth century, local color writers Sidonie De La Houssaye and Washington W. Cable clearly placed the triangle in the hands of blacks. Quoting these early accounts, Ryan Brasseaux suggests diffusion "across racial and ethnic boundaries from the Afro-Creole or African American traditions into Cajun arrangements," merely reasserting the commonly accepted stereotype that attributes rhythm instruments to the black population.[34]

The question of ownership also relates to specific songs, the focus of considerable debate. Ancelet notes that the song likely to have inspired C.C. Chenier's "Hip et Taïau" is of Acadian origin; a 1934 *juré* would have also been "borrowed" from the Acadian repertoire.[35] However, Joe Falcon, the first to record the song, indicated in two interviews—one with Ralph Rinzler in 1965, and the other with Lauren Post in 1970—that he learned "Hip et Taïau" from the son of Oscar Babineaux, a black sharecropper who lived on his father's farm in 1906.[36]

This concern about the origins of tunes is ubiquitous, but the notion of a shared repertoire and similar style brought to light in this process have not led to questioning the categorization of local music along racial lines.[37] In his liner notes to *Louisiana Cajun Music: The First Recordings*, Chris Strachwitz mentions that "En route chez moi (Going Home)" (1936), played by Joe Falcon, is "common to black Creole tradition" and similar to 1934 Lomaxes recordings of *jurés*. In another publication, he also says about the Hackberry Ramblers that they learned tunes like "Trouble in Mind," "Tiger Rag," "High Society," and "Eh la-bas" from "a Negro band who used to come every other weekend from New Orleans to play at a local dance hall."[38] This perception is maintained throughout the century. Ancelet notes in the Lomax recordings he edited that the song "Croix de ma tombe" as the Segura Brothers played it resembles "Les barres de la prison"—another example in which similarities are observed without prompting further questions regarding how a common regional repertoire might have been constructed.

In *Zydeco!* music writer Ben Sandmel immediately emphasizes the limits of music categories: "The distinctions between zydeco and Cajun music (and swamp pop) are guidelines rather than hard-and-fast rules." Illustrating his point with several examples, he continues: "These exceptions underscore the broader point that terminology has innate limitation in the world of traditional music. While useful as a point of reference, terminology is usually superimposed upon music long after its emergence. As such it is often imprecise, arbitrary, and overlapping. . . ."[39] Aware of the imperfection and conflicted dimension of music categories, Sandmel cautions his readers. As imperfect as music categories are, they still seem to serve for many writers a heuristic function that communicates with a wide public.

Beyond the acknowledgment of blurred boundaries, I argue that the enduring use of these categories by music writers and researchers contributes to the perception that racial distinctions are embedded in French Louisiana music. Les Back offers a similar reasoning to explain how blues, R&B, and soul arose as distinctly "black" phenomena within southern music: "My initial point is that such prototypical images of love and theft conceal the diversity of white involvement in black music. . . . Walter Benn Michaels questions the underlying racial logic that defines to whom blues, rhythm and blues and soul belong. He points out that when whites learn from blacks, this is understood as *imitation*, but when blacks learn the same chords, it is automatically a matter of *inspiration*, in which their heritage is claimed."[40] This attention paid to acknowledging a kind of musical debt toward black musicians often reinforces a racialized view of music styles by establishing the idea of musical ownership that Walter Benn Michaels describes as linked to what he calls "cultural geneticism." Discussions of the "black through white syndrome" in music suggest that the involvement of whites in black music is linked to a blend of pernicious desire and of exoticism that is reduced to exploitation and appropriation at blacks' expense. In Louisiana, the fear of being associated to this process seems to lead many white scholars, journalists, and music intellectuals to subscribe to the idea of distinct traditions and musical forms based on ethnic and/or racial identification as Cajun or Creole.

Cultural institutions readily echo this narrative. A permanent exhibition on Louisiana history and culture at the Louisiana State Museum in Baton Rouge called "Experiencing Louisiana: Discovering the Soul of America" includes a number of displays about southwest Louisiana music, some of which were written by one of the museum's historians, Karen Leathem, in collaboration with Ben Sandmel, who was contracted for the job. While they all share an awareness of the limitations of music categories, they are also constrained by the need for accessibility to a wide audience and the space available on each panel. Borrowing from scholarly work on French Louisiana music, the text reflects the ambivalence of the local musical imaginary in characterizing French Louisiana music as a "blend" or an "amalgam" separated into two distinct traditions with specific musical forms that are traceable to distinct origins: "Cajun and Creole music developed as true amalgams, borrowing elements from the many cultures that made up the region. Scholars trace these two related music traditions to a combination of the folk music of western France; Afro-Caribbean folk songs and drumming, African American blues, the Spanish guitar and the German/Austrian accordion and Anglo-American fiddle tunes." Along the same lines, southwest Louisiana blues is described as a unique combination of "Cajun music, with its Acadian and medieval French roots, and zydeco, with its Afro-Caribbean roots and rhythm"; this rhetoric of origins is consistent with the "cultural mosaic" described in books dedicated to local history and culture. The primacy of parallel traditions and difference over fusion echoes the local uses of the concept of creolization.

In fact, ascribing particular music skills and characteristics to racial and ethnic groups shapes French Louisiana music scholarship. Tellingly, in his essay, Austin Sonnier omits the many white musicians who composed big bands in rural Louisiana in the early twentieth century. Sonnier also defines rural jazz as "a combination of traditional New Orleans jazz, ragtime, African rhythms, Creole folk material, and the blues," clearly identifying it as "black music." Ryan Brasseaux insists on the heterogeneity of styles within Cajun music while maintaining that each style derives from a specific ethnic affiliation. Dennis McGee's style and his many reels are thus linked to its Irish descent, neglecting his French and Seminole Indian origins on his mother's side and, more importantly, his upbringing in Evangeline Parish. Similarly, the French roots (as opposed to Acadian) of Blind Uncle Gaspard and Delma Lachney are cited as explanations of his soft style and ballads from the 1920s, which are identified with an "older European style."[41] This neglects the fact that Gaspard also played cowboy songs and Anglo-American fiddle tunes such as "Ragtime Annie," however.[42] Individual creativity, and processes of borrowings, negotiations, and adaptation are not referenced, suggesting that music styles primarily reflect musicians' ethnic affiliations, whereas a variety of factors of great significance are involved such as regional environment and identification, influences of exogenous music styles, career opportunities, music market forces, outsiders' interest and mobility, and academic and cultural institutions.

Beyond the music realm, Gwendolyn Midlo Hall in her pathbreaking work about slave society in colonial Louisiana suggests evidence of African influences in Louisiana's cultural forms, a controversial interpretation according to eminent Louisiana scholars.[43] Among them, Tulane historian Sylvia Frey wrote: "the most important and controversial evidence for Africanization of Louisiana culture is the Louisiana Creole language. Drawing on the work of sociolinguists, Hall argues that although the vocabulary of Louisiana Creole was French, 'its grammatical structure is largely African' (p. 188), a sweeping statement for which she offers no grammatical evidence whatsoever. . . . Nor does she expend much energy on sustained analysis of some of her most important and certain to be most controversial points."[44] Linguist Thomas Klingler later reinforced Frey's critical point:

> Attempts to trace creole structures to African origins are fraught with difficulty even for those creoles that, like Haitian or Saramaccan, show the greatest structural distance from their lexifiers. . . . Even when suitable demographic and linguistic data are available, great caution must still be exercised in attributing a substratal origin to a particular feature, since many features could just as easily be attributed to universal principles of language change or acquisition in situations of contact, or to a particular variety of the lexifier spoken in the colonial setting.[45]

After an in-depth linguistic analysis, Klingler concludes: "Based on the evidence currently available, we may conclude that claims of widespread African influence on the grammatical structure of Louisiana Creole are unfounded."[46]

Other aspects of Hall's work have also been discussed, like her argument that the Bambara in Louisiana were truly members of this ethnic group. In his review of her volume, anthropologist Stephan Palmié questioned this interpretation: "Hall's Bambara could have been an entirely heterogeneous bunch of people who, in the course of enslavement, wound up with an imposed 'pseudo-African' identity which, in the end, they may have adopted as their own. This is not to deny that a community of Bambara existed in Louisiana; it is to question who they really were. For we cannot rule out the possibility that they may have become 'Bambara' only in the New World."[47]

Contested Creole Identifications

Processes of differentiation are not solely derived from music scholarship and institutional discourse. They also take place among musicians themselves, although their rhetoric is more ambivalent and contextual. The homogenization of French Louisiana until the late 1990s and the unequal access to economic and symbolic power through tourism that focused on Cajuns has led some Creole musicians to turn their demands for recognition into claims of ownership. These musicians acknowledge and value the musical collaboration between the older generation of Cajuns and Creoles in the early twentieth century, while associating them with two distinct styles. Dennis Paul Williams, a prominent zydeco musician and renowned painter in his own right, describes the music of Ardoin and McGee in the following way: "They both were beautiful musicians. I love their music. But if you listen real closely, they don't play the same at all. I could tell the difference between a black fiddler and a white fiddler. It's just that you can give me some of your blood, but it takes more than your blood to make me like you. I need your bones, I need your heart, I need your sensitivity. The soul, the subtlety of the soul ... that transparent element cannot be duplicated."[48]

According to Williams, then, although blood is not sufficient to pass on the sensitivity and soul that differentiate Cajun and Creole musicians, skin color—often associated with culture—tends to be perceived as crucial, a point frequently made by both Cajuns and Creoles, whether they are musicians or fans. The distinction between Cajun and Creole musicians even leads Dennis to attribute the origins of the Cajun style to Creoles, although he does not give Creoles a monopoly in terms of influence. According to this narrative, it was primarily the slaves who played this style of music, thus placing the Cajuns in a relationship of dominance on the same level as slaveowners, *Genteel Acadians*, who occupied the top rungs of the social ladder. Cajuns play a secondary role in the construction of a musical tradition of which the Creoles act as principal artisans.

For other Creoles, Cajuns are instead presented as lower-class people, as opposed to the Creole elite. A retired, light-skinned Creole raised in the vicinity of Lafayette, who dedicated his career to coordinating the state's educational programs for the promotion of higher education, explains his own reading of Cajun and Creole history:

See, the Creoles came from a connection with a line of Frenchmen, they were educated, they were polished, they were the *bourgeoisie*. Whereas the Cajuns, they were farmers, they went from France to Nova Scotia, then when England got rid of France, they kick the Frenchmen out of Nova Scotia and they came down to Louisiana. And the Parisian French, members of the *bourgeoisie*, says, we don't want you over here, you're ignorant, so they went to the bayous, and developed their own culture, their own food . . .[49]

Class consciousness among some Creoles continues to resonate in contemporary perceptions about music. While positioning the Cajuns at the bottom of the social ladder, class consciousness can also serve as a tool for creating hierarchies among Creoles themselves.

Present-day Louisiana is in fact criss-crossed by concurrent rival perceptions of Creole identity.[50] In south Louisiana, identifying oneself as Creole can associate an individual either with the white or the black population, depending on the region and on the identity of one's interlocutors. Those who proclaim to be white Creoles claim Spanish and/or French heritage, a prized social status. In the southwest, this mode of identification has become marginal, however, and Creoles are primarily associated with the black French-speaking population descended from free people of color and slaves. The Creole identification does not prevent them from feeling a powerful sense of commonality with African Americans, other than a few members of former enclaves of rural Creoles. Blackness and the francophone heritage are claimed together. Many Creoles vividly emphasize the discrimination that they have experienced as blacks regardless of the relative lightness or darkness of their skin tone, recalling that in either case, during segregation, "you knew your place."

By contrast, in New Orleans and the Cane River region around Natchitoches, as well as in the Creole diaspora (particularly in California), a sense of belonging to a specific culture resulting from a unique blend of Europeans, Africans, and Native Americans endures, along with a refusal to be identified as either white or black. The Creole Heritage Center in Natchitoches, which organizes annual conferences, events, and publications, advocates this perception of a mix that is superior to its constituent parts. Sybil Kein, a Creole scholar, poet, and musician from New Orleans, embraces this perspective.[51] As does Gary B. Mills, whose book on the Cane River Creoles of Isle Brevelle attempts to demonstrate the prosperity of the people of Cane River, their role in the "maturation" of Louisiana society, and most of all their distinctive status as "the third caste" up until the late twentieth century, a higher status rooted in social hierarchy and French ancestry that resonates throughout the realm of music and dance.[52] Mills argues: "Dancing was a pastime among all classes within Creole society—the French, the African, the free man, the slave. . . . The Isle Brevelle plantations were no exception, but for the African descendants who lived in the manor houses, the style of movement was decidedly French; the quadrille waltz and the *fais do-do* replaced Congo dance," drawing a line of demarcation between the primitiveness of ring shout dances and the sophistication of European dances.

Judged to be elitist by Creoles who identify themselves as African Americans, this uniquely Creole identification is closely associated with the desire to play a leading political role like that played by Creoles during Reconstruction. The desire to amplify Creole achievements and to attribute a defining role to them in the education, emancipation, and defense of the civil rights of black Louisianans is part of a celebratory official history that is in stark contrast with conflictual and troubled collective and individual memories.[53]

Depending on the interactional frames, social stakes, and regions, Louisiana Creoles can today identify themselves as African American and Creole, or as exclusively Creole.[54] In the latter case, their servile heritage is avoided in favor of the construct of mixing. Since the 1990s, zydeco music has earned increasing national fame and commercial success and is thus at the core of current power relationships among Creoles. James Caillier quoted above establishes the decisive role of Creoles of color while reassessing Clifton C. Chenier's contribution:

Zydeco really started from Creoles [of color]. . . . Creoles never wanted to expand their culture. And a guy like Clifton Chenier took advantage of it. He started taking it to the larger community. He took the Creole music and called it zydeco. Keep in mind, Clifton, their fans, many of their ancestors were slaves, Creole slaves. Some of the Creoles later married the slaves. But it was a slow process. So that was a mixture taking place.[55]

According to Callier, zydeco originated among Creoles of color, who passed it on to their slaves with no aspiration to celebrity, an aspiration that he implicitly deprecates. In fact, Chenier, the icon of zydeco music who owed his success to this very heritage, descended from Creoles of color. Moreover, since the beginning of the century, the ethnonym "Creole" refers both to descendants of freedmen and free people of color, as acknowledged in this quote, but without taking it into consideration in his argument. Whereas this Creole does identify as black, he nevertheless conceals a servile ancestry and overshadows the African ancestry. Whether Chenier's descent from Creoles of color is denied or simply not deemed plausible appears to stem from the often tacit association between Creole identification and being light-skinned, whereas Chenier was dark-skinned. Stigmatization of the Louisiana Creole speech variety that Chenier used in his songs might have been an additional factor, as it is positioned at the bottom of the range of language varieties in francophone Louisiana in large part because of its association with slavery.[56]

Indeed, Chenier's position as the "King of Zydeco" and the father of this music style is often contested, sometimes fueling the process of depreciation. This is the case of the Creole musician "Pap" DePass: "The thing with him [Clifton], he was a blues player! I mean, hey, what's the big deal! He didn't create anything! He just fed off of what was already there! And he was a typical example of a blues band that used an accordion and sang in broken French."[57]

In some cases, depreciation gives way to condemnation. A singer from Lafayette who mixes blues and swamp pop with some French songs criticizes the music and the musicians alike: "I don't like it . . . They're not musicians, they just pick up an instrument and play. It's too loud . . . *C'est chanté crié* [it's shouted] . . . They're drunk and don't know their music. They're ignorant." My interpretation of his virulence, however, is that he was primarily attempting to distance himself from zydeco in the eyes of a foreigner who was more likely to confuse local music styles.

When Differences Are Rooted in Origins

It wasn't until Clifton Chenier told me that Amédé Ardoin was the first colored to make French records that I realized Amédé was of African-American background. To my ears, the recordings of Amédé Ardoin did not sound all that different from . . . Cajun accordionists I had heard on records.
CHRIS STRACHWITZ, *ZYDECO: THE EARLY YEARS (1961–1962)*, LINER NOTES, ARHOOLIE CD307, 1989

Me, I never understood the difference between Creole music and French music, except that it's a white man who plays the accordion when it's Cajun, and it's a black man when it's Creole.[58]
FRED CHARLIE, VILLE PLATTE, MAY 1, 2001

The discourses of every social actor today converge by basing current musical categories on distinct ancestry. Music is not the only cultural phenomenon affected by this representation, which can be found in the different francophone speech varieties—Louisiana Creole and Louisiana regional French—that can be learned by the same person regardless of his or her origin. Among Cajuns and Creoles who speak Louisiana regional French, Cajuns define their language as Cajun, and Creoles as Creole. It is thus the group to which the speaker claims to belong that determines the meaning of the term that they use and not the nature of the language itself.[59]

The acknowledgment of shared musical traditions is not perceived to be inconsistent with claiming the existence of distinct styles. Throughout this process, old-time French music can be labeled either Cajun or Creole, depending on who plays it. Some of the arguments advanced by musicians to support a distinction between Cajun and Creole styles rely on musical techniques: the Creole style is commonly characterized by its more rhythmic, syncopated nature and its "crooked," "scratchy," "choppy" sound, distinct from the softer, smoother Cajun style.

Contradictions are always quick to rise within a single discourse or between individuals, however. The Creole accordion player Joe Hall is proud of his Creole style and has played and recorded with Mitch Reed. One morning in November 2004, while hanging out at Mitch's shop with his accordion as he often did, a music fan from the area decided to conduct an informal, filmed interview, which I eventually joined.

> JH: Have you ever realized that Creole is older that Cajun? Cajun is something new. It came from Creole. Creole is not a Black man. It could be a Black man or a White man. To me Creole is the purest of anything around here. The Creole music, you still have the European emphasis with certain tunes, especially with Bebe Carriere, Bois Sec, Amédé. You could still hear the European emphasis on their music....
>
> SLM: What's the difference between Cajun and Creole style?
>
> JH: The music is the same! The style is different. What may be different: the lyrics, the tempo, a lot of different things you could do to make a tune Creole . . . It depends on the person. It could be on the turn-around.
>
> SLM: How different is the Cajun bridge from the Creole bridge?

JH: It's how you put it. It's how you put it. It's not nothing you can explain. It's not nothing you can explain. It's just a style, it's just a style . . .[60]

Joe used the European emphasis to support the idea of Creole as a former music style that is understood to be the most "authentic." Moreover, his assertion that Creole music cannot be defined along racial lines seems more like a justification of Mitch's skills and talents, because in Joe's eyes, Mitch seems to be the only—or the best—Cajun musician able to play the Creole style. In fact, Joe finds the musical differences between Cajun and Creole styles impossible to characterize, arguing that the songs are the same, while qualifying one specific tune, "One Step du Chameau" by Ardoin, as "pure Creole."

In attempting to pinpoint the specific differences between Cajun and Creole fiddling, Reed spontaneously thought of approaches to bowing, as illustrated by Creole fiddler Bébé Carriere, who typically played every note on a single bowing, as opposed to slurring. Immediately after citing this example, Mitch added: "But Dennis too though, he definitely had like a Creole style. He was like a Creole fiddle player. . . . His waltzes tended to be quicker and more rhythmic." Mitch thus presents Dennis McGee as a sort of counter-example who qualifies as a Creole fiddler despite the fact that he is not himself a Creole—hence the cautious simile "like a Creole," which calls attention to dimensions that appear identical while not necessarily implying sameness. Musical style and musicians' identifications thus tend to become somewhat blurred. Mitch continued:

Where people start to really maybe get different was like when that whole swing influence came over, like J.B. Fuselier, where they'd keep 2 strings solid, like ringing. He was the most influential fiddlers, him and Leo Soileau. . . . As country music and Texas swing and stuff came here, people started hearing it on the radios, started dancing, the bowing became smoother, and it was more drones. . . .

Creole tunes tend to be modal, and they tend to have that one chord kind of thing. Like "Mme Fayette" or the "Bluerunner". This is one that Joe Hall plays all the time, he call it "Chicot de Bois sec." [laughter] [He plays Madame Fayette, then Eunice Two-Step] They're very different from each other, the first one being Creole, the second one Cajun. But to me the only thing that really separates the tunes is the influence from Texas. 'Cause I think before that, even listening to Leo Soileau playing, it was more Creole [i.e., French], you know. Like that stuff Leo did with Moise Robin, "Blues de Neg' français". That was Leo but what he was doing was really funky. But then he changed and became totally western swing.[61]

Mitch immediately pointed out that temporality is closely linked to the distinction between Cajun and Creole styles. As the old-time French music of the early twentieth century entered the swing era, styles diversified. The naturalization of Cajun/Creole differences results in fact from the evolution of aesthetic conventions. These distinctions are in reality linked to a greater extent to styles that come in and out of fashion depending on the time period than they are to musicians' origins. The influence of western swing created a more fluid style and helped spread, for example, the succession of violin and accordion solos that had previously been played simultaneously and against a more choppy rhythm.

Veteran fiddler Kevin Wimmer explains the generational context of this stylistic shift quite explicitly:

That's probably as much an older style of playing, more than Creole versus Cajun playing. The older Cajun musicians—Octa Clark, *Hector* Duhon—used to play the melody at the same time on the fiddle and accordion. The old records from the late twenties, the older style might have been more of that sort of playing, and it [trading off on playing melody] certainly developed in Cajun after the string band influence with the steel guitar, the influence of the western swing bands, where you pass around the solos. . . .

When I play with Preston [Frank], he's used to giving me fiddle rides; when I play with Keith [Preston's son], I don't get fiddle rides every time. It also depends on the tunes; there are some tunes I play backup on, and don't expect a fiddle ride. Certainly the more modern zydeco musicians are not used to having the fiddle alternate. . . . The fiddle and accordion are very complementary, the fiddle kind of slides, bends around the notes, and the accordion gets a percussive kind of punch. . . . In a smaller group, Preston and I, just the two of us, I might find I want to do more backup [seconding] to help, fill out the rhythm, but with a band, the rhythm is pretty full, so I double the accordion. That's sort of the context. In Cajun music too, if there is no triangle, you got more room.[62]

The configuration of the band, the musicians' generation, and the specific tunes are all factors that directly influence the sound. Kevin is most knowledgeable about the old-time French style and the different influences that contributed to its evolution. The fact that he is recognized as a highly talented fiddler for both Cajun and Creole styles, as well as other styles, makes his case particularly enlightening. Originally from New York City, he established permanent residence in Louisiana during the mid-1990s. He was mentored by Dewey Balfa, whose style he mastered during his first local gig with the band Balfa Toujours, but he has also regularly played fiddle with Preston Frank and is happily invited to play by Creole musicians. He was asked to teach Advanced Creole, Blues and Zydeco Fiddle at the 2008 Balfa Camp at Chicot State Park, a class generally taught by Creole musicians. Todd Mouton, who as director of Louisiana Folk Roots organized the music camp, ultimately hired two instructors for the advanced level. Todd expressed pleasure to have chosen to hire "a white guy and not even from here" to teach Creole fiddling. The ambiguity of the title of the class inspired a student to ask Kevin: "The Valse de Balfa, does it fit into that category? Just curious . . . it sounds bluesy to me." Kevin nodded and answered, "it *is* bluesy," before he began teaching it. When he opened the floor to his students one morning, I questioned him on the difference between Cajun and Creole styles:

> KW: There are some tunes that are more in the Creole repertoire, and then there is more the style of some of the Creole musicians. I mean, not to make generalizations but they tend to have more . . . some different rhythmic things going on. Like sometimes they're . . . more syncopated, and have some rhythmic punches, where some of the Cajun music is smoother. . . . I mean Cajun music has got syncopation too but . . . Sometimes the Creole music is a little more . . . bluesier, kind of sliding . . . I mean, some of these qualities are in Cajun music also, so it's hard to totally define, you know, define it. . . . Hmmm . . . I think a lot is in the rhythm, some of the Creole tunes have a funkier, deeper something in the rhythm. I'm not describing it very well, but . . .
> SLM: is it more a feel, a style…? More than a repertoire?
> KW: Right, some of these songs Canray wrote are more in the Creole repertoire, but then Canray and the Carriere brothers play tunes that are common to the Cajun repertoire also. You certainly have Cajun musicians that are bluesy and syncopated, I mean, the

> Cajun music ranges from more bluesy and syncopated to, let's say, more kind of fast or country rhythm.

A student came to his rescue by reminding him that he had answered a similar question the day before, demonstrating his answer by playing "Jongle à Moi" in the style of Dewey Balfa, followed by the style of "Bois Sec" Ardoin and Carlton Frank. Realizing that words were not doing justice to what he was attempting to express, Kevin happily switched to another mode of expression by replaying this musical demonstration for me.

> KW: So . . . the second way . . . Bois Sec would syncopate certain phrases, would put more accent, hmmm, I mean . . . I don't know how to totally describe it . . .
> A student: more syncopated and less smooth.
> KW: Definitely more syncopated, yeah. The Balfa rhythm, the triangle [he imitates the triangle vocally], it kind of rolls, you know, it rides on that rhythm, on that shuffle guitar of Rodney [he hums]. That kind of Balfa rhythm on the two-step . . . And Bois Sec just sort of punches more. I mean he does sort of slurring too but not necessarily . . . It has more accents or punches . . . you know . . .
> Another example is "Old Fashioned Two Step" which I learned years ago with Dewey and Robert Jardell, the kind of more Cajun way, and Preston and Beau Jocque have more of a syncopated take on the tune, that's another contrast.
> That Creole style, for some reason I play it in a lower key. If Preston is on a B♭ I'll play with G fingering, out of F [since the fiddle's tuned down]. I'm used to playing that one in this key. And the other one (Cajun) with A fingering. [He sings the song emphasizing the rhythm.] It's basically the same kind of melody, shape, a little different rhythm, and it has a different effect . . . does that make sense to hear that?

A specific approach to tuning is an additional technique associated with the Creole style. Because lower-key accordions (particularly B♭) are common in Creole style, some players tune their fiddles to match the accordion, turning the D into a B♭. Others refer to the structure, based on the view that Creole tunes do not include a B part but in fact contain several parts (like in "Bluerunner" or "Bee de la Manche"), although Canray Fontenot contradicts this argument. Different parts instead of a melody and a bridge can also be found in songs considered to be Cajun. "Lake Arthur Stomp," for example, has either three or four parts depending on the version. "Reel de Joie," and "Galop à Wade Frugé" also seem to be more structured on different parts.

Like other musicians, Kevin questions his own technical thinking even as he explains it, rambles, finds exceptions to the rules he is explaining, and seems to confess to the difficulty of defining musical characteristics. The distinctions most often remain indescribable, and are evoked using the language of subjectivity and feelings, through allusions to a distinctive "soul" or "feel" or "flavor." Physically integrated and lived through the act of playing, such distinctions finally leave little space for other arguments.

As the interview quoted above exemplifies, the specific interactional frame significantly influences the arguments that musicians articulate through their discourse. This sample of Kevin's discourse occurred during a music camp in front of an audience of fans who hold Louisiana musicians—whether native Louisianans or not—in high esteem and value their judgments, while at the same time expecting them to match particular representations commonly associated with the music. When a student and workshop participant asked whether "Happy One Step" or "Pop's Waltz" (by Dennis McGee) were considered Creole, Kevin answered: "Not strictly, but it doesn't mean we can't do it," leading another student to implore him: "I wanna do some Creole stuff!" Kevin compromised, trying to please everybody. "We'll do 'Pop Waltz,' it won't take too long, then 'Zydeco Hee-Haw.'"

Kevin did not seem completely at ease with either my questions or his answers. Although he expressed considerable hesitancy concerning his own arguments while he was developing them, other students functioned as safeguards, encouraging him to stick to the differentiation between Cajun and Creole styles and its associated points. However, the evolution of his discourse and his musical examples (such as the expressions "Dewey's," "Bois Sec's," or "Canray's version") suggested that individual styles are essential. In fact, this thorniest of issues in the Cajun/Creole distinction—made obvious throughout the discussion quoted above—does not mitigate racial fixations. "Creole style" commonly refers to a series of specific songs considered typically Creole, although Cajun-labeled songs can be eligible for the Creole style, like la "Valse des Balfas," and despite being part of the old-time French repertoire widely shared among Creole and Cajun musicians. In a back-and-forth movement between difference and sameness, the same aesthetic conventions are at times associated with a specific style—Cajun or Creole—and at other times with the entire French Louisiana repertoire, depending on the context of enunciation.

Instructional videos are highly informative in this respect. The rhythmic nature of French Louisiana music, rather than being strictly ascribed to Creoles and their musics, is typically presented as one of its most significant features, whatever the instrument. In his video, Steve Riley talks about "rhythmic" playing, a "poppy," "bouncy" rhythm of the Cajun accordion, while Dirk Powell describes the "Cajun feel as playing in octaves ("playing double"), playing bass with the left hand and holding a "bouncing rhythm." In teaching the Cajun fiddle, Michael Doucet cites Dennis McGee, who liked to bounce, and to the more percussive sound of modern players.[63] Fiddler and veteran teacher Tracy Schwartz has taught a class for decades devoted to teaching the distinctive looping rhythm of Louisiana French music at Augusta, one of the most popular Cajun music camps that is held annually in Elkins, West Virginia. To better illustrate the bouncy feel of that rhythm, Schwartz uses the image of "an egg-shaped wheel."[64] Mitch Reed chose to record a sequence of two volumes of instructional video entitled *How to Play Cajun and Creole Fiddle* (2011 and 2012) in which he promotes a single method and shared techniques for both styles. Double-stops, slides, drones, and chords are demonstrated without distinguishing between Creole and Cajun approaches. Because their identification is so widespread however, he does present certain emblematic tunes as either Creole ("Bonsoir Moreau") or Cajun ("Jolie Blonde").[65]

By contrast, D'Jalma Garnier published a method and video dedicated to what is described as the Creole style, the first of its kind, in the *Louisiana Creole Fiddle Method* (2010). A popular Creole fiddler originally from New Orleans who lived throughout the country before settling in southwest Louisiana in the late 1980s, Garnier comes from a musical family, beginning a classical education on the violin at the age of five with a teacher from the Minneapolis symphony. He decided to apprentice himself to Creole music and applied for a grant to study with Canray Fontenot. He selected fourteen songs commonly associated with Creole fiddling, mostly from Canray Fontenot ("La Danse de la Misère," "Tes Parents Ne Veulent Plus Me Voir," "Bonsoir Moreau," "Malinda," "Bernadette"), Bébé Carriere ("Blue Runner," "Blues à Bébé"), Amédé Ardoin ("Co Fah," also spelled Quo fé). However, he also included one tune from Cajun fiddler Dennis McGee ("Ville Platte Two Step"), two pieces of his own, and a lone New Orleans rag. Through this selection, Garnier situates the Creole style as "traditional" music and focuses primarily, if not exclusively, on Creole fiddlers.

As an iconic figure of the "roots" of French music, the inclusion of Dennis McGee—Amédé Ardoin's musical partner—seemed inevitable. Although the text itself does mention many similarities between Cajun and Creole fiddling, the specificity of the Creole sound is the object of his method. A number of "Creole fiddle techniques" are demonstrated, including bowing, cross-string bowing, fingering, sliding, double-stops, and scratching or bearing down. Most of these techniques are shared with Cajun fiddling, with the exception of the "scratchy" sound associated with Creole fiddling. Achieved by bowing, it is produced bearing down on the bow and playing closer to the bridge, and perhaps by applying excess rosin on the hair. The representation of the Creole style as a "rough," even "nasty" sound—as Garnier put it—is widespread and crosses over the origins of musicians. A Creole friend once told me that in his view, Louis Michot of the Lost Bayou Ramblers played "more Creole" than Mitch Reed. Both the way he expressed this opinion and the example he chose were significant, and expressed in a nutshell what seems to be at stake in the labeling of Cajun and Creole styles: they are principally a matter of sound more than they are a question of repertoire or of racial identification.

The persistent justification of two distinct Cajun and Creole styles is also fueled by the media, which perpetuate confusing reports and labels while generally focusing on the Cajun dimension. Although the national press is more likely to perpetuate such an imbalanced representation, local publications also contribute their share of biased reporting concerning local music styles.[66] In its "attractions" page, the 2004 edition of the Lafayette area phonebook defined zydeco as "a blend of Cajun dance music and African blues," a definition shared by an article entitled "Zydeco Fever in Lafayette" that appeared in the *New York Times* as well as several music textbooks and dictionaries.[67] Even the magazine *Billboard*, the bible of the American music industry, published a critical piece on the CD *Creole Bred* under the title "Cajun Music Gets Its Due" that was conceived by Ann Savoy as an hommage to Creole and zydeco music. A local journalist who is a specialist on zydeco, Herman Fuselier, never misses an opportunity to express his exasperation with this persistent, widespread media attitude, even within the music press, that presents zydeco as having its roots in Cajun music.[68]

More broadly than the question of French Louisiana music, the racial imaginary contributes to the assumption that there are similarities shared among black musicians around the globe, and particularly between contemporary Creole and African musicians. These parallels have become an object of fascination and have helped foster local consumption of African exoticism. During the 2008 Festival International, the Blue Moon inaugurated the series "Rhythm and Roots: Celebrating the Musical Bridge between Cultures" by inviting foreign artists featured at the festival to share the stage with local acts. In one 2010 show, for example, the Senegalese kora player Morikeba Kouyate played with Creole musician Cedric Watson for a standing-room-only audience. The owner of the Blue Moon produced the CD *Creole Moon: Live from the Blue Moon Saloon* (Valcour, 2010) that was nominated for the 2011 Cajun and Zydeco Grammy Award, including three tracks with Kouyate. The opening track was entitled "Afro Zydeco." "We're bringing the roots back into zydeco right here at the Blue Moon!" Watson shouted to the crowd when the song ended.

In the summer of 2008, Cedric had parted company with the popular Pine Leaf Boys, led by Wilson Savoy, claiming that he wanted to explore connections with other Creole populations from the Caribbean. A year later, his travel in Haiti was pictured on his website in a YouTube video, along with quotes that were explicit about his views about the music. "A lot of people think I mix my music with African music and stuff like that, but it's not really true. We were separated from the African part, and it was washed out of us. The only thing we have to tap into that part of our spirits is music,"[69] he stated. The band has appeared on his web page and sometimes on stage with colorful African-patterned shirts and Rasta headgear. Despite predictable criticism by more traditionalist music lovers, he was acclaimed by the local press and scholars for his determination to explore Afro-Caribbean traditions. Interestingly, this exploration seems to meet greater challenges when it comes from white musicians. Although their band included black members, Moïse and Alida Viator, two siblings from the Eunice area, were never able to attract a consistent following in Louisiana with their innovative style, which they called "Creole fusion" and which integrated a wide range of influences and musics, including old-time French music, zydeco, jazz, New Orleans R&B, salsa, cumbia, Jamaican ska, meringue, and zouk.

While Creole musicians like Cedric Watson who focus on their mixed ancestry refer more readily to Africa in connection with their intention of "bringing back the roots of Louisiana music," musicians who claim a "new" zydeco sound and their fans identify with a globalized, mass-mediated culture of blackness, achieved through practices of consumption. While the reference to Africa is always there, it remains overall somewhat distant and vague and often seems restricted to a predisposition for polyrhythm.

"It's All French Music . . ."

As much as the Afro element inspires his music, Cedric Watson is also acutely aware of the commonalities between the Cajun and Creole repertoires. When I met him in the fall of 2004, he was twenty-one years old and had recently moved to southwest Louisiana. Mentored by Creole musicians Ed Poullard and J. B. Adams, he was already highly confident about his musical views when I interviewed him at the Blue Moon:

> SLM: How do you call the music you play?
> CW: I call it French music. I don't talk about white music or black music, there is no difference. Close your eyes and just listen to the music, you can't tell if it's a black or a white band. But whites can play French music and blacks can play French music. A lot of people told me, you're black, you have to play zydeco music. Blacks play zydeco music, Cajuns play Cajun music. But a long time ago Creoles and Cajuns played French music. There is no difference....
>
> Dennis McGee was Cajun but when he played the fiddle he could play like European, he could play blues, that's Creole music. A mixture. But Bois Sec and Canray they were Creole too and they played Creole music. That's what it was. It's not about the color. When it comes to categorizing it as Creole music, it's not Creole music because it's black, it's Creole music because it's that style, that old Louisiana Creole style. And Leo Soileau, that's Creole music.[70]

When Cedric's first CD came out, however, the cover pictured him flanked by Canray Fontenot and Clifton Chenier, drawn as medallions in the background, almost as though they represented guardian angels who watched over him and inspired his music. This explicit identification with black musicians was a powerful statement that seemed to contrast his assertion when I interviewed him. Indeed, asserting sameness within old-time French music style regardless of musicians' skin color combines with efforts to draw on African influences within Creole culture. Cedric continues: "What makes us Creole people is that we are African, but we can speak French. That's why zydeco music has a lot of African influence in it. Because that's what we are."

At the 2006 Festivals Acadiens in Lafayette, local music journalist Herman Fuselier presented a workshop on accordion styles. Among his guests, Kristie Guillory was representing the Cajun style, Dexter Ardoin represented the Creole style, and Horace Trahan was the ambassador for a mix of the two. After questioning the first two musicians, who attempted somehow to articulate the differences between the styles, Fuselier asked Horace about his view: "It's a different flavor to it, but it all comes from the same place, Louisiana. Some people say to-may-to, some to-mah-to (laughter from the audience). I didn't mean to start any trouble, though . . ."[71]

Since his conversion to zydeco, which progressively evolved in his hands into a blend of southwest Louisiana music styles, Horace has made a point of reconciling the differences within French Louisiana music and of asserting the overarching importance of regional identification. In fact, the cover of his 2010 CD *Keep Walking* explicitly illustrates this synthetic approach by showing the Acadian flag and the Creole flag side-by-side, with a map of Louisiana astride the two.

Like Horace, one older musician consistently minimizes difference between Cajun and Creole styles. Ed Poullard continues to apply the label "French music" that was current in the first half of the twentieth century. Ed's brother, Danny, shared his views, as corroborated by his students, including music scholar Mark DeWitt and Blair Kilpatrick. Refusing to be pigeonholed as Cajun or Creole, he simply said he played French music.[72]

At the 2008 Balfa camp, during Ed's master presentation, the director of Folk Roots whispered in his ears to suggest that he address the perennial question of the differences between Cajun and Creole music:

> Mostly, I think, back in the twenties and thirties, and my dad told me, a lot of these older ones, I don't care who they were, they all played similar styles, they played same songs. There was no difference. You couldn't say who was playing what. When music started to dwindle around the fifties, those groups started listening to other styles of music. Blacks listened to R&B, Cajuns to Country and Western. When French music came back into play, a lot of these influences came back into the music. Me, Preston, Dirk, we play three different ways. You can hear our influences. I try to learn songs from Jesse Lége, I try to play just like he plays. That's my interpretation.[73]

Sharing the stage with him, Dirk Powell echoed Ed's point by telling the story of his then sister-in-law, Nelda Balfa, who grew up in the 1960s and was convinced at the time that the AM/FM options on her radio referred to the distinction between American music and French music. "That's where the divide was," he added, concluding an anecdote that was as amusing as it was startlingly clear. He pursued this argument with another story about his then wife, Christine Balfa, who wanted to learn the fiddle but wanted to sound different from her father. She went to visit the Creole fiddler Calvin Carriere and asked him where he got his style. "I just try to play like your daddy. I like his style too much." Dirk's punchline reinforced Ed's view through anecdotes that required no further explanation because they were presented as factual as well as humorous, a key element in the story-telling of Louisianans.

Far from being confined to the past, the label "French music" carries meaning for many present-day musicians and dancers in Louisiana. It characterizes a specific old-timey style and is also used as a generic term that evokes more of a regional—rather than racial—identification and therefore encompasses a range of southwest Louisiana music styles.

. . . and French Blues"

> I like blues a lot, because I was raised in potato fields with blacks and whites and we would sing. I can relate to it. When you listen to the blues, you always think that it's a black man singing. But they sing about the same thing that we went through too.
>
> [J'aime beaucoup la musique blues, parce que j'ai été élevé dans les clôts de patates avec les Noirs et les Blancs et on chantait. I can relate to it. Quand tu vas écouter la musique blues tu vas tout le temps croire c'est un homme noir qu'est après chanter. Mais il chante le même chose que nous autres on a passé à travers aussi.]
>
> FRED CHARLIE, MAY 1, 2001, VILLE PLATTE

The music producer Fred Charlie was born northeast of Eunice in Chataigner in 1949, growing up with black neighbors. His parents also worked for blacks as agricultural laborers (known as *récolteurs*). Don Cravins Sr., who belongs to the same generation, is a popular Democratic politician elected as a state senator in 1992, and grew up in the same period in the Creole of color enclave of Mallet, in Saint Landry Parish, where his parents were farmers and landowners. For Cravins, French music could be characterized as the Cajun and Creole people's blues, "because it talked about the suffering and the misery they endured during those hard times. It almost sound that they're wailing."[74]

According to Ronald Radano, the qualities associated with blues, and more broadly with black music, are "its soulfulness, its depth of feeling or 'realness,' its emotional and rhythmic energy, its vocally informed instrumental inflections." These are all qualities that, in Louisiana, are not specific to black or Creole music, but instead encapsulate the narrative of French Louisiana music. Anchored in collective memories of shared hardship, feelings come first in descriptions of the music, which is described most of all as soulful and emotional. David Greely remembers the first time he listened to the Balfa Brothers, who had been recommended to him by Jo-El Sonnier: "Oh my God, I had never heard anything like it. There wasn't anything I had ever heard that was more perfect for me. 'Cause it was great fiddle playing, soulful fiddle playing, great singing, lots of syncopation, good rhythm, and you didn't have to be the fastest, you didn't have to have the biggest collection of tunes, all you had to do is feel it, love it and play it."[75]

Far from the dexterity required in bluegrass music as he had previously experienced it, he discovered the power of emotions, although as he admitted, "it could be that any music can be played that way, but it's Cajun music that first taught me that lesson."

The Creole fiddler Canray Fontenot used to characterize Cajun and Creole fiddle playing as the sound of a crying baby.[76] In fact, sorrow and regret have been one of the French music's major themes, and even happy melodies can be a vehicle for heartbreaking lyrics. "Cajun music is kind of like singing the blues, dispelling the bad times for the good times,"[77] explained Michael Doucet to his students at the 2008 Balfa Camp. "The main thing about Cajun music, it must move you," he added, echoing countless musicians who insist on this intrinsic musical quality.

The description of French Louisiana music as bluesy is also ubiquitous in publications about music. According to Chris Strachwitz, improvisation is the common denominator: "On the whole, making a record was apparently much the same to a Cajun musician as it was to a blues singer. The Cajun would take an old tune or theme and deliberately change it or improvise new words to it."[78] He entitled one of his publications "Zydeco Music i.e. French Blues," in which he described zydeco as "a unique brand of blues" also called "French music" or "La La." The music of Clifton Chenier was characterized as "lowdown blues played on accordion with rhythm accompaniment and sung in English with a heavy Cajun accent."[79]

In fact, blues tunes are a defining element of the French repertoire, whether they are labeled blues or not. They are initially identifiable by their specific rhythm, slower than a two-step and different from the 3/4 waltz. The beat is typically pounded, based on a ternary rhythm. Countless blues have been recorded since the early 1920s, but waltzes can also sound like blues, like "Valse de Balfa" or "Barres de la Prison." Technically, blues or bluesy waltzes can (but do not necessarily) follow the chord progression of a basic blues (I-IV-V, i.e., the first, fourth, and fifth chords of a given scale).[80] Numerous French Louisiana songs are not always "square" or musically predictable because often the chords will change in unexpected places, usually due to beats dropped from measures of music. What makes a song bluesy is also the use of blue notes, particularly the flat third and the flat seven, and the slides between major and minor scales (the minor third sounding against a major chord), introducing the ambiguous tension of tones typically associated with blues. Most blues in French Louisiana music, whether old-time tunes or zydeco, are in a major key ("Blues de Bosco," "Blues de Tac Tac," "Blues de Cajun," "Let the Good Times Roll," "Paper in My Shoe," "Worried Life Blues," "Hungry Man Blues") as opposed to minor blues. This is partly due to the diatonic accordion, the dominant instrument in French music during the late 1920s that came back into fashion after the swing era. Although the accordion can play minor melodies by the use of modes, the French repertoire includes few minor songs other than old ballads and old-time fiddle tunes.[81] McGee's "Pa Janvier," the traditional "Danse de Mardi Gras," and the old Edius Naquin ballad "Je m'endors" are among the few examples of minor songs.[82]

Countless songs in this repertoire are in the keys of C and G. The key of G, played on a C accordion, means that the scale is not complete, lacking the F#. As Sam Broussard, the guitarist of Steve Riley and the Mamou Playboys explained to me, this involves the use of modes, which are types of scales superimposed onto a chord that is not its root (like a D major scale played over an E^m chord). The most common modes are Dorian, Mixolydian, and Aolian.[83] What they all have in common is the flat seventh. Most folk melodies and particularly French music tunes were originally sung without harmony or with just a single or double note drone as accompaniment. These songs are now usually harmonized by a modal harmony that is appropriate to the scales used in folk music. Like Irish, Scottish, and old-time music, French music primarily uses the Ionian and

Mixolydian mode.[84] Finally, many zydeco songs and fiddle reels employ a simpler structure than the twelve-bar I-IV-V, including one or two chords, and they may use a fifth chord but not for the purpose of resolving, like in other blues and non-blues music. "Oh Mom" by Preston Frank or Steve Riley and the Mamou Playboys is one example [I-IV-I-I] as are many fiddle reels, or zydeco tunes [I-I-V-I] , or any riff-based blues song like Howlin' Wolf's "Spoonful" or "Smokestack Lightning" that are just based on a single, repeated chord [I-I-I-I].

Chas Justus, songwriter and guitar player with the Red Stick Ramblers, explains the specificity of this bluesy sound and provides a technical description:

> One of the great things the Cajuns did is the blues waltz. "The Evangeline Waltz," that Lawrence Walker stuff, the Balfas and "The Criminal Waltz," those are just blues to a waltz and I never heard that so much in other kinds of music. . . . When you go to the four chord, the flat seven of the four chord is the minor third of the one chord. And there's this line between the minor third and the (major) third—the happy note and the sad note—it is this kind of blurring of the two that's so much of what the blues is, like technically, the blue note. [the use of the flatted third, fifth, and in those songs in particular the flat seventh of the associated major scale.]
>
> And "The Valse Criminelle" and "Evangeline Waltz" that goes to that four chord, it's like the flat seven and the four chord, so it's got the blues in it. It's really bluesy. . . . Even "J'ai été au bal" or "Bosco Blues," especially, so much of it has that influence and is part of what makes it interesting.[85]

As a result, many songs feel bluesy without being technically defined as blues. Sam Broussard illustrates further:

> "La Valse du Bambocheur," I would call this a blues even though there's no ♭7 or ♭3, and the chord progression uses 1, 4, and 5 like a normal Cajun waltz, not a blues. The central note of the melody is the fifth, which does not make it bluesy, but the singer's emotion leans that 5 toward the ♭5 very strongly. It is that, the rest of his singing, and the lyrics that make this song a blues. If you play this song for a black American blues musician, he will tell you that he "feels" this song to be blues. . . .

"Valse de Balfa" is very bluesy. There's a ♭7 and no minor 3, but as usual the major 3 slides up from a soupçon of the ♭3, like the "Mardi Gras song"—like almost every 3rd the Balfas sing.[86]

Such slides on vocals and the fiddle are typical of a bluesy sound and a soulful singing and playing.

The argument that blue notes and the pentatonic mode originated in Africa is deeply ingrained in musicians' understanding of southern music. This is how Sam explained his view of French blues in written correspondence with me:

> Creole music could not have avoided the sound of blues even if Canray and Clifton had not existed, because the flattened seventh sound and the indeterminate third are in the memory of the West African ear at the cellular level. The chord made by most of the notes when drawing or pulling [the accordion] is the fifth of the push chord—in the case of a C instrument, that would be a G chord.... If there is a rule here, it's this: if the instrument presents you with a ♭7, you will use it if you are a Cajun (older Cajuns are generally not wasteful). Not if you are an Acadian in Acadie hundreds of years ago. There were only fiddles and voices, and their European sensibilities probably would not have liked the sound of a ♭7. But the Cajun has grown up around black people and heard their music; he either liked it or he didn't. *Evidemment* (obviously) many, many of them did.[87]

Along with Creole musicians who are understood as bluesy by nature, the late Balfa brothers, Nathan Abshire, and Iry Lejeune have been the most emblematic of that style, while their songs "Valse de Balfa," "Pine Grove Blues," and "Valse criminelle" are presented as archetypal French blues. *Iry Lejeune: Wailin' the Blues Cajun Style* is the title of a book written about the legendary musician, whose powerful and distinctive voice left an indelible mark on the history of French Louisiana music, somehow associated with an ability to express the sadness and pain that are ascribed to every French Louisiana musician.[88] Through this association with blues as internationally successful, celebrated, and legitimized, French Louisiana music itself acquires increased legitimacy. However, although Cajuns and Creoles alike claim French blues as yet another music category associated with French Louisiana music, this commonality receives little attention in the French Louisiana musical narrative.

The different methods of tuning the accordion are sometimes advanced as a way to distinguish Cajun from zydeco musicians. Accordions can be tuned "wet" and "dry," and very few can do both, so the instruments tend to be chosen depending on the desired effect and sound. As Mark DeWitt explains, in "wet" tuning (which characterizes the French musette style), some of the reeds are sufficiently detuned that they produce a rich vibrato or shimmering effect because of the acoustic "beating" or interference that takes place between sound waves of slightly differing lengths. In "dry" tuning, the reeds sound tuned with each other, with little acoustical beating. Through tuning, Creole and zydeco players who use the single-row accordion are sometimes distinguished from their Cajun counterparts on the basis of a bluesier sound, although French Louisiana musicians today seem to use both regardless of their style, depending on their personal preference or the desired effect. It would be interesting to know how older musicians perceived the differences between these tunings and on what basis they made their choices. When I asked David Greely about "wet" and "dry" tunings in 2008, he mentioned that they no longer sufficed to distinguish between Cajun and Creole musicians. In Greely's opinion, the placement of the microphone was more relevant, because it tends to be inserted outside the accordion in Cajun music and inside in zydeco, where it yields a rougher sound by emphasizing the bass.

Interestingly, the bluesy character of French Louisiana music can also be used as an argument against its legitimacy as a distinct music style. Arnold DePass Jr., deploring what he perceives as an ersatz blues, explained:

> Some tunes just use the I and IV. What makes blues interesting is . . . in the C chord you got three notes, do (C), mi (E) sol (G), and they got inversions. So you got three inversions on each chord. So that's III, VI, IX. So you can get a lot of variety by inverting. You got C, E, G, then you can use, E, G, C, then G, C, E. That gives you twelve options. Now zydeco sometimes, they never get off one chord. They never got the I. And they go like that for five minutes![89]

Representing zydeco as blues does not cover the scope of its influences, however. Although the King of Zydeco drew mostly on rhythm and blues, many subsequent zydeco musicians have been inspired by other music styles. This was the case of the late John Delafose, who borrowed the strains of country from Dolly Parton, Randy Travis, and George Jones in tunes such as "Go Back Where You Been" and "La misère m'a fait brailler (Misery Made Me Cry)," to the delight of his white audience.[90]

Whereas blues is typically stereotyped as genuinely black, and country as typically white, the two styles actually share an ample, rich middle ground. In fact, Cecilia Tichi qualifies them as musical "cousins," including Cajun music within country music. Along with sharing identification with rural roots and economic privation, the blending of the two styles has also been constantly expressed in terms of instrumentation (banjo, mandolin, and fiddle) and technique (improvisation in both styles can shift from a country scale to a blues scale).[91]

Charlie Musselwhite and Charley Pride appear to exemplify the blurred lines between music styles and racial identification. Musselwhite was a white bluesman who played harmonica, and Pride was the first African American country music star, with twenty-nine number one hits to his name. When he arrived Nashville in 1965, he could hardly conceal his anxiety. He was criticized by his own family as well as others, leading him to pre-empt questions on stage by saying things like "I tell you, I get a lot of questions, like 'Why do you sound like you're not supposed to sound?' (laughs of the audience)."[92] Blues and country have been mastered by musicians on both sides of the color line. Ray Charles, the Supremes, and Howlin' Wolf contributed masterful renderings of country tunes, while Texas swing icon Bob Wills and country legend Hank Williams—known as the Lovesick Blues Boy—are just some of the most illustrious examples of the versatility of musicians in blurring the boundaries between identifications and implicitly interrogating conceptions of music styles as constituting black or white cultural legacies.

The description of French Louisiana music as "French music," and sometimes as "French blues," further illustrates the intricacy of musical influences and the fact that they cannot be reduced merely to an encounter between so-called white and black styles, or, for that matter, to skills that would be specific to white or black musicians. Arguing against a vision of soul as a "bi-racial" genre, Les Back considers that it "reduces the agency and creativity of the artists and pickers to some perverse form of racial alchemy. Rather, these musicians carried diversity of musical influences in themselves."[93] The musical context of the specific time frame, audience expectations, the quest for recognition and upward mobility, market-driven interests, outsider's interest, and geographical mobility of music and musicians are all additional factors in determining their musical choices and sounds, professional strategies, and personal projects.

It is worth considering whether the distinct collective memories of suffering and privation associated with Cajuns and Creoles might inform how the category "French blues" is used. On one hand, there is the Grand Dérangement, the term for the deportation of Acadians from Nova Scotia by the British in 1755. Scholars and activists have in fact borrowed or redeployed the lexicon used in discussions of slavery and the Holocaust. Carl Brasseaux, for example, has compared the conditions of the exile with those in the Middle Passage and the detention centers in Halifax to concentration camps.[94] On the other hand, there is slavery—for those who embrace a servile ancestry—and segregation. As suggested by the above quote from Fred Charlie in which he claims the blues and asserts the connection with the shared history of hardship of Cajun and black history, the appropriation of "French blues" and its correlative emphasis on hardship could also be interpreted as a rival demand for recognition as survivors of adversity.

Blackness and Eroticism

> There is soulfulness in zydeco music, it's more sensual . . . you feel it . . . on the inside. There is a lot of personal expression in the way you move that isn't there in the Cajun dance. . . . If it were a religion, Cajun would be the church and zydeco would be the Charismatic movement . . .
> FRANCES HAYMARK, LAFAYETTE, MARCH 30, 2001

Frances Haymark was born in 1954 and grew up in Lake Charles in a Baptist Scottish family that "had the mindset of staying away from anything that was not prosperous and in their mind well-bred." Frances heard only negative stereotypes about French Louisiana culture when she was growing up, but when her family moved east to Lafayette in the 1970s, she fell in love with Cajun dance:

> Somewhere in the late 1980s, a woman that I met from Quebec was teaching French, I met her at Randol's and she had gone zydeco dancing and told me "You've got to go hear Beau Jocque in Richard's in Lawtell!" "I cant' go there, it's a black club!" "Oh yes you can go!" (laughter). She brought me out to Richard's. And that was it, I was gone, I became . . . There was something of the way this music sounds. The music was much bluesy, it had a soulful sound. I just

loved it. I love the dance that goes with it. It's much more personal, you can express yourself more in that dance, to me. At that time it was a really risqué, wild thing to do. Because it was such a racial issue. I guess it was my own way of having some adventure.[95]

Frances was fully conscious of transgressing the social rules of the time, but she was fascinated by this the idea of rebelling against her family, and she began to dance regularly:

In the beginning, there was a group from us from Randol's, who would go to zydeco clubs. And the group felt we all needed to go as a group and needed to have some white men with us. One night, three of us went to a zydeco club with no white men, and one person from that group, the Crew de canaille, called us and told us we were setting ourselves up, it was so dangerous, so wrong to go! It's funny now, because it's so accepted.

Until the 1990s music clubs continued to be fairly segregated in Louisiana. Zydeco musicians performed in white clubs for dancers who were white except for their families. Missy Maloney, a native of New Orleans who lived in the region as a student during the 1970s, vividly recalls Clifton Chenier playing weekly at Jay's Lounge, a roadhouse in Cankton with low ceilings, no air conditioning, and giant four-foot-high fans blowing cool air coming from the open windows:

It was about probably three dollars to get in. Beer was, I can't even remember, like seventy cents. It was very cheap. Everything was cheap. And Clifton, once he would start, he would never take a break. I'm sure you heard that. So he had a saxophone player. I think his real name was John Hart. And they called him Blind John. Well, he was great. I mean, really good, like blues-style. And I loved that because that was familiar from my N.O. soulful music R&B experience. It was great dance music. So he would play the opening, you know, probably half an hour. He would lead the band. You know, there was just something very special about it. He would be there dressed in a suit, speaking like he could be in a sophisticated club in Chicago, or something, not in a roadhouse out on the prairie. The rest of the band, they might be in blue jeans and tee-shirts, but he was in a suit and he give a proper introduction of himself and the band, the tunes and all that. I loved that music. I don't remember the crowd being very mixed racially, but I do remember like today, the family, and the girlfriends would be sitting up front, maybe close to the band. The black people would be there.[96]

Along with a few fellow young, white dancers, out-of-towners were among the first whites to enter zydeco clubs, encouraged by the development of a tourism policy focused on French Louisiana culture. Dancehalls like El Sid O's in Lafayette, Hamilton's Place on Verot School Road, now absorbed by the city, Richard's in Opelousas, and Slim's Y-Ki-Ki in Lawtell were the major landmarks of the zydeco circuit at the time. In 1982 Hamilton's was officially integrated to some extent when the owner, William Hamilton, began what became known as White Night, hosting weekly Wednesday night performances by the Red Beans and Rice Revue. The oil slump of the 1980s that deeply affected the region slowed down his business, however, after about two years. Still, "that White Night started the white folks coming," says Hamilton, whose father had first opened the club in 1956. "After that, it was white and black until now."[97]

Everyone who experienced zydeco clubs when there were few white dancers refers to the friendly atmosphere that they encountered, but they also mention that they quickly learned a few tacit social rules. Single women recall the gendered organization of space that excluded them from standing at the bar, which was reserved for single men. Booking a table was the rule for everyone else, and most women came accompanied by male friends. Whether white patrons were introduced by a black friend or not, certain behaviors were not considered socially acceptable. Missy Maloney remembers her first time at a zydeco club when she went to Slim's around 1979. She and her dance partner felt extremely well received dancing together, but that changed when she got up to join the ladies' line dance. "I didn't feel welcomed at all," she says." I picked up the dance pretty quickly, but those ladies were bumping me and pushing me. It didn't have a good feel to it."

Like Frances and Missy, Michael Seider recalls being among the only whites when he started going to zydeco clubs. Raised in New York, he was a Unitarian Universalist minister who was passionate about international folk dancing and began teaching a dance class in 1986 before moving to Louisiana. Michael learned a hard lesson when he became aware of the importance of dressing appropriately after he showed up in shorts, a T-shirt, and sneakers when he came to Richard's one evening directly from the Festivals Acadiens with his girlfriend. It so happened that a wedding party was taking place that evening. Introduced by a Creole friend to the musicians, John Delafose and his band, he paid the price for stealing the show from the wedding guests with his incongruous clothing. "So that night we got bumped. Guys came walking on the dance floor, bumped into us," he said. At the time, and even today in some clubs depending on the band, audiences take great care in how they dress, like they would in church. Men might wear suits, and women wear decked-out dresses and sport sculptural hairdos. As with other dance styles, the dance floor can be a competitive space in which certain aggressive moves—bumping, pushing—explicitly signify disapproval.

Dance style is also a factor in the judgment of insiders. As a courtship space, the dancehall is also a space in which roles are quickly assigned depending on body language. The perception that white women are typically seeking affairs in zydeco clubs is common, and tight dancing (*danser collé*) is always interpreted as an obvious indication of availability. Lori, who began dancing in Louisiana in the early 1990s and befriended Michael before she moved in 2005, realized after a while that her red hair and shapely body were not the only reasons she was attracting seductive moves from black men:

> I was always being propositioned, but I didn't know why. Then I realized that I learned to dance in San Diego and in San Diego, people dance with no dance frame. You were like thigh-to-thigh, you were like going for . . . and I didn't have any dance frame. And now I'm realizing the people from down here don't dance like that. So the little foreigners coming in have that . . . no wonder they're thinking I want to go home with them or something, it was because I didn't have the dance frame. "You don't have a man? C'mon, I'll cook for ya. I got a horse." [laughter] . . .

Her technique of dancing close to her partner was perceived locally as an exhibition of sexual freedom and availability that was typically associated with visitors or tourists. She reports later learning a lesson about the rhetoric and tacit rules pertaining to infidelity:

> I'll never forget this. I was at Dog Hill [Lake Charles area] and I was probably a couple of years having come down here, and it was Labor Day weekend and Boozoo was still alive. I was dancing with this guy

and this other guy comes up and, "You know, man, it's been really nice seeing you, but I didn't see you." I was like, "What does that mean?" "Oh! It means he's with another woman, he's here at this club and he doesn't want his friend to say that he saw him. That's what it means." It's like, "Oh, he's with his wife tonight. You can't go ask him to dance tonight because he's with his wife." I'm like, "Oh-h-h- . . ." It's very common, you know, very common.

Such configurations were in fact so common that Missy, a close friend of Lori's, also learned her own lesson the hard way one evening at Hamilton's with a man she had often danced with:

I saw him. It was crowded, and I kind of made my way over to him. And around that time, more ladies would ask the men somewhat. Some people wouldn't, but I would. So I went up to him and I put my hand out to him, cause the music was so loud you we couldn't talk. And in a very fast moment, a lot happened. I could see out of the corner of my eye, this woman he was standing in front of her, she put her hand out to where I was, I was almost touching him, and she grabbed him, and gave me this really nasty look and pulled him on the dance floor, and he didn't hardly make eye contact with me at all. I was just really struck and really embarrassed. I talked to somebody, like "You wouldn't believe what just happened." I was struck that he blew me off and she obviously was with him, and it was not at all okay that I approached him, in any way. If looks could kill, one of those moments, you know. I kind of felt like I had to do something, so later I went up to her and said "I'm really sorry, I didn't realize that was your husband, or something. And I'm very sorry." And I mean, she just gave me a really nasty look and didn't say anything, like "You better pretty much get out of here." So I was like "Okay, I'm leaving!"

The courtship game is thus framed by specific rules in these clubs and applies to single white women who regularly dance, even if they are not necessarily seeking to flirt. Laura Jewett explored the construction of white femininity from the perspective of black masculinity as it circulates between prohibition and pleasure, and innocence and betrayal: "In conjunction with notions of white female interracial desire as dangerous, white Delilahs are perceived and treated with caution: they are trouble. . . .

[They] trouble patriarchal constructions of race and gender through their public embodiment of a semblance of interracial intimacy."[98]

A central social function of the region's dancehalls has always been as a courtship space. As a single woman in her fifties, Missy knows that for many white women of her age, the club scene is a favorite place to establish casual sexual relationships: "I have women friends who might want a sexual relationship, once a week, once a month, and they don't care if he's attached. In fact, they might want that. So there's a lot of the sexual aspect, the relationship aspect, because it's close dancing at night and there's drinking, and single people, some who are single for the night" [laughs].

These situations, however, are much more commonly associated with zydeco clubs and black men than white men. Courtship among white dancers, however, is a significant element of dancehalls and white men also show up with their mistresses. As a woman doing fieldwork and often single when I was in the field, I have experienced many situations where dancing in any club, regardless of men's skin color, almost systematically prompted a quiz within the first five minutes about where I was from, whether I was visiting, whether I was married, and where my husband was. Naïvely responding honestly at first, I eventually noticed that my wedding band—during the time that I wore one—was no deterrent to such attentions if I was unaccompanied by my husband or a male friend. My status as a non-resident may also have been an additional factor in this attraction by making the prospect of a temporary liaison more likely.

Whether married or not, many musicians have acquired a reputation as being flirtatious, and in some cases, their relationships have been open secrets. However, black men are typically described as disposed to flirt in a more overt manner, and black dancers and musicians more or less explicitly address and use this stereotype. In fact, one of the music camps that offers Cajun and zydeco classes outside of Louisiana invited a zydeco player one year and, according to rumor, his behavior with women would have discouraged the organizers from re-inviting zydeco bands in order to preserve the reputation of the camp (which includes teenagers). Of course, another justification—saving money—is offered for inviting bands that can play both zydeco and Cajun styles.

Peter Wade makes the point that sexuality is frequently present in representations of music and dance styles associated with creolization and *métissage*, which are etymologically tied to biological considerations. In his view, "ideas about 'race mixture,' since they imply sexual congress, are mediated by ideas about gender; the embodiment of music and especially dance has implications for the construction of sexual meaning about them."[99] Markers of "black music" are fueled by sexual fantasies, and as Radano argues, reexamining the modern representation of "hot" rhythms as dangerous, "the vast repetition of references to black music as a fever, drug, disease, and intoxicant indicate that the threat of black music related above all to fears of miscegenation, through which hot rhythm becomes a metonym of the black male body and, specifically, Negro semen or blood threat."[100]

Concealed within the narrative of cultural creolization, biological hybridization appears as a threat in the domain of music that is expressed through accusations of a dangerous strand of eroticism. Dancehalls, as spaces of seduction and promiscuity, are singled out for cultural sanction, and certain episodes have marked the French Louisiana collective memory. One example is Amédé Ardoin, who was severely beaten while playing in a dancehall for having accepted a handkerchief passed to him by a white woman so that he could wipe the sweat off of his face. Several different versions of the story are in circulation, however. Some musicians, including the zydeco artist Boozoo Chavis, are convinced that Ardoin would have avoided such a naïve transgression of the social boundaries, and believes he was poisoned by a white man. Denis McGee, Ardoin's musical partner, contends that Ardoin fell victim to a black man's jealousy, made more acute by the fact that he played with a white man. Regardless of which version reflects actual events, Ardoin never fully recovered from his injuries and died in a psychiatric hospital in 1941. Viewed as a symbol of musical creolization, Ardoin also embodies the risk represented by musical collaboration with a white man.

Later, during the 1950s, Creole swamp pop musicians also experienced very tense situations, and those who performed in Cajun clubs were forced to enter through the back door, were not permitted to leave the stage, and were escorted by police to go to the bar or the toilet.[101] An adventure with a white woman involving Huey "Cookie" Thierry, the leader of Cookie and the Cupcakes, provoked a threat from the local sheriff apparently so convincing that he moved to California in 1965. Lil Bob also had occasion to face the sanctions that were applied to blacks who played in Cajun clubs. Collaboration between Cajun and Creole swamp pop musicians did occur—Cajun musician Rod Bernard's national hit "This Should Go On Forever" was largely inspired by a King Carl composition—but King Carl's version received little attention and the two musicians never performed or recorded together. Dance very often crystallized, both locally and nationally, the phobias of segregationists, who felt that it encouraged "racial amalgamation" or miscegenetion.[102] Chep Morrison, the Mayor of New Orleans in the 1950s and 1960s, labored to improve the rights and working conditions of blacks while never questioning segregation. In 1960 he accused his opponent in the election for governor of having managed "an integrated nightclub" in Palm Springs.[103]

Women are perceived as vectors of transgression in this complex process. The widespread condemnation of the musician Horace Trahan referred to earlier also involves this same fear of biological mixing of the "races." Horace is not only perceived as embodying musical transgression by his musical choices, he also lived with a Creole partner for several years with whom he had a child born out of wedlock. Several years later, he married a black woman, cementing his role as the embodiment of both personal and professional transgression that awakened fears of racial mixing.

The potent sexual connotations of zydeco dance have been construed as expressions of primitivism that are threatening to morality, but this same quality has also been identified with more liberated sexuality seen as modern, particularly by the younger generation.[104] Within French Louisiana music, songs that evoke sexual themes, with varying degrees of explicitness, have met with considerable success. Boozoo Chavis was particularly well known for his songs with double entendre and some "colorful" late-night performances where his lyrics were more explicit.[105] Another example are the lyrics Clifton Chenier's rendition of "I'm a Hog For You Baby": "I'm a hog for you baby / I'm gonna root all around your door / I'm a keep on rooting around / Until you wanna love me some more / You can put a yoke around my neck / I'm a do like a snake / Cause I'm a hog for you." Then it turns into a French translation: "Mo cochon pour toi / Laisse mo ch'te dis / Mo j'va faire / Mo j'va faire comme un serpent / Mo cochon pour toi / J'va fouiller tout partout dans ton escalier / Mo fouillé, fouillé, fouillé . . ."

Among many other notable examples are "My Toot-Toot" from Rockin' Sidney Simien, among other musicians who had their own version of this sexual innuendo, as well expressed by John Delafose in the song "Ka-Wann"[106]: "Well now, you got Buckwheat talk about a Ya Ya / Then you got Boozoo talk about a Deacon Jones / Rockin' Sidney talk about a Toot Toot / But now myself, John Delafose, I want the best / Come on 'la ka-wann,' come on 'la ka-wann,' / 'Ka-wann' est la meilleure, come on 'la ka-wann.'"

Other examples of double entendre include "Tu Peux Cogner" (You Keep a Knockin'), "Keep Your Hands Off of It If It Don't Belong to You," and "Little Bitty Girl" by Lawrence Walker, and "Pine Grove Blues," which exists in a variety of versions, ranging from the racy original verse: "Hé negresse, ayou t'a été hier au soir / T'es arrivée à ce matin / Ta robe était tout déchirée / Ca m'fait de la peine pour moi" [Hey neg, where were you last night / You got back this morning / Your dress was all torn / It hurts my feelings] . . . to the Pine Leaf Boys' more salacious version: "Hé negresse, avec qui t'as couchée hier au soir? Arrivée à ce matin / Ta culotte était tout mouillée [your pants—or panties—were all wet]."

Young zydeco players today tend to sing lyrics that explicitly focus on sex, as exemplified by albums like *Thats Da Lick* (1994) and *Lick It Up* (1995, Maison de Soul) by Chris Ardoin, who goes by the nickname the Candyman, and appears surrounded by sexy girls on the album *V.I.P.* (2010). In Curley Taylor's two-CD set *Free your Mind* and *Close to Midnight* (2006), the second CD is dedicated to four steamy tracks: "You're the Only 1 4 Me," "Sexual Fantasy," "Gotta Have You," and "Lick It Stick It," with the following lyrics: "Your body's dripping wet, let's not waste no time / 'cause it's on my mind / I want to taste your body wine." Aware that such risqué lyrics contribute to strong CD sales, Taylor also situates them within the history of zydeco, referring to one of his founding fathers: "People might say 'That boy is singing some nasty stuff.' But if you listen to Boozoo singing about Deacon Jones, he's telling you what's going on. I guess because he was old and senile, people would just say he's crazy."[107]

Nicknamed the "Zydeco Sweetheart," Rosie Ledet, born in 1971, has been performing since 1994 throughout the Texas-Louisiana triangle, gradually extending the geographical range in which she tours. A skillful accordion player and one of the first women to carve herself a career in a male-dominated field, she has been expected to produce risqué songs ever since she released "Sweet Brown Sugar" and "I'm Gonna Take Care of Your Dog" (*Zesty Zydeco*, 1995), "Bring It On" (*It's A Groove Thing*, 2000) fits the same mold: "Baby bring it on, if you think you can / I'm starting to believe you're a two-minute man / If you want to get your point across / Stop putting' me on, if you can't get me off!"

Among male musicians, songs referring to women's posteriors have had enduring popularity. "That Butt Thing" propelled Horace Trahan into the top 40 of regional radio stations: "I don't like golf / I don't like swimmin' / I just like chasin' / Dem big butt women / We gonna do that butt thing / Kinda like that nookie thing / We gonna do that butt thing / And we gonna make that butt swing."

A single young man at the time, he was far from anticipating the craze that greeted the song, recalling that he was just "clowning around in the studio" when he recorded it. He reports: "The live performances of the song were met with lewd audience displays. Trahan, who was raised Catholic in a stable and loving household, had mixed feelings about performing the song live: "They had women at shows shaking their asses all up in my face."[108]

A member of the same generation, Travis Matte is far more comfortable with the overtly sexual appeal of his lyrics. After his hit "Vibrator" (*Zydeco Train*, 2005), he offered several posterior-oriented songs on the album *Booty Zydeco* (2006), including certain songs whose degree of explicitness excluded them from the radio, like "I'd Tap Dat," "Slap That Ass," and "Wam Bam Thank You Mam." "Let's get Nasty," "Bring Your Drunk Ass Home," "Hottie" pursued a similar theme. "Booty Call" (*Hip Hop Zyderock*, 2008) goes like this: "She's not my lady / She's just a girl on the side / She likes to rock my world y'all / She likes to take a little ride / She likes it in the kitchen y'all / She likes it up against the wall / But it's not like that y'all / It's just a bootie call . . ."

Travis is another musician who switched from "traditional" French and country music to zydeco (until he dropped the label in the band's name in 2008) and who obviously endured negative feedback as a consequence, particularly from his family, although this did not lead him to have conflicted feelings like it did Horace Trahan. In fact, Travis made a specialty of erotic songs for several years that have proven particularly successful with collegiate audiences and clubs. In his view, the controversy is of little importance:

> Like I told my mom, if Stephen King writes a murder movie, it doesn't make him a murderer. He knows there's an audience that likes murder movies and he's going to write a murder movie. Is he selling out because he writes a murder movie? I don't think so. I just think he's a good writer. And he knows what his audience wants to see and he creates what they want to buy and see. Same thing with me; I should be able to write any song I want. It doesn't make me a porn star because I wrote a song like that.

As a main product for sale, sex appears a legitimate topic and pushing it to the foreground seems like a strategic choice among others.

The implicit distinction between the racy eroticism of the architects of French Louisiana music and the pornographic prurience of young musicians that is more associated with a commercial approach echoes the distinction between the "folk" and "commercial" blues of the 1920s and is based on the very same arguments. Historian Marybeth Hamilton discusses the vexed relationship between sexuality and authenticity in how scholars have represented the construction of the blues tradition since the late 1950s.[109] The distinction between the salaciousness of "commercial blues" and the existential anguish of "authentic blues" echo the claim of certain French Louisiana music revivalists—and not only scholars—that sex, combined with urbanity, make the music into a commercialized perversion of folk purity, which is anchored in rurality, rawness, and emotions.

The mocking of such moralistic claims and the expression of inhibited sexuality in song lyrics is common to numerous rap singers across the country, a tendency that also appears to be increasingly frequent among zydeco players in Louisiana. As the case of Travis Matte illustrates, however, eroticism is not restricted to the imagery of blackness. In the Costeño regional identification on the Pacific coast of Colombia, for example, white women can embody the supposedly raunchy sexuality of black women through Costeño music. As Wade has asserted, "tropicality, sensuousness, and sexual openness can become part of everyone, not just the property of a region and much less a 'race.'" Pursuing this argument, I would argue that in Louisiana, the expression of a liberated sexuality that transgresses against constrictive religious norms can transcend the color line and appeals to the region's young people. Young white men can call for sensuality and hotness, although they initially do it under the zydeco label. In this sense, zydeco functions as a springboard for defying moral and sexual norms. Across regional borders, however, blackness encapsulates sensuality combined with novelty, sustaining the ongoing appeal of zydeco.

In Veracruz, the process of defying the moral and sexual norms of local high society entails negotiating among the different "roots" of *mestisaje* and expressing what French anthropologist Christian Rinaudo calls an "elective Africanity." The staging of physical traits, postures, gestures, and aesthetics that draw on representations of African heritage is a means of signifying one's empathy with *callejera* (street) culture that sustains an elective relationship with Africa and the black Americas. It is also a way of situating oneself within a class struggle that is expressed through signs attributed locally to the different "origins" of *mestisaje*. Dancing "like a black" is a means of differentiating oneself from "proper society" that simultaneously plays on social and ethno-racial registers.[110]

The perception of zydeco as more innovative than Cajun music, probably also encouraged by an emphasis on English lyrics, has contributed to its greater success outside Louisiana's borders. After the "Cajun craze" of the 1980s, when folk dancers discovered Louisiana French music and dance, zydeco began to become so popular in California during the 1990s that by the end of the decade, most "Cajun and zydeco" dances within the dance circuit in the Los Angeles area were almost exclusively devoted to zydeco dancing. Overall, zydeco bands have turned out the California crowds more than Cajun bands, with the exception of bands like Steve Riley and the Mamou Playboys, the Lost Bayou Ramblers, and the Pine Leaf Boys. Dancers tend to do their blend of Cajun and zydeco dancing, often just zydeco dancing regardless of what band is playing. As a dance teacher, Michael Seider spent a great deal of time with outsiders and, when I interviewed him in 2001, linked the success of zydeco to the novelty of the dance moves that dancers ardently asked him to teach them: "Zydeco has gone further away from tradition as far as dance moves are concerned. Much of the change in styling is coming from the younger kids who find new moves from hip hop. I know Creole people who've told me 'On Sundays, when we're all around the house, we'll dance and try out new moves that will look kind of cool.' There is that innovation." He continued:

> I see some styling around young Cajun dancers, too, and I've had to make up a name to describe the style. Some people call it the slide, I call it the Cajun cowboy jitterbug. It's because I heard a place in Lake Charles called Cowboys and the guys who dance there are really country and western dressed. Actually now I'm gonna teach it on the cruise in November. But since it's a zydeco cruise, I wrote them an email describing the style to the woman I teach with. But they renamed it the zydeco cowboy two-step, so people will not go "we don't wanna learn a Cajun dance!" So I don't know if there will be an interest in doing this variation of a Cajun jitterbug.

The greater appeal of zydeco among outsiders thus shapes the marketing of French Louisiana dance through the use of—and a preference for— the zydeco label as an implicit synonym for "black dance." Whereas fans of French Louisiana music from across the country tend to value zydeco as more sensual and modern, such representations contain an inherent ambivalence that becomes visible in specific contexts and time periods. In fact, the connection between dance skills and sexuality is closely related to stereotypes regarding class and race. Whether the question is exoticism or social marginality, "the Western view of others ceased being contemptuous only to become aesthetic," according to French anthropologist Marc Augé.[111] In this process, eroticism constitutes a shared reference: in the same way that exotic, black, ethnic, or popular dances are judged to be more sensual and spontaneous, marginal peoples are allegedly endowed with innate physical competencies and a sensuality that encourages the *encanaillement* (gutter-crawling) of middle-class audiences. In France in the late nineteenth century, delinquents were in fact explicitly associated with wildmen and called "Apaches."[112]

The ambivalence between attraction and repulsion is typical of how difference is represented via ethnic, racial and class-related stereotypes. Brasseaux notes that, in the English renditions of "Jole Blon" (Jolie Blonde), the Cajun woman is turned into "a sexually deviant, sometimes perverse seductress."[113] The expression of uninhibited debauchery and double entendre in these adaptations of the "Cajun anthem" represented the fear of rampant female sexuality, as much as the attraction for its innate and spontaneous character among females identified as ethnic (in this case Cajun), black, or from the working class. Instead, risqué songs of today come from within, claiming sexuality as modern, without necessarily tying it with blackness or with a specific ethnic identification. Rather than marginalizing French Louisiana culture, sexuality aligns it with the mainstream, across conservative stereotypes of the South, while maintaining a regional identification explored in the next chapter.

From Amédé Ardoin's death to the widespread and highly vocal disapproval of Horace Trahan, historical and contemporary examples illustrate the relationship between eroticism and the transgression of the color line. More broadly, it reveals the tension between attraction and repulsion as reflected in the exoticization and the marginalization of racial, ethnic, and class identifications. The ambivalent representation of blackness and the negotiation of ascribed stereotypes by black musicians and dancers themselves are situated within this logic.

Musical genealogy and the categories practiced in French Louisiana music are often legitimized by researchers via an omnipresent racial imagination grounded in an emphasis on African and European lineages that tend to obscure the multiplicity of factors at stake in the existence of different styles within French Louisiana music. The manner in which French Louisiana music is presented, conceived of, and experienced by those who practice and appreciate it within Louisiana society perfectly illustrates the flexibility of musical categories. Cajun, Creole, zydeco, French music, French blues, black and white music are at times viewed as distinct, at other times used in alternation, and at still others perceived as interlocked.

There is also a notable, permanent oscillation between the metaphor of cultural mixing, adaptation, and creativity on the one hand and the rhetoric of origins and naturalization of difference on the other. In this continual back-and-forth, the discourses and categorizations sometimes appear to enter into contradiction with reality, creating endless processes of adjustment and justification. The array of categories deployed by musicians and their situational use suggests that researchers need to be careful not to reify them, at the risk of ossifying ideas that social actors routinely use dialectically.

The Louisiana context illustrates that the logics used by regional actors should not be considered in conflict with each other but instead as inextricably bound together. While certain styles, techniques, and instruments are classified as black or white, Creole or Cajun, the narrative of creolization and the symbolic of mixture are only reinforced through this process, as Wade argues is the case for Costeño music of Colombia. "As is always the case with *mestisaje*, music is seen as a symbol of fusion, of the overcoming of the difference, but the representation of that symbol involves the continual reiteration of difference."[114] Wade demonstrates how the "symbolic of origins" is inseparable from a "symbolic of mixture." He does not restrict *mestizaje* to an ideology that masks strategies of exclusion, but interprets it more broadly as belonging to "a lived process" that is felt and interiorized, embodied by actors, and reveals the interactions between complementary processes.[115]

The polysemy of the term "black" in the context of music further complicates understanding of its meaning and of the multiple representations that it covers in Louisiana. As we have seen, the Creole style, although often linked to African origins, can be identified with "black music" but is also used to refer to a distinctive style that is independent of racial identification and is created and performed by either black or white musicians. By contrast, "black music" does have connotations as an urban phenomenon with respect to the "new" zydeco sound. In terms of dance, blackness evokes eroticism and novelty. The description of certain southwestern Louisiana music styles as "black" is thus invested with very different meanings that are not necessarily tied to a sense of belonging but serve as a resource according to different contexts, whether local, regional, national, or international. Musicians who self-identify—and are identified by the public—as performing black music are situated differently depending on the frame under consideration, with a range of consequences. For example, such musicians might achieve recognition at different levels, negotiate access to a specific music market, or be involved in conflicts of authenticity. In fact, as Radano contends, "authenticity is part and parcel of black music's constitution within American racial ideologies. As a matter of course, black music in the United States would not sound the way it does or carry authentic meaning had it not been for the idea of race. Nor, for that matter, would race have come to express what it has, had it not been for the idea and practice of black music." Southwest Louisiana demonstrates the multiple dimensions and complex ramifications of "black music," which functions less as a category of racial identification than as an operative category, a category of action that does not necessarily exclude other identifications.[116]

In fact, numerous studies bring to light the complex processes through which specific music styles are constructed as "black" at certain times and what political issues are at stake in this mechanism. Wade explains how in the 1940s, Costeño music was categorized and promoted as "black music" under the influence of the powerful Afrocubanism artistic movement. He outlined the significance of market-driven interest and of the record industry in this commodification process, qualified as the "musical tropicalization of Colombia."[117]

Other authors explained in different contexts the role played by cultural and academic institutions in the rediscovery of some regional repertoire as "black."[118] Such is the case of Mexico with *jarocha* music in Veracruz, *son de artesa* on Costa Chica, Coyolillo carnival, and even *zapateado* in Michoacan. As demonstrated by French anthropologist Odile Hoffman, the mobilization of a "black identity" in Mexico was largely stimulated by anthropologists through the development of "Afroamericanist" studies, particularly since the 1990s. She draws attention to the distinct logic of identification depending on the scale considered (interpersonal, collective, regional, national) but also emphasizes their mutual influence. While there is a space for black identification among Mexicans, it is combined with other identifications, and should be viewed as a positioning rather than a bounded and stable category. On a broader scale, in an article about the construction of an "Afro" cultural heritage, anthropologist Stefania Capone analyzes the mechanism of an international network of artists and choreographers, including key figures of the Harlem Renaissance like Katherine Dunham and others in Latin America.[119] She explores the impact of their exchanges in the creation of a "black" dance based on the stereotypical notion of the "black body," contributing to the emergence of national ballets in several newly independent African countries. "Dance, as the expression of an 'ancestral organic rhythm,' becomes the main locus of African memory and culture."[120] Cuba is yet another example: a classic textbook found in every art school focuses on "Cuban-ness" and "specificity" more than ancestral roots, while being combined with the assertion of a traditional heritage.[121] Son, rumba, danzón, and cha-cha are presented as emblematic of Cuban-ness. The author, folklorist, and musicologist Argeliers León founded the Institute of Ethnology in 1962 during the revolution.[122]

Although the nomenclature of music and the rhetorics of origin denote a powerful racial imagination, racial and ethnic identifications are by no means the only kind of identification and self-understanding used by Louisiana residents to position themselves or their music. Regional identification, with all its corollaries, is indeed a determining factor of connectedness within French Louisiana music.

4

Homegrown and Lowdown

A locally legendary bar and dancehall perched on a dock that projects from the levee over the waters of the Atchafalaya Basin, Whiskey River Landing is located near the small town of Henderson, Louisiana. The stage is backed by a large bay window that looks out over the vastness of the swamp, and on Sundays, gigs begin at four o'clock in the afternoon, allowing dancers to admire the sun setting behind the band. A gong resounds throughout the hall each time a waitress receives a tip. The wooden walls are plastered with articles and pictures of musicians and dancers, the bar is presided over by a trophy wild boar, and a stuffed deer, crawfish traps filled with empty beer cans, and a pirogue are suspended from the ceiling, along with tasseled lampshades. A sign in the toilet asks customers to flush only when necessary due to low water pressure. Bud Light and Coors Light advertising mirrors and neon lights provide additional embellishments, and a red neon light hangs suspended in front of the stage, while behind it, another neon light says simply "The Boyz." Flyers attached to the pillars supporting the ceiling of the long interior encourage customers: "Don't get thirsty, get a bucket of beer." A slightly elevated dance floor dominates the center in front of the stage, as customers sporting tight jeans and T-shirts form clusters or go out onto the outside porch for breaks.

Whiskey River's owner, Terry Angelle, who used to work in the oilfields, operates the dancehall as a family business, having bought it in the early 1980s and started a boat landing for fishing. He later organized swamp tours and now welcomes tour buses seven days a week. He eventually started dances that became weekly gigs in the late 1990s.

Beyond the distinctions between music styles based on racial and ethnic differences, a powerful attachment to rural heritage and a strong sense of place is a common element in the discourses and practices surrounding French Louisiana music. This chapter explores the meanings underlying the role played by rural heritage and the dichotomy between urban and rural contexts, revealing how these ubiquitous oppositions are reconciled among contemporary zydeco musicians. Hip hop influences become compatible with rural roots, respectability, and localism, making zydeco at once urban and rural and redefining it as "black music" that appeals to both blacks and whites. The ramifications of the rural legacy are numerous in terms of how certain characteristics are applied to the entire repertoire and throughout a music-making process that characterizes the music as simple, plain, and unpolished. These attributes are infused into technical descriptions as well as how the music is practiced, lived, staged live, displayed on CDs, taught, and recorded. The chapter will conclude by reviewing the ways in which French Louisiana music is rooted in a fundamental attachment to specific places and more specifically to south Louisiana, and shared by every Louisiana musician. I argue that the deployment of the survival theme and this sense of place are important responses to stigmatization, marginalization, and poverty.

Loyalty to Rural Heritage

Boozoo was a brilliant, brilliant man . . . He was so real. When you'd see him with his accordion, you could see his horse, you could see his chicken . . .
DENNIS PAUL WILLIAMS, MARCH 23, 2003, ST. MARTINVILLE

The ways in which French Louisiana music is depicted systematically invokes rural life. In fact, Dennis Paul Williams, who grew up in the town of St. Martinville, ties the success of zydeco pioneers such as Clifton Chenier and Boozoo Chavis to their ability to reflect and represent the agricultural lifestyle, thereby establishing an identification between musicians and their audiences. Says Williams: "People could relate to what Clifton was singing about, about cane cutting, potatoes diggers, people did that kind of work. . . . They could relate to that. Even as a boy, I picked okra, pepper, pecans. So he wasn't singing something about the big city, it was about the country."

French Louisiana music appears to achieve total "authenticity" when it addresses rurality and osmosis with nature that are conveyed through lyrics and musicians' own experience of rural life. This aesthetic of authenticity reflects the efforts of record companies and cultural middlemen during the 1920s to find the most appealing incarnation of "hillbilly" music by constructing "real" white trash performers, even though many of them were urban tradesmen.[1] In *Hot Pepper* (1973), Les Blank captured this rural imagery by using bucolic scenes that alternate with musical performances. The film begins in a dancehall, with Clifton Chenier playing "I'm Going Back to Grand Mamou" while dancers waltz. A series of images of the countryside follow, including a young girl walking on a railroad track, an old man gardening and attending its chickens, workers on railroad tracks, a man filling his wheelbarrow with stacks of wood, and Clifton on the road in his trailer. As we hear Clifton's reflections on life and watch him perform, the camera pauses to take in a sunset, birds gliding in the sky, cows grazing, and green oak trees. More than a decade later, Blank's *J'ai été au bal* (1989) follows a similar pattern. The setting chosen for Michael Doucet's lines is a pirogue in the swamps, and Marc Savoy is filmed playing outside under an oak tree surrounded by sheep, then on the porch with his wife Ann, singing harmony while the laundry is drying in the breeze.

Music producer Chris Strachwitz embraced this representation in his anthology *Louisiana Cajun Music*. While suggesting the possibility that the song "Gue Gue Solingail" was recorded by Dr. James Roach in 1925 for the OKeh label therefore preceding Falcon's first recording of Cajun music in 1928, Strachwitz also argues that Roach "could not be considered an authentic Cajun performer."[2] The authentic Cajun performer was above all considered a folk artist with little formal education. This definition perfectly fit "the professionalized music with an ethos of non-professionalism" that arose with the folksong revival in the 1940s.[3] Fueled by this ideology, popular folksingers of the 1960s embraced the public image of non-professionals, pre-industrial artisans, and minstrels.

In fact, one of the most popular rock bands of the sixties, Creedence Clearwater Revival, reflected the anti-establishment interest in south Louisiana culture.[4] The group, whose members hailed from the counterculture's epicenter, San Francisco, actively fostered a "Cajun" image, promoting themselves as rustic good old boys from Louisiana despite the fact that none of them had ever been there.

Closeness to nature, rural roots, a work-hard-play-hard ethic, and the working-class background of Louisiana music pioneers continue to this day to constitute the imagery of Louisiana "folk" (now called "roots") music. This image has attracted out-of-state musicians to move to Louisiana and pursue their musical careers. Multi-instrumentalist Dirk Powell, raised in Ohio, describes the similar perceptions of Appalachian old-time music and French Louisiana music while explaining his own musical roots. Deeply influenced by his grandfather, who remained in Ashland, Kentucky, after exploring a variety of music styles, Dirk immersed himself in old-time music out of a desire to "get back to a more working-man approach to life.... Mountain music and Cajun music share a similar spirit and functions,"[5] he noted, endowing his itinerary with a coherence that brought him to southern Louisiana in 1992.

The vivacity of this image strongly shapes outsiders' expectations. As a dance teacher in one of the Cajun music camps in the country, Don Brasseaux was once describing elements of his background to his students. Don grew up in the downtown area of a local town, where his dad was a shoe repairman. His dance partner at the camp had grown up on a cotton farm. "And the question came up, was I a Cajun? I said 'You want me to take offense?'" he recalls, still in shock.

Several music clubs exploit the rural aesthetic by turning fishing, trapping, and hunting tools into ornaments that hang from the ceiling and the walls or above the bar. Whiskey River Landing is particularly devoted to aestheticizing wildlife and the woodsman's lifestyle. The variety of approaches to decoration one encounters in the region's dancehalls reveals a degree of diversity that crosses the boundaries of country life and scenery, however: in the same town, the club Atchafalaya combines a mural depicting the local swampy environment with a bar evoking the 1970s and silver-specked red leather stools and large hanging light fixtures. The honky-tonk feeling of Lafayette's Blue Moon Saloon and Lakeview Park in the Eunice area contrasts with the more urban-looking Lafayette clubs such as Grant Street and Outlaws, and all offer a wide range of music styles. By contrast with these clubs that embrace the variety of "roots" music, others with more of a lounge feeling are strictly dedicated to Cajun music, like La Poussière in Henderson. There are only a few zydeco clubs functioning today, and bands are not even scheduled every week. Hamilton's, which was in the outskirts of Lafayette, no longer exists; Richard's in Lawtell and Slim Y-Kiki all date back from the mid 1940s, and are unimposing buildings located along Louisiana highways; whereas only one zydeco club, El Sid O's, is located in Lafayette, with more of a lounge feeling. The commonality of dancehalls, however, rests in their unpolished interior. At El Sid O's, vinyl 45s attached to strings are suspended from the ceilings, while musical instruments line the walls. The floors are linoleum, and strings of lights run along the bar, with music posters and Bud light ads (on mirrors or neon bar signs) decorating the wall behind it. At Hamilton's, the

4.1. CD, Boozoo Chavis, *Zydeco Trail Ride*. Maison de Soul CD 1034-2, 1990. Source: © Flat Town Music Co., Ville Platte, LA. www.FlatTownMusic.com.

decoration was similar with posters of musicians, and for Easter, Mardi Gras, and Christmas, additional ornaments included small paper bunnies and Christmas lights.

Clothing is evidently essential in the deployment of aesthetics and reflects the diversity of French Louisiana music imagery across styles.[6] The majority of local musicians favor a casual and laidback look, from T-shirts to long-sleeve shirts, sometimes one under the other, jeans, and caps or cowboy hats for men (such as Cedric Watson, Geno Delafose, Keith Frank or D. L. Menard), sometimes a beret. Depending on the context and the audience (club, festival, workshop), casual outfits give way to dressier clothes. Cedric seems to have favored these past few years a more

4.2. Clifton C. Chenier, Downtown Alive, Lafayette, 1981. Courtesy of Jacques Henry.

Caribbean look, exchanging his occasional cowboy hat or cap with a straw hat and bright-colored shirts. In the early 2000s, dancers too were neatly but casually dressed in jeans and cowboy boots. Women sometimes wore skirts, but more often wore ornamented jeans, occasionally pocketless on the butt featuring their posterior, along with careful attention to accessories like shoes, belts, makeup, and jewelry. Occasionally at El Sid O's, it was also possible to see dressy outfits, long frilly dresses, and shimmering tops.

These aesthetic choices are often reinforced on CDs, which give the opportunity to emphasize a specific aesthetic on the cover and in the booklet. Rural sceneries are still very common, whether through natural or architectural landscape (sunset, green oak trees, forests, swamps, barns, farms, fields), agricultural tools or the evocation of farm life. The Magnolia Sisters have developed a distinctive retro and feminine look, with flowery dresses

4.3. Buckwheat Zydeco. Source: Press kit, photograph courtesy of Joseph A. Rosen.

and opaque stockings evoking women's attire of the 1930s, on stage and in sepia photographs. Since the renewal of the Cajun music scene in the mid-2000s, however, there has been a trend toward a more personalized aesthetic, with the use of contemporary artwork, design, and band photographs more likely to display rock aesthetics than rural imagery.

Within the zydeco scene, some players favor hip hop aesthetics with sunglasses, baggy blue jeans, NBA jerseys over T-shirts, baseball caps, or doo-rags. The contrast with zydeco pioneers is stunning, although the older aesthetic was itself rather eclectic between the bluesman appearance of C.C. Chenier or Buckwheat Zydeco (dark glasses, jewelry, accessories, shiny accordion) and the western wear and cowboy hat of Boozoo Chavis. Overall, the aesthetics found today among musicians and in music clubs show a tendency for a casual, laid-back style, while negotiating different figures depending on the context (CD, web site, gigs).

The rural motif is further emphasized by the frequent reference to Cajuns' and Creoles' common hardship of sharecropping in the late 1920s, the era of the first recordings. This shared economic background led to competition but also to a common emphasis on hard work. Raised in the country in a family of *récolteurs* (farmers who owned their land), Don Cravins Sr.—a long-term Creole politician who served as state senator, ran a music and TV show on zydeco, and is presently the mayor of Opelousas—explained when I met him in 2001:

> There is a common bond, and almost an understanding. It could almost be described as a kinship that exists between Cajuns and Creoles. Because of the struggles that both groups endured. They lived very similar. There was a commonality in the way of life too, it was a struggling way of life. Our neighbors were white. If they needed help harvesting their crop or working their field we helped them and they helped us. So it was a relationship that went way beyond race, it was really a struggle to survive.

The Ardoin-McGee duo therefore happened to symbolize both a common musical heritage and a shared social status, class being presented as a source of cohesiveness beyond distinct racial identifications and tensions throughout the twentieth century.

Concealing these tensions, the romanticism of common hardship that emanates from Cajuns and Creoles alike is coupled with the enduring stereotype of French Louisiana population as living off of the land, an image that transcends time. Jacques Henry and Carl Bankston show the evolution throughout the twentieth century from an agricultural economy where Louisianans were mostly farmers and fishermen to a new economy in which they became service and office workers. The oil and gas industry has established itself as the core of Louisiana's economy throughout the twentieth century. The authors argue that the children and grandchildren of hunters, trappers, fishermen, and small farmers largely moved into working-class jobs that led to the association of Cajun ethnicity with blue-collar occupations.[7]

Fueled by the ongoing practice of hunting and fishing as a leisure activity, the longevity of French Louisiana's agricultural depiction reveals its strength in the collective memory of Southwestern Louisianans, and more broadly the image of an unchanging rural South. The shift toward a new mental world structured by industrialization, mass consumption and materialism has not altered a musical ethos based on "grinding poverty and agrarian, working-class lifestyle."[8]

Hip-Hop Cowboys

> Rap has nothing to do with my culture at all. I'm African-American, but rap, how do I say . . . rap ain't my culture. 'Cause I'm not from the ghetto, I'm not from the hood, I'm not a gangster. . . . And to me, that's not my culture, I'm from the country. I'm more into roots things. Mixing it with a little R&B and a little blues and stuff like that, that's good. Just leave the rap out of it.
> CEDRIC WATSON, LAFAYETTE, JANUARY 3, 2005

Respectability is a key notion in shaping musical tastes, involving interrelated factors such as the urban/rural division, education, family background, racial or ethnic identification, and morality. Even today in the contemporary Cajun and zydeco music scene, the claim of a shared social status is associated with shared values, which are expressed through perceptions of behavior and appearance. Both Cajuns and Creoles value musicians' politeness and grooming. Proper dress is a matter of pride for musicians, although this does not suggest high fashion but simply attention—jeans and clean, well-pressed, buttoned shirts. The amount of attention paid to the public is also particularly appreciated, and regardless of one's celebrity, remaining accessible and showing consideration for fans, smiling and offering greetings with neither arrogance nor weariness that belong to a culture of affability between musicians and their public. Hospitality, generosity, accessibility, and thoughtfulness toward the audience are all part of a requirement to "present well" and to "take care of your people" [*soigner son monde*], and forge the notion of respectability.

Emblematic of respectable values, the figure of the hard-working, self-made, self-sufficient Creole cowboy lies at the core of how zydeco is represented, an ethic epitomized by Boozoo Chavis. After he recorded zydeco's first popular single "Paper in My Shoe" in 1954, feeling despoiled by the music industry, he dedicated himself to training racehorses. Following in his footsteps, Geno Delafose pursues a similar path at his Double D Ranch in Duralde, near Eunice, where he raises cattle and horses like his late father John Delafose, himself an important figure of "traditional" zydeco. Geno often poses with a Stetson hat, with his horses in the background. His album *Le Cowboy Creole* (2007) fully exploits this image both through its title and its snapshot mosaic of horses, sunsets in the field, and Geno happily riding a tractor. As a French-speaking cowboy, Geno Delafose embodies the moral virtues associated with the notion of respectability.[9]

"People don't go to dance if the performers think they're too much. If you don't have time for the people you just down your own self," maintained John Delafose.[10] True to his father's advice, Geno is extremely attentive to his audience. His diligence is such that the photo gallery on his website does not provide pictures of him but instead, a series of snapshots of his fans dancing and enjoying themselves.

His popularity and reception among Cajuns illustrates the importance of respectability in justifying musical taste. When the owner of Whiskey River Landing explained his decision of hiring him as a regular band and the first Creole musician to play in his dancehall in 2001, he argued:

> I've had a lot of zydeco band, Keith Frank, I'm not stepping on nobody's toes. But I don't want them to play. Ca amène un [it brings a] different crowd. Ca amène [it brings] . . . parce que j'ai vu ça [because I saw that] they don't bring a trouble crowd, but they bring a loose crowd. Geno, le plus gros following que lui a c'est le monde blanc. Je veux pas faire quelquechose qui va casser mon business. [Geno, the biggest following that he got is white people. I don't want to do something that's going to break my business.] As a businessman first, I've gotta keep my business, so I've gotta watch what I do. Geno est respectable lui-même. Il te traite comme t'es supposé d'être traité. [Geno is respectable himself. He treats you like you're supposed to be treated.] He'll talk to you politely, he's clean, he ain't into no shit. He works hard at what he does. We go eat at his house, they call us, they can come sleep here if they want to, that's how much I like those people."[11]

Underlying the justification of the owner's music choices is the stereotype of black patrons as troublemakers who are construed as potentially dangerous to a white clientele. Respectability functions here as a trope for racial discrimination.

Respectability also suggests implicit rules between black and white dancers, especially for the generation born in the 1950s and 1960s. When accompanied by a male dance partner, a white female will rarely be asked for a dance. If she is accompanied, a prospective dance partner will acknowledge the presence of her partner and ask permission to dance with

4.4. Geno Delafose shaking hands with a fan. Balfa Camp, Chicot State Park, April 20, 2008.

her. Conversely, when Cajuns from that generation are at a zydeco club, they make a point of first sitting and watching unobtrusively, sometimes even asking permission if they focus on a specific couple, for fear of being found offensive. Each party establishes tacit rules, and inappropriate behavior can provoke penalties expressed through body language, as illustrated in the previous chapter in the example of incongruous clothing. Respectability is thus involved in interactions between black and white dancers, in a link to past memories of segregated clubs.

The importance of being respectable harks back to the heritage of Booker T. Washington and his actions to urge blacks to retain their dignity and raise themselves socially to the rank of whites, particularly by educating themselves. Historian Susan Smith discusses the impact of these views in the arts in the context of the policies of Motown, a black record label that invested heavily in efforts to tailor the public image of its artists, including their diction and appearance, according to its criteria of respectability.[12]

Jazz trumpet player Arnold DePass Jr. remembers the importance of "proper" behavior when he performed in the 1950s, first in the 63rd Army Band then in different bands in New Orleans and Opelousas. "Oh yeah,

4.5. The Hackberry Ramblers, from the era of the band's first recordings for RCA-Bluebird (circa 1935). L–R: Floyd Rainwater, Luderin Darbone, Lonnie Rainwater, and Lennis Sonnier. Photograph copyright Luderin Darbone, all rights reserved, used by permission, courtesy of Ben Sandmel (www.hackberryramblers.com).

you had to get it right. . . . This bandleader would say: I don't mind you guys drinking, you can drink if you play in my band, but don't never look like you're drunk! [Laughter.] You had to be a gentleman. After the job was over, the guy would look up the bandstand and see if you let any trash, 'cause they didn't wanna hear "Oh! that band we had was tacky, look at the trash they left on the floor!"[13]

As an enactment of whiteness, respectability led the way to emphasize appearance and behavior among early century Cajun swing musicians as well. Ryan Brasseaux notes that Cajuns distanced themselves from working-class stereotypes by underscoring their affiliation to the region's booming industrial sector. Most importantly, economic independence was considered a way to obtain the benefits available to the upper classes. Like Tejano musicians who performed in Mexican-American *orquestas*, Cajun swingers and hillbilly radio bands cultivated a class consciousness to escape "off-whiteness" (otherness) and subordination.[14] Historian David R. Roediger applies the notion of "in-betweenness" to working-class white immigrants in the late nineteenth and early twentieth century such as Irish, Italian, Hungarian, or Jewish who historically were regarded as nonwhites and situated in "in-between racial spaces."[15] "The processes of 'becoming white' and 'becoming American' were intertwined at every turn," he argues, "these immigrants gradually achieving whiteness and becoming 'white ethnics.'"[16]

Even today, respectability functions as a way for Creoles to achieve whiteness. Hence the expression still heard by Nick Spitzer during his fieldwork in 1986: "A rich Negro is a Mulatto, a poor Mulatto is a Negro."[17] With hard work, poorer, darker-skinned Creoles could ascend the social ladder to join lighter-skinned landowners. In fact, stereotypes went both ways even during the mid-1980s, as Spitzer attests: "Rural Creole culture and music was stigmatized as 'old time' and 'French' by urban blacks and black Creoles while the urban Creole culture was viewed as 'too black' by country Creoles and Cajuns." Even today, musical choices and behaviors reflect the ways in which musicians position themselves on the social ladder and which racial or ethnic identification best suits their career strategies and target market. These choices are not necessarily clear-cut, however. Whereas Geno Delafose caters to a white audience fond of French Louisiana music and "roots music," Keith Frank hedges his bets, targeting both young African Americans and "roots" fans. As seen in chapter 2, Delafose and Frank distinguish themselves from performers of the "new" zydeco sound aspiring first and foremost to an African American youth following.

Negative stereotypes are embedded in racial and ethnic identifications (black, white, African American, Creoles, Cajuns) that are entangled with respectability and the rural-urban dichotomy. The insistence on respectability contrasts with urban life, a context that is associated with a lack of respectability, including laziness and begging. The figure of the "urban bad guy" and the "hippie" are frequently cited as opposed to order and respectability, a rural-urban divide that rural jazzmen also emphasized in the early twentieth century. Trumpet player Hypolite Charles, who was born in 1891 in the small community of Parks east of Lafayette, was the son of a schoolteacher who played horn in the Parks Brass Band. At age seventeen, he went to New Orleans and played in the Silver Leaf Band before joining "Papa" Celestin's Tuxedo Brass and the Maple Leaf Band. Charles played for high society events like afternoon teas and dinner dances at the country club. Interestingly, he had also played in the New Iberia red light district, but a whipping from his father persuaded him to desist. He further established his reputation at the Francs Amis and Jeunes Amis dancehalls where, as he related in an interview, the dancers were "well-behaved," in contrast with other venues where people were not "decent."[13]

"You got to look clean. I don't like them damn hippies, with a scarf on their head, an earbob in their ear, their hair flyin' in their face. Them hippies make me mad. Me, I wear a cowboy hat everywhere I go. I got that from riding horses, training quarter horses and thoroughbreds," Boozoo Chavis declared proudly as an affirmation of his own respectability.[18] This insistence regarding the dubious character of the figure of the hippie, inherited from the 1960s and from negative views of the counterculture among most southern Louisianans, has contributed to the extension of meanings belonging to that specific political context to the broader, more recent negative image of the urban bad guy and more specifically of rap musicians.[19]

The country-city opposition provides the basis for negative judgments of "nouveau" zydeco. Although performers often claim rural heritage or origins, their detractors contest their eclectic influences, including rap, funk, soul, reggae, R&B, and rock. Objections are primarily associated with the hip hop scene while ignoring the music's diverse inflections and disparate influences. Moreover, the negative stereotypes associated with rap tend to remain vague and implicitly revolve around violence.

The late Joseph "Zydeco Jo" Mouton, who played in a plain zydeco style and often referred in his songs to his rural upbringing, made explicit reference to this association:

> Zydeco music doesn't make any trouble, it's not music with bad messages like rap music. I respect all musics, but I like zydeco and blues. It shows people that blacks are not animals, and that they can have a good time, they're going to respect you. So I'm glad it's here.
>
> [La musique zydeco ça fait pas de tracas, c'est pas la musique des mauvais messages, comme la musique des rap. Je respecte tous les autres musiques, mais j'aime le zarico et le blues. Ca fait le monde voir que le monde noir c'est pas du bétail et tu peux gain du bon temps, ça va te respecter. Ca fait je suis content c'est là.][20]

This representation is all the more surprising considering that, to my knowledge, zydeco lyrics do not include expressions of violence or references to racism, social degradation, or discrimination against black youth. The recent rise of the New Orleans brass band scene is the target of similar accusations among musicians themselves. Young trombone player Glen David Andrews played with the New Birth Brass Band, but after Katrina, he devoted himself to his band the Lazy Six and became a regular attraction at Preservation Hall, the sacred ground of "traditional" jazz: "I just don't want to be part of hip hop. I don't like all that 'nigga,' 'bitch' bullshit. It's violence. It's not music. It's one chord over the same groove over and over. No offense to the Hot 8. No offense to the Soul Rebels. I like those people as people. I don't want to listen to that," he told music writer John Swenson.[21]

In zydeco, however, most uncensored language has more erotic overtones that it does politically conscious lyrics or theme that contain commentaries on social or personal conditions. "Sweat" by Chris Ardoin is one illustration among many others: "Man I'm sweating / I'm sweating for sure / Since I first saw you / With that NewStep zydeco / . . . Meet me in my room / Meet me in the shower / Wet it's going down / And when we get to sweating / You know it's going down / But with the candyman / It's guaranteed to go down / I wanna make you sweat / Make you sweat / Get you all soakin' wet / I'm gonna make you sweat."[22]

In "Stronger," J. Paul seems to give primacy to love and courtship in order to dissociate himself from drug addiction. "My love is stronger than any drugs / I just can't get enough," goes the chorus. Keith Frank, whose musical choices are expressed through an eclectic mix of songs, some in the most innovative zydeco style and others in a plain Creole style, cuts short criticism and dismissive comments in his song "Haterz" on his double album *Loved. Feared. Respected*. Chorus: "Now raise one hand up / You know you got haterz / But raise both hands up / If you know that you're greater / They don't understand / What it takes to be a music man / If you gotta lot of haterz / You must be doing something right / I got big dog status / I expect dem to hate / If you shine like I shine / I know y'all can relate / I'm not tryin' to brag / I just got it like that / Even when I'm bragging it's a matter of fact / There is nothing I can do / If I was you I'd hate me too."[23]

For those who claim a "new" zydeco sound, their style draws on the commercial successes of rap and other music styles by promoting a "pop" form deemed more acceptable by record companies, radios, as well as by local audiences. In fact, zydeco echoes what is called "pop" rap, that is distinguished from "hardcore" rap whose lyrics invoke themes of social consciousness and racial pride.[24] New Orleans bounce sparks similar reactions to those inspired by "new" zydeco. Bounce, a dance-oriented sub-genre of rap whose lyrics emphasize enjoyment rather than political resistance, has attracted criticism for its allegedly regressive, simplistic nature, expressed through the repetitive use of particular beats or samples, sexually explicit lyrics, and other factors.[25] Sean Ardoin, Chris's brother and music partner early in his career, pushed this dissociation from rap's negative representations even further; since 2005 he has labeled his music "Christian zydeco" and his band Sean Ardoin + R.O.G.K. (Reflections Of God's Kingdom). "Sean believes his music will cross over all denominational, racial, and economic lines," spanning racial identifications and class struggle, and instead placing the emphasis on worship and Christian love. In fact, deference to "our Lord," "Savior," and "God" is very common among zydeco players regardless of their style, and many make a point to express their Catholic faith, for example through acknowledgments on CDs, sometimes from every single musician of the band, or by wearing a cross.[26]

Detractors of zydeco usually deploy musical arguments to signal what are considered evidence of obvious degeneration in lyrics and melody lines, considered to be scarce and minimal, if not entirely absent. Incidentally, rap songs tend to be loquacious and are usually associated with life narratives from the ghetto rather than with badly written and meaningless lyrics. Whether it involves New Orleans brass bands or zydeco, the stigmatization of these music styles often seems based on their allegedly simplistic musical structure or lyrics, supposedly objective criteria that are cited to justify distaste.

Regardless of its regional success among African American and white youth, the "new" zydeco sound continues to be stigmatized in Louisiana and viewed as at best a reality to be accepted or a symptom of a decline in authenticity relative to its "traditional" counterpart. Clifton Chenier's disciples also express contempt for these newer styles, including his son C.J. Chenier: "Today, you play a riff, you have a steady beat, you have a bass line, you have a rhythm, and you play a riff, an then you holler some stuff; [laughs] . . . To me, that's not what's supposed to carry zydeco . . . I'm not a one-dimensional player, man . . ."[27]

Folklorist and music expert Nick Spitzer objects to these allegations of impoverished form and content: "If you apply the same argument about lyrical simplicity to the relationship of country music—which is a lyric-focused form—with rock and roll—which is a rhythm-oriented form—you end up denying the undeniable, which is rock's power to move people."[28]

Even when not subjected to overt criticism, "rap influence" is dismissed based on its origins among poor inhabitants of the urban ghetto, as explicitly opposed to a rural context. For Cedric Watson, as formulated in the epigraph, which dates back to the beginning of his career when he was in his early twenties, rap simply does not belong to his experience. A few years later, when he joined the Pine Leaf Boys, he further developed his earlier views in an interview for one of the main regional music journal, *Offbeat*:

> The stereotype of black youth is all they care about is rap, but I felt that Cajun and Creole were bringing me closer to Africa than hip-hop ever could. Think about it: Creole music comes from a time when Africans first came to North America, so it brings you closer to the source. If you listen to Creole music, especially the old la-la music with the wooden rubboard, it has that same African beat like calypso or ska. If you turn on the radio now, you won't hear anything that has the same syncopated, groovy, African, rootsy feel.[29]

As the only black fiddler in French Louisiana music who is celebrated by fellow musicians, Cedric seeks to construct his singularity via a quest of Africanness, which he opposes to what he considers the more well-trod paths pursued by young, urban American blacks.

This rural-urban opposition is also reflected in the peripheral role attributed to the urban centers of the state of Texas. Southwestern Louisiana is presented in the local tourist literature, official narratives, and music publications as the cradle of French Louisiana music. This emphasis has given rise to powerful regional mythology that neglects the historic role and current vibrancy of east Texas, more specifically its industrial urban centers, including Houston, Beaumont, and Port Arthur, an area referred to as "Louisiana Lapland," revealing its image as an extension of southwestern Louisiana. The mobility of musicians between the country and the city was important in the early twentieth century, along with tourism, serving to establish and maintain links between rural Louisiana and New Orleans as well as other large southern cities. In 1929 the *Daily Advertiser* promoted railroad excursions to Lake Charles for $1.50, Beaumont, Texas, for $2.70, or Port Arthur for $3.20.[30] Indeed Texas played a major role in the diffusion of French Louisiana music. Iry Lejeune's first recording was on the Texas-based Opera label, and Huey Meaux, originally from Kaplan, Louisiana, became one of the most successful and significant record producers in Texas history. He eventually owned several labels, including Sugar Hill Recording Studios, and he became a key figure during the 1960s for two generations of Gulf Coast musicians from Baton Rouge to San Antonio.[31] It is also worth recalling that Harry Choates, originally from Rayne, Louisiana, grew up in Port Arthur, Texas, and recorded "Jolie Blonde" for the Houston-based Gold Star label.

The development of zydeco music is inseparable from the Creole migration to work in the oil industry and industrial centers of southeastern Texas, beginning between the wars but accelerating during World War II. In fact, during the 1920s, Houston's 5th Ward had the highest concentration of Creoles in the city and became known as "Frenchtown." It seems that zydeco thus emerged in Texas as a full-fledged style that combined Louisiana French music with rhythm and blues. Zydeco blossomed in the urban environment, becoming integrated into a commercial network that provided the traction necessary for its subsequent promotion nationally.[32]

The first appearance of the term in reference to a music sound includes many layers, but all writings concur on the significant role of Houston musicians in its popularization. Minton and Tisserand mention that the term was first used in its written form in commercial recordings of non Creole blacks from Houston, starting with the blues player Lightnin' Hopkins in "Zolo Go," recorded between 1947 and 1950. Hopkins, who was cousin by marriage to Chenier, mimics the sound of the accordion with an organ, and introduces the song with the following line: "I'm going to zolo go a little while for you folks. You know, the young and old likes that."[33] Ben Sandmel attributes the actual popularization of the term to Texas-based blues and R&B artists Clarence Garlow in his 1950 hit "Bon Ton Roula."[34] The genealogy of the term is telling about the various actors and processes involved in the creation of music labels when considering that the spelling "zydeco" was first used by cultural historian and record producer Mack McCormick in the album notes of *A Treasury of Field Recordings* dedicated to showcase the "folk" music of Houston. McCormick said that he decided himself on this spelling after studying the different spellings in existence, all different and unsatisfying to his ear. The success of the term was beyond all his expectations. McCormick reports that he was horrified when the word that he intended to apply to the music of Frenchtown in Houston crossed the Louisiana border through the efforts of the Louisiana tourist commission.[35]

Interestingly, the role of Texas still is controversial among researchers working on zydeco.[36] Contrary to the narrative that ascribes Louisiana origins to zydeco that then spread to Texas, John Minton and Roger Wood maintain that its development in Louisiana was a result of Creoles' return to their native state or recordings while they were touring in the state. Wood, in the first book-length research report on the subject, *Texas*

Zydeco, argues that innovations in terms of instrumentation as well as the recording history, leading figures, and stylistic evolution of zydeco all initially took place in Texas. Through the 1950s and well into the 1970s, Clifton Chenier resided in Houston once establishing himself as a full-time musician after initially working at a refinery in Port Arthur. By 1955 he was a regular in Houston's most prominent music venues for black music, including the Eldorado Ballroom, which was owned and operated by African Americans. He toured both in what Wood names the "zydeco corridor" and in the nation's larger cities. Many of his classics were recorded at Houston studios such as Gold Star. A further indication of Chenier's success and recognition was his recruitment by the Houston chapter of the American Federation of Musicians.[37] This circular mobility between east Texas and Louisiana continues, and some of the major figures on the current zydeco scene were born, grew up or lived in Texas, including C.J. Chenier, Brian Terry, Step Rideau, J. Paul, Corey Ledet, and Cedric Watson.

The tradition of zydeco trail rides and their tremendous following have clearly been instrumental in shaping the association of zydeco music and rurality. Trail rides began as family affairs before drawing hundreds of people belonging to fifty riding clubs in Louisiana and east Texas. Trail rides and campouts, as they are advertised, are held on weekends from November to May and either begin or end at a church, community center, or farm. These community events gather hundreds of RVs, horse trailers, and horse-drawn wagons loaded with coolers and people equipped to party all day in a huge horse parade, while the sounds of zydeco emanate from speakers and are orchestrated by popular DJs. Before the actual rides, campsites fill with the fragrance of ribs, gumbo, cracklins, and backbone stew simmering over low fires. At the end of the day, they give way to live music and dancing. The popular Step-N-Strut held in St. Landry Parish in early November has evolved into a several-day music festival that attracts thousands of people, although it is not well known outside the circuit. In fact, web sites are often not current, and the most reliable advertisements are fliers passed around at trail rides. Southern journalist Shaila Dewan, who participated in her first trail ride in 2006, describes the change that she observed five years later among riders participating in a trail ride over Labor Day weekend in Beaver, Louisiana. She noted changes that parallel the stylistic evolution of both the music and its audience:

> At my first ride, I had noticed a lot of old-timers—"originals," they call themselves—wearing . . . pressed Western shirts and string

ties. But at the Piney-woods ride, as more and more young people crowded the grounds, I noticed cargo shorts and rubber-soled boots with brightly colored uppers, some with an accumulation of paper wristbands from previous rides threaded through the pull straps in a display of trail ride status. Virtually everyone wore T-shirts proclaiming their allegiance to a particular riding club: the No Limit Riders of Mamou, La., the Spare Time Riders of New Roads, the Hip Hop Ghetto Riders of Breaux Bridge. Some clubs, like the Exclusive Steppers, showed loyalty to a particular kind of mount, the high-stepping Tennessee walker, considered the Cadillac of trail riding ("If you ain't steppin', you ain't reppin'"). Others, like the Wild Bird Riders, honored their favorite whiskey, while the Suga Riders were named to commemorate "one of the realest cowboys you would ever get to know," according to a Lafayette man who rode his horse to nightclubs. The Mixed Breed Riders, a youthful posse in short-shorts and tank-tops, gave a nod to the racial mélange so common in Acadiana.[38]

Reflecting a generational shift, this evolution is not necessarily at odds with the image of the cowboy, which maintains its aura and continues to be celebrated by a younger generation of zydeco fans, whether they are of rural origin or urbanites. In fact, the fans of J. Paul Jr. and Chris Ardoin attest to their strong attachment to trail rides and the cowboy tradition associated with them. YouTube videos of zydeco trail ride concerts generate numerous excited comments in which fans express a sense of belonging to "cowboys" or to "the boot" (such as "cowboy 4eva!" or "Gotta love dat boot"). Song themes help to sustain the prominence of this emblematic figure, exploiting its metaphorical potential for erotic double entendre. This is the case with J.J. Cailler's "Pop That Tuddy Cat," Chris Ardoin's "Stallion" (whose chorus is "All I want / All I need / Is the stallion in my life / All the time / By my side"), and J. Paul Jr.'s "Love in the Stable" (which includes the lines "Its been a long road on this trail ride / Let's go back to the barn tonight" and the chorus "Gonna have a little fun tonight / I wanna make love in the stable").

A specific ethnography would be needed to fully describe this fascinating scene and to reveal its contested meanings and possible authenticity struggles, and by no means do I mean to suggest that zydeco trail rides are restricted to the consensual celebration of the cowboy image. There is, however, an interesting combination of imageries that tend to nuance

4.6. Trap House Trailride Lacassine, LA, Sept. 6–8, 2013. Source: http://www.zydecoevents.com/trailriders.html.

the clear-cut rural/urban dichotomy. In fact, the cowboy motif is not perceived as contradicting urban sounds. In *Le Cowboy Creole*, Geno Delafose overtly combines an eclectic song list of Creole classics along with covers of Lionel Richie, Chuck Berry, and Van Morrison songs and images of his horses and ranch. Whether J. Paul Jr., Lil Nate, Brian Jack, or Step Rideau are providing the music, trail ride clubs insist in their flyers on the fact that security is provided (i.e. "full security"; "You fight! You go to jail! No weapons allowed!"), so as to dissociate the zydeco trail ride scene from incivility and confrontation.

From one end of the zydeco continuum to the other, the connection with the countryside and its associated trope of respectability is consistently reaffirmed, even when it overlaps with sensuality. Just as rap posses are careful to maintain connections with the 'hood, zydeco performers, through their involvement in trail rides, song lyrics, promotional blurbs, interviews, and marketing strategies, make a point of reminding their fans of this rural identification, whether they grew up on the prairie or in the sprawling suburbs of Houston. In conjunction with rap, the cowboy motif allows Creoles to position themselves in such a way as to appeal to black youth while also asserting their distinctiveness and cornering a niche market.

Boozoo Chavis prided himself that "I could have bought me a Cadillac, but I don't need it. I don't try to act proud, I'm still me. Some of them guys they want to change into five different color suits every night. I don't need all that."[39] Michael Tisserand, encapsulating their differences, asserts that Boozoo's musical choices and persona were in contrast to those of the King of Zydeco, Clifton: "For if Chenier always reminded his audiences that he came from the country, Chavis makes it plain that he never left. Instead of Chenier's crisp suit and tie, Chavis makes his statement in a Stetson hat and a plastic apron (to prevent sweat from drenching the accordion bellows). And while Chenier played the big piano accordion, Chavis stays with the old French single and triple-row boxes."[40]

Despite the divergent itineraries of Boozoo, who left music to train horses, and Chenier, who took his role as the ambassador of zydeco very seriously, they shared an eagerness to establish authenticity by convincing their audience that they had remained true to their rural roots and had not sold out despite their commercial success. Other musicians were similarly blunt in reminding fans about their origins and the skills associated with the rural lifestyle, which they maintained despite their success and national profile. "I used to go hunting rabbits with a stick. And that was a real meal for me, my brothers and my sisters, my mom and dad. You hear what I'm telling you? I used to hunt armadillos, possum, and nutria. I'm a woodsman. If nature is there, I will survive," Buckwheat Zydeco told music writer Michael Tisserand, reversing the image of the music star he became by accentuating his bold character and self-sufficiency.[41]

Although musicians who claim a "new" zydeco sound integrate rap and other contemporary urban trends, they ultimately share an attachment to the rural motif. Whether identified as "new", "nouveau," or "traditional" zydeco players and regardless of the strategies that govern their careers and enduring polarities in how they represent themselves, all zydeco performers achieve respectability on their own terms. From Boozoo Chavis to Brian Terry, regional identification and rural roots serve as driving forces and provide a springboard for their aspirations to recognition and upward mobility. On his website, J. Paul proclaims that "the Zydeco Nubreeds have taken the French Creole music of rural Southwest Louisiana and blended it with sounds of blues, R and B, Hip Hop, and Gospel. All the way from Houston, TX with this style and sound, they have 'CHANGED THE GAME' and taken zydeco to next level nationally."⁴² Asserting rural roots and southwestern Louisiana heritage while achieving success untangles Creole musicians from the enduring image—simultaneously romantic and negative—of rural southern Louisiana as primitive and archaic. Through a process of stereotype reversal, the rural heritage and images of "folk" or "roots" music function as the defining essence of musicians' achievement, a process articulated early on in a long interview by Ben Sandmel with Boozoo Chavis: "I come a long way from picking cotton and hoein'. I used to couldn't afford a book of matches. One can of pork and beans had to make it for the whole family. All the nice things I got now, music paid for them. . . . Now that we're traveling, we're opening people's eyes. They're sayin', "Where he come from, that little man? That joker can play."⁴³

Brian Terry, the leader of Lil' Brian and the Zydeco Travelers, bore this ambition still further, developing a distinctive, innovative music style that he called "funky zydeco" and that inspired the release *Z-Funk* (1997). His hometown of Barrett Station, Texas (B.S.T.), a hamlet outside Baytown not far from "H-Town" (Houston), is acknowledged as the birthplace of the style he promotes. "Funky Nation" (Lil' Brian and the Zydeco Travelers, *Funky Nation*, 2000, Tomorrow Recordings) explicitly affirms the close connection between this territorial identification and the emergence of a new sound: "If you ain't / Heard about it / You need / To crack it up louder / It's a brand new funk / Coming to your town / B.S.T. / Gonna get down / It's the Z funk / In a funky nation / We funk / Barrett Station."

A different version of the song is a remix with West Coast rapper Kurupt—known for his work with Death Row Records and rap group Tha Dogg Pound—is proudly announced on the cover of Lil' Brian's album *Worldwide* (Freh' Toi Records, 2007). Additional lyrics include: "Funky zydeco / That's us and everybody knows / Funky zydeco and we ain't ashamed / Coming out of H-Town / We're in the swamp in Louisiana / Tryin' to see what's cracking with this country grammar . . ." Brian Terry's musical choices and lyrics express his determination to take zydeco to the global stage, as related in "Worldwide": "From the East to the West to the North to the South / We repping zydeco and we repping it proud / From New England to New Orleans you all know I'm callin' / I ain't playing with this game, man, y'all know I'm bowling / We're worldwide / Worldwide y'all / We're worldwide / We're nationwide."

His instrumental choices also reflect a desire to elevate the diatonic accordion—associated with old-fashioned music outside of Louisiana—to the same status as the large piano-accordion that he also uses. Terry's musical style and lyrics exemplify the ambitions in terms of upward mobility and national—and in his case global—recognition of contemporary zydeco players on the basis of regional roots and rural heritage. Their efforts to transform zydeco into a style identified with eastern Texas and southwestern Louisiana is not merely coextensive with their ambitions of attracting an international audience. Instead, localism and rural roots are considered to be a *sine qua non*, a prerequisite, for the elevation of the music. By claiming and enacting the rootedness of their music within a specific region and heritage while recasting its musical forms and integrating mainstream musical influences, they have transformed zydeco into a site of empowerment. The fact that the success of zydeco music among African Americans has primarily been on a regional scale and that its appeal around the country is limited to mostly white fans does not diminish its symbolic power as a distinctive "black music" that is both urban and rural and influenced by hip hop but also respectable. In fact, more recent changes in the Cajun scene have tended to pursue similar directions through the exploration of new sounds, textures, and influences, opening up new horizons and seeking worldwide recognition and legitimacy. Cajun musicians, like their zydeco colleagues, have thus expanded their careers while sustaining the centrality of their claims to regional and ethnic identification. From the Pine Leaf Boys—who present their music as "worldwide" on their homepage and provide a Google Map link portraying their tours in the United States, Europe, and the Middle East—to Kevin Naquin and the Ossun Playboys who "are on a mission to bring their blend of Cajun, dance-hall groove to the world," bands that label themselves as Cajun as well as bands with a more diffuse identification with south Louisiana emphasize the potential of gaining international recognition.

Deceptively Simple

I remember one incident, I went to Mulate's in Baton Rouge, they knew me there because I played other nights of the week, the waitress walks up to me and says "David, do something! Listen!" Bois Sec and Canray were playing, and this little white redneck girl didn't hear it, she didn't get it. When we played it was smooth and in tune, there was no roughness. But that night she thought there was something wrong with the PA system!

DAVID GREELY, JANUARY 14, 2003

The strength of the rural motif, assigned to French Louisiana music by both natives and non-natives, ranks high among the shared characteristics of the different styles of French Louisiana music. Cajun and Creole styles are often characterized as simple, plain, with unpolished techniques, rhythm, and lyrics. Represented as spontaneous, raw, and even "lowdown for real" (as I once heard), the different ways in which the region's music is described tend to prize emotion, sociability, and conviviality over technical prowess.

This sub-chapter is not intended to provide an exhaustive view of French Louisiana musical techniques. In this realm, my personal skills are limited to the fiddle, and I have only an imperfect knowledge of music theory and the intricacies of technique. Instead, this section draws on descriptions of certain technical features to illustrate—but also to interrogate—depictions of French Louisiana music as "plain." This characterization as simple, unfussy music is routinely applied, not only to instrument playing, but also to the processes of teaching, composing, and recording. It should be noted, however, that I do not include zydeco and its variations in this section, because in my experience, only its detractors use the term "plain."

As Greely suggests, a number of musicians pay tribute to the harshness that defines Cajun music as it is played by its most distinguished icons, even when their own style does not reflect it. Certain contemporary bands appropriate this distinctive trait, also integrating elements of string band, avant-garde, or rock 'n' roll. In 2004, when the Lost Bayou Ramblers had established themselves as one of the most popular bands in the Lafayette area, local journalist and musician Josh Caffery argued that while others achieved success by making the music more modern and palatable to outsiders, "The Lost Bayou Ramblers take almost the opposite tack, distilling the music to its clear, exhilarating core." "I think the most traditional thing we do is that we don't practice, and we don't make arrangements," fiddler Louis Michot confirmed at the time, adding "We don't want to practice. We don't want to be refined" to further clarify the band's position.[44] Other young, established musicians like the Pine Leaf Boys envisioned their music pursuing similar lines. In fact, the band's leader, Wilson Savoy, perceives the music differently from his younger brother, Joel, who was one of the founding members of the Red Stick Ramblers. "We have practiced," admits Joel, "and that used to drive Wilson crazy. We'd sit here for three hours and talking about this and doing these meticulous things, or just swing tunes that we'd arrange."[45] Interestingly, practicing implies in this context a loss of harshness and spontaneity, which is construed as being opposed to sophistication.

Corey Porche, who plays accordion and the fiddle and is well connected to the music scene, expresses strong feelings about this harsh sound. Referring to a famous French Louisiana band, he confessed at the time of our first interview: "Their music is very pretty, refined, beautiful. . .I like a little bit more not so refined. To hear that wrong note coming out, that's realness. He's a technical genius, but it's too pretty for me," he continues, situating "realness" as a distinct quality relative to virtuosity.[46] The reference to iconic figures and the old-time French music style helps legitimize harshness. "At first, to the unpracticed ear, it sounded like Canray Fontenot was badly missing his pitches on the fiddle," says musician and music manager Peter Schwartz. Referring to Fontenot's song "Les Barres de la Prison," he explains it as "a song about the aching despair of a life behind the prison bars [which] was best reflected by a lost and slowly wandering blue note somewhere between disorder and a perfectly orderly major third."[47] Intentional dissonance is unarguably one of the notable features of French Louisiana music, even in its contemporary forms. In his accordion teaching video, Dirk Powell explains that in the key of G, the octave system of playing that characterizes what is called the Cajun accordion is not quite as clear as in C. Half the time, the left side is not playing the right chord, which creates the dissonance that in his view makes the charm of this style.[48]

A penchant for minimalism has often attracted outsiders to the sounds of French Louisiana music. Boozoo Chavis was among the most well-known practitioners of this style, according to Ben Sandmel: "[His music] is shamelessly repetitious; once a lyrical or melodic idea is introduced, further development is virtually nil." He gives the example of "Dog Hill," which is based on a single line and an accordion riff with no chord change or harmonic resolution: "Such minimalism is never dull, however, because what Boozoo Chavis lacks in complexity is counter-balanced by his ferocious, irresistible groove." The musician had a disarmingly quick wit as well: "Sometimes they [his band] say: 'Boozoo, you out of time!' My youngest boy, the drummer, he'll say, 'Dad, watch your beat, you jumpin' time' and I tell him, 'Don't tell me to watch my beat, you watch me. If it's wrong, do it wrong with me! If I'm wrong, you wrong, too!' he answered without budging."[49]

Chavis is also credited for introducing animal imitations. In 1986, "Dog Hill" started a fad for songs with canine themes, complete with barking.

Nicknamed "Zydeco Hog," Chavis also introduced mule noises, as he did in "Zydeco Hee-Haw," reflecting, as Sandmel puts it, "a swaggering sexuality that recalls such other songs of unbridled passion as 'I'm a Jockey,' by Chicago blues guitarist Jimmy Johnson, and Mel Tillis's country hit 'I Got the Hoss, and You Got the Saddle.'" After several verse-and-riff sequences, the band 'breaks it down' into a churning drum-and-frottoir segment, spurred on by snorts, whinnies, and hee-haws. Then the harmonic tension is finally resolved with a shout of 'Lâchez-les!' ('let them go!'), and the song gallops off in a dancing frenzy."[50] Animal themes echo the success of animal dances that blossomed in the 1910s—the turkey trot in the New Orleans scene featured flapping arm movements, and there were also the foxtrot, the bunny hug, and the lame duck.

Although this technique is primarily experienced as providing levity and entertainment value, French ethnomusicologist Victor Stoichita illustrates that animal imitations and sounds were deployed in twentieth-century American folklore as a way of demonstrating a type of virtuosity. Mostly expressed by the harmonica and the fiddle in country music and bluegrass, the practice centers on the imitation of non-musical sounds within musical performances. The fox hunting is among the most common imitations on the harmonica. In French Louisiana demonstrations of vocal prowess provide animal sound imitations.[51]

What is described as "crooked" or "dissonant" does present challenges to an unaccustomed ear, and practicing French Louisiana music requires careful listening and adaptation. Lisa Bourque and Joel Breaux had just graduated from the University of Louisiana at Lafayette when they moved to Los Angeles to establish themselves as architects. Joel had grown up in the small town of Loreauville, near New Iberia, with the stigma of a strong Cajun accent. He began buying Cajun CDs in California, found his way into the Cajun and zydeco dance scene there, and under the guidance of Lisa's father when he came home to Louisiana, he learned the basics and bought himself an accordion. "Why in God's name would I ever want to play a music that would just invite more criticism?" he wondered with fifteen years' remove, having returned to his native town. His first accordion came from the Rose Bowl flea market in Pasadena, and an older couple themselves transplants from Louisiana, encouraged his first performance, with their band the Brand New Old Time Cajun Band. As he developed his skills with other musicians, he noticed how challenging the music could be for newcomers to this music. He met the San Diego Cajun Playboys in 1998 and began playing with them:

The good thing with playing with the guys from San Diego was they already knew all the funky chord relationships, those extra two beats in songs, and that we'll stay on the G forever and then there'll be like a D on the end of a song for two beats and I mean, you know, things that are quirky about Cajun music that people around here take for granted, you know.... but people in L.A., that was foreign to them, right? So if you're playing with people in Los Angeles, then you're spending half your time just saying: "this is not where the chords change." And no matter how many times you say it and no matter how good of a musician these people are, they're still wanting to put the chords in a different location. I mean it was foreign to them. It's like relearning a language or something.[52]

Respecting chord changes and adapting to the fact that beats and even measures can be dropped or added are aspects of what is referred to as "crookedness" in characterizations of this music, particularly the old-time French style. Other challenges include, for example, the dragging of the vocals in waltzes, which requires that instrumentalists keep the tempo instead of following the vocalist and eventually slow down the entire song.

To the waitress at Mulate's who was put off by the sound of Canray Fontenot and Bois Sec, David Greely retorted: "You're listening to Abraham Lincoln!" calling attention to her lack of knowledge by referring to one of the most admired presidents in the history of the United States, not to mention an abolitionist. Within the musical register, Dennis McGee's peculiar style presents challenges to such an extent that he is compared with classical maestros. Andrea, a transplant from San Francisco to Louisiana in 2003, offers her perspective on this point:

You play that Dennis McGee stuff, if you haven't heard it before, you can't guess why it's gonna have like three measures, four measures, two measures... or how it's going to go. You basically have to learn it and memorize it or count it.... A lot of times playing with accordion, it is sort of like, "Okay..." But when you start playing the Dennis McGee stuff, it's more intellectually challenging because you have to figure out where the song's going all the time.... He reminds me of Mozart.

Dennis McGee is credited with transforming French Louisiana music into a high-level cultural expression, elevating it to the status of "art" music. Reversing the stereotype of plain or simple music, this comparison is suggestive of the existence of geniuses within French Louisiana music, like in any other genre.

The unpredictability in the structure of songs gives rise to a sense of distinctiveness. During a workshop at the 2008 Balfa Camp in Chicot State Park, Louisiana, Ed Poullard mentioned this claim to exceptionalism, citing the example of a song originally called the "Elton 2-step."

Guitarist Sam Broussard provides detailed explanations to his Cajun guitar students:

> Some Cajun songs are "crooked," meaning they drop and/or pick up beats. The opposite of crooked is square. Country songs are almost always square. The vast bulk of modern pop is square. This means that things happen more or less where you expect them to happen, informed as you are by your own familiarity with songs in general, the vast majority of which have no surprises about when chords change. If you listen to the old blues guys, Jimmy Reed for example, you'll hear him change chords when he damn well pleases, and if you listen close you can hear the other musicians trying to cope. The results are often pitiful in an organizational sense, but there you go. It still sounds great. Cajun music is vastly more organized, in that the dropped beats and added pauses have become part of the song in many, many cases. Not all, but many. And many melodies are written crookedly. After a while you don't notice it. (A "while" could be "years," but there you go. Cajun music is not for sissies.) A good example of a crooked song is Johnny Can't Dance.[53]
>
> Here are some adaptations to crookedness: Parentheses around a number means that the bar is cut in half i.e., has only one beat. Thus, if you're counting a two-step in 2/4 (which is best), that chord/bar will have only one beat. For example: the "Scott Playboy Special." This shape is: 1 1 (1) 5 (1) 1 1 (1) 5 1. This shape is the turn or B part of many songs, and is the entirety of others, like "Creole Stomp." It is a difficult thing to get if, like me, you're accustomed to squares, but once you get it you will see it repeated all through the repertoire. It's one of the most fascinating aspects of Cajun music—to me—appearing as it does so often. It's the only piece of Cajun crookedness that I would call a formula. I'll never know how it came about, but so many of the melodies seem to be written so that no other chord changes will fit.[54]

According to Broussard, then, crookedness becomes the rule more than the exception.

One of Sam's former students, Andrea describes the variety of guitar styles that contradict the cliché of Cajun guitar being boring and basic:

> There are choices you make when you decide how to back up Cajun music. There's like a Balfa style with open chords and D.L.'s style with bass runs and there's choke chords and bar chords and there's slightly different ways you put the rhythm to every song. . . . Like some of the Balfa stuff, it's like a little bit of runs, and some of it, it's like this really flowing style where the guitar never stops. It's just like fills in all the spaces, then there's that "boom-chuck" thing, which is mostly what anybody here does. . . . Like there's a Eunice style and then there's a Basile style and like a Christine style and what the Savoys want to listen to and it's all different. I use to think it was all regional, you know, but now I think it's really family.

Fiddle playing illustrates other dimensions of the individualization of music styles. Michael Doucet recalls that Canray Fontenot, for instance, did not touch his fingerboard with his left-hand fingers, instead playing on top of the strings. In "Adieu Rosa," a good example of what can be accomplished with a one-chord tune, Canray accentuated the shuffle bowing like in the early recordings: "Canray used it so nice in his song, you have to use your arm like a metronome," explains Doucet.[55] Specific bowing styles rendered the scratchy sound characteristic of the old style. Playing "La Malheureuse" in the film *J'ai Été au Bal*, Dennis McGee thrust his thumb but also his little finger between the stick and the horsehair of the bow, leaving his three other fingers resting above for support. "This allowed him to draw the bow hair to terribly high tension and to play, with great force, his rapid cascading sequences of eighth and even sixteenth notes without sacrificing articulation or phrasing," explains music collector and California musician Will Spires.[56]

At the first Balfa Camp in 2001, Mitch Reed, who was teaching advanced fiddle, insisted on the importance of the older style approach to bowing:[57]

> A lot of the rhythm I come up with, they come out naturally, because I'm around so many accordion players, I'm just making their rhythm. And I'm doing that with the bow. And really in the old days,

they would do that too, because you wanted to play together, you wanted to have the rhythm locked on, so . . . You have a lot of fiddle styles that are almost mimicking the accordion. You just jump on the tune, really. There is no clean start at all. . . . But in most Cajun tunes, there is a big Texas influence, so there is some tunes like "Jolie Blonde," where they'll have a walkup, but some of the older ones, you just jump on it!

It is worth recalling that the sound of French Louisiana music throughout the twentieth century was far from monolithic. As seen in the first chapter, the Texas influence of the 1930s introduced notable changes that, for the late fiddler Hadley Castille, contributed dense embellishments and fiddling acrobatics that were especially well exemplified by his mentor Harry Choates:

> He recorded a song called *Dragging a Ball*, he heard it from one of the best Texas swing player. That was a style he learned there. A number which has just 3 chords, one part of the song is simple, simple, then it gets to it, you can just feel he switches over, it's called *Hip et Taïau*. Listen to what happens on the second part. I'm sure you play Port Arthur Blues. Almost all fiddle players here are going to play it like this. Him, he would play it like that. When you're playing that it's a little bit harder. So a lot of fiddlers they learn it the simple way. He would go the second part like this. See it feels good, the movement makes you wanna dance. . . . A simple song like "Chère Toute-toute." Fiddlers who play with the accordion, no feeling. Watch the difference. Just two keys but, that's what you put in between that makes it so attractive.[58]

In addition to the range of styles this genre encompasses, certain instrumental methods can be highly technical, creative accomplishments. For the diatonic accordion, key modulations within a song are limited in particular by the impossibility of modulations by semitone, as described by ethnomusicologist Mark DeWitt.[59] These key modulations systematically have an exhilarating effect on the public and result in happy screaming. Fiddlers often provoke a similar reaction when performing a medley of fast twin fiddle tunes without interruption, as the band Racines traditionally does with Kevin Wimmer and Mitch Reed, an act that is uniformly greeted with a warm ovation.

As demonstrated by DeWitt, Barry Ancelet offers a somewhat tenuous theory that limitations of available notes and keys on the accordion tended to restrict and simplify tunes that were played when the fiddle dominated this music.[60] DeWitt provides a different interpretation based on rigorous investigation of the effects of the diatonic accordion on Cajun music. While the right hand can only play the diatonic scale in which the accordion is tuned, the left hand is even more restricted—two bass notes, two major triads—compared with the harmonic possibilities possessed by every key of a chromatic piano accordion. However, even though certain gestures are impossible on the diatonic accordion, musicians developed simulation tactics (like the blue third effect) to compensate for such technical limitations. Most accordions are C or D accordions, but they are not restricted to playing in one key. "The keys of C, G, and F prevail because they offer the greatest number of opportunities for the right hand to play chord roots and harmonic thirds, fourths, fifths, and sixths in support of the tonic, subdominant, and dominant harmonies, and for the left hand to reinforce those harmonies at opportune moments."[61] Cajun accordionists do not play melodies in minor modes such as Dorian, Phrygian, and Aeolian, despite the fact that the instrument would readily allow them, in part because minor keys have not typically been associated with the Cajun style. Numerous descriptions of musical effects further support DeWitt's argument based on "the relationship between how the music sounds or should sound (style) and how to play the instrument most effectively (idiom)."[62] Musicians negotiate the sound of their instrument beyond its technical limitations, according to their stylistic preferences and the capabilities of their instruments: ". . . one must recognize the importance of the choices that the musicians themselves make in fashioning their music. Simplicity in one dimension such as pitch selection can be compensated for with complexity in others, such as ornamentation, improvisation, demands on memory, and so on."[63]

Musicians themselves often argue that the music's simplicity is only superficial. In French Louisiana music, the fiddle is tuned "standard" or "classical" (GDAE) when playing with a D accordion, and tuned down to a lower standard G (FCGD) when playing with a C accordion. This allows the double open string effect, which is one specificity of Cajun fiddling. However, in the old days some musicians like Dennis McGee included other tuning. Will Spires reports that McGee could tune in GDAD, GDGD, DADD, ADAD, GDGB, and ADAE. Instead of seeing these tunings as a simplification of fingering, Spires emphasizes these techniques as highly specialized.

The limited number of keys found in most of the repertoire (mostly G, C, and D) figure among typical criticisms of Cajun music among its detractors, a point that has been internalized by some French Louisiana musicians, to the point that they joke about it. Although neither the melodies nor the chord progression are particularly complex in most songs, musician Josh Caffery also argues the rhythm is demanding and challenging. "I have seen a competent jazz guitarist shaking his head, confounded by the seeming facility of 'J'étais au bal' and heard trained drummers wandering down wayward rhythmic pathways, goodheartedly butchering a Cajun waltz."[64] David Greely also mentioned to me guitar players maintaining that they refuse to "be sawing wood all day long," whereas the guitar is actually the pillar of the music just as it is in Irish and old-time music.

Depending on their musical background and education, musicians use different musical practices. The most knowledgeable usually use the Nashville number system, a technique developed by Nashville musicians in early country recording sessions. Because it employs numbers instead of keynotes, it became useful as a way to avoid rewriting all of the chords when the key is changed. The number 1 chord is always the root chord of the key in which it is played. This system is clearly explained to students by Sam Broussard in a web document: "In the key of C, the 1 chord is C. To know what the 5 chord is, count the alphabet from C on your fingers; you will arrive at G on the fifth finger. The 2 chord is D, the 4 chord is F, and so on. If you need to quickly communicate a song to someone, it's unbeatable. For example: 'How does Quelle Etoile go?' It is 'Forty-one fifty five, fifty-five eleven,' i.e., 4155 5511, which in the key of C would be FCGG GGCC."[65]

When a guest musician is invited on stage and does not know a song, someone will show him the first chord with his first finger, then open his hand to show all fingers, meaning the 5th chord. Sam Broussard explains that most musicians do not make use of this technique, either out of embarrassment at exposing their lack of knowledge in music theory, or due to lack of interest. "(When) I moved here, I would hear a knowledgeable musician say 5 and a less knowledgeable musician say G," he recalls. "It didn't matter either way, and no one thought anything about it. It's just a language of convenience, and it would be spoken some at rehearsals, and a lot at recording sessions."[66] In fact, in my experience of jams among occasional musicians, I have not encountered anyone using the number system. Guitar players and fiddlers exchange keynotes to figure out the chords. And due to the limited numbers of keys within French Louisiana music, those who do not know the chords can also try to figure them out by ear.

Beyond practicing and playing, recording and production contribute to the representation of a "natural," "approachable" music and play a significant role in the construction of a distinctive sound. The insistence on a natural process is shared with country music. Cecilia Tichi notes that country songwriters downplay rigor and struggle in the process of song composition. The focus on everyday life scenes feeds the notion that songwriting is spontaneous: "The act of writing only formalizes what already is—or what already is gestating." Along the same line, Hank Williams is presented as a natural country genius without any mention of his collaboration with mentor/publisher Fred Rose. Even instruments appear as "living creatures in a natural world." According to Tichi, the description of Cajun artist Doug Kershaw as "screaming like a bayou wildcat" is consistent with this characterization.[67]

Several musicians use the expression "kitchen music," pointing both to its social dimension and to the style inspired by so domestic a setting. Balfa Toujours recorded *La Pointe* (1998) with vintage analog equipment in their kitchen and living room in order "to capture a feeling that often evaporates in the clinical environment of the studio." Linzay Young and Joel Savoy's 2008 recording of twin fiddle tunes on Valcour Records is an uncluttered CD with no title and minimal documentation and annotations that includes the following text on the cover: "In an age where everything seems to be way over-analyzed, it's nice to be able to just sit down and make a record on an afternoon with no fuss and no frill- the old fashioned way. This is our music. We hope you enjoy it."

Valcour Records is particularly representative of this minimalist process. Cofounded by south Louisiana natives Joel Savoy, Phillip Lafargue, and Lucius Fontenot, Valcour began in 2006 with the idea of capturing sounds on analog tape without resorting to digital editing. After two CDs, the friends changed strategy:

> SLM: And what made you change your mind?
> Joel Savoy: It got too expensive to do it. When friends come to me to record a record, almost always it costs less than $1500, which is like a third of the price a normal record costs, because my focus is to just set them up to where they're comfortable and then just capture what they do and not have to create and edit and do all this stuff to build something.... What I like to do is just capture somebody doing something. It's great to do that on analog tape because you don't lose anything in the continuous stream of audio

data, but it got too expensive to do that because the tape is expensive, they quit making it for a while, and so I just switched to the computer and I've been having fun with that. I'm very interested in honest music, music that . . . I just recorded a record this week with Jesse Lége and me and our friends from the Northwest, the Foghorn Stringband guys (*The Right Combination*, 2010). We do everything pretty much in one take or two takes. We sit down, play the song, make sure we know it, and then we play it how we want to play it. And it's not going to be perfect, you know, it's not going to be 100 percent perfect. What is perfect? I don't know. But it's exactly how we sound, and it's natural, and it's fun, and it's raw, and that's what I like—honest music. And I think people really appreciate that, when they hear recording that's honest, when it's straightforward, not perfect, sounds like a human made it—you have this instant connection with people. . . . The biggest thing is to make music that is not pretentious. It's totally approachable and very natural.[68]

However, while Joel Savoy feels strongly about these goals as a musician and producer, his label Valcour is not restricted to this approach: "Feufollet's album *Cow Island Hop* that we put out—I didn't mix, I didn't record, I didn't have anything to do with it. They did it in Lafayette. And Givers's stuff was mixed in New York, I think, the stuff we put out. That's great. We're not going for unification of the Louisiana music sound. That's not what we want to do. I think diversity is the most important thing we have."[69]

Indeed, other musicians express a rather different perception of the recording process. According to C. C. Adcock, a Lafayette prominent musician and producer of *Grand Isle* from the Mamou Playboys: "Around here bands think they should just play live and put a mic in front of it or else they're being fake. Cajun music is very much a 1980s music. It came to prominence in the 80s, and crossed over into a pop consciousness where teenagers were listening to it and it wasn't just an old man music anymore. I wanted to address that in this record."[70]

Beyond the recording process, the idea embraced and promoted by many musicians—especially the younger generation—is to perform music described as raw and energetic in order to provide the public with a lived experience. Although it yields very different styles and aesthetics, this perception is nonetheless widely shared. "It's not a languorous, sitting-around-playing-something pretty thing. It is a 'get after it' type of music.

I came here filled with gentle linger of gothic Richmond, Virginia and had to turn into a Cajun wild woman. It was like, 'come on, beat on it Annie. Beat on it Annie!'" recalls Ann Savoy about learning rhythmic guitar.[71] Kristie Guillory further pursues this idea on the websites of both of her two bands: "This isn't music to sit in your chair and listen to. This is music that plays as you press your cheek against someone while passing across a dance floor. This is music made by a band that works hard on stage to make music for people who work hard during the week," says the Lafayette Rhythm Devils site, whereas her other band, Bonsoir Catin, is described as four girls who "share the same vision that Cajun music should be unafraid and unabashed, full of energy and raw emotion."[72]

French Louisiana music is defined by its ability to move people, both literally and emotionally. It is meant to be lived, felt, sensed, and experienced from the inside instead of articulated or verbalized. The fact that the recording process often involves meticulous work, intense sessions, and long discussions and sessions spent reviewing tracks in order to make a final selection is not viewed as a paradox. It is the result that matters, the rendition, and the spirit that supports it. From those who stick with a traditional style to those who have embraced new sounds and textures borrowed from indie-pop to punk rock and contributing to the renewal of the Cajun scene, these eclectic approaches continue to support the perception of the need for raw, energetic music.

Thomas Turino distinguishes two fields within recorded music: "high fidelity recordings" are intended to index or be iconic of live performance, while "studio audio art" involves the manipulation of taped or synthesized sounds or digital technology. In high fidelity recordings, studio techniques are masked or downplayed, although he argues that sound manipulation is inevitable to create signs of "liveness." This ideology is also found in bands from Austin, Texas, and "ties liveness to musical authenticity (which is fundamentally linked to sincerity and personal expression) and recording to alienated, calculated corporate profiteering schemes."[73] However, high fidelity recording requires electronic manipulation and specific use of reverb, echo sonic spacing (panning), equalization, and compression. The lack of visuals and the aura of the musician's presence can be reflected solely through sound quality.[74]

Furthermore, even within the "high fidelity" field, approaches to representing liveness vary according to different genre frames, social context, and bands. While Turino recorded his zydeco band himself in Illinois, capturing first or second takes played just like at home or in performances, his experience with the Zimbabwean guitar band Shangara at the Shed studio was quite different because most musicians recorded their parts individually. Turino explains at length how his choice to record all of the instruments of his band together reduced the range of available possibilities at the mixing stage, like equalizing or changing the balance of individual parts that lacked textual clarity and part separation. Different personnel, technologies, and performance processes are required for making a successful recording according to the values of the high fidelity field.

South Louisiana bands involved in the renewal of the French Louisiana music sound seem to situate themselves between "high fidelity" and "studio audio art" recording. Although they share an attachment to live performance and to the lived musical experience, in the studio they have been able to explore uncovered territories within the genre, including a vast range of instrumental effects, overdubs, and studio distortions, unusual instruments, machines, and equipment. The decisive role of producers, co-producers and engineers in the new wave of recordings such as Feufollet's *En Couleurs* (2010), Steve Riley and the Mamou Playboys' *Grande Isle* (2011), and the Lost Bayou Ramblers' *Mammoth Waltz* (2011) is indicative of a new desire to explore the possibilities of studio recordings and to recast their sounds.

Jamming and Beyond

> I heard a rumor that Lafayette is number 4 in live music, after Chicago, New York, and New Orleans . . . Thanks for all the musicians here who support it! It ain't buying groceries, man! It ain't buying groceries! You can't buy dat! You make dat!!
> LINZAY YOUNG, OCTOBER 30, 2010, BLACK POT FESTIVAL, LAFAYETTE

The French Louisiana music-making context is an essential part of its meaning and value for musicians and fans alike. For them, music is something that fills the air, and is incorporated into everyday life, from stage to home and in public and private settings. Music can be an event, but it is valued above all as a lived practice. People incorporate it to every aspect of their life, they establish social ties around it, and fill their time with it; they not only inhabit a musical region but are inhabited by music.

Jams are a fundamental aspect of the region's musical practice. Whether total beginners or accomplished musicians, whoever wants to play can join a jam. Whether they take place in cafes, workshops, clubs, or restaurants or at somebody's house, jams are open to all interested comers. Based on acoustic music, they are typically led by one or two hosts who can invite special guests, one of whose roles is to kick off tunes, which are then followed by the participants who form a circle. The more advanced play the chorus, together or take turns, while the others, sometimes beginners, play the chords and get familiar with the melodies. In French Louisiana music, instruments take turns taking the lead, in other words, usually playing the chorus in the following order: accordion, vocals, fiddle (and other instruments). During the lead, in the context of a jam, the others commonly play the chords. The accordionist is the group leader and decides when a tune starts and ends and when to give the lead to instruments other than the most common (occasional amplified instruments like electric guitars, harmonicas, saxophones, banjos, etc.).

Throughout the last twenty years, a long list of jams have been formed and later either interrupted or abandoned, in part because opportunities to play with other people are so numerous. Nobody knows who or how many people will show up, except for the hosts who are always there; this unpredictability regarding the level of musicianship and attendance is an integral part of the experience and is suggestive of the flexibility required of every participant. On Wednesdays, the Blue Moon Saloon hosts a Cajun jam. On Saturdays, Ray Landry hosts another jam at Vermilionville. The Coffee Break in Breaux Bridge used to offer one led by various musicians; in 2012 Joie de Vivre Café took over, while another jam started downtown. On Sundays, Tom Pierce hosts a monthly "organic jam" in his shop Tom's Fiddle and Bow in Arnaudville. The Jam des Amis organized by Louisiana Folk Roots—an association dedicated to the preservation and promotion of southwest Louisiana's culture—takes place once a month in downtown Lafayette during Artwalk, with a different host each time, always an accomplished musician. One of the most popular jams until 2007 was hosted by Mitch Reed in the spacious back room of his shop Louisiana Gifts and Souvenirs, on Gloria Switch Road in the north Lafayette area. Numerous other jams that are not announced in the weekly paper, on specialized websites, or via mailing lists are nonetheless well attended by people in the vicinity. This was true of the jam held in an old gas station located on Highway 167 past the town of Maurice, south of Lafayette at Touchet's on Saturday afternoons, for a time in alternation with another jam at Morvant's in Youngsville.

Jams are put together on a variety of occasions and are part of the social life of the area, often combined with preparing and sharing a meal.

They also happen at various social gatherings, sometimes spontaneously when friends get together, or they can be planned ahead of time to honor visiting friends. Over the years, my own friends have organized numerous jams in my honor, either as a welcoming event or a farewell after a period of fieldwork. In that case I usually had the most comfortable role: I could kick off any song I wanted, have any special request, and invite anybody to choose a song. The host, in other words, is the leader and has the privilege of selecting what to play and when.

Some regular jams—like Tom Pierce's in Arnaudville—do not always have appointed hosts, in which case regulars assume the lead role, asking others to assume the lead when they feel ready. If they are full-time musicians, the hosts can be paid to come lead the jam. Tom Pierce, for example, had applied for a state-funded grant that enabled him to invite popular musicians and pay them $100 a piece. But full-time musicians also simply appear at jams without any money being involved if they are available.

The use of space during regular jams is often indicative of the skill level of the players and their seniority. Newcomers usually do not sit next to the host, leaving this space for regulars or more advanced musicians. Depending on the size of the jam, the core circle can be doubled by other seats aligned with it. Accordion players are the leaders except during rare string jams. The Coffee Break jam in Breaux Bridge, which used to be held on Saturdays between 11:00 am and 2:00 pm often became a string jam toward the end after most of the musicians had quit. Whenever possible, fiddlers try not to sit too far away from the host so that they can be heard, unless they are total beginners and simply want to second. The more accomplished musicians are, the closer they sit to the host. Regardless of their skills, newcomers, unless they are special guests, also tend to stand back (physically or musically) until the host makes eye contact or nods their head to allow them to play a chorus or "give them a ride." Body language acts as an essential means of interaction. Eye contact (or the lack of) and facial expressions are particularly meaningful. They can enact authority, or leadership, or they can suggest withdrawal, approval, pleasure, or timidity.

The success of a jam thus depends to a large extent on the way in which the host handles his or her role and on how participants respond to them. During smaller jams, participants, when they know each other, can demonstrate a song that they worked together. Most importantly, however, jamming requires flexibility and adaptation. Whereas many musicians have their own arrangements in terms of beginning and ending, structure, sequence of parts, or keys, in a jam one follows the leader and accepts changing habits. Moreover, participants who can play a chorus are expected to do so even when the song is unknown to them, a frequent occurrence because every musician carries his own repertoire beyond the body of standards, with different inspirations and favorites. Other than accordion players, who choose which songs they are able to play, to decline a chorus as an advanced fiddler is accepted but not considered appropriate. I have declined to play numerous choruses out of fear of playing poorly. The expectation, however, is to take any opportunity to play, regardless of the result. When I happened to be the only fiddler in a jam and could not avoid it, I practiced the melody during the singing or instead of seconding in order to prepare myself for the chorus. Musicians are evaluated primarily on their ability to adapt and play the game instead of being strictly judged on their skills.

Jamming ultimately requires playing by the rules, taking the space at the appropriate moment, and knowing the boundaries, regardless of one's skills or status. A full-time musician is subject to the same rules, and all the more appreciated when he or she does not take the opportunity to show off. Jams that some of my friends put together for me often included a working musician. Whether it was Mitch Reed, Eric Adcock, Christine Balfa, or Dirk Powell, among others, they always made sure to allow me to kick off the tune of my choice unless I addressed a special request to them. While engaged in their playing, they were nonetheless very careful about leaving space for the other participants and never expected to be the center of attention.

Some regular jams have better reputations than others, and leaders considered "out of place"—for example who do not share the rides—quickly attract the disapproval of participants, although it is not expressed to their faces. Leaving the jam or waiting in the back until someone else leads are possibilities. Criticism can concern the skill level of some players when they happen to lead the jam temporarily, for example somebody who is off-tempo or adds beats or bars, or who cuts off the B part, which results in suppressing the fiddle chorus and creates frustration among fiddlers. Most often, however, criticism addresses a lack of humility or generosity or excessively self-centered musicians, some of whom might be criticized for being too controlling. Occasional participants who draw attention to themselves and act inappropriately can be abruptly called to order. At the Blue Moon jam on Wednesdays, a young guitar player once came in and played a song that he had written. He received a compliment that compared him to Zachary Richard, to which he replied with contempt: "But

I sing in Cajun French, Zachary sings in French from Canada or whatever. . . ." Participants looked impatient, and some left while he was playing, until an accordion player joined the group and, as the songwriter was starting another of his songs, cut him off and played over him, followed by the rest of the players.

Music camps and group lessons illustrate the centrality of jams in the learning process. The Front Room, a working music and art studio in the town of Scott west of Lafayette, offers "Tune and Jam" sessions during which Steve Riley and Mitch Reed team up to teach the same song to accordion players and fiddlers. At the end of the lesson, both classes are combined in order to jam on the tune they just learned. For ten months in 2009, Tom Pierce interrupted his then-weekly jam in Arnaudville to organize "String Series" lead jams that were supported by grants from the Louisiana Division of the Arts, the Office of Cultural Development (DCRT), and the Louisiana State Arts Council.

Like all "roots" music camps, those related to French Louisiana music include numerous jams within their programs, in addition to the inevitable after-hours jams. Louisiana Folk Roots, which organizes the DBCCHW, promotes learning by immersion. It emphasizes experiential, intuitive learning. Some master class or workshops are run like jams, featuring teachers playing together, as a site of observation and immersion for students. For the first Balfa Camp at Lake Fausse Pointe State Park in 2001, daily "lagniappe sessions" featured older musicians considered pioneers of the genre, sometimes informally interviewed by other musicians in between songs. The late Carlton Frank, Calvin Carriere, and Rodney Fontenot, all older black fiddlers playing the old-time French style, were invited to play after the meal with one or two other musicians who taught at the camp. There was no formal stage, and the guest players just kicked off tunes without announcing them, as is often the case in jams.

Jams featuring older musicians are a tribute to iconic masters, but they also follow the idea of mutual benefit. Artists gain wide exposure and recognition among students from the country and abroad, and in return, students are exposed to a specific way of relating to music and to life. Encountering older masters also serves as a reminder of the origins of French Louisiana music as spoken exchanges draw attention to the rural environment of its interpreters, their farming occupations, the poverty of their youths, and for some, an interruption that lasted two decades while raising children. Numerous older musicians explain that they resigned themselves to quitting playing in order to provide for their families, thus preserving the status of respectable fathers and avoiding the disparagement associated with being a full-time musician.

At the DBCCHW in April 2008, which honored Dewey Balfa, one jam featured the Savoy Family Band. Ann Savoy evoked her family's relationship with Dewey as a "party buddy." In between tunes that they had recorded with him, each member of the family took turns telling stories about him. In 1978, for example, Mark and Ann received a phone call from the filmmaker of *Southern Comfort*, and they all drove to Shreveport to the headquarters. After a few stops at bars, they were finally about to be made-up. When they expressed concern about being ready, one of the film crew members replied: "Y'all gonna be fine just the way y'all are..." [laugh in the audience]. Then Dewey said there was a scene they did not want to be part of that involved incest, and eventually decided to quit. The moviemaker changed the script to keep them. "But the movie was bad enough without the scene" [laughs]. Wilson then quoted some of the dialogue with a dramatic tone: "Louisiana, land of hospitality. Unless you don't belong, and YOU don't belong! [laughs]." The performance was then filled with tunes as much as stories that in this case tackled the negative stereotype of Cajuns as backward, incestuous, and fiercely territorial that is systematically propagated in films and literature. By derisively appropriating these stereotypes, they only emphasized their inanity. Indeed, humor and storytelling are often incorporated into teaching and used as a rhetoric tool that reflects an integral part of regional identification.

In fact, as musicians often contend, there is a great deal more than the music itself during many social occasions, and musicians take every opportunity to broaden the meaning of French Louisiana and to illustrate the role of music in the region's socialization. Michael Doucet told his DBCCHW students:

> When I'd go see Dewey, sometimes we wouldn't even play, we'd drive the bus, and Dennis, we'd go fishing. That kind of stuff stays with you, more than why would you play that note or how. Canray is a great example, he had different degrees of soberness, and if you'd catch him sober, he would tell you a story one way, the more he's drink, he would loosen up, and you'd really feel the racism somebody Creole had to deal with, so you got a whole different prospective about his music. That's the best thing to do, just go visit people.

In keeping with this narrative, teachers include more than music in their classes, sometimes combining storytelling, jokes, and sometimes food, thus adding layers of meaning beyond the specific instrument or lesson. In the 2001 DBCCHW, Mitch Reed once brought boudin, *grattons* (cracklings), and beer to end the fiddle class, to the delight of his students.

Jams and other master presentations function as performed narratives by integrating stories and anecdotes that shape the image of French Louisiana music. Music camps, whether in Louisiana or elsewhere, offer a portrait of French Louisiana music not only through musical performance but also through the way in which the music is taught, the discourse that punctuates the songs, the vividness with which stories are recounted, the humorous punch line, or their picturesque stories. The combination of these elements enacts French Louisiana music as more than just a repertoire and finally as "a way of life."

The intensive individual and collective practice of working musicians is inseparable from this approach to making music. Depending on the timing within their careers, they practice daily for hours on their own, listening to recordings and joining the many jams available. Mostly, however, they jam or just hang out together, which inevitably involves eating, jamming, talking about music, listening to recordings, and exchanging tunes and techniques. These activities form an essential dimension of the process that can eventually lead to the formation of a band. Many young musicians, including members of the Pine Leaf Boys, the Red Stick Ramblers, and others, began as roommates in Lafayette who influenced each other and mutually boosted each other's musicianship through comradeship and daily practice. When Corey Ledet, a somewhat shy and reserved young man, was learning the accordion, he came to Mitch Reed's shop nearly every day and played in a corner for hours, meeting musicians who stopped by to visit.

Guitar player Chas Justus, who grew up in Vicksburg, Mississippi, recalls similar occasions in his childhood like "pickin'" (referring to playing the guitar). In his late teens, he moved to Baton Rouge and began his university studies at Louisiana State University, where he met Linzay, Joel Savoy, and Richard Burgess, all natives of the Eunice area. In their apartment on campus, they cooked and talked about the sauce they were going to fix, an activity inseparable in his mind from the formation of the Red Stick Ramblers. In fact, Chas compares Appalachian old-time music with Cajun music, which he describes as involved in a broader social context than just performance. Clifftop, a popular old-time music convention, illustrates this process according to Chas: "They have contests, but the contests are an afterthought. Really, it's just thousands of people who get together and just have one jam circle after another and nobody is really trying to impress anybody necessarily, or perform. . . . Just that scene around our campsite with that black pot, the smell of it, the music going, it makes this community thing. It's amazing."[75]

This is what led him to talk about the Black Pot Festival—a music festival, camp, and cook-off founded in 2006 by the Red Stick Ramblers—not just as a festival but as "a way of life." In fact, this communal dimension has come to be considered the essence of the ethos of southwestern Louisiana. Dirk Powell recalled with a chuckle seeing a sign at a benefit at which he played that encapsulated this value perfectly: "Private party, everybody's welcome!"

In addition to jams that are at the core of the learning and teaching process, other methods are applied as well. At the DBCCHW, band labs that group students into temporary "bands," make them work out songs and perform every morning under the eyes of working musicians who offer guidance and feedback. They provide input on various aspects of the process, including, for example, adapting volume to the performance setting (acoustic versus amplified, or a gig with a full band versus a workshop with a handful of instruments) and how to play strong without necessarily playing louder or the importance of the backbeat for rhythmic instruments that makes a song roll.

In addition to seasonal music camps and formal workshops, group and individual lessons are available throughout the year. At his shop in Arnaudville, Tom Pierce provides group lesson series taught by various musicians like Henry Hample, Mitch Reed, and the late Al Berard. The Front Room, which started in 2008 and is run by Mitch Reed and his wife Jen, offers group and private lessons for adults and children in fiddle, guitar, and photography, in addition to a band lab class open to any music style. The aim of their band lab is not simply to teach school-age students how to play in a group, but also how to succeed in the music business, including coverage of copyright laws, royalty payments, paying band members, marketing music, and placing music on online media websites. Although this dimension is seldom approached in teaching settings, the fact that the business aspect is now accessible to local school kids reveals a desire to better market music and to provide younger players with the tools that their musical endeavors will require.

Technical explanations, however, are not favored by the setting of camps or group classes. Although some teachers select the songs they will teach and have specific ideas about how to teach them, others, particularly in advanced classes, allow students to request what they would like to learn and then answer questions. In 1976 the Smithsonian Institution produced the first music method for learning to play French Louisiana music under the title *Traditional Cajun Fiddle: Instruction by Dewey Balfa and Tracy Schwartz* [Folkways Records FM 8361], and in 1977, *Cajun Fiddle, Old and New with Dewey Balfa*, recorded and annotated by Tracy Schwartz [Folkways Records FM 8362]. Schwartz, a member of the New Lost City Ramblers, was part of a group of pioneers in the resurgence of southern mountain and bluegrass music. He first met Dewey Balfa at the 1964 Newport Folk Festival and later at the 1974 University of Chicago Folk Festival, where he played second fiddle with Balfa, who approached him to collaborate on an instructional album.[76] Rather than a specific learning method, the record was designed "to serve the curious listener and the serious learner at the same time, without going too far in either direction." Played at normal speed but shortened, the sample songs on the second LP do not include written musical notation (as opposed to the first album). The method was thus deliberately based on listening and imitation. First, Dewey demonstrates specific left-hand methods: sliding note, rolling note, the trill sound, the drone sound, and the old lonesome sound. Balfa and Schwartz then explain how each technique contributes to the Cajun style and illustrate it with a tune. A full side of live performances by the Balfa Brothers is also included.

This approach of learning by imitation has continued as a model for all music teachers. At the 2008 DBCCHW camp, Michael Doucet, considered a virtuoso, taught a twin fiddle class with Mitch Reed. He was not eager to answer technical questions from the students.

> Student: can you talk about the rhythm a little bit?
> Michael: I don't teach, ask Mitch those questions. You know how I learned. I'd sit with these guys "How do you play that?" "Like this." So I don't think about it in logical terms. I just play it. So yes, there is a pattern [does the seconding]. But I know that because I have the melody in my head.
> Mitch: Of course this is a music camp, so you get things broken down, but when Michael was learning, and even me, when I'd meet these old guys, they didn't know what they were doing, so you had to just watch. But really, you actually learn so much better by just watching and not thinking about it. But you know, you pay to come here and get people to tell you about it [laughs]. But when you can, just watch.

Doucet's instructional video is consistent with this view in providing almost no technical explanation.[77] His approach primarily consists of playing each tune slow and fast, making use of slow motion and zooming in on his left hand in the upper left corner of the screen. While he names all his mentors and describes some of their style, including the statement "Dennis McGee's rhythm is unlike most modern players, he likes to bounce, octave sounds, before the accordion," he does not specifically explain how it is done (whether through bowing or fingering) except for modeling it in his performance.

There are degrees of imitation, and some musicians-turned-teachers elect to break tunes down more than others. Dirk Powell, for example, tends to provide more explanation to help students get the "Cajun feel": "One technique for adding embellishment is squeezing notes from the right side. These things don't have names here, that's the way I call it for this purpose. I'm slimming into a note, gradually getting there." Another specific technique is playing triplets by doing fast motion with the middle finger in an octave position.[78] These technical suggestions, however, are always offered cautiously, unlike standardized techniques.

Many fiddle teachers like Mitch Reed and David Greely adopt a similar teaching method. Other than announcing the key in which the tune will be played, no music theory is mentioned. In classes and instructional videos, Mitch first plays the whole tune at tempo. He then breaks it down at a very slow speed and without ornament: he first plays the A part, which is itself broken down in several phrases. He walks through each phrase very slowly, numbering the digits for each note. For example, in "Colinda," the A part I divided in 4 phrases. The first phrase is demonstrated while the fingering is called as follows: "Open A, third finger on the A, Open E, first (finger) slides on E, third on A, first slides on E." Students repeat after him, and this "call and response" is repeated numerous times until everyone is comfortable with the phrase. The other parts (B, sometimes C) are taught according to the same principle. Once each phrase of the part has been played, the teacher and the students play it together for a while. The phrases are then put together to form the parts. Once the melody is learned, Mitch shows the drones or double stops, droning the string below the melody string (droning the D string when on A, for example); he then demonstrates the chords before playing the melody while the students practice the chords, and he finally demonstrates ornaments that can be added like slurs, special double stops, fingering, putting up and down the first finger, and other techniques. In his most recent teaching videos, a graphic appears while he plays the chords and indicates precisely the position of the fingers on the strings for each chord. Additional resources included on the producer's website include tunes transcriptions with the number of the finger indicated above each note.[79]

While some teachers provide more technical tips than others, the choice not to intellectualize this music is widely shared. Many teachers insist on the value of repeatedly observing and listening. "This is what I recommend. After class, instead of going under a tree and playing these tunes, I think it's better to put your headphones and listen. Because then you get the tune instantly," Reed contended to his students at the 2001 Balfa camp. Unless people ask specific questions, musical theory is very seldom referred to, and anyone can take a class and have access to what is taught. In order to learn a song from a CD, people also use free software like Slowdowner, which allows songs to be played at any tempo, and in any key.

This accessibility is supported by the use of numbers instead of keynotes to teach a song. This also avoids further confusion for the fiddle, which can be tuned standard (classical) or tuned down. Instead of calling notes while breaking down a tune, the teacher will say: "Use your first finger on your A string, your third finger on your E string, etc...."

Mnemonic methods for bowing are also used for simplification. The shuffle's push and pulls on the bow are memorized with the line "I'm hap-py, you're hap-py" (borrowed from the Suzuki method) or "Dile, croco-dile, croco-dile."

In their instructional videos and classes, these instructors consistently remind their students that learning should be "fun," a notion that bears little relationship to music theory. "No pressure, fun lesson" is one of the expressions that is used. In fact, learning French Louisiana music does require little to no musical theory, and teachers easily adapt to students' prior knowledge. The primacy of imitation through observation and listening makes the learning process non-threatening for those with little formal musical education. My classical training spared me from learning from scratch, but like everybody else, I sat with musicians who taught me basic tunes and techniques, listened to the tapes and CDs that they recommended, and played along with recordings for hours. I had the good fortune to be given a copy of a very helpful tape recorded by Peter Schwartz, the son of Tracy Schwartz. Made for his friend Christine Balfa after Dewey passed away, it was intended to teach her the basics of the fiddle and was extremely clear and well considered for beginners. I progressively immersed myself in a style that was new to me, to the point of completely detaching myself from the sheet music and theory of my classical training.

Many younger musicians, whether native Louisianans or not, received a formal music education. This is the case of D'Jalma Garnier, who learned classical violin at age five; Mitch Reed, who started with the classical cello; Kevin Wimmer, who beginning at age four learned from his violinist mother using the Suzuki method; and Daniel Gale, whose initial training was also classical. These musicians' skills unquestionably contrast with the informal learning process of French Louisiana music's pioneers, contributing to a different sound. They adapted to this music, however, by jamming and practicing daily as well as socializing with accomplished musicians who taught them how to immerse themselves in its ethos and techniques, tailoring their earlier skills to this specific style.

The notion of fun is also found in French Louisiana dance teaching methods, where it refers to a debate regarding the codification of dance that often intertwines with the distinction between native teachers (or Louisiana residents) and out-of-state teachers (a question discussed in chapter 5).

The exasperation of Louisiana natives and residents toward what they construe as over-codification of dance moves and sequences is also situated within idealized values assigned to "folk" or "roots" music, including freedom, spontaneity, and authenticity. Very similar controversies are found in other "exotic" dances such as peasant, tropical, and popular dance, including the dance practices in *guinguettes* (dancehalls and clubs) along the Marne River in the region of Paris, France.[80] These debates oppose purity to dilution, and simple pleasure (i.e., fun) to elaborate coding systems. It seems to me that the opinion that these codes and rules are not present or are very reduced in such dance practices carry ideological judgments. Indeed, privileging simplicity, spontaneity, and pleasure should be considered itself a rule. These qualities are only possible if the dancer or musician masters the rhythmic codes and gestural conventions that regulate the specific dance. These moves require learning that can be experienced as constraining, even when they are learned *in situ*. The fact that in dancing, attention is paid to smoothness, sliding, or other steps and sequences of moves only signifies a different set of codes, and certainly not a lack of codes.

My own experience as an outsider in dancehalls only confirms the importance of knowing and eventually mastering the local codes. As I dutifully went to numerous dance clubs for the sake of my research, which by no means excludes pleasure, many native partners hastened to advise me on the "right" way to dance as soon as they took me in their arms, after noticing that I was not an expert (to say the least). Proficient dancer friends, when I asked about dancing, gave me tips: for zydeco, one insisted on hip movements and placing the weight on the third step; another referred to the alignment of the feet and the hips, without too much space between the feet, except for specific steps. All of my informants talked about the position of the upper body and the importance of avoiding bouncing the elbows. A retired friend who would never voluntarily miss a dance and went from one dancehall to the other on weekends once told me: "Don't think about it, that's the worst that can happen to your feet. They know what to do!" In fact, people who are not aware of these rules are the object of criticism and even run the risk of being expelled from the dance floor: regulars at La Poussière are known for bumping into novices who inadvertently enter the inside circle, where only fast, competent dancers circulate instead of staying on the outskirts. *Guinguette* regulars in suburban Paris used precisely the same tactics to sanction newcomers.

It is also true that, regardless of the dance style or the method used to learn it, every accomplished dancer went through a period of assiduous practice in order to become proficient. Corey Porche recalls the time when he became fond of zydeco dancing after he moved from his native New Orleans to Lafayette to attend college in 1993: "From the Friday to the Sunday, I danced and learned so much, that I couldn't even walk, my feet were doing crazy sheet, I can't dance like that now if I try. I was really transformed, that was it! . . . Every weekend all we did was dancing. I was 20, maybe. We'd go to Randol's during weekdays. We'd talk about dancing, music all the time. Then I started to go to zydeco clubs . . ."[81]

Like learning to play music, learning how to dance requires a degree of obsessional practice to acquire the necessary skills and comfort to perform in public and confront people's judgment. Pleasure and fun are inseparable in this process from assiduity, perseverance, and at times frustration.

"I'm Coming Back Home, 'Cause That's Where I Belong"

> What is it that we have here that sets us apart? What we do have in Lafayette is a character grounded by our homegrown and rooted sense of being, an undeniable sense of place; an uncommon respect for family and tradition, as well as an open mind to the good that the future can bring.
>
> DOMINICK CROSS, "ALLONS À LAFAYETTE, INDEED," *INDEPENDENT WEEKLY*, MARCH 30, 2012

Cultural geographers, anthropologists, philosophers, and landscape architects have all contributed to the development of the concept of place.[82] The emergence of humanistic geography developed as a meaningful component in human life, a center of meaning, and field of care that formed the basis for human interaction. From the 1980s onward, critical cultural geographers have demonstrated how places were socially constructed within contexts of unequal power relations.[83] The meaning and materiality of place are envisioned as social constructs that invite analysis of the processes of place making. Edward Soja developed the notion of *thirdspace*, which challenged binary oppositions between objectivity and subjectivity, real versus imagined. Thirdspace is practiced and lived rather than simply being material (conceived) or mental (perceived).[84] Pierre Bourdieu also developed this dialogic relationship in an article in which he argues that social scientists should "go beyond the opposition . . . between representation and reality" and "include in the real the representation of the real."[85] Representations are understood as "performative statements," and Bourdieu questions the division between so-called "objective" and "subjective" properties, defending the necessity of including "the reality of common representations into the scientific representation of reality." The issue of authenticity has been particularly well explored as a challenge to mobility and globalization, which have led to the notion of the erosion of place. However, the cultural distinctiveness of place has not suffered from erosion but has instead become more salient.

"Louisiana represents the heart over the intellect, spontaneity over calculation, instinct over reason, music over the word, forgiveness over judgment, impermanence over permanence, and community over the isolated and alienated individual." These are the words of Lafcadio Hearn, an Anglo-Greek writer who spent a single decade in New Orleans from 1877 to 1888 and whom Frederick Starr credits for best exploring this subject and, in the process, "inventing" the notion of Louisiana as both an idea and a symbol.[86]

Louisiana's culture, most commonly expressed through its unique music, cuisine, architecture, and people, is considered its greatest asset. In south Louisiana's music milieu, this distinctiveness is strongly related to family ties and musical dynasties, which are central to the legitimacy of musical choices and to the acquisition and transmission of musical skills and styles. Musical dynasties—the Ardoins, Carrieres, Cheniers, Balfas, Savoys, and Franks, just to name the most emblematic—are part of a veritable pantheon of French Louisiana musicians. Musical dynasties are often represented as one of the hallmarks of the city of New Orleans, but the role of kinship in southwestern Louisiana is similarly powerful. The dynastic character of musical tradition has been extensively documented in the Crescent City, particularly regarding contemporary musical families that include the Marsalises, the Nevilles, the Connicks, and the Bouttes.[87] Aided by interaction from a tender age with musicians who are members of their immediate and extended family, children were and still are exposed to performances and informal mentoring, have ready access to instruments at home, and are encouraged to pursue musical education.[88]

Musicians' connectedness to New Orleans and southwestern Louisiana is also expressed through the notion of home, epitomized by Chenier's famous song "I'm Coming Home," recorded in the late sixties: "You know, all of my friends / They're all sending it back home for me / And when I'm coming home and meet my dear old mother / That's one woman, I know she loves me, I know she do, I know she do / I'm . . . I'm coming home / I feel, feel so all alone / I'm coming back home and meet my dear old mother / 'Cause that's where I belong."[89]

Home is viewed as the heart of social life, and irrigates its every aspect, overlapping with the notion of "community," also equally present, for example in the following quotation from Joel Savoy: "Everybody shares personnel, you know, I'll go play with so-and-so if so-and-so can't make it. It's just this great, big community. It's a musical culture here unlike any place I've ever seen. And so we say 'Louisiana. Music. Culture' [in reference to Valcour Records slogan]. From New Orleans to Lake Charles, you know? All across, all over. We're just friends."[90]

This connectedness to a "community of musicians" in southwest Louisiana is shared with New Orleanians, who value the intensely rich interaction that characterizes the city's network of musicians.[91] Although nonnatives point out how easy it is to connect with this network and how welcomed they feel, natives are literally born into it.

Beyond the spatial unit, "home" refers to a network of relationships and mutual support that is assimilated to family ties. Chenier summarizes the nurturing, soothing role of home when he compares it with his mother in the song "I'm Coming Home," a sentiment echoed by Wynton Marsalis when he states, "home is like your Momma," capturing the ambivalent meanings of the concept in expressing both the obligation to leave and, ultimately, the indestructible ties with "home."[92]

Home is anchored within a space defined by musical practices and networks of interaction more than it is by its physical traits or even the meanings that have come to be associated with it historically. In southwest Louisiana, mutual assistance among musicians and music institutions is supported by the regular organization of benefits, fundraising performances in support of either individual or collective causes. Benefits provide financial assistance in the event of death, illness, and private or institutional musical projects (for example, annual events such as the Medicine Show in support of the Dr. Tommy Commeaux Memorial Endowed Fund for Traditional Music, Archive Aid for the Archives of Cajun and Creole Folklore at ULL, and Louisiana Folk Roots events).

Within south Louisiana, one was born and raised in a specific neighborhood (urban or rural, called *voisinage*), or town, and such spatial boundaries (neighborhoods, towns, sub-regions) are central in the place-making process. The ubiquity of references to place in French Louisiana music offers one illustration of the localized nature of the sense of place. The identification of particular bands with a specific town dates back to the earliest recordings of French Louisiana music, from the Hackberry Ramblers and the Rayne-Bo Ramblers to contemporary bands like Steve Riley and the Mamou Playboys, the Lafayette Rhythm Devils, Horace Trahan and the Ossun Express, or the Red Stick Ramblers (a reference to Baton Rouge or "red stick"). Song titles inspired by specific localities are even more numerous. Just a few examples of particular classics include "Allons à Lafayette," "Two-step de Ville Platte," "One step de Mamou," "Eunice Two-Step," "Two-step de Grand Marais," "La Valse de l'Anse au Paille," "Lake Arthur Stomp," "La Valse de Grand Basile," "La Valse de Grand Bois," "Port Arthur Blues," "Valse à Reno," "Dog Hill," "Perrodin Two-Step," "Lacassine Special," or "Church Point Breakdown." Current bands continually contribute new material to this corpus of geographical references within a tightly circumscribed region, including "Allons a Tepate" (Balfa Toujours), "A Saint Martin" (Feufollet), and "Ossun Breakdown" (Horace Trahan), among many examples. Every town has its own character beyond the common bonds of family and locality. Connectedness to a particular place, a home place that is intricately woven with family bonds, is comparable to what Karen Blu describes for the Lumbees in North Carolina.[93]

Specific towns are not only significant as birthplaces, hometowns, or places of residence. They are also constructed as central to the diversity of musical practices and music styles within French Louisiana music. Music is associated with highly specific places. Parishes, town, or rural settlements can be bound to a specific style, whether the tie is a question of a preference for particular instruments over others, a certain musical influence, or broader differences. Fred Charlie, a record producer and musician from Ville Plate, evokes a few of these localized musical identifications:

> There are different styles. If you go to Abbeville or Kaplan, they play music with a lead guitar. Here, they don't do it. But it's still traditional for us. In Houma, it's more country and western French, because there is no accordion player, they're very rare, and the music is very well done, polished. That's their way of playing French music. Around Ville Plate, I was raised with the music of Morris Berzas, on Wednesday evenings he played a dance in Mamou.[94]

Beyond regional diversity within the southern portion of Acadiana, the prairie region in the north, and the Bayou Lafourche area in the east, a broader distinction between city and country is emphasized. David Greely provided some additional context:

> I was just asking questions to Jay Cormier the other night, the accordion player. He was explaining to me the difference between Lafayette Cajun music, and around Mamou and Ville Platte. In my band [Steve Riley and the Mamou Playboys] we split our time between the Mamou prairie style and the Lafayette style. Jay describes it as being more relaxed, maybe more fiddle oriented. As opposed to the Lafayette style, which is very hard driving, boum, boum, boum [he mimics a triplet rhythm], walking bass, mostly accordion, fiddle is very much in the background. The music of Aldus Roger and Belton Richard. It's a little bit more . . . it's hard to say urbanized, 'cause Lafayette is not a big city, but . . .[95]

Travis Matte echoes this distinction between Lafayette and the prairie towns, drawing a parallel between them by referring to a specific sound: "They've got a dancehall style, what I would call it, or a Lafayette kind of style. And then you got the traditional folk style, more like what Dewey Balfa and 'em played, which is a totally different style than Tony plays. Tony Thibodeaux [his favorite fiddler] played more of a dancehall—you know Aldus Roger and Belton Richard?—he was their number one fiddle player."

Accordionists Nathan Abshire and Lawrence Walker became emblematic of what came to be called the "dancehall sound" during the postwar era, characterized by small, amplified rhythm sections (electric bass, electric guitar, steel guitar, and drums) and the drive of the accordion.

These differences perceived as styles or sub-genres contribute greatly to the place-making process and add an additional layer to the question of authenticity. Musicians' influences and choices are not only perceived as the result of their agency but as grounded in place. As a result, the local reception of the music is interpreted by the same pattern, as explained by Mitch Reed: "When I used to play with Balfa Toujours, we played in Basile at a place called the Office, and all the old guys were like . . . Dirk and Kevin played this awesome, the Balfa Brother music that put Basile on the map! And two of them would go 'Get the accordion out, we've had enough of that!' A lot of places, they're not in the traditional music at all. They want a lot of country songs with the Cajun."[96]

The intimate bonds between people and place in Louisiana needs to be understood within the perspective of a region long marginalized in terms of power and resources at the national level. Louisiana is a source of fascination on the part of outsiders that is driven by equal measures of attraction and repulsion. From New Orleans to Lafayette, south Louisiana has been portrayed as romantic and backward, simple, and given to excess. After Katrina and the levee failures, fundamentalist Christians and the political right were quick to cite the image of the sinful and depraved city of New Orleans inherited from the colonial past in order to justify arguments against reconstruction and even to contest the city's very existence. By contrast, musicians from New Orleans and southwestern Louisiana proclaimed unconditional love for their city and state and their indestructible bond with the region through both song and action. This perpetual need to give voice to their attachment to place can be attributed to the imminent threat of destruction that historically hangs over the region and that recently became considerably more immediate following the 2005 hurricanes and levee failures. The mismanagement of the disaster before, during, and after the events of 2005 only intensified the sense of fragility that haunts residents of the region.[97]

The widespread displacement of New Orleanians following Katrina had profound artistic consequences deeply affecting how music was interpreted and the aesthetics of playing. Robin Boudreaux, former saxophone player of the band the Other Planets (an experimental band inspired in particular by Sun Ra), provides his perspective on how this shift affected him:

> I feel better in a way, much more . . . a lot freer. A lot less compromised. Lately when I've been performing I feel a lot of urgency, bordering on an aggressive angry. An immediacy that I don't care what anyone has to say about it. I noticed before, I might have been much more careful of what I played, when I played it. But lately every time it's just so personal, it's almost like instantly I'm in another place, it kind of blocks out all that garbage anyway.[98]

I had the privilege of experiencing firsthand this reevaluation of playing practices and meanings on Halloween 2006, when the Other Planets who had then returned to New Orleans performed at Artmosphere, a downtown music club in Lafayette, where some of the band's members had stayed after Katrina. The band was dressed to the nines for the occasion: Dan Oestreicher, on baritone and bass saxophones, was sporting a goatee and a dark suit, his uniform as a member of the prestigious New Orleans Jazz Orchestra, combined for the occasion with an orange fur hat. Given to experimental sounds, with inventive rock instrumentation and electronic noises, the music provided ample space for improvisation. Jimbo Walsh on guitar and vocals proffered cynical social commentaries and absurd interludes. Dan did not play much, providing just the occasional riff and a few melodic lines. His involvement became highly focused, however, when he shouted aggressively into a microphone, rolling on the floor while managing to continue playing his bass sax. The outfits worn by the band for the occasion further materialized the transformation brought about by their displacement and its impact on their creativity and performance. The amplified shouts gave singular voice to the feelings expressed by Robin Boudreaux, embodying freedom and anger that were all the more powerful without the mediation of an instrument.

One of the most notable consequences of the aftermath of Katrina was a strengthened relationship between music and place, with the addition of a new layer of meaning to old songs connecting New Orleans with watery environments. Songs about the Mississippi River, rain, floods, and exodus have since become charged with renewed relevance by both performers and audiences. "Louisiana 1927," a 1974 song by Randy Newman about the Great Flood of 1927—widely played after the 2005 disaster—is an example of older song material given new life and reinterpreted with new lyrics. John Boutte's rendition of the song at the 2006 Jazz Fest was a particularly intense experience. The audience responded enthusiastically at every chorus, particularly when Boutte changed the original line "President Coolidge came down in a railroad train with a little fat man with a note-pad in his hand" to "President Bush flew over in an airplane with about twelve fat men with double martinis in their hands." Similar receptions and political commentary accompanied Paul Simon's "Bridge Over Trouble Water" and Bruce Springsteen's "My City of Ruins." The Dirty Dozen Brass Band titled their subsequent release after Marvin Gaye's song "What's Going On," tailoring its thirty-five-year-old social commentaries to the context of Katrina for the first anniversary of the disaster. Elsa Grassy argues that Katrina covers unite musicians and their audiences by expressing shared emotions in a way that contributes to "communal catharsis."[99]

The 2010 BP oil spill reopened this still-open sore, unleashing a new wave of activist songs and initiatives. While southwestern Louisiana musicians responded to the 2005 hurricanes primarily through benefit concerts, this time some committed themselves to the battle to restore the beleaguered marsh ecosystem along the Gulf Coast of the state, producing a number of songs that paid tribute to the coastal region. Musician and songwriter Drew Landry took this mission seriously, attending a meeting of the White House Oil Spill Commission. During a public comment period, he told the commissioners that the army of contractors brought in to clean up the oil flooding the gulf was largely wasting the region's limited financial resources considering the thousands of volunteers eager to help. He also invoked Cajuns' collective memory by alluding to the fact that the disaster could trigger another "expulsion" before taking his guitar and playing a song that he had composed, "BP Blues," while nobody stirred in the room: "Grew up on the southern shore / Louisiana now there ain't no more / Kickin' mud off up a crawfish hole / Barefooted with a fishin' pole / Make a living with my own two hands / Hell it's part of being who I am / Went to workin' in the oil fields / That's the only way to pay our bills."[100]

Landry subsequently dedicated a website to calls to action and field trips to the Gulf Coast in an effort to give a voice to coastal residents and workers, document the disaster, and organize benefit concerts.[101] Warner Brothers later released "BP Blues" as an iTunes single, and 75 percent of the proceeds were dedicated to the association saveourgulf.org for future testing. Landry also joined Mac Rebennack (a.k.a. Dr. John) to pursue a long-term environmental musical project that was the legacy of the late Bobby Charles, "Solution to Pollution."

Landry explained his involvement: "I don't know if I'm writing better songs or if people are just paying more attention, but I do know that there are many things I care about here in south Louisiana. If nothing else, I hope my music has inspired others to fight for the things they hold dear. Whether it's the Atchafalaya Basin or the Gulf, there's something about leaving this place that makes you really appreciate it when you come home."

Long-time activist and celebrated musician Zachary Richard was naturally eager to join the cause and collaborated with other North American francophone composers—Rocky McKeon from Cocodrie, Louisiana, one of the areas most affected by the oil spill; Ricardo Lamour (a.k.a. Emrical), a member of the Haitian community in Montreal; and Samian, a Native American of Algonquin heritage—to write two songs:[102] "Pelican" and "Grand Gosier" (Big Gullet), the Louisiana French name for the brown pelican but also the name of a village in southeastern Haiti. The lyrics in Haitian Creole expand the reference to the oil spill to encompass the Haitian earthquake of January 2010, establishing Louisiana as a springboard for the struggle against injustice and against other manmade disasters: "Le Grand Gosier is covered in oil / Le Grand Gosier is dying / The sky is red / The sea is black / If I told you / You would not understand / The disaster has happened, with no return / No concern for my well being, nor that of my community / Unable to fly, my wings stuck to the ground / While you are losing money, I am soaked in oil / Why is this happening to me this time? / But after all, I am nothing but a bird and I have no gravestone / You have soiled my memory and so I will always remember / That this catastrophe is 'natural' but that the error is 'human.'"[103]

Whether they are about New Orleans or southern Louisiana as a whole, these critical readings of the recent disaster transcend the state's singularity as the home of a unique culture. Musical reinterpretations cross the spatial boundaries of Louisiana, reflecting national and global issues and confronting relations of inequality throughout the country and the world (in the case of Zachary Richard). In this way, critical songs serve as an important modality in collective mobilization. The fact that national celebrities rallied to the defense of Louisiana and contributed their artistic creativity to the cause raised questions about the state's confinement to a subject position. I believe that this movement has helped reintegrate Louisiana as a locale for mobilization and has contributed, if only temporarily, to invert dominant power relations.

Other musicians like David Greely and Linzay Young were eager to express their outrage about the disaster on their band websites, often evoking sweet memories of childhood trips to the coast, fishing, crabbing, and watching dolphins. Songs that arose from this regional creative outburst were often battle cries: the Lost Bayou Ramblers recorded "Bastille" (initially produced as a single in two versions, one featuring Gordon Gano from Violent Femmes, and the other a remix by the Lafayette Indie-rock band the Givers) and "Marée noire" (Oil Spill) from the album *Mammoth Waltz* (2012); in 2010 the Mamou Playboys put out "Grand Isle," which gave its name to their eponymous CD, whose cover art featured an oil-covered seabird, and "C'est trop/Too Much": "C'est pas la première fois / ça nous fait ces chères promesses / C'est pas la première fois / Que ça nous vole et ça nous laisse / Asteur c'est tout gâté / C'est pas la peine brailler / Cette fois-là c'est assez / Et c'est trop tard pour pardonner . . . / Asteur nos cœurs ils sont cassés en tits morceaux / Cette fois là c'est assez, c'est trop, c'est trop, c'est trop" (This isn't the first time they've made us precious promises / This isn't the first time they've stolen, then abandoned us / Now it's all ruined it's no use to cry / This time is enough and it's too late to forgive . . . / Now our hearts are broken into tiny pieces / This time is enough, and it's too much, too much, too much).[104]

In February 2011 Marce Lacouture, producer of the KRVS radio show *Lagniappe*, invited David Greely to discuss the song that he composed in collaboration with Jean Arceneaux (Barry Ancelet's pseudonym for poetry and song lyrics):

> How does one take what is a very mournful subject and put it into song that people still wanna dance to it?
>
> That's one of our oldest traditions in Louisiana. . . . This is a place where times gets tough now and then, and it gets down to survival level. We're not talking about getting the blues, we're talking about survival [emphasis] . . . When you get to that point, You gotta make it, and you gotta come up with some joy. And it got to come from inside, it can't come from outside. And that's what people in Louisiana have been good at for a long time. The jazz musicians in New Orleans, the slaves in Congo Square, the Cajuns out here living off of nothing in the prairies. They had to come up with some joy. That's how it's done.

From the inhabitants of the marshy coastline to New Orleans residents, regardless of the damage and suffering that they endured and whether it was explicitly proclaimed or simply suggested, the survival theme is an omnipresent feature of the Louisiana landscape. Indeed, disasters are an integral part of the regional identification in the case of French Louisiana and are defined by Cajun and Creole narratives through references to their struggles against adversity, forced exile, and stigmatization. Presented as a "Second Grand Dérangement," Hurricane Rita offered a further opportunity to reaffirm this image of the resilient survivor. Drew Landry's reference to the "expulsion" that threatened Cajun Gulf Coast residents follows the same pattern, echoing the repetitive dimension of their destiny.

Cajuns have become emblematic of the notion of "self-sufficiency." Acadian historiography is replete with allusions to behaviors that demonstrate independence, resistance in the face of adversity, and adaptability, values that enable them to transcend their status as victims and to appear as agents of modernity. Their ancestors chose to leave the center-west region of France to escape the violence of the wars of religion that was particularly fierce in this bastion of Protestantism. In Acadia, their political independence encouraged them to resist the threats of the British government but also to avoid rallying to the French cause, resulting in their forced exile at the hands of the English during the 1755 Grand Dérangement. In Louisiana, their narrative is centered on economic independence and resistance to stigmatization as francophones at the bottom of the social ladder.

While the Cajuns appropriate the survivor image in their discourses, the poor black population of New Orleans also claims it. The construction of the opposition between being a survivor and being vulnerable is anchored in social stereotypes that derive from stigmatizing oppositions between rural and urban, especially among Cajuns, who define themselves as white, and New Orleans residents, often identified as black and poor. The former vaunt their mutual assistance networks, which are contrasted with the violence of urban blacks and juxtaposes Cajun autonomy and self-reliance with blacks' alleged dependence on public assistance. The result is a Cajun self-characterization based on the image of the survivor that applies specifically to rural, white inhabitants of south-central Louisiana.[105]

The Swiss geographer Jean-Luc Piveteau describes the value and function of place first as a landmark that enables one point to be situated in relation to another (i.e., the distinctiveness of Louisiana as compared to mainstream America). Second, in its anchoring function, place has connotations of permanence, stability, durability, and continuity that ensure transmission through time. Sharing a common place creates what he calls a "spatial anchoring community."[106]

Like the Native American Lumbees tribe in North Carolina, attachment to place is not simply an option for the population of south Louisiana.[107] For the Lumbee, the strong interconnection between people and place is ubiquitous and necessary and is a vibrant factor in the maintenance of a sense of belonging. "Indian identities have seemed to hinge crucially on their retention or reconstruction of and access to a home place, perhaps because displacement was so common and so devastating, so politically beyond the control of most groups throughout their histories. Whether one's group has a reservation or not is still a vital distinguishing feature among contemporary Native Americans."[108] Louisianans in general, and Cajuns and Creoles in particular, appear to follow a similar pattern in anchoring themselves and their sense of identification with south Louisiana.[109] This deep attachment provides a collective source of stability and continuity that could be considered a coping mechanism in the face of the array of displacements they have undergone over time (forced exile, disaster evacuations) as well as systematic stigmatization, marginalization, and poverty and the resulting vulnerability of the region's people.

"Louisiana is a land apart—a land of striking geographical and topographical contrasts shaped by the nation's most complex rural society and America's most colorful urban population. The links on this page provide the best available guide to Louisiana's vast cultural resources." One of the missions of the Center for Cultural and Eco-Tourism of the University of Louisiana at Lafayette is to promote Louisiana culture, while also focusing on archival and research efforts related to the state's southwestern region. The center houses the Archives of Cajun and Creole Folklore, established in 1974 and the most comprehensive collection of recorded and transcribed materials on French in Louisiana. The center also produces CD series based on its archives, organizes music benefits, and offers a free monthly series promoting cultural and environmental awareness in Acadiana called "In Your Own Backyard." The driving idea behind the center's activities continues to be to encourage Louisiana residents to become aware of the state's rich heritage and its specificity.

The implementation of tourism policies intended to highlight the cultural heritage of southwest Louisiana dates from the early 1990s and was designed to help close the gap between the region's touristic potential and its image in the eyes of tourists, which had focused on New Orleans.

Many cities in the United States and abroad have been associated with musical sounds, such as Nashville, Chicago, and Liverpool. In a paper analyzing the construction of a "Liverpool sound," Sara Cohen demonstrates how the production of locality through music functions as a political strategy, a resource through which relations of power at local, regional, national, and international levels can be addressed.[110] The strong sense of local identity fuelled by the national media, the differentiation from the rest of the country, the distinctiveness of specific sub-regions and cities, the webs of kinship surrounding musicians, and the sense of sharing history and fate that are part of this place-making process are also singularly relevant in south Louisiana.

Although the exoticization of southern Louisiana portrays the southwest and the city of New Orleans as unique, distinct, and therefore alien places and people even within their own country, Louisianans exploit and reshape this image to their advantage, reclaiming agency through claims to resiliency and presenting themselves as a "laboratory of innovation and change," to quote New Orleans mayor Mitch Landrieu in his speech to commemorate Katrina's sixth anniversary. Although this claim is closely tied to efforts to reconstruct New Orleans, it also converges with the reconfiguration of the southwest Louisiana music scene in terms of innovative energies and its strategies to gain international recognition. In an article dedicated to a critical analysis of the notion of region, French sociologist Pierre Bourdieu addresses the mechanism of regionalism:

> ... Regionalist claims are a response to stigmatization that produces the very territory of which it seems to be the product. ... It is because it exists as an entity that is negatively defined through symbolic and economic domination that some of those who participate can be led to struggle (and with objective prospects for success and profit) to change the definition, to invert the meaning and value of stigmatized traits, and that the revolt against domination in all of its aspect, even economic, takes the shape of regionalist claims.[111]

Regionalism functions as a tool to bolster the position of Louisiana residents as citizens rather than "subjects." Faced with the economic, political, social, and environmental vulnerability of the region, which were dramatically emphasized in the aftermath of the disasters of the 2000s, Louisiana musicians have embraced the regionalist narrative as part of their quest for legitimacy. From "new" or "nouveau" zydeco to "roots" zydeco, and from the old-time French style to the latest transformations in the sounds of Cajun bands, the French Louisiana music scene cultivates distinctiveness, defying or at least blurring the boundaries between polarities like rural-urban, mainstream-roots, and white-black, and founding ambitions for worldwide recognition on this very singularity.

1. Horace Trahan performing at Festivals Acadiens for the first time in 1996. The young man's haunting, heartfelt voice and music style was then situated in the legacy of "traditional" Cajun music.

2. Horace Trahan and the New Ossun Playboys, Blackpot Festival 2010, Lafayette. In 1999 Horace branched out to zydeco and encountered virulent opposition. After years of turmoil, his success with the CD *Keep Walking* (here performed on stage) marked his full return on the music scene.

3. *Keep Walking* (2010, BMI, The Redemptine Process) CD by Horace Trahan and the New Ossun Playboys. Horace has made a point of asserting the overarching importance of regional identification in French Louisiana music. On this CD cover, the Acadian flag and the Creole flag are explicitly side by side, with a map of Louisiana astride the two.

4. *Cedric Watson* (Valcour 0004, 2008). On his first CD, Watson is flanked by Canray Fontenot and Clifton Chenier as major inspirations of his music, establishing an identification with Creole musicians and African influences, combined with the assertion of sameness within old-time French music.

7. Joe Hall defines his and Mitch Reed's old-time style as Creole. "Creole is not a black man. It could be a black man or a white man. To me Creole is the purest of anything around here. The Creole music, you still have the European emphasis with certain tunes."

5. BeauSoleil with Dexter Ardoin and the late Zydeco Joe's washboard player, Festivals Acadiens, Lafayette, 2006. Cajun bands increasingly incorporate old-time Creole tunes or zydeco numbers and perform with Creole musicians.

6. Master Presentation: Kevin Wimmer, Ed Poullard, Preston Frank, Dirk Powell performing French music at the 2008 Balfa Camp. The label "French music" characterizes a specific old-timey style and is also used as a generic term that evokes a regional identification.

8. Rosie Ledet on the cover of *Hé! Toi Zydeco Magazine*, May–June 2000. Nicknamed the "Zydeco Sweetheart," Ledet has been performing since 1994 and is often associated with risqué songs.

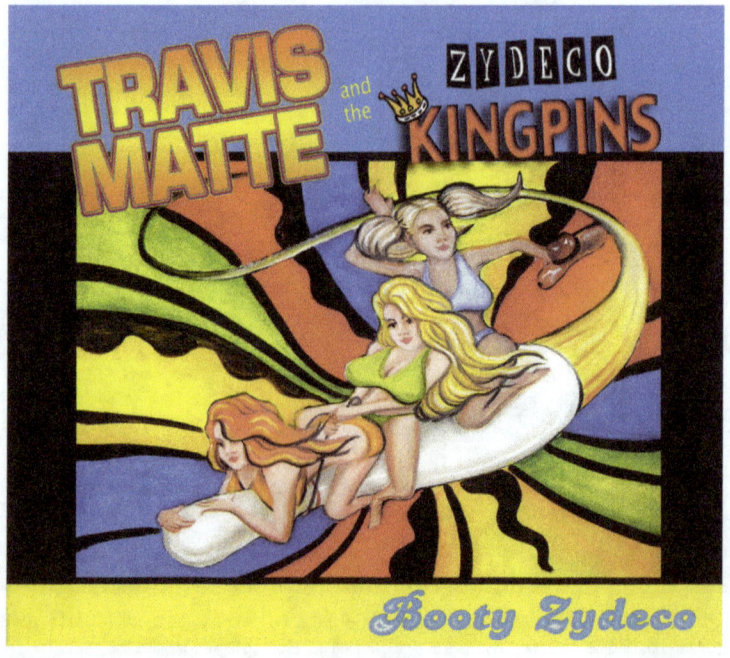

9. *Booty Zydeco* by Travis Matte and the Zydeco Kingpins (Mhat Productions, 2006). Eroticism is not restricted to the imagery of blackness. Young white musicians such as Matte can call for sensuality and hotness, although he initially did it under the zydeco label.

10. CD covers and press photos emphasize various aesthetics. Rural sceneries are still very common. Since the renewal of the Cajun music scene in the mid-2000s, there has been a trend toward a more personalized aesthetic, with the use of contemporary artwork, and band photographs sometimes veer toward rock aesthetics. Within the zydeco scene, some players favor hip hop aesthetics with sunglasses, baggy blue jeans, NBA jerseys over T-shirts, baseball caps or doo-rags. Keith Frank situates himself in two distinct styles conceived as a whole but tangibly separated into two distinct CDs.

10a: *La Pointe* by Balfa Toujours (Rounder 11661-6086-2, 1998)

10b and c: *Le Cowboy Creole*, Geno Delafose and French Rockin' Boogie (Times Square Records 9063, 2007)

10d: *En Couleurs*, by Feufollet (Feufollet Records, 2010)

10e: The Pine Leaf Boys, press photo

10f and g: *Follow the Leader* and *Boot up* by Keith Frank (Soulwood Records, 2012)

10h: *V.I.P.* by Chris Ardoin (Maison de Soul, 2010)

10i: *Who Do You Love?* By J Paul Jr. & the Zydeco Nubreedz (Louisiana Red Hot Records, 2001)

11. The Whirlybird. Jam with Joel Savoy, Jesse Lége, Linda Castle, October 2009. Functioning as mediators, Jim Phillips and Christy Leichty brought together different circles—fans, transplants, and Louisianans—at their saloon/dancehall.

12. Lâche Pas at Nunu's, Arnaudville, November 1, 2009. L–R: Daniel Gale (special guest), Linda, Andrea. In 2009 Andrea Rubinstein, Linda Castle, and Madeline Powers formed a trio called Lâche Pas that eventually disbanded. Their promo emphasized their old style and passion for this music: "Their driving, back-porch style reflects the rhythms and emotions of Cajun and Creole music of long ago. Playing 2-steps, waltzes, twin fiddles tunes, and singing in French, Lâche Pas plays from the heart, the way it was meant to be."

13. Sunday Jam, Tom's Fiddle & Bow, Arnaudville, November 1, 2009. Lori Henderson, who hosts the monthly jam with her husband Tom Pierce, sings with Shane, a regular California visitor. While the Cajun jam happens in the front room, an old-time music jam takes place in a screened porch overlooking Bayou Fuselier.

14. Sunday Jam, Tom's Fiddle & Bow Shop, Arnaudville, August 3, 2008. Joel Breaux (accordion), Madeline Powers (fiddle), Linda Castle (fiddle), Eddie Bourque ('tit fer), and Mark Normand, who usually is on the back porch playing bluegrass and country. All are regulars at the jam.

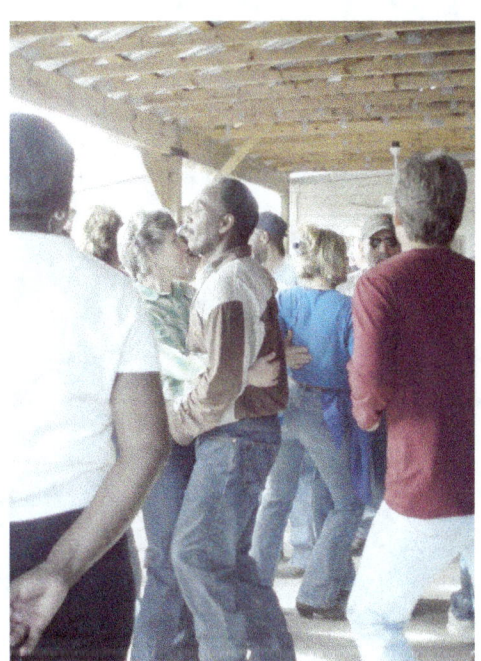

15. Missy Maloney dancing to Geno Delafose, Gerry Spanger's annual Mardi Gras party, Breaux Bridge, February 2, 2008. Originally from South Africa, Gerry lives in the Northeast and is a part-time resident in Breaux Bridge.

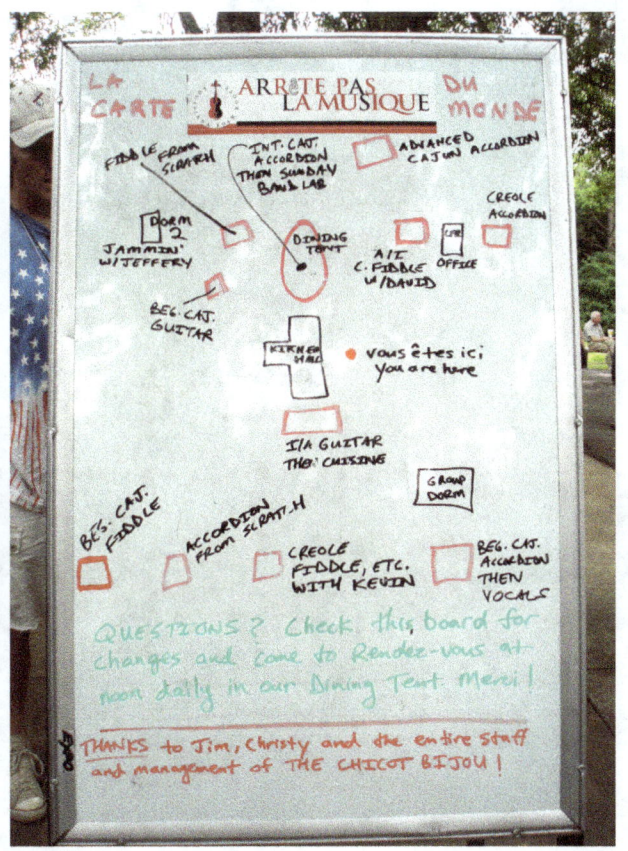

16. La carte du Monde (World Map), Balfa Camp 2008, Chicot State Park.

17. Jam with the Red Stick Ramblers, Ashokan Fiddle and Dance, New York State, August 2008. "Southern Week" includes both Appalachian old-time and Cajun and Creole workshops, and the Red Stick Ramblers regularly perform and teach there.

18. Jam with Tracy Schwartz, Ginny Hawker, and Suzy Thompson (on the porch steps), Blackpot Festival, Lafayette, October 2010. The festival has been instrumental in strengthening the connection between old-time and French Louisiana musicians by bringing major figures of this alliance.

5

Choosing French Louisiana

JANUARY 13, 2007, 12:30 PM
TOM'S FIDDLE AND BOW, ARNAUDVILLE, LOUISIANA

In small print, the sign hanging in front also announces the workshop's secondary function: "Organic Acoustic Jam." The first people to arrive for the Sunday jam can be seen from the outside, with players grouped in a circle around a cowskin rug and non-players seated on a sofa in an adjoining alcove. A mannequin sporting a wig and a shimmering gown and bedecked with Mardi Gras beads extending a hand in welcome toward visitors as they enter the door. To the left, fiddles hang in single file from the ceiling. The walls are covered with Lori's artwork—puppets contrived from baseballs and small, colorful birds on springs with long, slim legs made out of twigs, painted fabrics, album covers, umbrellas, and brightly-colored strings of lights. The people attending today's jam are a diverse group, a mix of transplants and natives, regulars and passers-by, musicians and spectators. On this particular winter day, a local accordionist is leading the players, joined by fiddlers, a few guitars, and a snare drum. Waltzes, two-steps, and reels alternate while Linda and Madeline sing harmony. From time to time, somebody unhooks the bass from the back wall, and the rhythm of most songs is punctuated by the *'tit fer* (triangle). Other instrumentalists join in with essential instruments like mandolin and banjo, and when not playing the snare drum, Missy uses rapid pencil-line drawings to capture the motions of a musician within the time of a single tune, one of her favorite activities.

Beyond the front room facing the street, the studio continues back toward the bayou, and a small, improvised kitchen on the right holds a table loaded with covered dishes brought by jam participants. The menu today includes a white bean and pork stew, deviled eggs, stuffed bread, salads, and vegetarian pies. People drift in to serve themselves whenever they are hungry. Further back on a screened porch overlooking Bayou Fuselier, old-time, bluegrass, and country music players create their own separate jam. Rick, an experienced bluegrass guitarist, is often present, and this week a Danish dobro player visiting the region for a few weeks has joined Rick on the porch, where Lori is strumming her ukulele and belting out a plaintive country song, "Cold Cold Heart." The concurrent jams, snacking, and conversation continue into the early evening.

For the first time, I was encountering a circle of people who had settled in southwest Louisiana because of their love of local music. My friends Joel Breaux and his now ex-wife Lisa, who were returning to their native region after a decade in northern California, had piqued my curiosity when they told me about this jam and other events organized by newcomers with whom they felt close as ex-residents of the same region. After I sat down and pulled my fiddle out of its case, Lori kindly asked if she could feed my hungry newborn, who was sitting in his car seat in the middle of the jam. Everybody welcomed me, and I instantly sensed a friendly, laid-back atmosphere that I would come to rely on over the next nine months. I had transplanted myself to the area in the fall with my family and was immersed in a new circle of friends with whom I felt a natural affinity. I shared with them the experience of having two homes, two lives, the experience of mobility; overall, we seemed to share similar political opinions that contrasted with the strong conservatism of the region; we were primarily raised in urban environments; I could relate to some of the challenges that they had faced; like them, I was not from the region and was acutely aware of it, experiencing throughout the years a shifting identity made up of degrees of inside-ness and outside-ness. At the same time, I was the only native French speaker and European among Americans. My relationship with Louisiana had begun earlier, in 1991; I was younger, and I first experienced the region's music as a student discovering the field, not as a fan of the local culture. In fact, I was not initially attracted to local music, and my immediate impression was that it sounded old-fashioned and dull. My love for the music had not predated my presence in Louisiana, nor was it initiated by French Louisiana music fans in France. Instead, it grew out of lived experience over years of fieldwork trips and encounters with musicians. Another difference lay in the fact that I had just started a family, whereas many transplants then were either single or had grown-up children. Finally, my circle of friends initially developed among people not necessarily involved in music and included a variety of Louisiana residents from different background and lifestyles. I was thus one of theirs, and yet I held a peculiar status and had followed a different itinerary.

Ever since French Louisiana music was first recorded by national recording labels in the late 1920s, the diffusion, validation, and promotion of the French Louisiana repertoire have been the result of a continuous circulatory movement in which the local music scene has responded to outside influences, in turn stimulating increased local interest. As demonstrated in previous chapters, academic and cultural institutions have played important roles in this process under the influence of folklorists, among them both nationally known figures (John and Alan Lomax, Ralph Rinzler) and regional specialists (Lauren Post, Harry Oster).[3] Other key actors have included music producers and film directors as well as musicians and dancers whose paths have intersected, leading to collaboration and mutual influences that ultimately have defined how the French Louisiana repertoire has evolved and changed.

This chapter demonstrates the decisive role of outsiders' interest and mobility in the development, evolution, and reconfiguration of French Louisiana music. Starting with professionals, collectors, and fans in the 1960s and 1970s and particularly in northern California, a historic migration destination for Louisianans, it shows the process and network of fans that eventually laid the ground for the establishment of a wave of transplants in the early 2000s. Arjun Appadurai and Akhil Gupta and James Ferguson, among others, have cautioned anthropologists to challenge the notions of neatly bounded, geographically distinct peoples, cultures, and territories, calling for a disjunction between place and space. The Gupta and Ferguson argue for a re-evaluation of the "assumed isomorphism of space, place, and culture" and in favor of an approach to place grounded in the realities of a world of diaspora, transnational cultural flows, and increased mobility.[1] Transplants in southwest Louisiana vividly illustrate the essential role played by non-natives in the validation, circulation, and remapping of French Louisiana music. I will focus on a few interconnected itineraries to show the driving forces of how these individuals became established in the region, what meanings they attached to their projects, how they inhabit their new home, what kind of network they have developed or joined, and how they interact with natives and working musicians. My specific interests are in revealing the changes in status and new hierarchies involved in this process as it regards music and musicians and describing the configuration of relational networks and the ways in which they overlap and grow, in other words, the processes through which the mobility of French Louisiana music shapes its reconfiguration locally, in Louisiana.

Outsider views of French Louisiana Music

They call me a Cajun mama in Denmark [laughter]. . . . I guess I've kind of mothered a lot of Cajun music.

ELSEBETH KROGH, LAFAYETTE, APRIL 30, 2008

As demonstrated by Mark DeWitt's thorough study of the Cajun and zydeco scene in northern California, this region constitutes a central node in the development of a vibrant French Louisiana music network that has been decisive in its diffusion and visibility throughout the country.[2] The mobility between south Louisiana and northern California was based on the migration of Creoles and southern blacks beginning in the 1940s through the 1960s and mid-1970s to work for wartime industries building aircraft and naval vessels. During World War II, there was a massive influx of blacks, especially from Louisiana and Texas, into the San Francisco Bay area, among them a significant number of Creoles.[3] California's liberal reputation offered an escape from the powerful grip of racial discrimination that prevailed in the South. Among the musicians who developed a career in California, Ida Guillory, a.k.a. Queen Ida, became one of the best known and established a role as spokesperson for French Louisiana music.

As French Louisiana music was becoming more common in California and in the South, music producer Chris Strachwitz was instrumental in the development of a strong French Louisiana music network in northern California. Based throughout his career in Berkeley and El Cerrito, in 1960 Strachwitz founded Arhoolie Records, initially specializing in blues but later one of the major recording labels for "folk" music. A major collector of 78 rpm commercial recordings of Mexican-American music, blues, and Cajun and zydeco, Strachwitz did field recordings in south Louisiana in the 1960s, rediscovering some older musicians who had made few if any commercial recordings, including Wade Frugé, Austin Pitre, Cheese Read, and others. He produced an album by the Hackberry Ramblers in 1963 and in 1965 released *Louisiana Blues and Zydeco* by Clifton Chenier. In 1970 he issued *Louisiana Cajun Music*, a series of LP compilations in five volumes that became an inspiration to local musicians.

Also based in Berkeley, filmmaker Les Blank reinforced the Bay Area connection to French Louisiana through his documentary films and has collaborated with Strachwitz since the 1970s. He made six films devoted to pioneer figures in French Louisiana music, including *Spend It All* (1971) with the Balfa Brothers, Nathan Abshire, and Marc Savoy; and *J'ai été au Bal* (1989), about Ann Savoy, which was followed by the release of an eponymous soundtrack recording on Arhoolie (1990). Strachwitz and Blank kindled an interest in the Bay Area through their work and the exposure they provided for French Louisiana musicians, but also because of visits to the area by musicians to play local gigs, festivals, and speak at radio shows.

The 1970s saw several California musicians interconnected to each other spend extended periods in south Louisiana. Will Spires, Eric and Suzy Thompson, and Delilah Lee Lewis were all practicing "folk" music before ending up staying for months and even years in south Louisiana in their late twenties and early thirties. They learned from master local musicians during these long visits. At a time when few outsiders came to southwest Louisiana to learn French Louisiana music, Will Spires and Suzy Thompson both received folk apprenticeship fellowships from the National Endowment for the Arts to study fiddle, Spires with Dennis McGee and Thompson with Dewey Balfa.

The distinctive character and lifestyle of rural southwest Louisiana by comparison to California very likely played a role in their attraction. Missy Maloney came from much closer, New Orleans, and settled in Lafayette in 1972 to study at the University of Louisiana at Lafayette. She recalls feeling like she was in foreign territory when she first found out that people actually spoke French and, because she enjoyed dancing at local clubs like Jay's in Cankton, when she first felt fascination on discovering cockfighting:

> Another one of the fun things about Jay's Lounge was that they had the cockfighting in the back. Oh yeah, well I was a city girl, and I didn't know the first thing about cockfighting. I'd be all involved in the dancing. But sometimes, maybe just following other people, you'd enter in the back and you could walk across the bar, the length of the bar was the width of the building, and close to where the ladies' room was, there was a back door. And it would take you out into this little . . . probably it was more like being outside, with the dirt floor, but they had a cover and these small bleachers for people to sit. It was one dollar for the guys and free for the girls to go watch

the cockfighting. I guess it's kind of like going to bull-riding now, people say "You like that?" and I love it! It's a terrible thing for the animals, but I was just fascinated. So I remember what the men were doing with the birds. It was a raucous environment, hootin' and hollerin' and screaming. They'd pick up the birds and put the bird's beak in their mouth like to wet it maybe, I think to irritate the bird, and they'd hold it like this, by the neck, pull them by the tail feathers. They were trying to agitate the bird. And then they'd throw them down on either side, like they were in a boxing ring. And then they would go at it. People talk about how cruel it was and bloody and all, and it was. It is. But it did happen so fast, it didn't seem like a torturous experience. But I would just kind of breeze through, just sit for ten or fifteen minutes, then go back to the dancing. So that was an adventure . . .[4]

During that same period, a handful of French "folk" musicians and fans were discovering south Louisiana. Music filmmaker Jean Pierre Bruneau first traveled to the area in 1971 from New York, where he was living at the time, and met the major figures in local music, an experience that persuaded him to make the cult film *Dedans le Sud de la Louisiane* (1974). During his stay, he recorded jam sessions in Mamou and Tepatate, at Dewey Balfa's home, later released under the name *Les Haricots sont pas salés* (1997, Cinq Planètes). In the early 1970s, Gérard Dôle became a fan of Hank Williams after a stay in the United States. In 1974, he started a band, Krazy Kajun, the first of its kind in France, and in the summer of 1975, he travelled to Louisiana.[4] He has since produced numerous recordings of his own band and in 1995 published the *Histoire musicale des Acadiens, de La Nouvelle-France à la Louisiane: 1604–1804*. A resident of Brittany, Eric Martin also traveled to Louisiana, where he lived in the early 1980s before establishing himself as an accordion maker in France and a member of the band Vermenton Plage, creating a solid reputation in France, Europe, and Louisiana. These early contacts provided the foundation for the creation of a circle of *Francadiens*, French Louisiana music fans in France, who organize their lives around events dedicated to this music in France, organizing gigs, workshops, and private or institutionalized festivals, the most important of which is the Nuits Cajun et Zydeco de Saulieu in Burgundy, which welcomes bands from Louisiana and throughout Europe.[5]

In England, John Broven, from the journal *Blues Unlimited*, explored French Louisiana music with his colleague Mike Leabitter, who began writing his "Cajun Corner" column in the late 1960s. Broven made his first trip to Louisiana in 1970 and embarked on the publication of a book on New Orleans rhythm and blues before publishing his well-known work, *South to Louisiana: The Music of the Cajun Bayous* (1983).

The early 1980s also signaled Elsebeth Krogh's encounter with French Louisiana music in Denmark. She was involved in a folk music band at the time and learned a few Balfa Brothers tunes through a friend who had heard them on Swedish radio. Because she was in music school training to become a music teacher, she decided to write her final paper on the history of Cajun music. She made her first trip to Louisiana in 1985 with a girlfriend and ended up staying for a year, an extended stay made possible when accordion player Sheryl Cormier offered to let her play fiddle in her band. Building on her experience, relationships, and encounters with "legends," she began teaching music and dance in music associations throughout Denmark, Finland, and Norway and created her own band, Cajun du Nord; she also published a book on French Louisiana Music in 1993 and wrote a "Cajun newsletter" for a period of ten years.[6] Her keen involvement in Louisiana music spawned a dozen bands in Denmark. She also organized dance and music workshops in Louisiana for her students for seven years, providing them with a unique experience based on her network of relationships there and contributing to the internationalization of musical tourism in the region.

These encounters with southwest Louisiana music among "folk" music fans from across the country and abroad coincided with the Louisiana French renaissance. CODOFIL had been established in 1968 and over the years became a powerful organization in the promotion of French in Louisiana. CODOFIL also created controversy, which in turn prompted publications that questioned the future of the French language in Louisiana and the transcription of Cajun French. With *Lâche pas la patate* (1976), Revon Reed founded the field of Cajun literature, which now includes plays, poetry anthologies, essays, and a journal published by the University of Louisiana at Lafayette (ULL). An additional milestone of the period that provided legitimacy for French Louisiana culture within academia was the creation of the Center of Acadian and Creole Folklore in 1974 at ULL (renamed the Center for Louisiana Studies in 1980). That same year, A Tribute to Cajun Music, now called Festivals Acadiens et Créoles, formally initiated the revival of French Louisiana music locally, with the financial support of the Newport Folk Music Festival. A decade later, the French Movement was in full swing, boosted by culinary successes like Chef Paul

Prudhomme's "blackened redfish" and the internationally acclaimed feature film *Belizaire the Cajun* (1986), which was directed by Cajun filmmaker Glen Pitre. In terms of music, outsiders' interest was welcomed locally by some major figures of the music revival, who hastened to introduce newcomers to old-timer musicians, fulfilling a mutual desire to foster the reach of French Louisiana music outside of Louisiana and locally. Marc and Ann Savoy, Dewey Balfa, and Revon Reed were among the key actors in facilitating outsiders' connections to local music circles, offering them housing and providing them access to numerous music events and encounters.

In return, music "experts" and "enlightened" amateurs from around the country played an increasingly significant role in producing records and reissuing early recordings. In 1999, Yazoo produced a CD compilation of classic recordings from the 1920s by overlooked musicians from a poorly documented area, Avoyelles Parish. Ron Brown of Athens, Tennessee, drew on his own archive to compile *Blind Uncle Gaspard, Delma Lachney, John Bertrand: Early American Cajun Music* (Yazoo 2042, 1999). European record labels have also played a central role in widening the reach of French Louisiana music, including JSP, Proper, Krazy Kat, Ace, and Acrobat in England, Bear Family in Germany, and Frémeaux and Associés and Expression Spontanée in France (on which Dôle released several albums). Other labels associated with recording during the period include Asterios Productions, through their subsidiary Cinq Planètes, which was directed by producer Philippe Krümm, a major figure in the promotion of traditional music in France. This non-exhaustive list reveals the impact of outsider collectors on the reissuance of vintage material in collaboration with independent recording labels.[7] Collectors of French Louisiana music also provide a mine of information to French Louisiana music fans due to their encyclopedic knowledge of recordings, specific discographies, and sometimes elaborate websites. Neal Pomea from Colesville, a librarian at the University of Maryland University College, launched the website np-music.org in 2002 "Cajun Music mp3: Hadacol Is Something!" "to foster enjoyment, appreciation, and understanding of the history of Cajun music." The site is a treasure trove of early French Louisiana music from the 1920s to the 1960s that makes rare 78 LPs available to listeners. The site was also contributed to by other major collectors such as Joe Bussard from Frederick, Maryland, owner of more than 25,000 78s of old-time music, including French Louisiana music. Lyle Ferbrache of Brentwood, California, has become known as the source concerning the 1950s and 1960s. The most recent production of a 78 collector, *Mama, I'll Be Long Gone*, was masterminded by record producer Christopher King based in Charlottesville, Virginia, and features the complete works of Amédé Ardoin.

Beyond question, non-native music fans have been key actors in documenting, circulating, and disseminating French Louisiana music throughout the United States and abroad. Other non-natives have made the decision to settle in south Louisiana, their interest in the music being in some cases contributed to by marital alliances with natives of the region. Ann Savoy made this choice very early on and has been an unflagging promoter of French Louisiana music ever since and the subject of numerous profiles in regional magazines.[8] A native of Richmond, Virginia, she brought back an unconditional love for the French language from a year spent in the Swiss Alps as a teenager. Before even going to Louisiana, she heard a 45 of Clifton Chenier on Arhoolie. "It just knocked me cuckoo," she recalls. She heard French Louisiana musician and accordion-maker Marc Savoy at a festival and eventually returned with him to Eunice, Louisiana, where she settled in 1976 and married Savoy. Already an accomplished guitarist, she met numerous old-timers and learned the music through her husband. Her landmark 1984 publication, *Cajun Music: A Reflection of a People*, was the first comprehensive book documenting French Louisiana music based on interviews and photographs of Cajun and Creole music pioneers, transcribed songs with written musical notation, and bilingual lyrics. With her friend Jane Vidrine, she founded the all-women band the Magnolia Sisters while raising four children, joining a series of other bands shared with her husband and family; since the 2000s, Ann Savoy and Her Sleepless Knights began to explore other repertoires, including gypsy swing, southern blues, and popular standards. Among many musical endeavors, Ann Savoy collaborated with producer T Bone Burnett on the soundtrack of *The Divine Secrets of the Ya-Ya Sisterhood* (2002), an adaptation of the best-selling novel by Rebecca Wells, and played a role as a Cajun woman leading a string band in the 1940s with her son, Joel. Her consulting role in the Cajun and zydeco segment of the *American Roots* PBS series (2002) is just another of her contributions to the national recognition of French Louisiana music. She also produced *Evangeline Made* (2002) and *Creole Bred* (2004) on Vanguard Records, tributes to Cajun and Creole music that were based on interpretations of Cajun and Creole music by rock and pop stars accompanied by native musicians. Internationally acclaimed stars Linda Ronstadt, John Fogerty, Richard and Linda Thompson, Rodney Crowell, and Nick Lowe, among others, interpreted Cajun music, while

Taj Mahal, Cyndi Lauper, and Michelle Shocked were among the musicians who played Creole music on the second of the two CDs. Ann Savoy continued her partnership with Ronstadt on *Adieu False Heart* (2006, Vanguard), and her collaborations with nationally acclaimed pop stars, moviemakers, and producers exemplify a desire to move French Louisiana music up the social scale and to validate it as an integral part of American popular music instead of comprising a single, bounded category.

In the 1990s, several young and highly accomplished working musicians active in the roots music scene eventually found their way to southwest Louisiana.[9] Dirk Powell, who was imbued with the traditions of old-time Appalachian music due to his grandfather, first encountered live French Louisiana music in Washington at the 1985 Smithsonian National Folklife Festival, where Dewey Balfa was playing with his youngest daughter Christine. Powell eventually moved to Louisiana, and after Dewey passed away in 1992, he and Christine founded the band Balfa Toujours, which became one of the most popular Cajun bands in Louisiana and across the country. Dirk did not simply remain an old-time musician who resided in Louisiana, he literally immersed himself in a local culture that echoed his bond with the Appalachian mountains of Kentucky, where his grandparents lived. He was eager to learn French and soon developed a strong attachment to the area. Among the band's other founding members, fiddler Kevin Wimmer, originally from New York, apprenticed himself to Dewey Balfa, played in the Bay Area–based California Cajun Orchestra, and, like Dirk, moved permanently to south Louisiana. While touring internationally with Balfa Toujours, Dirk pursued his projects in old-time music and began a career scoring movies. The film that gave him the most publicity in the media was the Academy Award winner *Cold Mountain* (2003), based on Charles Frazier's novel, for which he was involved in the filming and soundtrack produced by T Bone Burnett. His other prestigious collaborations have included Jack White, Joan Baez, Anthony Minghella, Loretta Lynn, and Spike Lee.[10] While Dirk's international career led him to spend a lot of time on the road, Kevin has been a member of numerous Louisiana bands and, since 2010, is the fiddler for the Mamou Playboys.

Although Dirk is currently an acclaimed figure at every level of the French Louisiana music scene, his reception by folklorists working on Louisiana has not always been smooth. At the time of his move to Louisiana, few other young musicians from out of state were doing the same thing. Although Peter Schwartz was a non-native, he had a unique status as the son of Tracy Schwartz and a cherished student of Dewey, who left him one of his most precious fiddles, named "The Old Man." Dewey's partnership with his father seemed to have left Peter invulnerable to criticism for being a non-native who played, composed, and managed the Mamou Playboys for nine years during the 1990s. Dirk, however, recalls experiencing this struggle for legitimacy the hard way when an authority in Louisiana folklore declined to allow him to play with Dewey Balfa at the Mall in Washington, apparently because he was an "outsider." Inspired by this story, Louisiana resident and filmmaker Tom Krueger collaborated with Dirk on a 36-minute movie named *The Folklorist*, in which Dirk played a professor from New York who journeys to the Appalachian mountains in search of "authentic" old-time musicians.[11] Although both Kevin and Dirk were apprentices of Dewey Balfa, their musical legitimacy was not achieved until they stayed long enough to fully demonstrate their talent.

Today, it would be far less likely for an outsider to face such a reception. Since that time, several young working musicians have settled in Louisiana: Daniel Coolick, Eric Frey, Kelli Jones, Chas Justus, Anya Shoenegge, and Daniel Gale, among others, are all versatile musicians involved in some of the most vibrant French Louisiana bands. Daniel Gale began taking violin lessons with a Suzuki teacher at age four after seeing Itzhak Perlman play violin on *Sesame Street*. At the same time, his bluegrass guitar-playing father encouraged him to figure out by ear the fiddle parts on his bluegrass and country records.

His first memory of Cajun music dates from high school:

> My parents took me up to a little violin shop in the Michigan countryside in a man's house to buy me my first full-size violin. Before letting me try a violin, he would take it out of the cabinet and play a few notes on it to make sure it was in tune. As the shopkeeper took a violin out of the case for me to try, he played the intro to a fiddle tune . . . my ears perked up—what was that, I wanted to know? The intro to a Cajun fiddle tune, he said. Ever since I heard that three-second-long Cajun groove and melody, it's stuck in my head.[12]

Daniel also remembers the first time his dad played Emmylou Harris's recording of "Lacassine Special." "I liked the song, especially the groove." His father was highly instrumental in exposing Gale to music and, when he went to the Augusta Heritage Festival of Davis and Elkins College in West Virginia to take a bluegrass flatpicking class for the first time in 1998, he thought his son might enjoy coming along and jamming:

Neither of us realized there was a Cajun/Creole week happening at the same time as guitar week. While we were standing in line to register, we noticed registration was happening across the hall for Cajun/Creole week. This piqued my interest, and, not knowing anything about Cajun music, I got permission from the director to sit in on the first couple days of the beginning Cajun fiddle class to see if I wanted to enroll. So instead of sitting in on my Dad's bluegrass guitar class, I went to Mitch Reed's beginner Cajun fiddle class. I didn't know any repertoire yet, but I caught on quickly and enjoyed seconding behind the folks who know the songs. That summer I enjoyed sitting in big jams on the porch playing along with dapper, smiling Bois Sec Ardoin.

Daniel took home his first Cajun CD: *Allons Danser: Bois Sec Ardoin with Balfa Toujours* (Rounder, 1998), which he listened to incessantly, learning the songs from his stereo. He returned to Augusta in the summer of 2000 and took accordion classes with Dirk Powell.

While majoring in music at Oberlin College in Ohio, he tailored his major and designed a Cajun music "topic course" with his advisors' support, which allowed him to receive academic credit for his work on Cajun music. During these years, he contacted people who played Cajun music and formed the Oberlin Playboys, a successful band that performed at clubs around Cleveland such as Fat Fish Blue and Redfish and the Oberlin Folk Festival, as well as opening for Louisiana musician Terrence Simien at the Beachland Ballroom and later for the Mississippi harmonica player James Cotton. Seeing the Mamou Playboys performing live prompted his first trip to Louisiana:

> It was a big deal for me when all of the sudden the Mamou Playboys came to perform at Oberlin College at a venue called the 'Sco (short for "Disco"). They were my favorite Cajun band at the time, probably my favorite band, PERIOD. I was obsessed with Cajun music at this time. For me, it was like the Beatles coming to play in my own backyard, and I was their biggest fan there. You can hear in the recording of the show as they were introduced, my yell is the loudest in the house. I approached Steve [Riley] during their set break, I told him I wanted to come visit Louisiana to learn Cajun music, how do I do that? Steve told me to talk to Peter [Schwartz, who played with and managed the Playboys at the time].... He told me to come down to Breaux Bridge in January, stay at Bayou Boudin [a B&B in

Breaux Bridge], and he could give me some lessons. This is exactly what I did that January 1999.

Jimmy Usie and his musician son Gary lived outside of Breaux Bridge, Louisiana, and heard that a "boy from up north came down to learn Cajun music." The family took him under their wing, and Gary introduced him to musicians throughout the region. Daniel took lessons with Peter Schwartz, Mitch Reed, and David Greely and began sitting in at Mulate's, a local restaurant with daily live Cajun music. After this one-month initiation to Louisiana, he enrolled at the Blair School of Music at Vanderbilt University in Nashville. The owners of Bayou Boudin had told him that their cousin Jo-el Sonnier lived in Nashville, and he began working on his fiddling with Sonnier nearly every weekend and performed with him. Eventually, Daniel moved permanently to Breaux Bridge and then to Lafayette before the 2005 disasters. Since that time, he has built a solid reputation as a musician that led him to record with David Greely, perform with Greely's trio Gumbo Jet, and found the band Low Maintenance, which performed at the 2010 Festivals Acadiens et Créoles. He also began teaching at the Acadiana Symphony Conservatory of Music where, inspired by his own musical education, he requires his students to read music as well as learning to play by ear. Over the years, he has written a collection of original Cajun songs and is working on an album.

In a similar timeframe, during the early 2000s a wave of French Louisiana music fans coming from an entirely different circle—dancers—gradually began to filter into the area.

Getting The Bug, Joining The Dance

I knew my life changed that day. I can't even emphasize it enough. It was like a magical day for me, I was so excited. So, as soon as I went home, I'm looking up the dance lessons and all the dances and I'm getting on the websites and I'm like, "Oh, my god." In the San Francisco Bay area, there were probably eight bands playing this style of music Cajun-zydeco. There'd be three or four hefty dances a week and then there were festivals going on and, so it's like, "Oh, my god." So I just dove in head first like a lot of people do when they get the bug.
LINDA, JUNE 11, 2008, HIDDEN HILLS, ARNAUDVILLE

Promoted on the national music scene and revived locally, and the core of Louisiana's tourism policy, French Louisiana music aroused keen interest among "folk" dancers. Across the nation during the 1990s, groups formed to celebrate and promote Cajun and Creole dance through courses, dances, concerts, festivals, and websites. The most extensive fan networks formed in California in the Bay Area and New York State, and beginning in the early 2000s, a number of members of these networks decided to move permanently to the Lafayette area. Mostly now in their fifties and older, they tend to be members of the urban middle class some of whom retired early with comfortable incomes, while others have portable professions that allow them to continue to work. Within the space of a few years, this circle of transplants widened to approximately forty to fifty people. Their itineraries and the webs of interactions among them illustrate the mechanisms of the process of circulation and the repercussions of these circular movements. This process of reterritorialization has contributed to the creation of new social hierarchies and contributed to the evolution of the status of French Louisiana music and to how it is configured on both local and national levels.

Those who settled permanently in southwest Louisiana for their love of French Louisiana music sometimes call themselves "transplants." One meaning of the term refers to a plant that has been uprooted and replanted, but it also denotes a medical procedure. The verb *to transplant* is synonymous with displacement and relocation, and the notion of a graft, whether plant or human, is also a means of understanding the physiological aspect of such a change—the risks inherent in it and the different stages of the trajectory, from the moment of uprooting to implantation and eventual adaptation to a new host environment.

Among transplants, Lori, Linda, and Andrea have made names for themselves in the area since they arrived. Lori has moved repeatedly since she was a child and her father worked in the aerospace industry. In our first interview in Louisiana in the winter of 2008, she made a point of emphasizing her exposure to rodeo, beginning when she was eight years old. Her first record album was by Eddy Arnold, a famous country singer. When she left Long Island, where she was born, she scrupulously listed the many places where she could conceivably consider living in the United States, a country that she pictures as a collection of "foreign countries," many of which arouse her curiosity. She has remained faithful as an adult to this peripatetic vision, regularly moving between Florida, the Northeast, Colorado, and California, while criss-crossing the country on numerous business trips that also took her to Asia and Europe. The single mother of a daughter by the age of twenty, Lori specialized in echocardiography and had a complex career working for different laboratories and later for Hewlett-Packard. She explains:

> My daughter is now thirteen and I'm thirty-three and I'm now getting exposed to all kinds of things. New York City has like the No. 1 country music radio station. So now I'm like tying it back being ten years old again, cause I'm like going back to my rodeo days. I'm like really into country music. My company sends us to Texas for a conference. And we get to dance with these cowboys. It's like, it's kind of like a trail ride, a company-sponsored trail ride. We go and there's country music, cowboys, dressed with the cowboy hats, the belts, and the boots. And I'm like in heaven. I learn how to two-step dancing around a fire, with my company, with my job. I was using that quick-quick, slow-slow as my mantra. I wanted to learn to dance so bad. But I'm still really focused on my career. So the dancing, it started a spark, but I didn't really pursue it. I have a thirteen-year-old I'm trying to raise, and a career, and my marriage isn't doing good.[13]

Managing her career and raising her daughter were her primary focus, and Lori devoted half of her narrative to describing the different jobs, activities, and business trips that preceded her move to San Diego, where her encounter with Cajun and zydeco music dramatically altered her priorities.

> There's this huge dance scene in San Diego. So I get involved with swing dancing almost immediately and I'm learning to swing. I'm taking East Coast Swing, West Coast Swing, Lindy Hop, and then I got really involved with Scottish Country Dancing . . . In the meantime, all this whole Scottish country dancing and my feet hurt, there's this other dancing, this Cajun/zydeco thing and I was like, "Wow! What is that?" I show up, I kind of figure out it's from Louisiana, I didn't know quite what it was, but I had seen a Pepto-Bismol commercial and it was like, that looks really good.

The pivotal moment for her coincided with her first trip to Lafayette:

> I think the first festival I came to, it was a combination of Festival International and Crawfish Festival. I was 38 . . . and it was like, that

was all over for me. It was like this is where I want to live. Right away. I just knew. I'm there it was like Mecca to me. It was whenever I was coming here, I was so excited to come, I did never want to leave. The musty smell when you get off in that airport in Lafayette, it's just like, "Ahhh, heaven. Home."

Among the many places she has lived, she chose Louisiana as her home before even moving there permanently.

My daughter is already grown up and ready to be on her own. So I'm going to move from San Diego to the Boston area. And my yoga teacher says, "If you move to Boston, I'm going to go to Lafayette. I'm going to go home" cause her mother was kind of sick and she wanted to be closer to Thibodeaux and she was also into the Cajun/zydeco thing. So she moves here to Lafayette and I move to Boston. So now, I have somebody that's really a dear friend of mine that lives here and I have a job where I'm traveling all the time. . . . But what was really great is that they didn't care as long as you saved them money on airfare. So, at every opportunity, I was staying over the weekend in Lafayette. So people here thought I lived here for years and years before I ever lived here because I was here all the time. If I had to go to Texas, I'd come to Lafayette first and go to Texas, come back over the weekend and fly home. So I was here all the time. Here for festivals, here before festivals, here not for festivals, just here.

Linda was also about thirty years old when she discovered French Louisiana music at about the same time as Lori. Unlike Lori (and most Californians), however, Linda has long-standing ties to California, where her family has lived for five generations. Linda was not a dancer, but she did grow up listening to Benny Goodman and other big bands with her father, an amateur musician who played guitar and trombone.

He was really into big band stuff and Benny Goodman, clarinet, all these big band guys. He also played a lot of Hank Williams and Kingston Trio and the guy that yodels, Jimmie Rodgers, so a lot of folk-style music. No black music, though. I think the only black music he was familiar with was, which I always find interesting, was, like Louis Armstrong and stuff. But, you know, he listened to all this music that had all these black roots, but he never really talked about black musicians that much. And I'd gotten familiar with them with my music stuff so I thought that was kind of interesting.[14]

As if to distinguish herself from her father and from what she seems to perceive as a gap or even a contradiction in her narrative, she explains that she was initially a zydeco aficionado before switching her affiliation to Creole style. Linda's father became a more prominent figure in her life after her mother died when she was very young. Her father was an engineer who encouraged her to focus on the hard sciences when she began college: "I was just so serious. I studied. You know, again, influence from my dad, I think. He would try to get me in a good career. He was an engineer and so he was like, 'You should do engineering.' Of course, he wanted me to do some hard science. I was doing pottery and art for a while. He was like, 'You know, all that's great for a hobby, but you need to study something, some hard science or something so you can get a good job.'"

She graduated in biochemistry and took a job with a company that manufactured equipment for genetics laboratories popping up at the time in the Bay Area, a position she kept for seventeen years. She often traveled to conferences and, during a business trip to New Orleans, was amazed by the dizzying array of music groups and styles. She started to recognize tunes her father had played for her and, shortly afterwards, she attended a music festival in California that initiated her into what was to be her new passion:

> It was 1993 and I went with a friend to a big thing they used to have in the Bay Area called New Orleans by the Bay. This is just a big thing Bill Graham put on, kind of a mini-Jazz Fest. They had like four stages and four bands a day and it would be like for two days. So, we went for like two days. I remember standing in line with her, she was kind of really cute, Kay, and there was this guy standing in front of us with a little bag, a little duffle bag and he kept turning around, he was clearly hot for my friend, so he kept trying to make conversation with us.
>
> He's like, "I'm going to dance and I got like my extra T-shirts in here." He's got a water bottle, and it's like, "Who is this geek?" I had no idea what he was talking about and then we go in. And later in the day we go to the big stage where they have a lower stage and an upper stage where the band is and on the lower stage, I think it was

BeauSoleil or somebody playing, I don't even know, I didn't know who the bands were in those days. And there's all these people dancing on the lower stage and they're partner dancing and they're having the time of their lives. I'm just like, I'm feeling like, I don't know. I've got so much energy running through my body watching this and I just knew that this like was something for me. I was so excited. I waited 'til the guy came off the stage and just sat in a chair to rest and I said, "I'm going down there and I'm gotta to go talk to him." I made a beeline down there and I'm asking him all about the dance, how did you learn and what is this and so he's telling me how there's lessons in the Bay Area and there's this huge dance scene and they dance to live music and it's really fun and I should go to these dance lessons. And then the music starts back up and he wants to dance and he actually asks me if I want to try it, which was, in hindsight, unbelievable since I'd never done it before. But, it's easy for me to dance. It's really easy for me to dance and I pick up things really easily, so I did OK...

I got really fanatical. The first couple of years, I had to go to every dance and I had to dance all the time.... How old was I? My mid-to-late thirties. And a lot of my friends at work were getting married and having babies and I wasn't doing that, I was living the single life.

So, this was a place I could plug in, there was all kinds of people who were available to, as a community, of single people, or people who wanted to socialize that way. Their kids were grown, or they're divorced, or they're . . . there's tons of recovering alcoholics there. There's all kinds of people who are on their second life kind of thing. So I made a lot of very good friends in there. Huge community. I met my husband in there.

Lori and Linda belong to a circle of fans—mostly single women—whose social schedules enabled them to become deeply involved in networks of dancers who develop powerful bonds and see each other constantly, deriving intense pleasure from this passionate commitment. Several years went by that were punctuated by various adventures, balls, parties, and pilgrimages to Louisiana to attend festivals, festivities, and workshops: the Festival International in April, the Zydeco Festival in September, the Festivals Acadiens et Créoles in October, and Mardi Gras in the spring.

Joining this network entailed the acquisition of a new status that was entirely separate from their professional identities. Linda and her husband frequently hosted parties for several hundred people that became very popular, while Lori became an accomplished dancer, bringing new dance steps back from her trips to Louisiana that she shared within her group and later starting to teach zydeco dancing at Ashokan. Their activities provided psychological benefits as well. Lori, a "woman of substance," as she put it, discovered that she exerted unexpected seductive power over Louisiana Creole men. "Here, you know, the more you got, the more they like it and you feel very accepted and cherished and admired. So it was like, I had never had that experience where your abundance is like, 'ooh. . .'"

After eight years of frenetic dancing, Linda developed an interest in playing music, even as she recognized that dancing was fundamentally therapeutic. Danny Poullard, a Creole fiddler who had moved to California in the 1970s, was highly supportive of her new interest. Over the years, Poullard has played a prominent role in the early careers of a series of musicians by mentoring fans. His former students unanimously praise his unfailingly encouraging approach and his skill in nourishing their passion for learning to play.[15]

Linda confided, weighing her words and gazing into the distance with a serious expression:

> My husband passed when we were in California, he died. And after he died, like I said, Danny [Poullard] had played at our wedding, Ed and him were pretty, they didn't hang around all the time, but they were tight. Danny was really great. I don't know, I felt like he was being one of my big brothers, at that time, because it was pretty hard for me. And I wasn't going out to dances and things like that.
>
> So, he would start coming by my house, like just drop by. Like on his motorcycle to see if I wanted to go out for a ride. Or, he'd like, him and Gary Thibodeaux was another friend of ours. They'd be, "C'mon. Come to the dance with us." They started to pull me out and Danny was really great that way. He was genuinely concerned about me and he took the time to call me, or just stop by, or just pull me out back into life again. . . .
>
> But playing music, I started playing at a really hard time in my life. Like I said, I had a lot of loss and things like that and just a lot of, "What am I doing?" and a lot of doubts about where I was and what I was going to do. Playing fiddle is so hard. You have to concentrate so much just to get one note right. It used to take me right to the present moment and I would forget about all of my worries. And it really has helped me that way. It saved my life. The fiddle saved my life. I know that.

Dancing and French Louisiana music became an indispensible source of energy that helped to lift her out of isolation and turmoil.

Forming a Circle

> There was just something about this place that just drew me to it, I was just like, "I want to do this." Maybe it was my parents and part of it was the music and there was just something that drew me down here and I don't know what it was. Now, I think I was crazy, because I look at what my life is now and the entire extended community, but it wasn't like that back then. I don't know what I was thinking. I guess maybe I needed a change, too.
> ANDREA, LAFAYETTE, 2008

The plan to settle in southwestern Louisiana came together after several successive years of round-trips and encouragement from relationships with other fans that developed over the years. For some of them, the move was made possible in material terms by particularly lucrative professions, while others were able to relocate because they sold property whose value was considerably higher than in Louisiana or changed professions. Most permanent moves initially took place by degrees and followed a long period of increasingly frequent out-of-season visits to become familiar with daily life. After several relationships with men who, like her, were either regular visitors or residents in Louisiana, Lori met her future husband, a native of New York State, at a zydeco dance in Rhode Island. At the time, he was working as an engineer at a naval facility and had been living in the same house for thirty years. Together, they made plans to both take early retirement and move to Louisiana. Their first step was to purchase a home in a gated community on the edge of a lake about ten miles outside of Lafayette, which they then rented for four years before moving there permanently.

Linda, for her part, let herself be persuaded to take the plunge by a couple who had moved before her, Jim and Christy, who "planted the seed for moving down here in my head." She initially rented a small house while continuing to travel back and forth for two years before deciding in March 2004 to move her possessions from California to Louisiana, where she purchased a house next door to Lori's lakeside home.

Adapting to local life was not without its difficulties. The contrast with the lifestyle and social relations of a politically liberal region of California is such that new residents often wondered if they would be able to successfully adapt. Two distinct themes are especially recurrent in their narratives—racial relations and nutritional habits.

Andrea, who met Linda in California and began dancing at about the same time, was one of the earliest transplants to move to Lafayette. She expressed what many future residents experienced when they first encountered the local social dynamics:

> My first trip, I was aware of the racial differences. And I was just like ... I didn't know if I could ever come back again based on some of that whole cultural context, you know. ... I was actually at the point of thinking, "Am I going to be able to move down here?" Not only is it a foreign culture and a tight family culture, it is a Catholic culture. And here I'm a nice Jewish girl from New York, what the hell am I thinking about coming down here, you know?[16]

The few Californian musicians who settled in the area in the late 1970s and early 1980s encountered identical difficulties, challenged by the attitudes and discourse of whites toward blacks or Jewish.[17]

The contrasts between California and Louisiana lifestyles are often mentioned, even after several years, as well as moving from a sunny, dry, temperate climate to the stifling heat for five months of the year, and the quality of the food and its impact on health. For both Andrea and Linda, the decision to settle in Louisiana was not an easy one, and their enthusiasm did not prevent them from experiencing mixed feelings. A fear that she would lack a sense of affinity with local residents prompted Andrea to create a discussion group even while she was living only intermittently in Louisiana. But frustrations with her life in California and the attractions of the Louisiana music scene helped dissolve any remaining doubts. She was tired of having to drive in her car for an hour whenever she wanted to visit friends, and the work she did at home for IBM further isolated her. Her desire to move closer to her aging parents in Florida finally convinced her.

> In San Francisco, I had really great food and great restaurants and world-class entertainment and I had season tickets to the opera and then my cousins were there and you know, there was certain stuff that was there and the weather was gorgeous and I still love San Francisco. ...

As of here, yeah, I didn't have the best food in the world, it got hot. But on the other hand, I had company all the time and if I got out of work and it's 5 o'clock, I'm just going down to the Blue Moon and see whose there. Or there were jam sessions and Sunday there was Louisiana Heritage or go up to Eunice, play there, and I was still doing a lot more dancing back then. And at that time, if I look at the people around me now that I hang around with, almost none of them lived here when I first got there. My friends, Jim and Christy weren't here full-time, Linda hadn't come here yet, Madeline hadn't moved here, Woody and Clarity, Susan Keifer, hadn't moved here. . . . I knew Sam [Broussard], and some of my zydeco dance friends. I knew Lisa [Trahan], go to Lisa's house on Mondays, they were all local people. That was about 2002, 2003, something like that. I knew Philip Gould and Sam was one of my buddies and dance people and, I mean mostly it was musician people. When I remember my first six months, I was like, "What did I do moving down here?" I had no old friends, everybody was new, they were friends but they were acquaintances more than friends.

As for Linda, she was crushed by her husband's death, and her life was made even more difficult by other complications—she had serious health problems and quit her job, which was exhausting her, only to find herself alone in a large house several hours away from her friends, with a heavy mortgage payment and growing impatience with the competitive atmosphere in the area. "The stress was all piling up. It was all kinds of things. You know, what have I got to lose? It felt like I didn't have anything to lose at that point. Maybe that's what I needed to pull my roots up and go." Her regular attendance at dancehalls quickly led to the realization that in the mid-1990s, the white population still rarely frequented the region's zydeco clubs, a situation that subsequently changed as tourism increased but that Linda found particularly striking at the time. However, as she reflected on her first reactions a few years after she moved to Louisiana, she considered the contrast between California and Louisiana in a new light.

I lived in Berkeley for a long time. Berkeley is like the most liberal place in the entire country. And everybody likes to think of themselves there as so tolerant and accepting. And you know, you want to experience tolerance? Come live here and live among people who you don't agree with and then you can tell me you have tolerance.

It's easy in Berkeley, they all agree. They have very progressive ideas which I really like. But they all agree with each other. So, coming here and being a minority in terms of political things, you know politics, progressiveness, racial things, whatever, gay marriage, whatever social issue you want to throw out there. I'm pretty progressive, so I'm very different from most people who live in this area. So, being that minority, it's been another very interesting experience.

As new arrivals streamed in, the circle of transplants began to widen beginning in the mid-2000s, alleviating fears about the prevailing conservatism in the region that are systematically expressed by new arrivals. As the circle expanded, it began to be called a community by its members, a term that is especially prized among Americans. Most Americans claim to belong to one or often several communities founded on such identifying factors as age, sex, religion, race or ethnicity, place of residence, or leisure activities. An idealistic project based on shared common interests, the community provides the bond. The term takes on several meanings, ranging from a residential area, to a feeling of belonging, to political strategies.[18]

In addition to their shared passion for dance and music, the members of the circle constituted a network of interaction and mutual assistance in moving (by helping locate housing or garage sales), sharing sources and supplies of organic food, helping locate services and activities centered on personal development and well-being such as Chi Qong, Tai Chi, yoga, shaman consulting, back flower remedies, and health cleansing), ultimately maintaining connections with certain aspects of their previous lives and supporting each other in their new project. Once the process of adaptation was well engaged and alternatives had been found, they humorously pointed out the contrast between the values emphasized in their narratives and the predominant lifestyle in southwest Louisiana. Linda, for example, cheerfully used self-derision when evoking her green smoothie as a fall daily cleansing while eating cracklins (fried pork skin) at the Blackpot Festival.

The system of value emphasized evokes alternative practices particularly widespread in the San Francisco Bay Area and known as New Age practices, although nobody ever used that designation with me.[19] French cultural anthropologist Christian Ghasarian explored how the idea of *possibility* is at the core of the New Age system of logic. Four interrelated dimensions in the everyday life are systematically evoked: spirituality, personal development, natural health, and global change (implying social change and ecology). This system of meaning is based on the idea that "if it is impossible to change the world, it is at least *possible to change one's own life* . . . Everyone can involve themselves in a process of *transformation* in order to find his/her 'raison d'être' that is *inner peace*."[20] The New Age world of meanings opens up a whole range of possibilities: well-being and health, inner strength, forming a community, (re)connecting with nature, mixing of ancient wisdoms and modern science, developing spirituality beyond religion, exploring the unknown, developing one's feminine side. It is precisely this cluster of possibilities that encouraged a number of transplants to undertake the move to Louisiana, because although some aspects of daily life in Louisiana appear to distance them from the New Age process (rich food, pollution, corruption, the lack of environmental policies in spite of rampant erosion that exacerbates vulnerability to hurricanes), other elements contribute to it, such as the promotion of cultural traditions and music, perceived as a form of energy in the same way as are food and vitamins. The Louisiana lifestyle is thus incorporated into this process, and the choice of settling there embodies, through the life change that it implies and the migration that follows, the personal transformation that is often sought and the quest for well-being and empowerment (regardless of the initial triggering factor, general dissatisfaction level, health issues, personal dramas, and professional changes).

Transplants' choice to settle in Louisiana is furthermore situated into the imaginary that roots music and its practitioners inevitably carry with them. Experienced as an alternative to consumer society and fierce competitiveness, southwest Louisiana appears to them to be a place to live in which culture is more important than money and status is not awarded based on career or material possessions. Like the folk revival of the 1960s, which saw the urban middle class re-appropriate representations associated with the working class and poorer African Americans, French Louisiana music responds to a quest for authenticity, conviviality, and simplicity nourished as much by the rural origins of the pioneers of the genre as by its musical characteristics. The primacy of sociability over performance and claims regarding a music that "comes from the heart," a quality considered intrinsic by transplants as well as locals, responds to the expectations of personal transformation of transplants who make the choice of southwest Louisiana.

Forging Connections

In their search for a "community of friends," transplants used regional musical events as opportunities to see each other and to develop relationships with both other new residents and locals. The Blue Moon Saloon is a major focal point. Combining a hostel with an outdoor bar presided over by a music stage, its rooms are often rented to tourists who are fans of French Louisiana music and often stay for long periods; some of them ultimately settle in the area themselves. The many weekly jams in the area, a central feature of local music practices that play a key role in the assimilation of newcomers into networks of local interaction, are also particularly appreciated by transplants and satisfy their desire to learn to play the region's music.

Louisiana Heritage and Souvenir shop, which was owned by Mitch Reed and his ex-wife Lisa Trahan, used to draw a mix of locals and visitors at the weekly jam hosted by Mitch, but also as a transient place where people would chat with Mitch and jam in the back room with whoever was around. In the early 2000s, I would go every Friday when I was doing fieldwork, always greeted with strong coffee that Mitch fixed in the back, chatting about all sorts of things, playing with him and occasional visitors, learning songs. Together with his reputation as an outstanding fiddler, Mitch's affability and sense of humor attracted newcomers who were passing by. He would act as a mediator, introducing visiting musicians to older local veterans, recommending the most appropriate recordings, playing them in his shop, catching his fiddle to share tunes.

Such places act as points of convergence, connecting music fans together and with local musicians. Some new residents took the initiative of creating places of sociability that play an important role in consolidating the transplant circle but also in opening the circle to local residents. This is the case with Lori and her husband Tom. They decided in January 2007 to launch a new music jam in Arnaudville, a small town fifteen miles northeast of Lafayette that has attracted a number of artists during the past decade, as well as an art school and a dancehall/art gallery that exhibits local arts and crafts (see ch. 2). They had recently purchased a workshop in the center of town, and Tom occupied one side with his fiddle-making activities, which he began before moving to Louisiana. Lori initially used the other half for her artistic creations, ranging from stitched fabric compositions to puppets, later deciding to move her studio to their home. With the encouragement of Ashokan coordinators, they initially established their Sunday afternoon jam as a way of promoting Tom's fiddle-making activities. Tom's Fiddle and Bow now offers teaching lessons given by working musicians (transplants and natives).

It was via virtual space that Andrea first began to play an important role among French Louisiana music fans. She created one of the very first websites in the country that was devoted to Cajun and zydeco music in 1995 while still living in California (there are hundreds of them today). Through the site, she developed warm contacts with the Louisiana musicians whom she promoted, among them Sam, guitar player of the Mamou Playboys, from whom she later rented a room during her first extended visits to Louisiana.

Once she became a resident, she announced that she was planning to host a jam for string instruments such as the fiddle and guitar, using a mailing list that gradually grew in size. Sam asked if he could post an announcement for her, and after other musicians also appealed to her with similar requests, she decided to create a more extensive list that would diffuse daily announcements about concerts, workshops, performances, and benefit events, but would also feature other kinds of announcements, including exhibits, miscellaneous for-sale items, real estate deals, and garage sales.

The list's reputation expanded to the point that the region's musicians began to systematically correspond with her to announce their schedules, confident that she was reaching a wide French Louisiana music fan base. The increasing profile of her mailing list enabled Andrea to become a key player in promoting regional dance and music and gain recognition among the area's musicians. This earned her privileged status as a local music expert, information source, and resource for visiting fans and new residents. It also helped her play an important role in Linda's itinerary during a long visit to Louisiana in April 2003.

> Andrea had just moved here, not permanently yet, but she was half here and half there. And so she had already plugged into the community and met a lot of people and her and I were not like hangout buddies before that. We knew each other, but we didn't hang out all the time. But she said, "Oh, come on down, I'll take you around." She just gave me the red carpet treatment. She took me to the Blue Moon and introduced me to a million people and took me here and we gotta go there and you gotta see this. Just gave me the whole tour.[21]

Like Andrea and Lori, Jim and Christy have devoted themselves to promoting local culture through their saloon/dancehall called the Whirlybird, where the couple periodically organize events.[22] They directed a Montessori school in San Francisco, where they became closely involved in the Bay Area circle of fans before deciding to sell the school and establish a new one north of Lafayette. The new school opened its doors in 2009.

In exchange for an optional donation, the Whirlybird also hosted a number of other initiatives, including concerts given by amateurs or visiting musicians, theatrical events, and music video productions. Through the Whirlybird and their support for local musical creativity, Jim and Christy brought together several different circles—California fans based in the Bay Area, transplants, and Louisianans—mastering the different codes in use in each region and thus functioning as mediators and facilitators, opening their welcome and networks of acquaintances to newcomers as well as residents and locals. This was how in 2007 the clip "Made in the Shade" was recorded by the Red Stick Ramblers, a popular group that plays Cajun, Texas swing, and traditional jazz. Recorded by Tom Krueger, a young New York filmmaker with a brilliant career behind him (including music videos for U2, Bruce Springsteen, Bob Dylan, and R.E.M.) who has since settled in Louisiana, the video was later shown on the CMT (Country Music Television) and GAC (Great American Country) networks. They eventually had to shut down the dancehall and sell it, but an opportunity later arose to recuperate the original building. As of this writing, Jim and Christy have a Whirlybird Community Building Fund in the hope of reopening it.

In return, their connections also enabled them to fund their school initiative through fund-raising events and volunteer participation as well as financial gifts from residents. The funds allowed them to renovate old buildings on their property, install the necessary infrastructure, and pay for the training of three health teachers to help combat the region's alarming rates of child obesity. Jim and Christy's Stonewood website,[23] which was inaugurated in the spring of 2009, provides a good illustration of the scale and significance of the network that they founded. Within the initial ten days, over two hundred members, both residents and outside fans, had registered for the site and had been grouped into clusters of friends based on invitations, with forums, chats, event announcements, and discussion groups, mostly related to music but also to other attractions and topics such as health, food, and the environment. Several months after this rapid beginning, the site began to lose steam, however, ultimately ceasing activity, primarily because it was dethroned by Facebook, which many fans use prolifically (LinkedIn, a professional networking site, is also among frequently used). It became clear that fans prefers to focus its interactions on these broader platforms, honoring their commitment to the French Louisiana fan community without necessarily being restricted to it.

Jim and Christy's Montessori school ultimately also suffered because of the difficulty of persuading parents to travel twenty minutes outside of Lafayette. Another factor was a certain skepticism (or lack of familiarity) with alternative education in the context of one of the poorest areas in southwestern Louisiana.

One year after it opened, Jim decided to look for a new location for the school, and financial problems also prompted the couple to move the Whirlybird building onto the land adjoining the school and their residence. Christy took a position as program director of the Cité des Arts in Lafayette, a highly active local arts center and theater center whose objective is to "connect cultures" through the visual arts, and Jim began organizing theater workshops and improvisation sessions and developing an artistic career as an actor, photographer, storyteller, and designer. Although fully aware of the culture gap between Louisiana and California, Jim and Christy had nevertheless not quite anticipated the number of obstacles that gradually forced them to change their plans.

They also encountered problems mobilizing the Creole population, who rarely attended their events, a further indication of one of the fundamental limitations on sociability among the French Louisiana population. During the 2008 Presidential campaign, musicians from the group Balfa Toujours decided to record a song in support of Obama and to ask a famous Creole accordionist to play with them. They made an agreement with Jim and Christy for the filming to take place at the Whirlybird and invited the entire network to attend.[24] Within three days, the song "*Oui on peut!*" (Yes We Can!)—or "Zydeco Obama"—had been composed, filmed, and broadcast on YouTube before being shown twice on the national television network MSNBC by Rachel Maddow, a well-known figure among American progressives. The film was virulently opposed by some Louisianans who voiced their sentiments through letters accusing the songwriters (with a single exception Louisianans) of not representing the opinion of the local population in a region heavily dominated by Republicans.

Jim and Christy enabled an entire network of pre-existing relationships to become more firmly established by providing a wider discursive space. This wider network thus prospered through lists and websites that were grafted onto each other, creating interactive spaces on local, regional, and international levels and multiplying the potential for the transmission of information, for mutual assistance, and even fundraising. New media and web technologies like podcasts, videos posted on YouTube, Facebook, SyncLive, and the fundraising website Kickstarter, among others, have tremendously expanded the scope and density of these exchanges, promoting numerous local projects and events, helping organize them and in some cases fund them.

In these key events and key places (camps, jams, clubs, festivals), French Louisiana music lovers converge regularly.[25] Together, they form what urban anthropologist José Guilherme Cantor Magnani named a circuit.[26] In the example of French Louisiana music, this circuit includes virtual places (websites, mailing lists), their significance demonstrating that a specific practice is not only territorialized but can use other channels. Depending on the situation, the circuit constituted through this process unites several circles that intersect and connect transplants, Louisianans, and outside fans. Through their initiatives, the transplants play a central role in constituting and maintaining this circuit. Some of them tend to involve themselves more in this process than others, particularly those who aspire to a wider role than simply music fans with the purpose of building a "community." For example, Andrea calls her website "A Transplant's Guide to Acadiana" and her Google group the "Acadiana Community," both defined by a regional identification.[27]

Jim and Christy have become pivotal figures among transplants, fans as well as a number of the region's musicians. They serve as the focal point of a network of individuals who constantly see each other, in which some connections procure greater social prestige than others, and which is supported by an array of well-known musicians who function as mascots.

While some never miss a single event organized within the network, aspire to gain the attention of a particular renowned musician, or to become involved in the board of a particular workshop or festival, others attempt to distance themselves from this network and create their own. These dynamics contribute to a process of hierarchization among both local musicians and transplants.

From Fanatical Dancers to Resident Musicians

New residents easily recognize themselves in their own descriptions of fanatical dancers. Linda recalls with a smile her first group trips, when she felt consumed by the urge to dance and repeatedly stayed up night after night in dancehalls: "It was so exotic to us. It was so foreign and so beautiful in so many ways. Its funkiness was just beautiful, you know. And we were just enamored with every single zydeco musician. I mean, we just thought they were gods. And we just we'd just go berserk and dance for three or four days and get completely exhausted and go home so happy."

For locals, these visiting dancers are immediately identifiable. One Sunday afternoon, on March 24, 2001, at Whiskey River Landing, while Geno Delafose was playing on stage, his family who was sitting at a table near the stage stared at a young woman jumping and bouncing with stockings and legging on this beautiful day where the outside temperature was 75 degrees. Her grunge look and her moves were in stark contrast to the other dancers, most of them dressed in jeans, boots, shirts, and cowboy hats and smoothly revolving on the dance floor. Geno's family members and others felt unable to restrain their giggles and whispers. At La Poussiere, regular dancers are quick to notify occasional dancers and tourists by bumping into them to clear the way that they should position themselves with slower dancers on the edge of the dance floor. Some dance moves that are taught outside of Louisiana are inconsistent with local practices and considered inappropriate by locals. In San Diego, Lori only learned the Cajun jitterbug, but when she came to Louisiana she discovered the two-step and its different variations. She also gradually found out that turns and a tight position from knee to thigh were not the norm in zydeco dance, as opposed to what she had been taught, and at times elicited disapproval and at other times flirtatious response from men in local clubs.

Fans visiting the area are in fact often criticized for their expectations that local practices conform to their own standards as inveterate dancers. Mark Falgout, owner of the Blue Moon Saloon, was somewhat irritated by the immediate complaints and demands of these outside dancers when I interviewed him in 2008:

> As soon as they get here, they want to tell you how they do it, where they come from and what would make it better. You know, like "You need to have a space reserved for us and you need to have a cooler of water for the dancers and you shouldn't smoke because we don't smoke in Massachusetts or California . . ." And I'm like, "Well, you're not there, number one. And you see it, there's people dancing, there's enough space to dance even when it's crowded. But this is not a dancehall."[28]

I have heard some musicians use the terms "Cajun-" and "Zyde-nazis" or more broadly "folk-nazis" to express their frustration with such opinionated outsiders. The different approach to dance encountered outside of Louisiana only further increases the gap between out-of-town dancers and local musicians. In 2003 David Greely could not conceal his exasperation:

> When you play outside of Louisiana, there will be a dance instructor. Often. So you have somebody down there from New Jersey, with a little microphone, it looks like a mosquito in front of their mouth, they're like "Rule number one!" [he mimics a northern accent]. And I'm back stage thinking, you're killing it! Because half of the crowd is gonna be looking at their feet and counting. Let them learn music somewhere else! I learned to dance in the kitchen, I didn't learned to dance at a dance![29]

Closely tied to the distinction between permanent residents and fans or tourists, these differing views over dance styles constitute an important dimension of the local dance scene. My goal is not to explore the details of footwork that can be found on numerous websites and in instructional videos, but rather to outline the process and the stakes involved in naming steps and codifying dance moves. Just the nicknames "chicken-," "limping-," or "broken leg-" steps reveal the debates about authenticity that surround what is more neutrally called the "Cajun jitterbug."

Originally from New Orleans, Missy went to what was then called the University of Southwestern Louisiana in Lafayette in 1972. She has witnessed the evolution of the dance and music scene since then, ultimately quitting her therapist practice in New Orleans to move to the area in 1996.

> People started teaching dancing. I don't know if you've heard of Randy Speyrer. Well, Randy, soon after he became Rand, he became the Cajun dance expert. And that was a kind of Cajun dancing that not too many people are doing now, I guess. That's what I would call, in a not-very-complimentary manner, call the chicken leg type, where you—as far as the dance style, it's not a six-count jitterbug dancing to Cajun music. It's more like, some people call it, the hobble step or the chicken step, or something, where you put your right foot down and push up on the ball of your foot and your left foot's flat and it's strenuous. To me, it just doesn't look as nice and it definitely doesn't feel as nice. I did it, but I don't like to admit

that I did it [laughs]. Because that's what a lot of people were doing anyway. It was partner dancing, and it was very heavy on the twirls and the turns, which is something I will almost refuse to do now.

The style described above—most commonly called Cajun Jitterbug or jig, is based on a one-step that keeps the dancers constantly going up and down, arms extended in elaborate twirls, crossing and exuberantly interweaving, leading the dancers' bodies to face each other, dance side-by-side, or turn their backs to each other.[30] Windmill, Little Window, Big Window, Sweetheart Chain, Pretzel, Crawfish, and St. Charles are among the names given to some of these moves by Randy Speyrer, the first to offer an instructional video on Cajun dance, *Allons Danser* (1987). This style, which later included an enhanced form of waltz, is inseparably tied to the image of Cajun dance outside of Louisiana and is featured in every tourist brochure and website. Like Missy, Lori dislikes the Cajun jitterbug intensely, which she describes as a "limping step with pretzel turns," an opinion shared by numerous other Louisiana dancers and musicians who deride its ostentatious and expansive movements, in contrast to the sobriety of local dance practices, which are characterized by a focus more on footwork than on turns. Bending the knees on back (or down) beats, keeping resistance in the arms and working on a push and pull to better feel the back steps are among the basics that are taught locally. The waltz, for example, has nothing in common with the Viennese waltz, nor with the *musette* waltz. Couples travel the floor counter-clockwise, their feet sliding in constant contact with the dance floor, and the few turns they perform are accompanied by no ornamentation or large moves. Everything resides in the harmony and synchronization of the dance partners. Even fast dances, like the two-step and the jitterbug, conform to this principle.

Heddy and Philip Nunez remember their experience when this dance style emerged in the 1970s. At the time in their twenties, they frequented Mulate's, then a small dancehall that had not evolved into the major tourist stop it eventually became. They met Rand Speyrer and his cousin and together, week after week, they recall the fun they had creating turns and figures on the basis of the one-step suggested by their cousin. Life interrupted their weekly collaboration, and Rand Speyrer subsequently began to teach in New Orleans, while his cousin taught in Lafayette. As she recalled witnessing this dance developing and taking shape, testing each figure and turn week after week, her perception was that she was attesting to its authenticity. Louisiana natives disagree about the "traditional" nature of this dance but, whether natives or not, dancers who perceive this dance as incongruous tend to be far more vocal in their criticism.[31]

Although the Cajun jitterbug epitomizes the commodification of Cajun dance, what is more broadly at stake in this debate is the codification of dance, intricately bound to the distinction between Louisiana residents and outsiders. Indeed, Louisiana teachers clearly position themselves against codification. At the 2001 DBCCHW, Christine Balfa and Don Brasseaux were teaching the Cajun dance class. After Christine explained that there were two ways to teach the two-step, the 6-count and the 8-count, and that they were going to teach the former, a New Yorker who had recently moved to Louisiana to learn how to dance asked how these styles were named. Christine was quick to answer that there was no such thing as naming steps in this area. "People are not analytical here," she added. To his reference to the "Mamou two-step," a name sometimes applied to the two-step, she answered that they would not use that name in their class. She continued the class, emphasizing the importance of the resistance in the arms, through the use of push and pulls to better feel the back step and to assist in turning. Don explained how people always start dancing in a close position to be certain they are together and then open up, just holding hands for the jitterbug. Another point was the primary importance of sliding the feet. She referred to La Poussière in Henderson, where regulars have become models of the smoothness and fluidity required for dancing appropriately. In fact, the club attracts many older couples that have been dance partners for years and, beyond very personal styles, glide smoothly and expertly around the dance floor as if on water, forming a single silhouette. In an interview, Don confirmed the value of this club as an illustration of the ingenuity of Louisiana dancers:

> I like to watch people dance. The beauty of the dancers is by far the best. I just go get a Diet Coke. Especially the weekend before a dance camp, I go there to get another shot of what I need to be like, to remind me where I come from. To let them know what I do is just my version. . . . It's not aerobics. What I see is an expression of feelings. They're an individual, they do their own things, they don't mimic. I see today too much people trying to copy other dancers, to the details. I think they loose their individuality, the fun part of it. Maybe that's the fun to them. . . .[32]

And to those who questioned him on the differences between Cajun and zydeco dancing, he responded unambiguously: "I call it dancing."

Seven years later, at the same camp, this position against codification and the reluctance to name specific steps was again reinforced by the choice of calling a dance workshop a "dance party" instead of a "class." Having fun was explicitly cited as the ultimate goal, as opposed to following rules. "Keep in mind, people would work hard all day long and on weekends they'd let go. It's about having fun. Don't think too much about it, you'll miss the point," insisted Christine Balfa.

As in music, immersion becomes the rule. Dance teachers also insist on the individualization of style and fear any standardization. At the same time, the reference to copying implicitly addresses debates regarding authenticity. The strong codification practiced by the many out-of-town dance teachers who train thousands of dance fans around the country is frowned upon by Louisiana residents, who see it as too "sophisticated" and opposed to the notion of simplicity and informality associated with the music.

Zydeco teacher Mona Wilson makes this topic particularly obvious by promoting herself as "truly authentic." A financial analyst who was raised in Louisiana but who lives in Texas, she has won several dance contests and teaches zydeco dance during camps and in workshops throughout the country. She defines authenticity on the basis of her Creole identification and status as a Louisiana native, and she was adamant about the uselessness of counting in teaching zydeco, which she presented as a corollary to jumping and bouncing that is the opposite of genuine dancing. "Nobody learned zydeco by counting. You dance to have fun. I teach the way I learned, by doing," she argued when I talked to her in 2001. Instead of codes and complicated naming systems, she uses simple words to explain dancing steps (such as "step-step-step-touch" for the basic step).

Her website continues to the present day to make the same claim: "Mona 'Zydeco Queen' Wilson® offers you the cream of the crop when it comes to authenticity—straight from Southwest Louisiana. Learn the way we did in the heart of Creole Country—having fun without the worry of counting. *NOTE*: Louisiana Creoles *DID NOT* and *DO NOT* learn to zydeco dance by counting, and if you take our workshops, you won't either—it's all about fun!!"[33] Her method, named "Monarobics," is trademarked, a sign that she positions herself as an authority among zydeco dance teachers and claims ownership of her teaching technique, while protecting herself from being appropriated by those whom she views as fake zydeco teachers and who are neither Creoles nor Louisiana natives.

Her fierce defense of her authority also addresses the minority of Creole dance teachers in Louisiana, a market dominated by white teachers. The involvement of white transplants can therefore generate powerful resentment among Creole natives, who are involved in a struggle over a lucrative and valued status for economic and symbolic power in a growing market across the country and within Louisiana.

Many non-natives teach French Louisiana dance styles elsewhere in the country, and in Louisiana, transplants are among the pool of dance teachers who are in high demand. A Unitarian Universalist minister from New York, Michael Seider was involved in international folk dancing until he eventually began teaching Cajun and zydeco dancing in 1986 in Pensacola, Florida, "probably before I should have," he avowed. He eventually moved to Baton Rouge before settling in Breaux Bridge, where he was living in 2001 when I interviewed him, dividing his time between his job and teaching dance in Louisiana as well as at music camps across the country.

As Michael explains, both Cajun and zydeco dance are described as East Coast swing, a six-count dance integrated into an eight-beat pattern:

> Cajuns tend to jitterbug to Cajun music, which is East Coast swing, when they're not doing a two-step in the "ball room" position. I think the reason is that the people about my age [fifty in 2001] and older learned to jitterbug and then danced it to Cajun music. So I'm not sure what the earliest Cajuns, how they danced to the music. I call East Coast swing a jitterbug. As opposed to West Coast swing. West coast swing is done in a slot, as I understand it. The female or the follow travels in a slot, in relation to the man or lead. East Coast swing has a lot of complicated little steps that you will see done on the dance floor here.

According to Lori, West Coast swing, which is danced to slow music and blues, is harder to dance to without a regular partner and involves a range of hip movements.

With Lori, Michael closely observes the style of locals in clubs like Whiskey River and Cowboys. After breaking down the steps, he started teaching across the country what he called the Whiskey River Jitterbug. Lori describes these distinctions: "It is a dance done by very cowboy type of guys and gals, we taught it at Ashokan and he went to Seattle, New York, New Jersey, all over teaching it. It is based on country: the posture in country dance is very structured and upright. Whiskey River jitterbug posture is also very upright. When doing East Coast jitterbug the posture is more relaxed and hunched over like lindy hop dancing."[34] Eventually, the use of this term for the dance attracted controversy with his dance partner, who quit dancing with him. As shown in the example of Mona Wilson, dance moves and teaching methods have become prized commodities among dance teachers, whatever their origins, generating conflicts over legitimacy, defined as personal ownership and copyright.

In the mid-1990s, when Lori, Linda, and Andrea first began to learn Louisiana dance, the popularity of zydeco outside of French Louisiana exceeded that of Cajun music. In New Orleans, the Rock 'N' Bowl accommodated this interest, packing the house on Thursdays with Boozoo Chavis or Beau Jocque. Whether in New Orleans or across the country, zydeco dancing predominated, no matter what style of music Louisiana musicians were playing. This practice later expanded to Louisiana, and in several clubs, certain characteristics associated with Cajun dance, such as traveling the floor counter-clockwise, fell into disuse. Numerous dancers remain rooted to a single spot when dancing to Cajun music. In fact, the Whiskey River Jitterbug can be danced to any music style. Remembering her experience in the early 1970s, Missy explains that what is now differentiated into zydeco and Cajun dancing was then based on the two-step and waltz. Today, certain new styles like the Whiskey River are also based on a certain attitude common to so-called Cajun or zydeco dancing:

> In the "Whiskey River," you're kind of straight up, hands down or maybe out, kind of close. But the footwork is the same, one two three, one two three, one two. And in the traditional jitterbug, it's the same thing. They're turning you, it's the same but in Whiskey River, you don't turn as much. And it's the same as the black girls' attitude, the kind of aloof, I'm-just-putting-up-with-you, real cool and a little bit more sexy, whereas the traditional jitterbug is more fun loving. You can make eye contact and stuff like that. I make jokes with my black friends about, in some zydeco communities, how when girls are looking for a partner, you absolutely don't make eye contact and you chew gum [laughs]. That's the attitude. Whereas, the white women come in and they're smiling and making eye contact, and looking like they're having a good time. That's not the custom that you generally see with the black women.

As the demand for learning zydeco grew, white teachers became more solicited. This is Lori's impression as someone whom Arnaudville townspeople addressed with requests for zydeco classes: "So they kept saying to me, you've got to teach zydeco. I was like, 'Why do you want me to teach zydeco? This is your local culture. There's people that grew up doing it here. Why do you want me?' The local white people want to learn zydeco from a out-of-towner, I think white person."

Michael soon realized that zydeco moves were in high demand and that people would "zydeco" on every music style, including Cajun music. He gave a name to each new style and innovation that he observed, priding himself on being a successful teacher because of his ability to break down steps.

On his website, zydecoach.com, Michael lists and provides a written description of more than sixty different steps, each with a specific name and organized into categories such as Closed position moves, Opens position moves, Advanced, Hot and Sleazy, Miscellaneous, Line dance, and Waltz. Whether outsiders or Louisiana residents, dance teachers struggle not to capitulate in the face of insistent requests from their students. At Ashokan, where she taught for two years with Michael, Lori eventually broke things down and named steps and moves:

> Everyone that takes a class basically thinks they're more advanced than they are. They want the most advanced, newest moves. So essentially, everyone wants the latest here. So you're always talking about what the newest trend is. And so last year [2007], I brought up the Cupid Shuffle because nobody had seen it. So you're always thinking about what can you do that's inclusive, what can you do that people can really learn and learn easily. . . . In the Cajun dancing, the last few years, it's like "I want to learn how to do the Whiskey River, I want to learn how to do that swing thing you're doing." In zydeco, the in thing is the slide. "I want to learn how to do that slide. I want to learn how to do some of those funky freeze moves and the funky moves, you know, hip hop."

Although Lori felt more constrained at music camps, she takes a different approach in her classes in southwest Louisiana:

> I've learned all different styles, there's all different styles, there's no right way, this is an organic dance that changes all the time. This is like capturing a piece of time and then trying to bring it forward to teach somebody. Whenever I'm teaching a class, I always say there is

no right way to do this. There's an eight count, there's four beats and there's two four-beats in a phrase of music and that's how zydeco music is played. And it needs to be danced with two holds. Where those holds go, it could be on two, you know, six, could be, you know, I don't know. It's all different. No way is the same and everyone does it different.

To Louisiana residents, she recommends the zydeco aerobics class that she would never miss at the time, in 2008, every Thursday evening on Highway 182, at the Judson Walsh exit, and now in Opelousas. The Zydeco Ballers Dance Program consists of a group of Creole volunteer instructors from ten to sixty-five years old, who also invite people to join their "zydeco ballers fan club" to support music bands at music events.[35]

If you don't know how to do it, they come and stand by you. It's not like a real lesson because if you're screwing up, it doesn't really matter. It's just a great way to learn it 'cause you're learning it like how they learn it. You're learning how a Creole learns how to dance. They don't go to dance lessons and they don't have the boys over here and girls over here and left foot, right foot, touch, touch. . . . No. They call it out, you know, but it's very, it's a really wonderful thing. I tell everybody to go to that. It's great.

As they negotiate the transition and become bona fide Louisiana residents, transplants achieve a new status that is opposed to that of the fans that they all previously were who never went to Louisiana or only experienced the region during festivals. In fact, Ashokan only began to consider Lori a paid staff member once she moved to Louisiana. Until that point, she taught as a scholarship teacher, receiving free tuition in exchange for teaching. Transplants who happen to teach dance incorporate their knowledge of local dance styles into their teaching methods, gaining authority as locals. But because they do not possess the same degree of legitimacy as native dance teachers, their latitude in terms of what and how they teach is probably not as broad. Consequently, those who choose to teach at music camps and seek the income have to negotiate with their students' expectations, adapting to their requests and to their appetite for new moves and names.

In parallel to these kinds of changes in dance practices, transplants evoke the rudimentary knowledge of the musical repertoire that they held as former fans. They recall that dance was an obsession for which the music mostly provided the supporting sounds and rhythms. Most of their narratives tend not to refer to the first regional group that they heard, or the style of music or musicians, but instead to the atmosphere, the dancers, their euphoric feelings, and their joy upon discovering a new passion. They recall having begun to listen to the regional "top 10," which they now perceive as "crap," "commercial," or "California-style." Lisa Bourque, a South Louisianan who lived in California for over ten years before returning to her native town, emphasized the frequent lack of knowledge about music that she encountered among the dancers whom she frequented, one explanation of her disappointment that her appreciation of certain local bands was not shared:

> A local band will play the very basics and it's disappointing because being so far away, any little bit of any little nugget of it is, you just cherish it. But then it becomes disappointing after a while for it to be the same sort of boiled down and it becomes a bit of a battle with the dancers because the people who really support the dance community are generally not Cajun. They're from outside the culture and they just want the drums to be on time so that they can dance.
>
> So it becomes apparent to you that they don't know the andouille's missing from the gumbo and they don't realize that it's dried shrimp and not fresh shrimp. They don't know it's missing and well, as long as the drummer's playing . . .[36]

Stylistic distinctions dissolve under such circumstances, and neophyte dancers learn Cajun and zydeco as though they belonged to a single style, which becomes apparent when fans refer to "CZ (Cajun/zydeco) bands" and the "CZ community." The relationship with Louisiana thus creates a fissure between residents and fans as they adopt increasing distance from their earlier perceptions of music and dance. The more time one spends in Louisiana, the more remote the fan network becomes. Even before moving to Louisiana, Andrea felt this gap beginning to widen:

> People would just go, "I don't like this Louisiana stuff." Or they'd listen to a band that came from Louisiana and it was like, "My favorite band is Tom Rigney" or somebody who's playing popularized, Americanized, California-ized version of music that is like, well, yeah, it's sort of Cajun but it doesn't sound like what it's supposed

to sound like. I mean it's fine, he's Harvard educated and he's a great musician, but he doesn't sound . . . it's not that . . . sometimes the best I could say, "Have you ever been to Louisiana?" and they'd say, "No." I wouldn't even engage in conversation because how do you explain some of that stuff?

As the project of a possible move to Louisiana slowly formed, the idea of starting to play an instrument became more obvious. Andrea remembers when she started staying for an extended period of time, after the Balfa Camp.

You met all these people, you know, local people. And then you'd walk around Lafayette and everywhere you'd go, you'd run into somebody from camp. You know, you'd see Courtney Granger on the street and you'd go, "Oh, hi! How ya doing?" and he'd give you a hug. I'm going, "Oh, my God!" You'd see Christine in the grocery store or, I mean, it just became like much more familiar than just passing through and going to the clubs 'cause you'd spend so much time talking to all these people when you're at camp. And you also got to see the culture from a different perspective, particularly, as I was getting more and more interested in Cajun music and not just zydeco music. All of a sudden I wanted to play something and participate as opposed to just dance.

Moving to Louisiana appears to prompt this transfer of interest from dance to music, which becomes an infallible distinction between fans and transplants. Each of these three transplants ultimately switched their passion to learning an instrument: Andrea rediscovered the guitar, which she had abandoned forty years earlier; at the age of forty-four and with no musical background, Linda took up the fiddle; and Lori was inspired to learn the ukulele at Ashokan. Each of them regularly attends existing weekly jams, and Lori and Andrea also founded their own jams. This shift in tastes combines with their resident status to even further distance them from the mass attraction to French Louisiana dance, and they come to associate an exclusive focus on dance with superficiality. They continue to take pleasure in dancing when the opportunity presents itself, but they have become immersed in the practice of music, attending jams, organizing parties that focus on music and performance, and increasing the number of recordings of courses and workshops that they circulate among themselves, sometimes assembling in small groups to rehearse specific songs.

Favorites in this corpus of songs are usually not standard tunes that fans can easily identify, but instead, unusual songs that are off the beaten path. In fact, my friends were particularly appreciative of the songs I played at jams because they were often not familiar to them and they were eager to expand their repertoires with new songs. This was particularly true of fiddle tunes, which are not frequent in jams that often are dominated by accordion. Because I am particularly fond of rare fiddle tunes by Dennis McGee, Dewey Balfa, Varise Conner, and Wayne Perry, I would play numbers like "Reel de Frugé," "Galop à Wade Frugé," "Reel de Cajun," "Reel de joie," "Indian on a Stomp," "Lake Arthur Stomp," "Reel de Berzas," "Valse à Pop," "Torchon's Reel," "Reel de Coquin," "Gumbo Waltz," or "Quand les Fleurs Fleurissent," which few people in this circle played at the time but that they were delighted to learn, sometimes figuring out unusual chord changes.

Transplants are particularly appreciative of the accessibility of French Louisiana music and the encouragement they have received from local musicians. Linda emphasizes her frustration with learning an instrument when she was a teenager: "I was very envious of people who could play music and I always just thought it was the coolest thing. I just always thought I couldn't do it. Yeah, I thought I kind of couldn't do it, so I didn't do it." Later in her narrative, echoing this intimidation and describing how the unfailing support of Danny Poullard and his brother Ed encouraged her to persist, she adds: "I'd see him a couple of times a year, but every time I'd see him . . . I could hardly play, he'd be 'How's that fiddle going?' Here's this guy who's like this incredible player, he's like, 'How's that fiddle going?' . . . And he gave me nothing but encouragement."[37] The sense of not being judged, the primacy of sociability over performance, and the accessibility of professional musicians encourages apprentice musicians to take a step that previously would have appeared virtually insurmountable. After several years in Louisiana, she never misses an opportunity to accompany well-known Louisiana musicians as solo fiddler, whether it is Ed at the 2008 Balfa camp during a workshop, the accordionist Jesse Lége in 2009 in small concerts or participation during workshops, or regular gigs with the late Al Berard, roles that give Linda intense satisfaction.

In fact, the constant encouragement of locals is emphasized in every outsider and transplant narrative and provides a major incentive for the labor involved in learning an instrument. Coming from a classical training and an approach to music focused on passing levels and performing properly, I, too, felt comforted by the encouragement of my Louisiana friends. I began with the *'tit fer*, an instrument that, in spite of appearances, requires control and technique. The late Wilson Gaspard patiently played with me over recordings, and he quickly nudged me into joining his band during jam sessions. It took me much longer to convince myself that I could pick up the fiddle, but regardless of how clumsily I initially played, I was always pressed to pursue my efforts. Teachers and listeners remarked on my improvement and never doubted my ability to "get it." As I gradually learned that French Louisiana music was less about proving skills than sharing collective pleasure, playing music proved increasingly rewarding. Further, I was finally able to give, and not only receive, which compensated for my position as an observer.[38]

In June 2009 Andrea, Linda, and Madeline, another transplant from the state of Washington, performed as a trio called Lâche Pas (from the regional expression "Lâche pas la patate," meaning "don't give up" or "hold on") for the first time and were warmly encouraged by well-known local musicians. One musician offered to help them interpret songs and become established as a group. The Blue Moon, the most prominent local music venue in the Lafayette city limits, staged them seven months later, and the host of *Lagniappe*, a local radio show, invited them on the air to discuss their itineraries and play live songs. After going back to school to become a midwife, Madeline eventually moved to New Mexico where she found a job, and Lâche Pas disbanded.

Through their interest in music and devotion to local musicians, transplants have contributed to the valorization of Louisiana working musicians and to a polarization of status between exclusive involvement and leisure activity. Their desire for legitimation has repercussion for musicians, granting them prestige that is much more difficult to obtain from the local public who, as seen in chapter 2, tend to be much more casual and critical with local musicians. Musicians' accessibility, even the most prominent, does not diminish the sensation of euphoria felt by transplants when in their presence, hanging out with them, or playing by their sides. Their proximity to pillars of the Louisiana music and old-time scenes and their integration into the roots music networks confers a role and recognition on them that are completely out of the reach of novices in other musical genres. In fact, there are power struggles among members of the transplant circle that often remain unaddressed, when particular bonds or involvements—in such and such a festival, gig, or as a member of a particular cultural organization—confer greater prestige than others. In a process that is parallel to this increase in status, natives can also be differentiated from transplants in particular contexts. Friendship, complicity, respect, and gratitude are sometimes blended with mixed feelings. "Wannabe Cajuns" or "Born again Cajuns" are among the terms sometimes applied to non-natives, blending fans, and transplants in an amalgam with non-natives.[39] The perceived distance seems less, or people are less conscious about it, with respect to those who are permanently settled in Louisiana to work as musicians and who have inserted themselves in the more fashionable groups. Often in their twenties when they arrive, far younger than most transplants, this label is rarely applied to these younger settlers. Beyond this generational difference, a process of distinction appears to take place among non-native residents, between those who make a living from music and those for whom it remains a leisure activity.

The change in the center of the transplants' interest in music and learning to play an instrument has infused local music practices with new energy by encouraging well-known local musicians to multiply group and individual lessons, contributing to the development of jams open to other musical styles such as bluegrass and old-time, stimulating the production of instructional DVDs, and encouraging the trend toward more seated concerts. Although the music continues to be experienced as dance music, it is also recognized as listening music. David Greely, for example, began to organize sit-down gigs for twin fiddles and an annual event, Fiddlers on the Bayou.

This process differs from fan networks that developed in the 1960s and that initially focused on the musicians, and later international folk dancers, who integrated Cajun and zydeco into a diverse choreographic repertoire before forming separate groups. Although they existed in parallel with each other, these circles did not interact, and they constituted distinct networks of shared knowledge. By contrast, in the current Louisiana configuration, the same individual displaces his or her center of interest and moves from being a dancer to becoming a musician. Furthermore, while earlier networks of French Louisiana music fans were an outgrowth of the folk movement, 1990s fans came from diverse horizons, and both musicians and dancers brought with them eclectic musical tastes and experiences. Andrea, for example, was a Beatles and Rolling Stones fan and was exposed to Peter, Paul and Mary, Bob Dylan, and other bands from the 1960s revival in summer camps, and later discovered an interest in Bruce Springsteen and Frank Zappa before finally discovering the Cajun group BeauSoleil in the 1980s.

The annual music camps and conventions in Louisiana and across the country play a vital role in this process and constitute sites of encounter and learning that are particularly prized by fans and transplants, who continue to attend them long after settling in Louisiana. Ashokan Fiddle and Dance in New York State and its Southern Week; the Augusta Heritage Festival at Davis and Elkins College in West Virginia and its Cajun and Creole Week; the Festival of American Fiddle Tunes in Port Townsend Washington State (directed by Suzy Thompson); and the Appalachian String Band Music Festival at Clifftop, Virginia, have become key events for French Louisiana music enthusiasts. Augusta had a major impact on Daniel Gale's involvement in French Louisiana music. Linda recalls the first time she went to Augusta in August 2001, before moving to Louisiana. Encouraged by her mentor Danny Poullard, she went with a friend and was "blown away." "It opened up a whole new world of people," she recounts, opening another circle of fans devoted to learning an instrument instead of exclusively focusing on dance. Linda attended Augusta for five consecutive years before enrolling in the Balfa Camp in Louisiana, and she has subsequently alternated years between attending Augusta and Ashokan. Not a year passed without her attending one or even several workshops. Christine Balfa founded the Balfa Camp in 2001. Originally meant to offer people from Louisiana an opportunity to learn local music on their own turf instead of having to go to music camps across the country, it attracts a vast majority of out-of-towners (90 percent in 2008).[40]

These key events create a particularly intense nexus for interactions through total immersion in daily musical activities over the course of a week, including group and private class, jams, and practice sessions. These are complemented by evenings devoted to dance, concerts, and other jams that often continue until the wee hours of the morning, with interruptions only for meals and a few hours' sleep, as well as occasional volunteer stints. The events bring a hundred or more people together, who interact with each other nonstop for an entire week, year after year (and sometimes several times a year), often reliving past memories, exchanging information, meeting different Louisiana music groups, jamming, learning new songs and new styles, and creating new musical projects, or even life projects that involve moving to Louisiana. The notion of "family" and "community" are often used with reference to the powerful bonds created during the camps. In her gospel class at Ashokan in 2008, Ginny Hawker, an acclaimed old-time singer and partner of Tracy Schwartz, defined family as "those people whose faces light up when you come in a room. And this is what this place is like too, it's a family, like a family reunion," she said before singing a song named "Family Reunion" before an audience silenced by emotion. The last day of the camp, Molly Mason, who has run the camp with her companion Jay Ungar since 1982, encouraged people who felt down during the winter to call people of the "community," get together, and play.

Experiencing these events, rubbing shoulders with famous musicians, and being able to claim them as teachers encourages the nurturing of plans to become a transplant, subtly elevating still further the status of those who have already made the move. Filmmaker Tom Krueger met the Red Stick Ramblers at Ashokan, fell in love with their music, and decided to make a clip about the band; he eventually transplanted himself to Lafayette, where he is now highly involved in the music scene and artistic community. Transplants construct their legitimacy through these processes and exchanges, demonstrating the intensity of their commitment through a new level of involvement as musicians, a status that is highly prized on the Louisiana music scene. Significant events such as the camps foster encounters and stimulate geographic mobility that contributes to the construction of transplants' legitimacy. The choice of living in Louisiana transforms their status, not only toward Louisianans but also within a broader circle of fans, nationwide and abroad.

The shift in taste from dance to music is mirrored in another change, from zydeco toward so-called Cajun and Creole styles. Transplants' passion for dance was directed primarily toward zydeco. In fact, many viewed Cajun music as "boring" and "has-been" and associated it with declining, elderly musicians. Once established in Louisiana, their musical interests completely reversed their tastes: For Lori, Linda, and Andrea, zydeco served as the "hook" for dancing. Although in her narrative of her first visits to Louisiana, Linda talked about zydeco musicians like "gods," her register changes dramatically when she describes how her interests in terms of music have evolved: "zydeco music is dance music, in my opinion. That's it. It's really not that great to listen to, most of it." Without denying their earlier passion, each of these transplants concur that zydeco, although it inspired them to move, holds little interest at the musical level. In this way, transplants reinforce a process of hierarchization between these two styles that is already hard at work in Louisiana.

From the sensuality of zydeco to the heartfelt and leaner style of Creole music, black exoticism is no longer embodied in dance but is applied to the music as well. Instead of evoking the sensuality and eroticism of zydeco dancing, the "naturally" syncopated rhythms of Creole style are vaunted, as well as its poly-rhythmic character and links to Africa and the Caribbean. Other musical characteristics are advanced, such as dissonance and asymmetrical structure, a characteristic more often associated with Creoles. These characteristics exert all the more attraction in suggesting a sense of marginality to which that many transplants can relate. Linda feels especially touched by Creole songs:

> I mean listen to Canray play. It's so, it's so, it's just coming out of their feeling. It's not, "Oh we do four beats, you know, here, and dit, dit, dit . . ." You know, it's not, there's nothing straight about it. It's just coming out of the heart all the time, I think. It's just oozing. And I love the dissonant sounds of it, like some of that Creole fiddling, you know. You know, that first year at Augusta, D'Jalma Garnier was there and he got up and did a little lunchtime concert and he just played solo fiddle. That was it. . . . That's my love right there. They're crooked, they're slippery, they're slidey, they're bluesy, they're beautiful. I just love their inconsistency. It's not inconsistency. I just love the styling.

Deceased and living Creole musicians who claim a Creole style, from the late Canray Fontenot to the young Cedric Watson, are praised as masters of an endangered tradition that embodies "the genuine earthiness of the rural working-class African American life, the earthiness of a forgotten and vanishing world," as Hugh Barker and Yuval Taylor asserted in relation to the exoticization of bluesmen.[41] Indeed, Taylor shares with readers an introspective analysis of his encounter with bluesman Jack Owens and the thrill he derived from seeing him in his native habitat in Mississippi in 1992. As a fan of rural blues, he interrogates this otherwise unforgettable experience: "When we view musicians as exotic animals, can condescension be far behind? I feel certain that my appreciation of Jack Owens was quite unlike my appreciation of, say, Wayne Shorter. For rather than appreciating Owens only for his artistry, I was appreciating him in large part for his authenticity. And in that, I was much like the blues fans of the 1960s."[42]

Creole music and zydeco dance have been objects of fascination that are incorporated into a process of aestheticization. At the same time, the shifting attraction from dance to music contributes to a new process of hierarchization between dancing and listening music.

Connecting with Appalachian Old-Time Music

Beyond the evolution in transplants' tastes in French Louisiana music, another trend that has increased since the early 2000s is the sense of connectedness between French Louisiana musicians who play Cajun and Creole music and Appalachian old-time musicians. The overlap of these two circles dates back to the beginning of the nationwide exposure of French Louisiana music in the context of the national folk movement. The collaboration between Dewey Balfa and Tracy Schwartz embodied this convergence in the 1970s. The incorporation of Cajun and Creole music classes in music camps encouraged this alliance, especially at Ashokan, where Southern Week includes both Appalachian old-time and Cajun and Creole workshops. Jay Ungar started his Ashokan Fiddle and Dance in 1981 and incorporated Cajun and Creole a few years later. A renowned "roots" musician, he formed a duo with his companion Molly Mason. They gained national exposure most notably through their involvement in the radio show *A Prairie Home Companion*, their own live performance show *Dancing On the Air*, and their composition for Ken Burns's documentary on the Civil War which turned "Ashokan Farewell" into their best-known composition, along with "The Lovers' Waltz," a violin solo and duet from an album of romantic fiddle music from various traditions. The song has become a classic in French Louisiana.

Through the years, these relational circles have intertwined not only outside of Louisiana but also through new events and marital alliances within French Louisiana. Coming from old-time music, Dirk has introduced some of his fellow old-time musicians to the music scene with his occasional band Donna the Buffalo and has performed at well-attended regional musical events like Louisiana Crossroads since he settled in Louisiana in the early 1990s. When I was staying at his and Christine Balfa's house, I met a number of members of his extended circle of old-time musician friends, not realizing at the time to whom I was being introduced. Christine and Dirk's wedding at Terre Haute, their home, was a huge gathering of old-time and local musicians. Dirk thus drew numerous old-time musicians into the fold of French Louisiana music. Jay Ungar and Molly Mason attended the first Balfa Camp as guests, jamming after classes until the wee hours with Dirk Powell and his old-time music friends from around the country. The Whirlybird also always welcomed old-time jams and gatherings, and the Red Stick Ramblers have also been

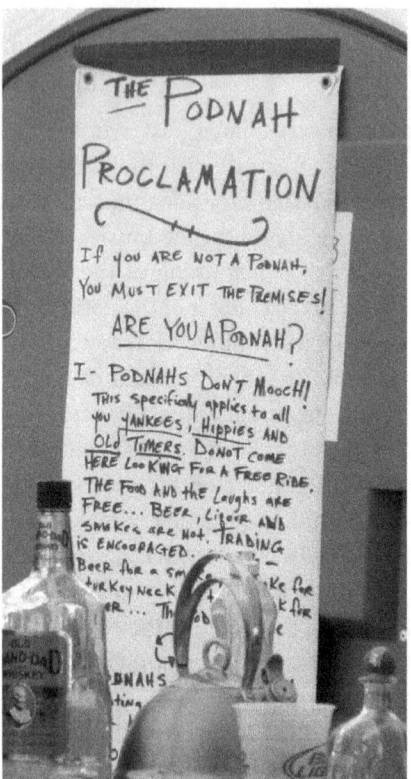

5.1. "The Podnah Proclamation," Black Pot Festival, Lafayette, October 29, 2010.

instrumental in bringing old-time musicians and strengthening this connection through the festival they founded, the Black Pot Festival. Inspired by Clifftop, which assembles over 3,000 string band music lovers for a five-day convention, the organizers of Black Pot Festival have extended the camp aspect to include pre- and post-festival events and a larger camping location at Lakeview Park and Beach near Eunice. The interactions and jamming offered by camping opportunities were a deliberate choice, extending the numbers of participants and the intensity of the social and musical exchanges. Intersections between the two circles are imbued with humor and friendly stereotypes. In 2010, a handwritten sign was posted under the jam tent, the "Podnah Proclamation," that listed distinctions between podnahs and "yankees, hippies, and old-timers." Among the eliminatory factors was the fact that "podnahs don't mooch!" encouraging trading for the consumption of alcohol and cigarettes.

Officially celebrating "roots" music of every stripe, performers and fans of old-time music constitute a significant part of the festival's attendance. Duos Jay Ungar and Molly Mason, Mike and Ruthie (Jay Ungar's daughter), Ginny Hawker and Tracy Schwartz, are regulars at Black Pot. Jams during the festival are principally focused on the old-time and French repertoire. Ira Bernstein, a well-known dancer considered an authority on clogging and Appalachian flat-footing, has been coming to Louisiana since 1981 and has watched these connections grow. In his view, Black Pot significantly contributed to this evolution and is considered by old-time enthusiasts an old-time event spiced up by the addition of French Louisiana music. A new musical project was born out of this alliance under the name Jesse Légé, Joel Savoy, and the Cajun Revival that includes members of the Foghorn Stringband from Portland, Oregon. The album they recorded together in October 2011, just before Black Pot, pays tribute to the mutual influence between honky-tonk and Cajun.

Moreover, the younger generation has formed marital alliances between the children of prominent figures on both music scenes, themselves artists: Linzay Young from the Red Stick Ramblers married Emma Leahy-Good, daughter of Sharon Leahy and Rick Good, a performing duo who have been teaching at Ashokan for years; Joel Savoy married Kelli Jones, who was raised in North Carolina and is the daughter of musician Carl Jones; other young couples include Richard Burgess and Anya Shoenegge, who grew up in New England and opened a violin repair shop in the Arnaudville area. All of them made southwest Louisiana their home and have, through new lineages and artistic collaborations in various bands, firmly rooted old-time music on Louisiana turf. Here again, the notion of circuit as Magnani uses it seems appropriate to describing the itineraries of the various actors involved in the connections between old-time music/French Louisiana music. Opening new paths and building new bridges, they extend distinct established networks.

The growing connectedness between French Louisiana music and old-time music does not encompass every French Louisiana music style. As these links are situated within the broader field of "roots" music, Creole musicians are included as long as they interpret the old-timey French music style, but not as zydeco musicians. While musical events, places, and alliances have multiplied between old-time and Louisiana "roots" musicians, they have also helped to strengthen the segmentation of French Louisiana musical categories: Louisiana "roots" music in all its various forms (Cajun, Creole, swing, country, blues) has distanced itself from local bands that situate themselves within the popular music market. As for contemporary zydeco musicians, regardless of their style, they do not at this point seem to share in these connections.

Whether regular, long-term visitors or transplants, outsiders have played a crucial role in the validation, circulation, and reconfiguration of French Louisiana music. This process results from various mobilities and flows. International musical tourism to Louisiana, and what has been called "virtual" or "sonic tourism" (the development of networks of fans outside of Louisiana studied by DeWitt[43]), have combined with the mobility of Louisiana musicians in the country and abroad, and the mobility of American and Europeans fans. These circulations create the conditions for the upward mobility of Louisiana musicians and bands, many of whom now promote their appeal worldwide.

Attracted by a geographic, social and cultural elsewhere, stimulated by an urge for change in their lifestyle, transplants' decision to move to southwest Louisiana accompanies their progressively greater involvement in the promotion and evolution of French Louisiana music, providing transplants with enhanced status and even, for some, a degree of local celebrity, that endows their lives with greater meaning.

Functioning as mediators, they have also contributed to, kindled, or reinforced the interest of south Louisiana residents in French Louisiana music and culture. Through the connections they forge and the networks they nourish and extend, transplants act as a driving force in shaping French Louisiana music locally, in its global appeal, and in the establishment and growing influence of circuits constituted by key places and events, whether they are territorialized or not. They participate in a process of hierarchization that changes the status of music practitioners, of the music itself, and of the specific styles associated with it. Their itineraries also show how their own status transforms itself, from fan to resident, from dancer to musician, but also from transplant moved by passion and eager to become involved as an established resident to a successfully transplanted individual who has put down roots and can exist independently of fellow transplants.

The circles they form not only overlap with other pre-existing circles but also stretch beyond the realm of music. Transplants have supported an increased emphasis on the protection of the environment, the consumption of fresh, local produce, and the development of eclectic practices from diverse traditions, from Buddhism to specific nutritional therapies and medical Chi Qong. They retain their progressive political stances although surrounded by a vast majority of conservatives, supporting Obama in 2008 and 2012 against a 65.9 percent Republican majority.[44] The evolution of local practices and lifestyles makes the appeal of the region even stronger for those who envision living there. The increased number of short-term rentals both sought by visitors and offered by homeowners to coincide with festivals reflects growing interest in south Louisiana and the development of a new real estate market.

While they take pride in their new roots and seem fulfilled by their new lives, transplants remain aware of their distinctive status and value their transformation without identifying as Louisiana natives. However, what they undeniably share with natives is a strong sense of place. Instead of the all-purpose and confusing concept of identity, Roger Brubaker argues in favor of a more differentiated analytical concept, among which the idea that "commonality denotes the sharing of some common attribute."[45] Following his perspective, it has become possible to talk of a Louisiana "commonality" that encompasses every resident, whether native or not.

Conclusion

The goal of this book is to question certain established notions and ideas that tend to mask processes of differentiation and hierarchization at work in a complex and evolving musical field. I also apply critical analysis to the representations of French Louisiana music, arguing that they tend to conceal the interstices between binary oppositions such as black-white, urban-rural, differentiation-creolization, and local-global. More broadly, this project also seeks to contribute to the positioning of music as an important field within anthropology that enables the exploration of crucial issues such as the production and management of difference.

Music offers a powerful vehicle for exploring the variety of registers within which French Louisianans identify themselves, including "French," "French Louisiana"; "Cajun," "Acadian," and "Coonass" for those who self-identify as white; and "Creole," "black," and "African American" for those who consider themselves black. The French Louisiana repertoire acts as a site in which social actors play among these often contradictory, conflictual, or competing senses of belonging by mobilizing them serially or layering them.

These identifications resonate with musical categories, and both reveal themselves to be remarkably flexible. They also echo the ways in which French Louisiana music is represented, thought about, and experienced by its practitioners and its fans in Louisiana society. This produces permanent oscillation between the metaphor of mixing, adaptation, and creativity on one hand and, on the other, the rhetorics of origins and the naturalization of difference. Musical practices in Louisiana reveal continuous interaction between these two positions. Like other musicians, French Louisiana music practitioners embody this diversity and are capable of combining a plurality of styles depending on the context, the timing in their careers, or the situation. They navigate between different registers of legitimacy, between French Louisiana heritage and modernity, between rural and urban legacies, and between mass-mediated popular music and "roots" music.

Several researchers who work on the region have adopted the notion of creolization, confining it to a seamless, smooth process that seems culturally beneficial and wholly valorizing, devoid of divisions and restricted to the francophone heritage. On the contrary, in my view the concept of creolization appears as a confusing tool for understanding the social dynamics at work in Louisiana society. The intricate interactions between analytical categories and vernacular categories demand that these notions be systematically recontextualized by taking into account every actor who makes use of them—from musicians and dancers to scholars and activists and from the music industry and cultural institutions to tourist organizations, music experts, and the media. The examination of these categories also entails a consideration of their circulation from one register, domain, or scale to another.

Musical genealogy and the categories used in French Louisiana music are legitimized through an omnipresent racial imaginary that frames African and European lineage as the foundational factors in the process of differentiation while enacting musical interactions across the color line through their practice. My experience as a musician allowed me to adopt a perspective that proved to be indispensable in seeing, hearing, and experiencing the diversity of musical identifications, categories, and contents that these discourses tend to fossilize. Instead of seeing the discourses of origins and mixing as contradictory, the field and the way music is practiced show that, on the contrary, they are continually confronted, reconciled, alternated, and superimposed. Being French allowed me to cross implicit boundaries by daring to ask sensitive questions without arousing suspicion or being found irritating while benefiting from the image of France as less inclined to "racial" discrimination.

The ubiquity of "racial" and "ethnic" factors in the process of differentiation is situated within the celebration of "diversity" that has become inescapable in American society. Distinguishing Cajun and Creole heritages by resorting to European or African origins as a means of grounding categories and musical contents arises from a persistent desire to "respect" racial and ethnic identifications and to capitalize on "cultural" differences that are seldom understood as sources of tension or discrimination. Numerous researchers, activists, and musicians have denounced past and present manifestations of racism and discrimination. However, the underlying representations and racial imagery of musical categories remain mostly unaddressed.[1]

In a parallel process, some social actors still refer to the notion of class as a cohesive factor and the source of a shared status by Creoles and Cajuns that is anchored in rurality, while some scholars have analyzed social stratification and inequalities between or within these two identifications, although this topic would benefit from extensive fieldwork on contemporary musical practices.[2] While musical styles and creativity are endlessly depicted as the fruit of a specific heritage or tradition, there is a need to inscribe them within a quest for upward social mobility and legitimacy. Market forces, outsider's interest, and geographical mobility of music and musicians also powerfully shape musicians' career strategies and musical choices.[3]

In 2007 the Smithsonian Institution launched the traveling exhibit that is still being shown, entitled "New Harmonies: Celebrating American Roots Music." The exhibit pursues the idea that music is an essential part of American national identity across the country.[4] Ray Allen contextualizes the enthusiasm for American grassroots music in his book *Gone to the Country*:

> We like to see ourselves as forward-looking, intrepid, explorers of the frontier, space, and, most recently, cyberspace. But there is also a residual Jeffersonian agrarian spirit in us that draws us back to some imagined pastoral past. Likewise, we need to temper our rugged individualism with a sense of democratic communitarianism that binds us to one another in a broad array of kinship, ethnic, religious, neighborhood, and affinity groups. Oral-based music perceived to be rooted in an idealized past and imagined community has played and continues to play a vital role in this balancing act.[5]

The ever-expanding experimentation of French Louisiana musicians and their eagerness to embrace and appropriate new styles and sounds while remaining faithful to a regionalist narrative only serve to consolidate this balance, foreshadowing growing interest in French Louisiana music.

Regional identification with all its corollaries remains one of the most significant determiners of connectedness in French Louisiana music. While its global attraction is celebrated locally, local cultural institutions have strongly reinforced the perception that it is "indigenous to south Louisiana." Reflecting on the meaning of rootedness in a particular place, Liisa Malkki notes that, "like the nation, culture has for long been conceived as something existing in 'soil.' Terms like 'native,' 'indigenous,' and 'autochthonous' have all served to root cultures in soils; and it is, of course, a well-worn observation that the term culture derives from the Latin for cultivation (see, e.g., Wagner 1981:21)."[6] The deterritorialization of French

Louisiana music and regionalist claims are in fact intimately bound to each other. Embedded in south Louisiana, French Louisiana music is often invoked through comparison to a tree shape. Its imaginary is nurtured by the south Louisiana natural environment, foodways, lifestyle, and French legacy, which combine to configure its singularity. French Louisiana music is meant to be lived, not merely practiced. It is cherished in part for the ways of life associated with it, both past and present, whether they are enacted, appropriated, honored through the memory of pioneers, or imagined from afar. For all those who enjoy and practice this music, no matter where they are from, it bears particular textures, smells, and savors. It is damp and sweaty, and it echoes with the sounds of storytelling and self-derision, combined with intense emotions, and sense of distinctiveness. And all of these feelings inspire and transpire in and among those who live this music.

Yet this soil has been fertilized and shaped since the earliest recordings of French Louisiana music by a circulatory movement in and out of Louisiana that involved a host of actors—folklorists, music producers, filmmakers, collectors, musicians, and dancers—who sparked local awareness. This circulation has been central to the ways in which French Louisiana music has been represented and to how it has evolved and been legitimized and reconfigured. The attachment to south Louisiana as a place, a unique geographic locale, and the homeland of French Louisiana music, is inseparable from this process of mobility, diaspora, and transplantation.

Some journalists have maintained that the regional identification of French Louisiana musicians hinders their aspiration to social mobility and changes in scale and status. The assignation of a singular and inalienable identity circumscribes Louisiana music within its native region, in spite of growing national attention, as if musicians and French Louisiana people as a whole were reluctant to define themselves as full-fledged Americans. *Garden and Gun* echoes precisely this view: "Feufollet has already gotten more national attention than most, but they're playing their cards a little closer to the chest, eyeing that bigger stage with caution even as they gather all the weapons they need to take it. As is sometimes the way with the Cajuns, the biggest question for Feufollet's conquering the rest of the country might be whether or not they want to have anything to do with the rest of the country."[7]

Cajuns are thus ultimately portrayed as quintessentially distinct, even exotic, and as a consequence as belonging to the nation's periphery due to characteristics deemed almost inbred in them. As theorized by Arjun

Appadurai, the attachment to south Louisiana is transformed into confinement or incarceration that contains French Louisiana residents within a bounded space and a specific "mode of thought."[8] The metaphor of "internal colonialism" that Ann Laura Stoler rehabilitated is helpful in undergirding efforts to explore relations of domination inside the United States, beyond oversimplified narratives of resistance versus control. In order to understand what makes the processes of categorization and differentiation viable and enduring in Louisiana, they need to be situated within relations of power that reveal the intricacies of political domination and regionalism within a context of economic, political, social, and environmental vulnerability that was dramatically placed in relief by the 2000s disasters.[9]

French Louisiana music helps us question "the unity of the 'us' and the otherness of 'the other'" in various ways, to borrow a phrase from Gupta and Ferguson.[10] The negotiation of difference involves both a ubiquitous racial imaginary and the metaphor of cultural mixing, which complexify the process of differentiation; the otherness of non-natives can be reconsidered in light of the role of outsiders and transplants in contributing to the vitality of French Louisiana music throughout the twentieth century. Finally, south Louisianans' otherness with respect to the rest of the country is both nurtured and endured. The production of cultural difference occurs in interconnected and interdependent spaces, traversed by economic and political relations of inequality. As Gupta and Ferguson argue, ". . . what is needed is a willingness to interrogate, politically and historically, the apparent 'given' of a world in the first place divided into 'ourselves' and 'others.' A first step on this road is to move beyond naturalized conceptions of spatialized 'cultures' and to explore instead the production of difference within common, shared, and connected spaces."[11]

As I am closing the examination of music categories and ethnic, racial, and regional identifications in French Louisiana music, Michael Doucet's provocative, humorous statement at the 2008 Balfa Camp echoes in my head: "There is no such thing as Cajun music. It's a fallacy. There is no such thing as Cajun. It doesn't exist." Later, as he was ending his fiddle workshop, he concluded: "So this has been fun!" which caused this wittily call-and-response with a student:

"And Cajun music doesn't exist!"
"And you're not here!"

Notes

INTRODUCTION

1. Hyena, a trickster character found in Louisiana folktales.

2. Lafayette is projected to experience the highest growth in employment (8.8 percent) in the region and the second-highest growth in gross metropolitan product (7.5 percent) of 363 urban areas in the nation (IHS Global, July 2012). In 2000 the population of the region called Acadiana, which includes Lafayette and the surrounding parishes, was 512,720, which was projected to grow to more than 552,000 by 2012. In its demographic snapshot report, the 2010 census indicates that over a state population of 4,533,372, Louisiana counted 62.6 percent white, 32 percent black, and 1.6 percent of two or more races. For Acadiana, the numbers are 68.69 percent white; 28.07 percent black; 1.23 percent two or more races. Income of less than $10,000 describes 10.1 percent of Louisiana households, but 20.5 percent of Acadiana households are under this level, an indication of statewide and regional poverty.

3. Parts of this section borrow from my article "Créolisation, imaginaire racial et marché musical dans la musique franco-louisianaise," in *Parallaxe transatlantiques. Vers une anthropologie réciproque*, dir. Anne Raulin and Susan C. Rogers (Paris: Editions du CNRS, 2012), 79–108.

4. Cécile Vidal, "Usages et appropriations du terme créole en Louisiane: des colons français du XVIIIe siècle aux historiens états-uniens du XXIe siècle," presentation, 4th conference of the French Atlantic History Group: "Histoires créoles—Creole histories: pratiques et poétique," McGill University, May 1–3, 2008.

5. James Dormon, 1996, "Ethnicity and Identity: Creoles of Color in Louisiana," in *Creoles of Color in the Gulf South*, James Dormon (ed.) (Knoxville: University of Tennessee Press), 166–79; Frances J. Woods, *Marginality and Identity: A Colored Creole Family Through Ten Generations* (Baton Rouge: Louisiana State University Press, 1989); Gary B. Mills, *The Forgotten People: Cane River's Creoles of Color* (Baton Rouge: Louisiana State University Press, 1977).

6. Carl Brasseaux, *French, Cajun, Creole, Houma: A Primer on Francophone Louisiana* (Baton Rouge: Louisiana State University Press, 2005), 112.

7. See Sara Le Menestrel, 2006, "Déclinaisons et enjeux de l'identité créole en Louisiane," in Carlo Célius (dir.), *Situations créoles. Pratiques et représentations*, Québec, Editions Nota Bene.

8. For an exhaustive study of the history of the Acadians in Louisiana, see Carl Brasseaux, *The Founding of New Acadia: The Beginnings of Acadian Life in Louisiana*

1765–1803 (Baton Rouge: Louisiana State University Press, 1987); Christopher Hodson, *The Acadian Diaspora: An Eighteenth-Century History* (Oxford: Oxford University Press, 2012).

9. Brasseaux, *French, Cajun*, 45.

10. Gilles Havard and Cécile Vidal, *Histoire de l'Amérique française*, 2nd ed. (Paris: Champs Flammarion, 2006), 641–45.

11. Christopher Hodson, *The Acadian Diaspora: An Eighteenth Century History* (Oxford and New York: Oxford University Press, 2012), 8, 211.

12. For an analysis of the emergence and evolution of this ethnic label, see Jacques Henry and Carl Bankston, *Blue Collar Bayou: Louisiana Cajuns in the New Economy of Ethnicity* (Westport: Praeger, 2002), ch. 1.

13. Marc David, "Memory's Warp: The Cultural Politics of History and Race in South Louisiana," diss. (University of North Carolina at Chapel Hill, 2005), 196–97.

14. Brasseaux, *French, Cajun*, 68. See also Brasseaux, *Acadian to Cajun*.

15. About the founding of and issues raised by CODOFIL, see in particular the analysis of J. Henry, "Le Mouvement Louisianais de Renouveau Francophone. Vers une nouvelle identité cadjine?" diss. (Paris: Université Paris, René Descartes, 1982); "The Louisiana French Movement: Actors and Actions in Social Change," in *French and Creole in Louisiana*, Albert Valdman (ed.) (New York: Plenum, 1997), 183–213; Shane Bernard, *The Cajuns: Americanization of a People* (Jackson: University Press of Mississippi, 2003).

16. For an analysis on the gradual Cajunization of French Louisiana and of the regional culture, see Cecyle Trépanier, "The Cajunization of French Louisiana: Forging a Regional Identity," *Geographical Journal* 157, no. 2 (July 1991): 161–71.

17. About the origin of the term and the expressions related to it, see in particular Ancelet, "Zydeco/Zarico"; Spitzer, "Monde Créole" and Tisserand, *Kingdom*.

18. Ancelet, "Zydeco/Zarico," 127.

19. See the CD *Cajun and Creole Music 1934–1937*.

20. Barry J. Ancelet, *Cajun Music: Its Origins and Development*, Louisiana Life Series, No. 2 (Lafayette: Center for Louisiana Studies, University of Southwestern Louisiana, 1989); Barry Ancelet and Elemore Morgan, *Cajun and Creole Music-Makers: Musiciens cadiens et creoles*, 2nd ed. (Jackson: University Press of Mississippi, 1999); Shane Bernard, *Swamp Pop: Cajun and Creole Rhythm and Blues* (Jackson: University Press of Mississippi, 1996); Ryan A. Brasseaux and Kevin Fontenot, *Accordions, Two Step, Fiddles and Swing. A Cajun Music Reader* (Lafayette: Center for Louisiana Studies, University of Louisiana at Lafayette, 2006); Ryan Brasseaux, *Cajun Breakdown: An American-made Music* (New York: Oxford University Press, 2009); John Broven, *South to Louisiana: The Music of the Cajun Bayous* (Gretna: Pelican, 1983); Mark F. DeWitt, *Cajun and Zydeco Dance Music in Northern California: Modern Pleasures in a Postmodern World* (Jackson: University Press of Mississippi, 2008); Mark F. DeWitt, "The Diatonic Button Accordion in Ethnic Context: Idiom and Style in Cajun Dance Music," *Popular Music and Society* 26, no. 3 (2003): 305–30; Raymond E. Francois, *Ye Yaille Chere: Traditional Cajun Dance Music* (Ville Plate: Swallow, 1990); John Minton,

"Creole Community and 'Mass' Communication: Houston Zydeco as a Mediated Tradition," *Journal of Folklore Research* 32 (1995): 1–19; "Houston Creoles and Zydeco: The Emergence of an African-American Urban Popular Style," *American Music* 14, no. 4 (Winter 1996); Rick Olivier and Ben Sandmel, *Zydeco!* (Jackson: University Press of Mississippi, 1999); Ann Savoy, *Cajun Music: A Reflection of a People* (Eunice: Bluebird Press, 1984); Rocky Sexton, "Zydeco Music and Race Relations in French Louisiana," in *Multiculturalism in the United States*, eds. P. Kivisto and G. Rundblad (Thousand Oaks, CA: Pine Forge Press, 2000), 175–84; Nicholas Spitzer, "Zydeco and Mardi Gras: Creole Identity and Performance Genres in Rural French Louisiana," diss. (University of Texas at Austin, 1986); Michael Tisserand, *The Kingdom of Zydeco* (New York: Spike/Avon, 1998); Roger Wood, "Southeast Texas: Hothouse of Zydeco," *Journal of Texas Music History* 2 (2001): 23–45; Roger Wood and James Fraher, *Texas Zydeco* (Austin: University of Texas Press, 2006).

21. See in particular M. Mattern, "Let The Good Times Unroll: Music and Race Relations in Southwest Louisiana," in *Accordions, Two Step*, eds. Ryan A. Brasseaux and Kevin Fontenot (Lafayette: Center for Louisiana Studies, University of Louisiana at Lafayette, 2006), 97–106; *Acting in Concert: Music, Community, and Political Action*, chap. 6 (New Brunswick and London: Rutgers University Press, 1998); R. Sexton, "Cajun Mardi Gras? Cultural Objectification and Symbolic Appropriation in a French Tradition," *Ethnology* 38, no. 4 (1999): 299–313; Bernard, *Swamp Pop*, ch. 3; Spitzer, "Zydeco and Mardi Gras"; B. Ancelet, "The Limits and Directions of Creolization: From Mercier's L'Habitation St. Ybars to the Eunice Mardi Gras," *Louisiana Folklore Miscellany* 14 (1999): 15–26.

22. For further development, see Bernard, *The Cajuns*, 79.

23. Cajun patronyms reveal the multiple origins of this category of identification: German (i.e. Hoffpauir, Shexnayder), Spanish (Castille, Domingue, Romero), Scottish (McGee, Melançon), White Creole (de la Houssaye, Fontenot, Vidrine, Louviere), Foreign French (François, Faul, Dubois, Jacquemoud, Herpin), and Acadian (Leblanc, Broussard, Arceneaux).

24. Brasseaux, *French, Cajun*, 2.

25. In fact, Glenn Conrad contends that the variety of what he calls Gallic subcultures calls the very idea of a French Louisiana culture into question: "What is perceived as French Louisiana has been and perhaps remains nothing more than a loose and sometimes antagonistic relationship between socially disparate Francophone communities. . . . At no time following their introduction into Louisiana did these Gallic subcultures merge into what might be labeled a 'French Louisiana' culture." "Potpourri français: Varieties of French Settlers in Louisiana," *Revue de la Louisiane* X, no. 1 (Summer 1981): 1.

26. Véronique Boyer and Sara Le Menestrel, "Introduction," special issue, "Race, ethnie, communauté," *Journal de la société des américanistes* 95, no. 1 (2009): 113–16.

27. As the French sociologist Loïc Wacquant noted, "the sociology of 'race' typically takes for granted the existence of these groups as such and misses the dynamic process whereby they were fabricated at the cost of a complex work of group-making that

inscribed ethno-racial boundaries in the objectivity of social space and in the subjectivity of mental space." "For an Analytic of Racial Domination," *Political Power and Social Theory* 11 (1997): 225. Thanks to Cécile Vidal for providing this reference.

28. Rogers Brubaker, *Ethnicity Without Group*s (Cambridge and London: Harvard University Press, 2004), 80.

29. Ibid., 41.

30. Ibid., 47.

31. Ibid., 10.

32. Bernard Lahire, *La culture des individus. Dissonance culturelle et distinction de soi* (Paris: La Découverte, 2004). See also his article in English: "The Individual and the Mixing of Genres: Cultural Dissonance and Self-distinction," *Poetics* 36 (2008): 166–88, 10.1016/j.poetic.2008.02.001.

33. Lahire, B., "The individual and the mixing of genres," Ibid., 180.

34. Gabriel Segré describes the implications of Lahire's approach in the study of musical practice in his comments to Lahire (paper presented at the international colloquium "Anthropologie de la musique et de la danse: une approche des mondes contemporains," coordinated by Sara Le Menestrel and the ANR Musmond, EHESS, Maison Suger, Paris, June 8, 2010).

35. Claude Grignon and Jean-Claude Passeron, *Le Savant et le Populaire. Misérabilisme et populisme en sociologie et en littérature* (Paris: Gallimard/Seuil, 1989); Nathalie Heinich, *Ce que l'art fait à la sociologie* (Paris: Editions de Minuit, 1998).

36. Heinich, *Ce que l'art fait à la sociologie*, 43.

37. Richard Peterson, "Understanding Audience Segmentation: From Elite and Mass to Ominivore and Univore," *Poetics* 21 (1992): 243–58.

38. Hervé Glevarec, "La fin du modèle classique de la légitimité culturelle" in *Penser les médiacultures. Nouvelles pratiques et nouvelles approches de la représentation du monde*, Eric Maigret and Eric Macet (eds.) (Paris: Armand Colin, 2005), 92–93.

39. For more on this subject, see Sara Le Menestrel et al., *Des vies en musique. Parcours d'artistes, mobilités, transformations* (Paris: Hermann, 2012).

40. See in particular Charles Stewart (ed.), *Creolization. History, Ethnography, Theory* (Walnut Creek, CA: West Coast Press, 2007); "Syncretism and Its Synonyms: Reflections on Cultural Mixture," *Diacritics* 29, no. 3 (Autumn 1999): 40–62.

41. "Creolité" is defined by the authors of the manifest as a dual process of adaptation to the New World and of cultural confrontation resulting in the creation of a syncretic creole culture. Jean Bernabé, Patrick Chamoiseau, and Raphaël Confiant, *Eloge de la créolité* (Paris: Gallimard, 1993 [1989]).

42. Robin Cohen and Paola Toninato, "Introduction," in *The Creolization Reader*, R. Cohen and P. Toninato (eds.) (London and New York: Routledge Student Reader, 2010), 7.

43. Special Issue: Creolization, Issue Editors: Robert Baron and Ana Cara, *Journal of American Folklore*, 116, no. 459 (Winter 2003); "Forum: Locating or Liberating Creolization," *American Ethnologist* 33, no. 4 (November 2006): 549–88; Cohen and Toninato, *The Creolization Reader.*

44. Robert Baron and Ana Cara, "Introduction: Creolization and Folklore-Cultural Creativity in Process," *Journal of American Folklore* 116, no. 459 (Winter 2003): 5.

45. Stewart, "Syncretism," 44n3.

46. Ibid., 44.

47. Stewart, *Creolization*, 7, 18.

48. Stephan Palmié, "Creolization and Its Discontent," *The Creolization Reader*, 54.

49. Aisha Khan, "Feats of Engineering: Theory, Ethnography, and Other Problems of Model Building in the Social Sciences," *American Ethnologist* 33, no. 4 (November 2006): 569.

50. Amselle 2001, 21–22.

51. Ronald Radano and Philip Bohlman, *Music and the Racial Imagination* (Chicago and London: University of Chicago Press, 2000), 37, 39.

52. Ibid., 5.

53. Simon Frith, "The Discourse of World Music," in *Western Music and Its Others: Difference, Representation, and Appropriation in Music*, Georgina Born and David Hesmondhalgh (eds.) (Berkeley, Los Angeles, London: University of California Press, 2000), 305–22.

54. Brasseaux, *Cajun Breakdown*, ix. Brasseaux follows in the footsteps of Ronald Creagh, *Nos cousins d'Amérique* (Paris: Payot, 1988), who confers to French Americans an incomparable capacity to adapt to frontier conditions.

55. Brasseaux, *Cajun Breakdown*, 6.

56. Roger D. Abrahams, with Nick Spitzer, John F. Szwed and Robert Farris Thompson, *Blues for New Orleans: Mardi Gras and America's Creole Soul* (Philadelphia: University of Pennsylvania Press, 2006), 28.

57. Along similar lines, Spitzer views creolization as an alternative to the assimilationist model: "A creole approach to American society . . . would describe it as constantly forming new cultural wholes, while accounting fro the continuity of elements that remain distinct in local communities." Spitzer, "Monde Créole: The Cultural World of French Louisiana Creoles and the Creolization of World Cultures," *Journal of American Folklore* 116, no. 459 (Winter 2003): 59.

58. For a comparative approach of this process, see Le Menestrel et al., *Des vies en musique* (Paris: Hermann, 2012) ch. 3.

59. In a literary analysis, Jordan Stouck suggests an alternative understanding of creolization in the Louisiana context. She shows that the tension involved in the practice of "passing" is accompanied by the psychic costs of maintaining fictive identities. She interrogates the dynamic, creative potential that underlies the notion of creolization while also revealing the contested set of meanings carried by the term Creole in southern states. "Identities in Crisis: Alice Dunbar-Nelson's New Orleans Fiction," *Canadian Review of American Studies* 34, no. 3 (2004): 269–89.

60. Daniel Cefaï, "Introduction," in *L'engagement ethnographique*, Daniel Cefaï (ed.) (Paris: Editions de l'Ecole des hautes etudes en sciences sociales, 2010).

61. Peter Wade, "Rethinking *Mestisaje*: Ideology and Lived Experience," *Journal of Latin American Studies* 37 (2005): 255; Peter Wade, *Music, Race, and Nation: Música Tropical in Colombia* (Chicago: University of Chicago Press, 2000).

62. See Jacques Henry and Sara Le Menestrel (eds.), *Working the Field: Accounts from French Louisiana* (Jackson: University Press of Mississippi), xii–xvi.

63. Cefaï, *L'engagement*, 7, 8.

64. Le Menestrel, "Tourist and 'Cajun from France,'" in *Working the Field*, Henry and Le Menestrel, 98–117.

65. Le Menestrel, "Introduction," special issue, "Musiques 'populaires', catégorisations, et usages sociaux," *Civilisations* LIII, nos. 1–2 (2006): 7–22. See http://civilisations.revues.org/index513.html

66. See Le Menestrel and Henry, "Figure du *survivor*: usages de la mémoire et gestion de la catastrophe en Louisiane après les ouragans Katrina et Rita," *Ethnologie française* 3 (2010): 493–506; Le Menestrel and Henry, "Sing Us Back Home: Music, Place and the Production of Locality," *Popular Music and Society* 33, no. 2 (2010): 179–202; Le Menestrel, "'I can't leave New Orleans more than it can leave me.' Place attachment, Displacement, and Musical Practices in Post-Katrina New Orleans. Direction for Research," paper presented at the international conference Saint-Louis du Sénégal et La Nouvelle-Orléans: Histoire comparée et croisée de deux cités portuaires de part et d'autre de l'Atlantique du XVIIe au XXe siècle, St. Louis du Sénégal, June 5–7, 2012; Le Menestrel, "From Commemorating to *Healing*: Coping with the Scars of a Katrina" (paper presented at the annual meeting of the American Anthropological Association, session "Traces Of Tragedy: Reshaping Differences, Reinventing Communities And Retracing Social Ties at the Scene of Disaster," Montreal, November 16–20, 2011); Le Menestrel, "Memory Lives in New Orleans: The Process and Politics of Commemoration," international conference From American Sodom to American Phoenix: The Destruction and Rebirth of New Orleans, EHESS, Lyon II, March 1–2, 2011.

67. Unless otherwise indicated, all interviews quoted are the author's.

68. See ch. 1 of Le Menestrel, *Des vies*.

69. Le Menestrel, "Tourist," 103–4.

70. Additional sources were consulted at the New Orleans Public Library, but without finding any hints of interactions or exchanges between southwest Louisiana musicians from the 1920s to 1940s. On this subject, I consulted the Jambalaya Program Records (1977–1980), the Friends of the Cabildo Oral History Project, and the Louisiana New Index, which lists articles of six New Orleans newspapers from the late nineteenth century through the 1960s.

CHAPTER 1

1. Interview with Geno Delafose, D'Jalma Garnier, Don Vappie, and John Brunious by Nick Spitzer, "Traditional Jazz and Zydeco: Identity and Impact of Louisiana Creole Music," colloquium, Deep South Regional Humanities Center, Tulane University, New Orleans, April 22, 2004.

2. For more details on his role and itinerary, see ch. 5.

3. Johnny Allan, *Memories: A Pictorial History of South Louisiana Music, 1910–1990s, South Louisiana and East Texas Musicians*, volume I and II, Lafayette: Johnnie Allan/Jadfel Publishing.

4. Doucet conducted interviews with Bradford Gordon, man of color from New Orleans who taught fiddler Leo Soileau, and with Hypolite Charles, that were unfortunately lost. Doucet also had a band in the 1970s with Austin Sonnier named the Black and Tan Creole Orchestra that recorded the song "Bunk's Blues" in tribute to Bunk Johnson on the album *Bayou Cadillac* (1989) and his 2008 album *Now On* gives a rendition of "Saint Louis Blues" and of Hoagy Carmichael's "New Orleans."

5. Another publication of his is *Willie Geary "Bunk" Johnson: The New Iberia Years* (New York: Crescendo, 1977).

6. Sonnier, *Second Linin'*, v; Austin Sonnier, *Willie Geary "Bunk" Johnson: The New Iberia Years* (Crescendo, 1977).

7. Broven, *South*, x.

8. The only exception to my knowledge is Shane Bernard, who interrogates the "swamp pop" category and argues for its inclusion as an integral part of the Cajun and Creole musical heritage. See Bernard, *Swamp Pop*.

9. *Histoire musicale des Acadiens. De La Nouvelle France à la Louisiane 1604–1804* (Paris: L'Harmattan, 1995).

10. Darensbourg, *Jazz*, 35–37.

11. Ibid., 36.

12. *Daily Advertiser*, January 8, 1918.

13. In a survey submitted to the readers of the *Daily Advertiser*, more than 160 clubs are listed from the teens to the fifties. See Jim Bradshaw, "Readers recall clubs where they danced to Louisiana music," *Daily Advertiser*, December 29, 1998, accessed October 20, 2011. http://RememberWhen.carencrohighschool.org/LA_Studies/ParishSeries/FrenchMusic/AcadianaDanceClubs.htm.

14. Al Kennedy, *Chord Changes on the Chalkboard: How Public School Teachers Shaped Jazz and Music in New Orleans* (Lanham, MD, and Oxford: Scarecrow Press, 2002).

15. Brasseaux, *Cajun Breakdown*, 53.

16. *Daily Clarion-Progress*, February 16, March 14, March 16, 1923.

17. *Crowley Signal*, February 7, 1925.

18. *Clarion News*, January 30, 1930.

19. *Weekly Iberian*, October 6, 1938; December 8, 1938.

20. Broven, *South*, 56–57.

21. Darensbourg, *Jazz*, 84.

22. Brasseaux, *Cajun Breakdown*, 122–23.

23. Bruce B. Raeburn, email correspondence, July 26, 2012. For an in-depth exploration of this context, see his book *New Orleans Style and the Writing of American Jazz History* (Ann Arbor: University of Michigan Press, 2009).

24. In *The New Grove Dictionary of Jazz*, 2nd ed., the term "big band" is defined as describing "swing bands of the 1930s and 1940s, which consisted of ten to fifteen instruments, although it may be applied to any large ensemble" (vol. 1, 218).

25. Sonnier, *Second Linin'*, 54 et seq.

26. Author interview with Orres Leblanc, New Iberia, January 7, 2005.

27. Sonnier, *Second Linin'*, 38.

28. Many references date Thomas's murder from 1932. He was in fact murdered by John Guillory on November 21, 1931. Acadia Parish Clerk of Court, Indictment #4298.

29. Steve Picou, the grandson of the Berro's Club owner in Eunice, owns a picture of Armstrong playing there in the early 1950s.

30. Darensbourg, *Jazz*, 143.

31. Ibid., 29.

32. Bruce Boyd Raeburn, "Stars of David and Sons of Sicily: Constellations Beyond the Canon in Early New Orleans Jazz," *Jazz Perspectives* 3:2 (2009): 146.

33. Alex Bigard, interviewed by William Russell, Richard B. Allen, and Ralph Collins, April 30, 1960, Reel III, 19–20, Transcript, Hogan Jazz Archive, Tulane University.

Paul Martel, a descendant of the Martels, teaches at North Central High in Opelousas. He created a website dedicated to his family and mentions the band, using similar sources. See http://martelfamily.com.

34. His music was preserved through two numbers recorded by the Lomaxes. See ch. 2.

35. Denise Hebert, "The Hebert Family and the Music of Acadiana," *Attakapas Gazette* 23, no. 3 (Fall 1988): 99–110.

36. Thanks to Joel Breaux for providing me with a copy of this recording.

37. Hypolite Charles, April 13, 1963, Parks, reel 2, Oral History Collection, Hogan Jazz Archive, Tulane University.

38. Brasseaux, *Cajun Breakdown*, 16.

39. Ibid., 19.

40. Ancelet, *Cajun Music*; Savoy, *Cajun Music*.

41. Malcom Comeaux, "Introduction and Use of Accordions in Cajun Music," *Louisiana Folklore Miscellany* 14 (1999): 27–40.

42. Rocky L. Sexton, "Cajuns, Germans, and Les Americains," diss. (University of Iowa, 1996).

43. Al Rose and Edmond Souchon, *New Orleans Jazz: A Family Album* (Baton Rouge: Louisiana State University Press, 1984 [1967]).

44. Edward "Kid" Ory, April 20, 1957, 27, Oral History Collection, Hogan Jazz Archive, Tulane University.

45. *La Nouvelle-Orléans, capitale du jazz* (New York: Éditions de la Maison Française, 1946). Thanks to Bruce Raeburn for finding these references. Drummer Bill Phillips also corroborates Bolden's skills on the accordion (May 24, 1961, Oral History Collection, Hogan Jazz Archive, Tulane University).

46. Ibid., 72, via Emmanuel Perez interview, his words, my translation.

47. Ibid., 79, Goffin's words.

48. Ibid., 35.

49. Ibid., 52, via Bob Lyons interview, his words.

50. Jack Stewart, "The Mexican Band Legend, Part I," *Jazz Archivist* 6, no. 2 (December 1991): 1–11; Stewart, "The Mexican Band Legend, Part II," *Jazz Archivist* 9, no. 1 (May 1994): 1–17; Jack Stewart, "The Mexican Band Legend, Part III," *Jazz Archivist* 20 (2007): 1–10.

51. Email correspondence with Jonno Frishberg, August 1, 2009.

52. Author interview with Gil Lejeune, New Iberia, December 8, 2004.

53. Brasseaux, *Cajun Breakdown*, 243.

54. Incidentally, the song also crossed the Atlantic and was incorporated into the *musette* style.

55. Miller, *Segregating Sound*, 179–84.

56. Benjamin Filene, *Romancing the Folk: Public Memory and American Roots Music* (Chapel Hill and London: University of North Carolina Press, 2000), 35.

57. Interview with Varise Connor, Lionel Leleux, and Michael Doucet by Barry Ancelet, May 26, 1977, Lake Arthur; Ancelet collection, AN1.002, Archive of Cajun and Creole Folklore, University of Louisiana at Lafayette.

58. For a detailed account of Falcon's recording and first Cajun recordings in general, see Brasseaux, *Cajun Breakdown*, 49–50, 58–64.

59. Chris Strachwitz, "Cajun Country," in *The American Folk Music Occasional*, Vol. 1, Strachwitz and Pete Welding (eds.) (New York: Oak, 1970), 15.

60. Strachwitz, "Cajun Country"; Brasseaux, *Cajun Breakdown*, 127.

61. Interview of Leo Soileau by Ralph Rinzler, Rinzler collection, RI1.025, Leo Soileau (October 20, 1965), Archive of Cajun and Creole Folklore, University of Louisiana at Lafayette.

62. Savoy, *Cajun*, 128.

63. Michael Doucet, personal communication, January 6, 2005.

64. *Clarion News*, October 3, 1929; *Daily Advertiser*, September 19, 1929.

65. The implications of this collaboration in the historiography of French music and more particularly in the creolization paradigm are analyzed in chapter 3.

66. Tisserand, *Kingdom*, 73.

67. Dewey Balfa Cajun and Creole Music Workshop, twin fiddle workshop with Michael Doucet and Mitch Reed, April 22, 2008.

68. Canray Fontenot, *Louisiana Hot Sauce: Creole Style* (Arhoolie 381, 1992).

69. Tisserand, *Kingdom*, 90.

70. Savoy, *Cajun*, 115.

71. Ben Sandmel, "The Hackberry Ramblers," in Brasseaux and Fontenot, *Accordions*, 392.

72. Ibid., 393.

73. Ibid., 403n9, 395.

74. For an analysis of "Jole Blon" ("Jolie Blonde")'s impact and contribution to American music, see Brasseaux, *Cajun Breakdown*, 161–78.

75. Cajun fiddler and string band leader J. B. Fuselier, for example, who was at the center of the string band movement, always carried his accordion with him to dances and played it. Kevin Fontenot, "Foreword," in *When Fiddle Was King: Early Country Music from the North and West Regions of Louisiana*, Ron Yule (ed.) (Natchitoches, LA: Northwestern State University Press, 2007).

76. Broven, *South*, 21.

77. Tony Russell, "Leo Soileau," in Brasseaux and Fontenot, *Accordions*, 386.

78. Charlie Seeman, *A Cajun Music Anthology: The Historic Victor-Bluebird Sessions, 1928–1941*, Country Music Foundation, 1990–93, vols. 1–3.

79. Brasseaux and Fontenot, *Accordions*, 426.
80. Ancelet and Morgan, *Cajun and Creole*, 26.
81. For more information, see Brasseaux, *Cajun Breakdown*, 61–62.
82. Charlie Seeman, *Raise Your Window: A Cajun Music Anthology: The Historic Victor-Bluebird Sessions, 1928–1941*, vol. 2, Country Music Foundation, 1990–93.
83. Broven, *South*, 409.
84. Russell, "Leo Soileau," 384.
84. Barry Mazor, *Meeting Jimmie Rodgers: How America's Original Roots Music Hero Changed the Pop Sounds of a Century* (Oxford: Oxford University Press, 2009), 102.
86. Ancelet and Morgan, *Cajun and Creole*, 47.
87. On August 10, 1936, Victor recorded "Dixie Hottest," "I've Got a Gal," "Put On Your Old Gray Bonnet," "Bar Room Blues," Cottage on the Hill," "Loveless Love," "I Took It," and "Under the Moon with You." Ancelet and Spitzer, liner notes, *Octa Clark and Hector Duhon: The Dixie Ramblers: Ensemble Encore* (Rounder Records 6011, 1982).
88. It is worth noting that many song titles on the original recordings can lead to confusion in that they appear either in (misspelled) French, or in English, even when the lyrics are in French, like for example "Mama Where You At" (Oh Mom).
89. Author interview with Luderin Darbone, Sulphur, January 16, 2005.
90. "Moi j'aime cousin, moi j'aime cousine, mais moi j'aime mieux la cuisinière / Samedi au soir j'étais au bal et j'mai saoulé comme un vieux cochon / Dimanche matin, j'étais tout manière malade / Passez-moi un verre de limonade." Nathan Abshire, "La Danse de Limonade," *Les haricots sont pas salés* (Cinq Planètes 022652, 1997).
91. Louisiana Music Collection 230, Box 2, File 31, Amistad Center, Tulane University. The lyrics are: "Vou zen connin tit' la maison qui proch' coté l'église / Quan' mo ouar li, ça don' frisson, c'é la maison Denise / Mo Chèr cousin, mo chèr cousine, mo l'aimé la cuisine / Mo mangé bien, mo boir' bon vin, ça pa' couté moi a rien / Denise aimé gombo filé, mo l'aimé gumbo filé. / Denise aimé bon vin bourgogne, Mo l'aim' bon vin Bourgogne."
92. Darensbourg, *Jazz*, 140.
93. Author interview with Melva Patton and Zenobia Verdun, Grand Marais, February 2, 2005.
94. Stephen R. Tucker, "Louisiana Folk and Regional Popular Music Traditions on Records and the Radio: An Historical Overview with Suggestions for Future Research," in Brasseaux and Fontenot, *Accordions*; Shane Bernard, "J. D. Miller and Floyd Soileau: A Comparison of Two Small Town Recordmen of Acadiana," *Louisiana Folklife Journal* 15 (December 1991).
95. Broven, *South*, 38–39.
96. Yule, *Iry*, 5960.
97. Interview de Shane Bernard avec Floyd Soileau, BE 100.3, 1991, Bernard collection, Archive of Cajun and Creole Folklore, University of Louisiana at Lafayette.
98. Bernard, "J. D. Miller."
99. Broven, *South*, ix.
100. Some Creole of color, however, played an essential role in the struggle for equal civil rights for the black population during segregation: among other activists, Louis

Martinet and Rodolphe Desdunes founded the "citizen committee" to denounce as a violation of constitutional law the legislation of Separate Car Act (1890) applied in the trial of *Plessy v. Ferguson*.

101. Anthony Arthe Agnes, "The Negro Creole Community in New Orleans, 1880-1920: An Oral History," diss. (University of California, Irvine, 1978), 165.

102. Michael S. Martin, *Historic Lafayette: An Illustrated History of Lafayette and Lafayette Parish*, Historical Publishing Network, 2007, 26.

103. Hypolite Charles, April 13, 1963, Parks, reel 2, Oral History Collection, Hogan Jazz Archive, Tulane University.

104. Quoted in Michael Eugene Crutcher, *Tremé: Race and Place in a New Orleans Neighborhood* (Athens: University of Georgia Press, 2012), 34–35.

105. Paper written by Vana J. Plaisance, given by Denise Hebert, no reference.

106. *Weekly Iberian*, October 6, 1938, "LaVail to open music store here"; December 8, 1938.

107. Author interview with Arnold DePass, November 22, 2004, Port Barre.

108. Author interview with John Potier, January 11, 2005, Parks.

109. Sonnier, *Second Linin'*, 26.

110. *Daily Iberian*, May 23, 1998, front page.

111. Austin Sonnier, personal communication, January 19, 2005.

112. Sonnier, *Second Linin'*, 42.

113. Author interview with Joyce Menard, Lou Louvière, and Helen Hebert, January 7, 2005, New Iberia.

114. Hebert, "The Hebert Family."

115. See Carl Brasseaux, *In Search of Evangeline: Birth and Evolution of the Evangeline Myth* (Thibodaux: Blue Heron Press, 1989).

116. *Clarion News*, June 6, 1929.

117. Pellerin's selections in this ad are "Five Feet Two" and "Grand Galle Son Of Uncle Pierre." Brasseaux, who identified the records through a different local paper, mentions another recording by this musician, a banjo rendition of African American standard "Ain't Misbehaving." Interestingly, the owner of the New Drug Store didn't include it in his ad, as if he had wanted to exclusively promote the Acadian roots of these records. In Brasseaux, *Cajun Breakdown*, 74–75.

118. *Weekly Messenger*, June 13, 1936.

119. *Clarion News*, August 1, 1929.

120. Brasseaux, *Cajun Breakdown*, 137, 150.

121. Curney J. Dronet, *A Century of Acadian Culture: The Development of a Cajun Community: Erath (1899–1999)* (Pelican, 2001), 89–90. Bayou Bijou Dancehall was located on the corner of Broadway and Edwards. The building was destroyed in a fire in 1938; Stacy Bodin, "The Spirit of Erath Articles," accessed September 10, 2012. www.vrml.k12.la.us/vpkids/vp/Erath/erathhistory/ErathSchools/erathschoolsystem.htm.

122. According to a reader of the *Daily Advertiser*, who participated in a survey conducted on dance clubs. Bradshaw, "Readers recall."

123. Lawrence Levine, *Highbrow/Lowbrow: The Emergence of Cultural Hierarchy in America* (Harvard: Harvard University Press, 1988), 9.

124. Ibid., 86.

125. Lauren Post, "Joseph C. Falcon, Accordion Player and Singer: A Biographical Sketch," in Brasseaux and Fontenot, *Accordions*, 321–37; Yule, *Iry*.

126. Brasseaux, *Cajun Breakdown*, 25.

CHAPTER 2

1. Regina Bendix, *In Search of Authenticity: The Formation of Folklore Studies* (Madison: University of Wisconsin Press, 1997).

2. Karl Hagstrom Miller, *Segregating Sound: Inventing Folk and Pop Music in the Age of Jim Crow* (Durham: Duke University Press, 2010), Kindle edition, emplacement 143.

3. See, among many examples, Ancelet and Morgan, *Cajun and Creole*, 51; in an interview in *The Mamou Playboys Rockumentary*, Ancelet sings the band's praises, pointing out that one of their greatest forces is that "they're inventing from the inside of the tradition."

4. On the nature of debates over cultural representation within the Cajun French Music Association, see R. Sexton, "Too Loud, Too Wild? Negotiating Cajun Cultural Representations," *Ethnology* 50, no. 2 (Spring 2011): 117–34.

5. As early as 1929, the *Clarion News* presented the music played in the accordion contest of October 3 in Opelousas as ". . . a delightful contrast to the jazz tunes of modern days."

6. Kali Argyriadis and Sara Le Menestrel, *Vivre la guinguette* (Paris: Presses universitaires de France), 140.

7. *Opelousas News*, November 1, 1928, "Life of 'jazz age' ruins girl's health." "Physical breakdown threaten the modern American girl because of her intensive pace in the whirl of the present jazz age, according to the US public health." The article argues that the study from health services physicians demonstrate a slight increase of tuberculosis.

8. Raeburn, *New Orleans Style*, 40.

9. Bruce Raeburn, email correspondence, September 14, 2009.

10. *Weekly Messenger*, June 2, 1934, 6.

11. Lomax recordings, number 8, Archive of Cajun and Creole Folklore, University of Louisiana at Lafayette. 2 songs, one of which is a waltz, were recorded.

12. Lomax recording, listed as "Jazz Orchestra/Brass band-clarinet, trombone, cornet, baritone?" Evangeline Band, 6/13/1934," AFS-41 A side, Archive of Cajun and Creole Folklore, University of Louisiana at Lafayette; Joyce Menard, the daughter of Lucien Landry from the Louisiana Six, thinks it also includes a bass and a piano and therefore Wilton and Noah Hebert. The tunes are also referenced in Brasseaux, *Cajun Breakdown*, n38.

13. Filene, *Romancing*.

14. Neil V. Rosenberg, ed., *Transforming Tradition: Folk Music Revivals Examined* (Urbana and Chicago: University Press of Illinois), 8.

15. Karl Koenig, "Musical History of Donaldsonville and Claiborne Williams 1868–1952: Gentleman Musician of Donaldsonville, La.: Leader, St. Joseph Brass and String Band" (Abita Springs: Basin Street Press, 1996), 53–54.

16. Ibid., 54.

17. For more on the historical context of this diversity of styles and against the myth of cultural isolation, see Brasseaux, *Cajun Breakdown*, 97 et seq.

18. Brasseaux and Fontenot, *Accordions*, 14.

19. Harry Oster, "Acculturation in Cajun Folk Music," in Brasseaux and Fontenot, *Accordions*, 54.

20. The Federal Writers' Project was created in 1935 as part of the United States Works Progress Administration to provide employment for historians, teachers, writers, librarians, and other white-collar workers. Among the areas of interest was rural and urban folklore.

21. Filene, *Romancing*, 139–49.

22. Jacques Henry and Carl Bankston III, *Blue Collar Bayou: Louisiana Cajuns in the New Economy of Ethnicity* (Westport: Praeger, 2002), ch. 3.

23. For a development on these debates, see Ray Allen, *Gone to the Country: The New Lost City Ramblers and the Folk Music Revival* (Champaign: University of Illinois Press, 2010).

24. Thomas Turino, *Music as Social Life: The Politics of Participation* (Chicago: University of Chicago Press, 2008), 156.

25. Ancelet and Morgan, *Cajun and Creole*, 151.

26. Mark DeWitt, *Cajun and Zydeco*, 119.

27. Allen, *Gone to the Country*, 244.

28. Thanks to Christian Rinaudo for bringing up this comparison.

29. Allen, *Gone to the Country*, 246.

30. Akhil Gupta and James Ferguson, "Space, Identity and the Politics of Difference," *Critical Anthropology* 7, no. 1 (1992): 7.

31. Frédéric Martel, *De la culture en Amérique* (Paris: Gallimard, 2006), 475.

32. Barry Ancelet, "The Theory and Practice of Activist Folklore: From Fieldwork to Programming," in *Working the Field*, Henry and Le Menestrel (eds.), 62.

33. Filene, *Romancing*, 116.

34. Olivier and Sandmel, *Zydeco!*, 54–55.

35. *Louisiana Cajun Music*, (Old Timey 109, vol. II, 1970). Liner notes by Chris Strachwitz.

36. *Louisiana Cajun Music*, vol. IV.

37. Paul Tate, "The Cajuns of Louisiana," in Strachwitz, *American Folk*, 12.

38. See Brasseaux, *Cajun Breakdown*; Bernard, *Swamp Pop*. Sexton initiated the discussion in "Cajuns, Germans."

39. Bernard, *Swamp Pop*; *Cajuns*; Brasseaux, *Cajun Breakdown*.

40. Brasseaux, *Cajun Breakdown*, ix.

41. Caffery's *Traditional Music in Coastal Louisiana: The 1934 Lomax Recordings* (Baton Rouge: Louisiana State University Press, 2013) was unfortunately published too late to include in this book. He offers for the first time a comprehensive examination of the 1934 corpus and provides a musical history of Louisiana that extends beyond Cajun music and zydeco to the rural blues, Irish and English folk songs, play-party songs, slave spirituals, and traditional French folk songs.

42. *Louisiana Folk Masters: Varise Conner*, recorded by Barry J. Ancelet in 1975–77, Archive of Cajun and Creole Folklore, University of Louisiana at Lafayette.

43. *The Complete Recordings of Dennis McGee, 1929–1930* (Early American Cajun Classics, Yazoo 2012). Liner notes by Ann Savoy, produced by Richard Nevins and Ann Savoy.

44. Rosan A. Jordan and Frank De Caro, "In This Folk-Lore Land: Race Class, Identity and Folklore Studies in Louisiana," *Journal of America Folklore* 109, no. 431 (Winter 1996): 33.

45. Fabian Holt, *Genre in Popular Music* (Chicago: University of Chicago Press, 2007), 160.

46. Jean-François Sirinelli and Jean-Pierre Rioux (eds.), *La Culture de masse en France de la Belle Époque à nos jours* (Paris: Fayard, 2002), 17.

47. Levine, *Highbrow*, 164–65, 234.

48. Bill C. Malone, "Nashville Sound," In *Grove Music Online. Oxford Music Online*, www.oxfordmusiconline.com/subscriber/article/grove/music/19589 (accessed February 1, 2012).

49. Holt, *Genre*, 72–73.

50. Ancelet collection, AN1.030, Interview with Lionel Leleux for Indiana University, Jan. 7, 1975, Archive of Cajun and Creole Folklore, University of Louisiana at Lafayette.

51. Broven, *South*, 62.

52. For a short biography on Thibodeaux, see Kevin Fontenot, "People Buy the Feel: Cajun Fiddle Master Rufus Thibodeaux," in *Accordions*, Brasseaux and Fontenot, 435.

53. Ancelet and Morgan, *Cajun and Creole*, 28.

54. Tate, "The Cajuns," 11.

55. Bernard, *Swamp Pop*, 75.

56. Ben Sandmel, email correspondence, March 7, 2006.

57. See Peterson, *Creating Country Music*, 209.

58. Barry Ancelet, "Cajun Music," in *Accordions*, Brasseaux and Fontenot, 204.

59. Author interview with Chas Justus, June 17, 2008, Lafayette.

60. Turino calls the recording fields "high fidelity music" and "studio audio art." The first one "refers to musical sounds heard on recordings that index or are iconic of live performance" like ethnographic field recordings (Turino, *Music*, 67); the second one "involves the manipulation of taped sounds, synthesized sounds, or digital technology for the creation of sonic art objects that exist only in electronically reproducible form and in which the goal is the creation of the recorded piece itself," like electroacoustic music (78).

61. Barry Ancelet and Philip Gould, with Benny Graeff and David Simpson, *One Generation at a Time: Biography of a Cajun and Creole Music Festival* (Lafayette: Center for Louisiana Studies, University of Louisiana at Lafayette, 2007), vii.

62. See Bernard, *Cajuns*, ch. 3.

63. Broven, *South*, 233. For more on the itinerary of Graeff, see Bernard, *Swamp Pop*, 169–75.

64. Bruce Raeburn, personal correspondence, July 2012. Although Bruce was not playing with Benny Graeff for the germination of the song, he was the drummer of the band in 1970.

65. Bernard, *Cajuns*, 73.
66. See also Sexton, "Too Loud."
67. "The Wisdom of Wilson Savoy," Valcour Records, Podcast, 26 min., August 2008.
68. Wilson Savoy, email correspondence, April 11, 2014.
69. R. Reese Fuller, "Marc of Distinction," *Times of Acadiana*, April 4, 2001, 23. For another development of the same argument, see also Leslie Berman, "Savoy Fare: The Real Family Values of Marc and Ann Savoy," *Sing Out!* 47, no. 3 (Fall 2003): 22–33.
70. Author interview with Joel Savoy, October 28, 2010, Black Pot Festival.
71. Quoted in Steve Redhead and John Street, "Have I the Right? Legitimacy, Authenticity and Community in Folk's Politics," *Popular Music* 8, no. 2 (1989): 177–84.
72. Olivier and Sandmel, *Zydeco!*, 38.
73. In fact, Sean Ardoin would have said that he did not like this term, which sounded to him like "nouveau riche."
74. Wood and Fraher, *Texas Zydeco*, 194; Sandmel, *Zydeco!*, 152.
75. Bruce Raeburn, "Faith, Hip Hop, and Charity: Brass Band Morphology in Post-Katrina New Orleans," paper presented at the international conference From American Sodom to American Phoenix: The Destruction and Rebirth of New Orleans, Tulane University, New Orleans, October 21–22, 2010, and Paris, EHESS, April 1–2, 2011.
76. Peterson notes similar authenticity claims in the country music scene, 209.
77. Quoted in Tisserand, *The Kingdom*, 209.
78. Ibid., 208.
79. For more musical details on this distinction, see Turino, *Music as Social Life*, 165.
80. Ibid., 162.
81. Author interview with David Greely, January 14, 2003, Breaux Bridge.
82. Tisserand, *The Kingdom*, 336.
83. Olivier and Sandmel, *Zydeco!*, 159.
84. Turino, *Music as Social Life*, 32–33.
85. Author interview with Mitch Reed, December 6, 2004, Carencro.
86. Ryan Brasseaux and Kevin Fontenot, "Saving Culture with a Song: Cajun Music and the Twenty-First Century," in *Accordions*, ed. Brasseaux and Fontenot, 501–6.
87. On how the CFMA exerts control over musical representation, see Sexton, "Too Loud."
88. Although there has been in recent years a development of listening gigs, dance music performances are the norm within French Louisiana music.
89. Brasseaux and Fontenot, "Saving Culture with a Song," 503.
90. Lahire, "The Individual and the Mixing of Genres."
91. Ibid., 174.
92. Ibid., 186.
93. Discouraged in 1974 to the benefit of "Cajun" and "Acadian" as the only acceptable labels, "coonass" was more explicitly condemned in 1981 as "offensive, vulgar and obscene" (see Bernard, *Cajuns*, 138).
94. One could argue, however, that the regional use of "Cajun" interchangeably with "Acadian" clearly establishes those labels as "white" identifications by focusing on the

Acadian heritage; furthermore, the comparison with "nigger" made by those who identify themselves as "coonass" could also suggest through this commonality of register a connectedness of some sort.

95. Shana Walton, "Louisiana's Coonasses: Choosing Race and Class over Ethnicity," in *Signifying Serpents and Mardi Gras Runners: Representing Identity in Selected Souths*, C. Ray and L. E. Lassiter (eds.) (Athens and London: University of Georgia Press, 2003), 38–48.

96. Sexton, "Cajun or Coonass? Exploring Ethnic Labels in French Louisiana Regional Discourse," *Ethnology* 48, no. 4 (Fall 2009): 291.

97. Mitch Reed on *Quoi Y A* radio show, hosted by Corey Porche, KRVS, spring 2008.

98. Author interview with Mitch Reed, December 6, 2004, Carencro.

99. David Greely, *Quoi Y A* radio show, hosted by Corey Porche, KRVS, 2008.

100. davidgreely.com/?page_id=4 (accessed July, 13, 2012).

101. Born and Hesmondhalgh, *Western Music*, 33.

102. *Learn to Play Cajun Accordion*, taught by Dirk Powell, DVD 1 and 2 (Homespun video, 1998 and 2005), directed by Happy Traum.

103. "400 years of Cajun music," lecture by David Greely (Ville Platte, March 1, 2008).

104. Email correspondence, July 12, 2013.

105. Ancelet and Morgan, *Cajun and Creole*, 8.

106. "A 'bridge' in normal popular music is almost always a third part added to a song that already has two, a verse and a chorus (refrain). It almost always happens only once. In this sense it is a C part." Sam Broussard, email correspondence, June 12, 2013.

107. For a detailed description of accordion playing techniques, see the teaching videos listed in the bibliography, and Mark F. Dewitt, "The Diatonic Button Accordion," 325.

108. Valcour's website, www.valcourrecords.com/artist-of-the-month/artist-of-the-month-2010/ (accessed November 2010).

109. For a description of his itinerary and influences, see Ancelet, "The Cajun Music Festival: Genesis and Legacy," in *Accordions*, ed. Brasseaux and Fontenot, 301–20.

110. Geoffrey Himes, "Cajun String Bands: The Next Big Thing?" NPR, May 5, 2011, www.npr.org/blogs/ablogsupreme/2011/05/07/1360252 (accessed May 9, 2012).

111. Dege Legg, "Stepping Out the Box," January 26, 2011 www.theind.com/cover-story/7663-stepping-out-the-box (accessed January 30, 2011).

112. Tisserand, *The Kingdom*, 319 et seq.

113. Liner notes, *Coteau: Highly Seasoned Cajun Music*, Rounder, 1997.

114. Author interview with Chas Justus, June 17, 2008, Lafayette.

115. Le Menestrel and Henry, "Sing Us Back Home."

116. Toynbee, *Making Popular Music*, 128.

117. This rejection also applies to club owners who are too controlling of the repertoire, as was apparently the case at Whiskey River Landing, causing the Mamou Playboys to quit playing there.

118. Ryan Brasseaux, "Fabricating Authenticity: The Cajun Renaissance and Steve Riley and the Mamou Playboys," in *Accordions*, ed. Brasseaux and Fontenot, 487–94.

119. Sam Broussard, "Ryan Brasseaux: Fabricating Content," November 3, 2008. www.sambroussard.com/writing/rant19.html.

120. This notion is borrowed from Jayson Toynbee, *Making Popular Music: Musicians, Creativity and Institutions* (London and New York: Bloomsbury, 2000).

121. Quoted in Tisserand, *The Kingdom*, 338.

122. www.keithfrank.com/.

123. Author interview with Billy McGee, February 1, 2005, Eunice.

124. Wilson Savoy, *The Corey Ledet Instructional Triple Accordion DVD for Beginner and Intermediate*, Almena Pictures, 2006.

125. David Simpson, "Contemporary Cajun, Creole and Zydeco Musicians," web.lsue.edu/acadgate/music/zydecokingpins.htm.

126. Tisserand, *The Kingdom*, 338–39.

127. Ibid., 350.

128. Olivier and Sandmel, *Zydeco!*, 29.

129. www.pineleafboys.com (accessed August 15, 2010).

130. www.lostbayouramblers.com (accessed August 15, 2010).

131. Dominick Cross, "Jolie Blon Steps Aside for Mammoth Waltz," *Independent Weekly*, April 18, 2012.

132. Rosenberg, *Transforming Tradition*, 50.

133. Dan Willging, "Review: Keith Frank: Follow the Leader/Boot Up," *Offbeat*, www.offbeat.com/2012/07/01/keith-frank-follow-the-leader-boot-up-soulwood-records/.

134. Larry Starr and Christopher Waterman, *American Popular Music: From Minstrelsy to MTV* (New York and Oxford: Oxford University Press, 2003), 407.

135. Since the census count is inadequate in capturing the Creole phenomenon in Louisiana—few individuals claim Creole as a race, ancestry, or language—Jacques Henry combined the dimensions of race (black) and second language use (French) to draw a fuller picture. Creoles were then analytically defined as French-speaking blacks, which allowed for comparisons with Cajuns, non-Cajun whites, and non-French-speaking blacks. Creoles were shown to have the lowest median household income ($19,400) and the lowest proportion of university graduates (6.2 percent). They are also the most likely to occupy the lowest-skilled and lowest-paid positions in the workforce: one half of Creoles are employed in construction and maintenance (20 percent) and service occupations (30.9 percent). See Henry, "Pourquoi les Cadiens disparaissent et les Créoles restent invisibles," in *La Louisiane*, ed. Guy Clermont (Limoges: Presses Universitaires de Limoges), 179–95.

136. Spitzer, "Zydeco and Mardi Gras," 537.

137. Tisserand, *The Kingdom*, 387–88.

138. *Louisiana: Where Culture Means Business*, prepared by Mt. Auburn Associates, July 31, 2005, funded by the National Endowment for the Arts and the State of Louisiana, Office of the Lt. Governor, Department of Culture, Recreation and Tourism, Office of Cultural Development, Louisiana Division of the Arts.

139. Livio Sansone, "The Localization of Global Funk in Bahia and Rio," in *Brazilian Popular Music and Globalization*, ed. Christopher Dunn and Charles A. Perrone (London: Taylor and Francis, 2001), 154–55.

140. Santelli et al. include in "roots" music jazz, blues, black spirituals, hillbilly, country, zydeco, Cajun, tejano, Native American, and rockabilly. Robert Santelli, Holly George-Warren, and Jim Brown (eds.), *American Roots Music* (New York: Harry N. Abrams, 2001).

141. DeWitt, *Cajun and Zydeco*, 202.

142. Wade, *Music, Race and Nation*, 143.

143. Herman Fuselier, "He's Chubby and gets Little Respect," *Times of Acadiana*, April 6, 2001, 24–27.

144. Author interview with Don Brasseaux, April 16, 2001, Breaux Bridge.

145. *Louisiana: Culture Is Business*, 64.

146. For further development on that context, see Sara Le Menestrel, *La voie des Cadiens* (Paris: Belin, 1999).

147. Louisiana Cultural Economy Foundation, *Our First Five Years*, December 2010.

148. Mat Sakakeeny, *Roll with It: Brass Bands in the Streets of New Orleans* (Durham: Duke University Press, 2013), 86.

149. Ibid., 87.

150. tipitinasfoundation.org/.

151. In 2011, the LED Lafayette office was working on a project of communal artist's workspaces and equipment, a format similar to that offered by Tipitina's Co-Op.

152. louisianaentertainment.gov/.

153. The sound recording investor tax credit program was implemented in 2005 and provides a 25 percent tax credit for sound recording projects made in the state of Louisiana with a minimum investment of $15,000. The investment may include multiple projects to reach the $15,000 minimum. This same approach extends to live performance since 2007 and filming since 2002. Louisiana was in fact the first state in the country to offer tax incentive packages for these entertainment industry sectors. See louisianaentertainment.gov/index.php/music/why-record-here/incentives/ (accessed October 9, 2012).

154. *2010 New Orleans Cultural Economy Snapshot*, Mayor's Office of Cultural Economy.

155. Author interview with Todd Mouton, LEDA, March 29, 2001, Lafayette.

156. *Louisiana: Culture Is Business*, 160; *Building a Permanent Entertainment Economy*.

157. Chery L. Baxter, "Fiscal and Economic Impact Analysis of Louisiana's Entertainment Incentives," in conjunction with the Louisiana Economic Development Office of Entertainment Industry Development and the Legislative Fiscal Office in accordance with the LA Motion Picture Incentive Act, 4/18/2011; Economics Research Associates, Louisiana Motion Picture, Sound Recording and Digital Media Industries, prepared for Louisiana Economic Development, February 2009.

158. tipitinasfoundation.org/; Office of Entertainment Industry Development, *Building a Permanent Entertainment Economy*, report prepared by Louisiana Entertainment, April 2010, 18.

159. The intended use of LCEF grants described by the recipients illustrate this trend. Most of the funding (52 percent) go to equipment purchase, marketing, product development, workshop or education opportunity, and website construction, whereas only 3 percent is used for CD production. In 2007, the Mamou Playboys would receive $1.50 on each CD sold at a national record shop, as opposed to $9 on their website or at a festival.

160. Ann Markusen and Ann Gadwa, *Creative Placemaking*, Markusen Economic Research Services and Metris Arts Consulting for the Mayors' Institute on City Design, National Endowment for the Arts, with the United States Conference of Mayors and American Architectural Foundation, 2010, 3–6.

161. See ch. 5.

162. Author interview with Mark Falgout, the Blue Moon, August 2008, Lafayette.

163. Out of thirty students, Daniel Gale, who teaches at the conservatory, says that about half are interested in learning fiddle tunes along with their classical studies. Email correspondence, September 2012.

164. Timothy Taylor, *Global Pop: World Music, World Markets* (London: Routledge, 1997), 21–23; for more on the politics of authenticity in country music and the different meanings attached to this notion, see Peterson, *Fabricating Authenticity*, 211.

CHAPTER 3

1. Author interview with Horace Trahan, April 30, 2001, Scott, Louisiana.

2. The song "Don't Worry About Horace" explicitly addresses his detractors, while "Reach Out and Touch a Hand" sends a message of peace regardless of skin color.

3. Wilson Savoy and Bennet Rhodes, *Horace Trahan: Hard Press But Never Crushed*, Almena Pictures, BackPorch series.

4. Dege Legg, "The Gospel According to Horace," *Independent*, October 27, 2010. www.theind.com/living-ind/7173-the-gospel-according-to-horace.

5. Wade, *Music, Race*, 2005.

6. Miller, *Segregating Sound*, 188.

7. Hugh Barker and Yuval Taylor, *Faking It: The Quest for Authenticity in Popular Music* (New York: W. W. Norton, 2007), 74.

8. Miller, *Segregating Sound*, 243.

9. Ibid., 189; Miller adds that in the late 1920s, controlling "old-time" artists to have them record as many "old-time" songs as possible was less a process of racialization than a strategy to maximize profits. The recording of "traditional" songs was then more profitable than popular tunes, which demanded royalties from the recording companies to the artist.

10. Barker and Taylor, *Faking It*, 78.

11. Interview conducted by Shane Bernard with Floyd Soileau, 1991, ACCM, BE-1.003.

12. Author interview with Mitch Reed, December 6, 2004, Carencro.
13. Bernard, *The Cajuns*, 63.
14. See Trépanier, "Cajunization."
15. "'Si longtemps séparés': le sentiment d'appartenance à la diaspora acadienne (Louisiane, Provinces maritimes du Canada)," communication at the French Colonial Historical Society, Toulouse, May 15–17, 2003.
16. Bernard, *The Cajuns*, 142.
17. Lomax 1987, *Louisiana Recordings*.
18. See for example Broven, *South*; Tisserand, *The Kingdom*; Wood, "Southeast Texas"; Sexton, "Zydeco Music and Race Relations"; Ancelet, *Cajun Music*.
19. Ronald Radano, *Lying Up a Nation: Race and Black Music* (Chicago: University of Chicago Press), 10.
20. See, for example, Sexton, "Zydeco Music and Race Relations," 179.
21. Spitzer, "Zydeco," 339.
22. An African American woman was turned away at the door of La Poussière in Breaux Bridge. Visiting from Chicago for a convention, she happened to be an attorney and brought a civil suit against the owners; several months later, a tourist from Kentucky was declined access to the Mardi Gras *courir* in Eunice.
23. Ancelet, "The Limits and Directions," 17, 19.
24. Ibid., 177.
25. Wood, "Southeast Texas," 25.
26. Wood and Fraher, *Texas Zydeco*, 91.
27. Bernard, *Swamp Pop*, 8.
28. Philip Tagg, "Open Letter about 'Black Music,' 'Afro-American Music' and 'European Music,'" *Popular Music* 8, no. 3 (1989): 285–98.
29. Ibid., 7–10.
30. Ibid., 10; "Scotch Snaps: The Big Picture," 2011, www.youtube.com/watch?v=3BQAD5uZsLY.
31. Ronald Radano, "Hot Fantasies: American Modernism and the Idea of Black Rhythm," in *Music and Racial Imagination*, 459–80.
32. See Dole 1995; Jared M. Snyder, "Squeezebox: The Legacy of the Afro-Mississippi Accordionists," *Black Music Research Journal* 17, no. 1 (Spring 1997): 39.
33. Minton, "Houston Creoles and Zydeco," 490.
34. Brasseaux, *Cajun Breakdown*, 17.
35. Ancelet, *Cajun Music*, 132.
36. Post, "Joe C. Falcon"; Rinzler, RI1.025, interview with Joe Falcon (10 October 65), Archive of Cajun and Creole Folklore, University of Louisiana at Lafayette.
37. Charles J. Stivale, *Disenchanting Les Bons Temps: Identity and Authenticity in Cajun Music and Dance* (Durham and London: Duke University Press, 2003), ch. 5, takes on practices of exclusion according to racial identification, but stays very cautious and limits its demonstration to lyrics and films (Les Blank's *J'ai été au bal*, for its misrepresentation of zydeco compared to Cajun, and Alan Lomax's *Cajun Country: Don't Drop the Potatoe*, for showing distinct practices of Cajun and Creole Mardi Gras rides). His analysis of the exclusion of a black woman from Chicago at La Poussiere is rather

sketchy and ambivalent: "The problem is not one of race, but of any other from outside the community," he argues, giving his own experience as an outsider at La Poussiere. "My experience and that of the tourists from Chicago recounted by Tisserand hardly constitute anything more than examples of local exceptions to the general rule of hospitality that one finds in most locations. Yet the example of Chicago tourists suggests the extent to which that hospitality may be specific to race" (153).

38. Strachwitz, *Louisiana Cajun Music*, 16.

39. Sandmel, *Zydeco!*, 29.

40. Les Back, "Out of Sight: Southern Music and the Coloring of Sound," in *Out of Whiteness: Color, Politics and Culture*, eds. Vron Ware and Les Back (Chicago and London: University of Chicago Press, 2002), 230.

41. Brasseaux, *Cajun Breakdown*, 79–80.

42. Ron Brown, liner notes, *Blind Uncle Gaspard, Delma Lachney, John Bertrand: Early American Cajun Music* (Yazoo 2042, 1999).

43. Hall, *Africans in Colonial Louisiana: The Development of Afro-Creole Culture in the Eighteenth Century* (Baton Rouge: Louisiana State University Press, 1992).

44. Frey, "Review of *Africans in Colonial Louisiana*," *American Historical Review* (April 1993): 454–56. The author adds: "A minor case in point is her imaginative proposal that the origin of the term 'coonass' used by poor whites of southwest Louisiana, 'derives from Louisiana's Afro-Creole traditions' (p. 236) and represents a defiant identification with the 'behind of the raccoon,' whose survival by its wits in the Louisiana swamps was reminiscent of eighteenth-century maroons." In fact, various theories circulate about the origin of the term "coonass"; to my knowledge none is based on Hall's interpretation, and no consensus has been reached.

45. Klingler, *If I Could Turn My Tongue Like That: The Creole Language of Pointe Coupee Parish* (Baton Rouge: Louisiana State University Press, 2003), 61–62.

46. Ibid., 67.

47. Stephan Palmié, *Africa*, 1, 64, 168–71.

48. Author interview with Dennis Paul Williams, March 21, 2003, St. Martinville.

49. Author interview with James Cailler, March 8, 2003, Lafayette.

50. For more details on these different representations, see Dormon, "Ethnicity and Identity: Creoles of Color in Louisiana," in *Creoles of Color in the Gulf South*, ed. James Dormon (Knoxville: University of Tennessee Press, 1996), 166–79; Sara Le Menestrel, "Déclinaisons et enjeux de l'identité créole en Louisiane," in *Situations créoles. Pratiques et représentations*, ed. Carlo Célius (Québec: Editions Nota Bene, 2006).

51. See her edited volume *Creole: The History and Legacy of Louisiana's Free People of Color* (Baton Rouge: Louisiana State University Press, 2000).

At the 2003 Creole Studies conference organized by the Creole Heritage Center in collaboration with Tulane University, Creoles in the audience claimed to "write their own story from their own perspective." In fact, the choice of anthropologist Nick Spitzer as the keynote speaker sparked strong criticism. Different petitions emanating from Creole activists from Los Angeles circulated. One was urging to resist the "Neo African American movement" and to support the cause of Creoles presented as "a dying breed" (Letter from Caesar Guyot, President of the Society for the Preservation of

Creole Heritage and Identity, Los Angeles, October 23, 2003). The other from the same association was a petition of protest against the identification of Mother Henriette Delille as "Native Born African American by the Sisters of Holy Family." Her canonization process generated a claim to identify her instead as "Native born Creole American."

52. See Mills, *The Forgotten People*. Mills described the Creoles of Isle Brevelle as attractive, educated, healthy, among the finest cooks, and holding astute business judgment, among other virtues, with a self-respect instilled from early childhood, and a focus on family solidarity (164–91).

53. See Shirley Thompson, "'Ah Toucoutou, ye conin vous': History and Memory in Creole New Orleans," *American Quarterly* 53, no. 2 (June 2001): 232–66.

54. Andrew J. Jolivétte, a scholar of Creole origin, introduced another perception of Louisiana Creoles and the Creole diaspora in the United States as mixed-race Native Americans or Creole-Indians. See *Louisiana Creoles: Cultural Recovery and Mixed-Race Native American Identity* (Lanham, MD, and Plymouth, UK: Lexington, 2007).

55. Cailler interview, March 8, 2003.

56. See A. Valdman, "The Place of Louisiana Creole among New World French Creoles," in *Creoles of Color*, 144–65.

57. Author interview with Arnold Depass Jr., November 22, 2004, Port Barre.

58. Original quote: "Moi j'ai jamais compris la différence de la musique créole et la musique français, except que c'est un homme blanc qui joue l'accordéon quand c'est cadien, et c'est un homme noir quand c'est créole."

59. For further development on the notion of Louisiana Regional French introduced by Thomas Klingler, see *If I Could Turn My Tongue*; on the sociolinguistic situation of French Louisiana, see Valdman, "The Place of Louisiana Creole."

60. Author interview with Joe Hall, November 12, 2004, Carencro.

61. Advanced Cajun and Creole fiddle class, DBCCHW, Chicot State Park, April 20, 2008.

62. Author interview with Mitch Reed, June 25, 2008, Scott.

63. *Learn How to Play Cajun Fiddle*, taught by Michael Doucet, Homespun video, 1993; Powell, *Learn to Play Cajun Accordion*; Wilson Savoy, *The Steve Riley Instructional Cajun Accordion DVD*, Intermediate, Ameda Pictures, 2009.

64. Reported by Blair Kilpatrick, *Accordion Dreams: A Journey into Cajun and Creole Music* (Jackson: University Press of Mississippi, 2009), 68.

65. Mitch Reed, *How to Play Cajun and Creole Fiddle*, vol. 1 and 2, Fruge Records, 2011 and 2012.

66. See Sara Le Menestrel, "French music, Cajun, Creole, Zydeco: hiérarchisations et ligne de couleur dans la musique franco-louisianaise," special issue, "Musiques 'populaires' catégorisations et usages sociaux," *Civilisations* 53, nos. 1–2: 117–44.

67. Aaron Latham, "Zydeco Fever in Lafayette," *New York Times*, 30 May 2004, www.nytimes.com/2004/05/30/travel/zydeco-fever-in-lafayette.html?pagewanted =all&src=pm.

68. He published his note "Zydeco Is Not Cajun" in *Zyde-zine Newsletter* (2004), a disabled zydeco fan's electronic publication, encouraging its readership to reproduce his paper and "educate" people.

69. www.cedricwatson.com/component/content/article/16-acadiana-profile (accessed July 15, 2011).

70. —Comment t'appelles la musique tu joues?
—Je l'appelle musique français. Je dis pas musique black ou musique blanc. Musique noire, blanc, c'est pas la différence. Fermer tes yeux et juste écouter la musique, tu peux pas dire si c'est un band noir ou blanc. Mais les blancs peut jouer la musique français et les noirs peut jouer la musique français.
—Y a du monde qui pense que quand t'es cajun ou créole tu joues pas la même musique.
—Y a un tas de monde, ça m'a dit, t'es noir, il faut tu joues la musique zydeco. Les noirs jouent la musique zydeco, cajun joue la musique cajun. Mais longtemps passé les Créoles et les Cajuns jouaient la musique français. C'est pas une différence....

Dennis McGee était cajun mais quand il jouait du violon il peut jouer comme European, il peut jouer blues, c'est du musique créole. Mixte. Mais Bois Sec et Canray they were Creole too and they played Creole music. That's what it was. It's not about the color. When it comes to categorizing it as Creole music, it's not Creole music because it's black, it's Creole music because it's that style, that old Louisiana Creole style. Et Leo Soileau, c'est musique créole.

71. Horace was making reference to the song "Let's Call the Whole Thing Off," written by George and Ira Gershwin (1937). The phonetics are /təˈmeɪtəʊ/ and /təˈmɑtəʊ/.

72. DeWitt, "The Diatonic Button Accordion," in Kilpatrick, *Accordion*, 232.

73. DBCCHW, April 21, 2008, Lagniappe session with Ed Poullard and Preston Frank.

74. Author interview with Don Cravins, April 4, 2001, Lafayette.

75. Interviewed by Corey Porshe on *Quoi Y A*, KRVS, spring 2008.

76. Broven, *South*.

77. Les Blank, Chris Strachwitz, and Maureen Gosling, *J'ai été au bal (I Went to the Dance): The Cajun and Zydeco Music from Louisiana* (El Cerrito, CA: Brazos Films, 1989 and 2002), narrated by Michael Doucet and Barry Ancelet, 84 min., DVD.

78. Strachwitz, "Cajun Country," 15.

79. Strachwitz, "Zydeco Music i.e. French Blues," in *American Folk*, 22–24.

80. Many thanks to Sam Broussard for explaining these music theory issues, and to Vincent Blin and Sarah Savoy.

81. As explained by Sam Broussard, "minor melodies are possible on the accordion by the use of modes, or placing its major chords and scales on top of progressions in keys that are distant from the scales provided by the two (push or pull) chords of the accordion. When players of the harmonica (a similar, two-chord instrument) do this, they call it "cross harp," meaning that they are playing their instrument in a key foreign to it, crossing over to other keys." Email correspondence, June 12, 2013. See also DeWitt, ch. 4, 3.

82. See Dennis McGee, *Himself*, recorded by Gerard Dole, Valcour Records, VAL-CD-0011, 2010.

83. According to Sam Broussard, the main blues scale is the Dorian mode.

For example, in Dm, the C scale will be played, starting on its second note, D. It is a minor sound, but used in major songs; sometimes an F♯ is added for the sweetness of its major 3 sound if the song uses a D major chord occasionally or exclusively. Very few blues musicians use the entire scale; instead they use a pentatonic variation of 5 notes only. In Dm, those notes are D F G A C D. All of those notes are in the C scale, although the ♭5 of D, which is G♯, is almost always added as a passing tone. (email correspondence, July 24, 2011)

84. Although there are many opinions on the subject, modal harmony describes chord progressions that use a ♭7 chord as a leading chord for the 1 chord. (A leading tone is the note or chord you hear before the return of the 1. It "leads" or "points" to the 1.) Songs in G that make use of F chords are using modal harmony. www.harmony.org.uk/book/pop_and_rock_music_blues_modal_progressions.htm (accessed July 26, 2011).

"The Ionian mode is the one that an accordion gives you on the push. On the pull it gives you the Mixolydian, which is the major scale with a flat 7th, which is the second most common mode in Cajun music, found in almost all songs based on the pull chord of an accordion." Sam Broussard, Email correspondence, June 12, 2013.

85. Author interview with Chas Justus, June 17, 2008, Lafayette.

86. Email correspondence with Sam Broussard, July 22–25, 2011.

87. Email correspondence with Sam Broussard, July 22–25, 2011.

88. Yule, *Iry Lejeune*, 75, 97.

89. Author interview on November 22, 2004, Port Barre, Louisiana.

90. Olivier and Sandmel, *Zydeco!* 163.

91. Cecelia Tichi, *High Lonesome: The American Culture of Country Music* (Chapel Hill: University of North Carolina Press, 1994), 7.

92. *American Routes*, public radio program, October 5, 2005, produced by Nick Spitzer, Tulane University's School of Liberal Arts, New Orleans.

93. Back, "Out of Sight," 247.

94. Brasseaux, *Cajun, Creole, French, Houma*, 58–61.

95. Author interview on March 30, 2001, Lafayette.

96. Author interview with Missy Maloney on April 28, 2008, Arnaudville, Louisiana.

97. Reese Fuller, "A Sense of Place," *Independent Weekly*, June 2005, www.theind.com/cover-story/183.

98. Laura M. Jewett, *A Delicate Dance: Autoethnography, Curriculum and the Semblance of Intimacy* (New York: Peter Lang, 2008), 123–24. The term *white Delilah* was coined by anti-lynching activist Wells as an inversion of the black seductress Jezebel figure and an evocation of Delilah, who was used by the men of her country to seduce the other and then betray him. The author used the term "to highlight zydeco as a racialized and sexualized locale, in which historical as well as contemporary relationships of race and gender are (re)articulated and shaped through dance." (6) I thank the reviewer for suggesting this reference.

99. Wade, *Music, Race*, 2.

100. Radano, "Hot Fantasies," 474.

101. Bernard, *Cajuns*, 66.

102. This threat is felt on a national scale: in 1943, the Bureau of Public Relations of the U.S. military banned pictures of black GIs dancing with British women published in several American magazines, such as *Life* (Ware and Back, *Out of Whiteness*, 187).

103. Adam Fairclough, *Race and Democracy: The Civil Rights Struggle in Louisiana, 1915–1972* (Athens: University of Georgia Press, 1995), 179.

104. Wade, *Music, Race*, 142.

105. Thanks to the anonymous reader for sharing this data.

106. See Tisserand, *The Kingdom*, 198. As reported by the author, Ka-wann can mean a good turtle meat around Ville Platte (north of Lafayette) but refers to a woman around Morgan City (southeast). Thanks to the anonymous reviewer for suggesting this song.

107. Herman Fuselier, "A Different Place," *Daily Advertiser*, February 17, 2006.

108. Legg, "The Gospel."

109. Marybeth Hamilton, "Sexuality, Authenticity and the Making of the Blues Tradition," *Past and Present* 169 (2000): 132–60.

110. Christian Rinaudo, "Métissage et africanité élective dans la musique populaire de Veracruz, Mexique" (paper presented at the international colloquium Anthropologie de la musique et de la danse: une approche des mondes

contemporains, Paris, EHESS, ANR Musmond, June 8, 2010.

111. Marc Augé, *Génie du Paganisme* (Paris: Gallimard, 1982), 11.

112. Kali Argyriadis and Sara Le Menestrel, *Vivre la guinguette* (Paris: Presses universitaires de France, 2003).

113. Brasseaux, *Cajun Breakdown*, 176.

114. Wade, *Music, Race*, 66.

115. Wade, "Rethinking *Mestisaje*," 255.

116. Elisabeth Cunin, "Introduction: L'ethnicité revisitée par la globalisation," *Autrepart* 38, no. 2 (2006): 6.

117. Wade, "La mercantilización de la musica 'negra' en Colombia en el siglo XX," in *Circulaciones culturales. Lo afrocaribeño entre Cartagena, Veracruz y La Habana, México*, eds. F. Avila Domínguez, R. Pérez Monfort, y Ch. Rinaudo (México: Ediciones de la Casa Chata, CIESAS/IRD/ANR/Universidad de Cartagena/El Colegio de Michoacán, 2012), 14764.

118. Thanks to Kali Argyriadis for indicating these references.

119. Stefania Capone, "Conexiones diaspóricas: redes artísticas y construcción de un patrimonio cultural afro," in *Circulaciones culturales*, 269–96.

120. Ibid., 242.

121. Argeliers León, *Del canto y el tiempo* (La Habana: ed. Pueblo y Educación, 1974).

122. Kali Argyriadis, "Les batá deux fois sacrés," *Civilisations* 53 (2006): 45–74.

CHAPTER 4

1. Barker and Taylor, *Faking It*, 58.

2. *Louisiana Cajun Music*, vol. 1, LP Edition, Editor's note.

3. Rosenberg, *Transforming Tradition*, 8.
4. Bernard, *Cajuns*, 76.
5. Todd Mouton, "Louisiana Crossroads," *Artworks* (February-March 2001): 5–6.
6. See also Sexton, "Too Loud."
7. Henry and Bankston, *Blue Collar Bayou*, 87–113.
8. Brasseaux, *Cajun Breakdown*, ix.
9. On the dialectical relation between respectability and reputation as a central value system among Creoles, see Spitzer, "Zydeco."
10. Quoted in Spitzer, "Zydeco," 397.
11. Author interview with Terry Angelle, May 18, 2001, Henderson.
12. Suzanne E. Smith, *Dancing in the Street: Motown and the Cultural Politics of Detroit* (Cambridge: Harvard University Press, 1999), 121.
13. Author interview with Arnold Depass Jr., November 22, 2004, Port Barre.
14. Brasseaux, *Cajun Breakdown*, 137–38.
15. David R. Roediger, *Towards the Abolition of Whiteness: Essays on Race, Politics, and Working Class History* (London and New York: Verso, 1994).
16. David R. Roediger, *Colored White: Transcending the Racial Past* (Berkeley, Los Angeles, and London: University Press of California, 2002), 141.
17. Spitzer, "Zydeco and Mardi Gras," 233.
18. Sandmel and Olivier, *Zydeco!* 79.
19. Spitzer argues that this perception also results from a shift of ethnic affiliation from Afro-French to Afro-American, which undercut the prevailing Creole notion of respect as a whole and the dialectical nature of values—hence the revulsion of what Creole elders see as the rise of Afro-American-oriented canaille, tou'fou youth ("Zydeco," 294).
20. Author interview with Zydeco Joe, May 18, 2001, Lafayette.
21. John Swenson, *New Atlantis: Musicians Battle for the Survival of New Orleans* (New York: Oxford University Press, 2011), 119.
22. Christ Ardoin and NuStep, *Sweat*, Maison de Soul Records, 2011.
23. Keith Frank and the Soileau Zydeco Band, *Loved. Feared. Respected*, Soulwood Records, 2009.
24. See Michael Eric Dyson, "The Culture of Hip-Hop," in *That's the Joint! The Hip-Hop Studies Reader*, M. Forman and M. A. Neal (eds.) (New York and London: Routledge, 2004), 61–68.
25. Matt Miller, "Bounce: Rap Music and Cultural Survival in New Orleans," *HypheNation* 1, no. 1 (April 2006): 28.
26. See, for example, the most recent site of Chris Ardoin, www.officialchrisardoin.com/about.html.
27. Wood and Fraher, *Texas Zydeco*, 195.
28. Quoted in Olivier and Sandmel, *Zydeco!*, 153–54.
29. Geoffrey Himes, "The Boys' Life," *Offbeat* 19, no. 10 (October 26, 2006): 26.
30. *Daily Advertiser*, June 20, 1929.
31. Joe Nick Patoski, "Huey P. Meaux: The Crazy Cajun. Sex, Drugs, and Rock and Roll," *Texas Monthly* 24, no. 5 (May 1996): 116.

32. Ibid.; Wood, "Southeast Texas"; Wood and Fraher, *Texas Zydeco*.
33. See Minton, "Houston Creoles and Zydeco"; Tisserand, *The Kingdom*, 17.
34. *Louisiana Stomp: Clifton Chenier with Clarence Garlow*, JSP Records, 2009. Quoted in Sandmel, "Bon Ton Roula."
35. Tisserand, *The Kingdom*, 22–23.
36. Among those who are skeptical about the predominant role of Texas in the development of zydeco is the anonymous reader of this manuscript.
37. Ibid.
38. Shaila Dewan, "Louisiana's Zydeco Trail," *New York Times*, April 22, 2011, www.nytimes.com/2011/04/24/travel/24zydeco.html?pagewanted=alland_moc.semityn.www.&_r=0.
39. Sandmel and Olivier, *Zydeco!*, 67.
40. Tisserand, *The Kingdom*, 293.
41. Olivier and Sandmel, *Zydeco!*, 127.
42. www.nubreeds.com (accessed July 4, 2012).
43. Olivier and Sandmel, *Zydeco!*, 91.
44. Josh C. Caffery, "Lost and Found," *Independent* (December 1, 2004): 14.
45. Himes, "The Boys' Life."
46. Author interview with Corey Porche, April 12, 2001, Lafayette.
47. Peter Schwartz, "Canray Fontenot and Bois Sec Ardoin," *Routes to Roots* 1 (2001): 11.
48. Powell, *Learn to Play Cajun Accordion*.
49. Olivier and Sandmel, *Zydeco!*, 67.
50. Ibid., 83.
51. Victor A. Stoichita, "Entre prouesse et dérision," *Ateliers d'anthropologie* 35 (2011), ateliers.revues.org/8793 (accessed Jan. 12, 2012).
52. Interview with Lisa Bourque and Joel Breaux, February 11, 2008, Loreauville.
53. The chords of "Johnny Can't Dance" in the number system are [111(5)(1)]2 Turn [[1 (5)(1)][1 (5)(1)]]2 Turn; or in the letter system [GGG (D)(G)]2 Tune [[G (D)(G)][G (D)(G)]]2 Turn.
54. cajunzydeco.net/CajunGuitar/SBroussard.htm (accessed January 11, 2011).
55. Mike Doucet and Mitch Reed, DBCCHW, April 24, 2008, Lagniappe session, twin fiddle workshop.
56. Will Spires, liner notes, *The Complete Recordings of Dennis McGee, 1929–1930, with Ernest Frugé and Sady Courville*, Early American Cajun Classics, Yazoo 2012, 1994.
57. Mitch Reed, April 24, 2001, DBCCHW, Advanced fiddle class, Lake Fausse Pointe State Park.
58. Author interview with Hadley Castille, November 16, 2004, Leonville.

Il a recordé une chanson qui s'appelle "Dragging a Ball," il entendu ça avec un des meilleurs joueurs de swing au Texas. Ca c'était un style il a appris là-bas. Un numéro qu'est juste 3 chords, une partie de la chanson, simple, simple, then it gets to it, you can just feel he switches over, it's called Hip et Taïau. Listen to what happens on the second part. J'suis sûr tu joues le Blues du Port Arthur. Presque tous les violoneux d'icite va le jouer comme ça. Lui il l'a jouerait comme ça. Quand t'es après jouer ça it's a little bit harder. So a lot of fiddlers they learn it the simple way. He would go the second part like. See it feels good, the movement makes you wanna dance. . . . Une chanson simple comme Chère Toute-toute. Les violoneux qui jouent avec l'accordéon, no feeling. Guette la différence. Juste 2 clés mais c'est, that's what you put in between that makes it so attractive.

59. DeWitt, "The Diatonic Button Accordion," 325.
60. Ancelet and Morgan, *The Makers of Cajun Music*, 23.
61. DeWitt, "The Diatonic Button Accordion," 322.
62. Ibid., 313.
63. Ibid., 306.
64. Josh Caffery, "Courir de Mardi Gras," *Artworks* (February–March 2001): 20.
65. Sam Broussard, cajunzydeco.net/CajunGuitar/SBroussard.htm.
66. Sam Broussard, email correspondence, March 23, 2011.
67. Tichi, *High Lonesome*, 198.
68. Author interview with Joel Savoy, October 29, 2010, Black Pot Festival.
69. Dege Legg, "Indie Cajun," *Gambit Weekly* (February 1, 2011): 13.
70. Dege Legg, "Steppin Out the Box," *Independent Weekly* (January 26, 2011), www.theind.com/cover-story/7663-stepping-out-the-box (accessed March 2012).
71. Dan Willging, "Ann Savoy: Cajun Music's Cultural Ambassador," *Offbeat* (April 2002), www.offbeat.com/2002/04/01/ann-savoy-cajun-musics-cultural-ambassador/ (accessed May 24, 2012).
72. www.lafayetterhythmdevils.com/lrd_band.html; www.bonsoircatin.com/about-us.html (accessed February 10, 2012).
73. Porcello (2005: 111) quoted in Turino, *Music as Social Life*, 76.
74. Turino, *Music as Social Life*, 71–75.
75. Author interview with Chas Justus, June 17, 2008, Lafayette.
76. Allen, *Gone to the Country*, 212.
77. Doucet, *Learn How to Play Cajun Fiddle*.
78. Dirk Powell, *Learn to Play Cajun Accordion, Starting Out*, DVD 1, Homespun Video, 75 min., 1988, directed by Happy Traum; *Lear to Play Cajun Accordion, Intermediate and Advanced*, DVD 2, Homespun Video, 75 min., 2005, directed by Happy Traum.
79. See demonstration on the sample video on "Bonsoir Moreau." sites.google.com/a/frugerecords.com/fruge-records/home/mitch-reed-vol-2-dvd (accessed August 31, 2012).
80. Argyriadis and Le Menestrel, *Vivre la guinguette*.
81. Author interview with Corey Porche, April 12, 2001, Lafayette.
82. Steven Feld and Keith Basso, eds., *Senses of Place* (Sante Fe: School of American Research Press, 1996).
83. Tim Creswell, *Place: A Short Introduction* (London: Wiley-Blackwell, 2004), 49.
84. Ibid., 38.

85. Pierre Bourdieu, "L'identité et la représentation. Eléments pour une réflexion critique sur l'idée de région," *Actes de la recherche en sciences sociales* 35 (1980): 65n17.

86. S. Frederick Starr, *Inventing New Orleans: Writings of Lafcadio Hearn* (Jackson: University Press of Mississippi, 2001), xii.

87. Le Menestrel and Henry, "'Sing Us Back Home,'" 191–92.

88. For further development on this topic in New Orleans, see Le Menestrel and Henry, ibid.; Le Menestrel, "Place attachment, Displacement."

89. Clifton Chenier, King of the Bayous, "I'm Coming Home," Arhoolie, 1993.

90. Author interview with Joel Savoy, October 29, 2010, Black Pot Festival, Lafayette.

91. For further development, see Le Menestrel and Henry, "Sing Us Back Home."

92. Glen Pitre and Michelle Benoit, *American Creole: New Orleans Reunion*, co-produced by M. Vappie, A Côte Blanche, Louisiana Public Broadcasting and Vappielle Production, 2006.

93. Karen I. Blu, "'Where Do You Stay At?' Home Place and Community among the Lumbee," in *Senses of Place*, 197–227.

94. Author interview with Fred Charlie, May 1, 2001, Ville Platte: "Y a différents styles. Si tu vas à Abbeville ou Kaplan, ça joue la musique avec un *lead guitar*. Ici [in Ville Platte], c'est pas fait. Mais c'est toujours traditionnel pour nous autres. A Houma, c'est plus Country and Western French, parce que y pas de joueur d'accordéon, c'est bien rarement, et c'est beaucoup bien fait, polished. Ca c'est leur style de musique français. Alentour de Ville plate, j'ai été élevé avec la musique de Morris Berzas, le mercredi au soir il jouait le bal à Mamou."

95. Author interview with David Greely, January 14, 2003, Breaux Bridge.

96. Mitch Reed, April 25, 2001, DBCCHW, advanced fiddle class, Lake Fausse Pointe.

97. Le Menestrel, "Place attachment, Displacement."

98. Author interview with Robin Boudreaux, November 19, 2005, Lafayette.

99. Elsa Grassy, "'Tradition Can Be a Verb': Covering Songs in the Post-Katrina Era," *Revue française d'études américaines* 120 (2009): 10–22.

100. *BP Blues*, Warner Bros. Records, 2010.

101. www.dirtycajuns.com.

102. www.zacharyrichard.com/francais/parolesetpoesie.html (accessed July 8, 2012).

103. This is the English translation of the following text in French:

> Le Grand Gosier est couvert d'huile
> Le Grand Gosier après mourir
> Le ciel est rouge
> La mer est noire
> Si je te dirais
> Tu comprendrais pas.
> [Samian:] Le désastre a eu lieu, quasiment irreparable
> Sans se soucier de mon existence, à moi et mes semblables
> Incapable de m'envoler, j'ai les ailes collées au sol

Pendant que vous perdez de l'argent, je suis imbibé de pétrole
Pourquoi cette fois c'est sur moi que ça tombe.
Mais je ne suis qu'un oiseau, y'aura rien sur ma tombe
On m'a sali la mémoire juste assez pour que je me souvienne
Que la catastrophe est naturelle mais que l'erreur est humaine!

104. Give and Go Music BMI, Flat Town Music BMI.

105. For a development on these stigmatizing oppositions, see Le Menestrel and Henry, "Figure du survivor."

106. Jean-Luc Piveteau, "Lieu et territoire: une consanguinité dialectique? (entretien avec Aline Brochot et Martin de La Soudière)," *Communications* 2 (2010): 87, 153.

107. Blu, "'Where Do You Stay At?,'" 224.

108. Ibid., 224.

109. Sexton and Guidry show that Cajun-ness is rooted in place, the prairies and bayous of South Louisiana, and that place is salient to identity. See "You Might Be a Cajun If . . . The Tenacity of Place in a Changing World," in *Worldview Flux: Perplexed Values among Postmodern Peoples*, eds. J. Norwine and J. Smith (Lanham, Boulder, New York, and Oxford: Lexington, 2000).

110. Sara Cohen, "Identity, Place and the 'Liverpool Sound,'" in *Ethnicity, Identity and Music*, ed. Martin Stokes (Oxford and New York: Berg, 1997).

111. Bourdieu, "L'identité et la représentation," 70.

CHAPTER 5

1. Akhil Gupta and James Ferguson, "Space, Identity and the Politics of Difference," *Critical Anthropology* 7, no. 1 (1992): 7.

2. DeWitt, *Cajun and Zydeco*, 107–16.

3. Ibid., 69.

4. Author interview with Missy Maloney, April 28, 2008, Arnaudville. All subsequent quotes from this interview.

4. gerarddole.free.fr/ (accessed July 9, 2012).

5. About *Francadiens*, see Christine Louveau de La Guigneraye, "Ma Louisiane: Ces Français qui interprètent la musique cajun," diss. (Presses universitaires du Septentrion, 1996).

6. Elsebeth Krogh (with Karen Vinding), *CAJUN, en kultur-og musikhistorisk rejse gennem Cajunland i Louisiana, USA* [a cultural and music historical journey through Cajun Country in Louisiana], Lyren, 1993.

7. Ryan Brasseaux compiled a discography of early Cajun music reissues on compact disks in *Cajun Breakdown*, 219–28.

8. Dan Willging, "Ann Savoy."

9. Gina Forsyth is also an accomplished and celebrated musician who somewhat stands between the previous generation of musicians moving to Louisiana in the 1970s and this new generation in the 1990s, and chose to establish herself in New Orleans

rather than Southwestern Louisiana. In the mid-1980s, she moved to New Orleans to study classical and jazz violin at Loyola University and developed a passion for Cajun music.

10. Silas House, "Dirk Powell: Family Traditions," *No Depression* 51 (May-June 2004). archives.nodepression.com/2004/05/family-traditions/ (accessed July 10, 2012); www.dirkpowell.org/Bio.

11. To my knowledge, this movie did not come out on the market.

12. Daniel Gale, email correspondence, September 17 and 23, 2012.

13. Author interview with Lori Henderson, March 12, 2008, Lafayette. All subsequent quotes in this chapter are from this interview.

14. Author interview with Linda Castle, June 11, 2008, Hidden Hills.

15. See Kilpatrick, *Accordion*, and the essential role of Danny Poullard throughout her learning experience of the accordion and vocals.

16. Author interview with Andrea Rubinstein, June 24, 2008, Lafayette. All subsequent quotes from this interview.

17. DeWitt, *Cajun and Zydeco*, 153.

18. Miranda Joseph offers a critical vision of the romantic discourse on community, founded on processes of exclusion and practices of production and of consumption that regularly lead to the legitimation of social hierarchies. See Joseph, *Against the Romance of Community* (Minneapolis and London: University of Arizona Press, 2002).

19. Christian Ghasarian, "Vivre dans un monde de 'Possibilités'. Une version New Age d'un mythe américain," in *Parallaxes transtlantiques*, 239–59.

20. Ibid., 248–49.

21. Author interview with Linda, June 11, 2008, Hidden Hills.

22. thewhirlybird.com/The_Whirlybird.html.

23. The original site no longer exists: stonewood.ning.com/.

24. www.youtube.com/watch?v=FLvgwHGlpdQ (accessed January 2, 2009).

25. In the transnationalization of religions, Argyriadis et al. define the notion of *key event* as "ceremonies (or any kind of regular or renewed gathering place) attended by adepts of distinct ethnic or national origin and distinct faith. These events build interactions among these various actors and generate communitarian imaginaries across the local and the regional. New alliances are formed, as well as tensions and power struggles among the different groups and/or trends." Kali Argyriadis et al., *Religions transnationales des Suds* (Louvain: Harmattan-Academia, 2012).

26. José Guilherme Cantor Magnani, "O circuito neo esoterico na cidade de Sao Paulo," in *A Nova Era do Mercosul*, ed. M. J. Carozzi (Petrópolis: Editorial Vozes, 1999), 27–46; "a circuit is defined as the distribution and linkage pattern of places that enable the practice of sociability from regular users, which does not necessarily imply a spatial contiguity, but a linkage through typical practices."

27. www.sfbayou.com/.

28. Author interview with Mark Falgout, August 2008, Blue Moon Saloon, Lafayette.

29. Author interview with David Greely, January 14, 2003.

30. For a detailed description of the Cajun jitterbug, see M. DeWitt, "Heritage, Tradition, and Travel: Louisiana French Culture," *The World of Music* 41, no. 3 (1999): 64; Stivale, *Disenchanting Les Bons Temps*, ch. 4.

31. See also Sexton, "Too Loud," on debates regarding the jig as a "traditional" dance form.

32. Author interview with Don Brasseaux, April 16, 2001, Breaux Bridge.

33. www.zydecoqueen.com/ (accessed March 28, 2011): 11–13.

34. Email correspondence, November 2008.

35. See for example www.youtube.com/watch?v=5nzQIzYg9tg.

36. Author interview with Lisa Bourque and Joel Breaux, February 11, 2008, Loreauville.

37. Blair Kilpatrick narrates a similar experience with Danny Poullard. See Kilpatrick, *Accordion*.

38. Le Menestrel, "Tourist," 110–11.

39. Another one is "Yankee Chanks," in reference to "chanky chank," applied to French Louisiana music.

40. Todd Mouton, director of Folk Roots, reported in an unrecorded interview on June 9, 2008, that out of 100 full-time participants, five to eight were locals. Another five to eight were part-time participants. Outsiders were from twenty-three different states across the United States and seven other countries (Netherlands, Denmark, Canada, Australia, England, Germany, France).

41. The parallels between the appeal of blues and the "Creole" style in French Louisiana music is also illustrated by the interest of French Louisiana artists on New Jersey's De Luxe record label and California-based Modern Records, both of which specialized in blues and rhythm and blues.

42. Barker and Yuval, *Faking It*, 94.

43. DeWitt, "Heritage, Tradition."

44. 32.2 percent voted for Obama.

45. Brubaker, *Ethnicity*, 47.

CONCLUSION

1. With the notable exception of Bernard in *Swamp Pop*.

2. See in particular Ancelet, "The Limits and Directions"; Bernard, *Swamp Pop* and *Cajuns*; Dormon, *A People Called Cajun* and *Creoles of Color*; Sexton, "Cajun or Coonass" and "Cajun Mardi Gras"; Walton, "Louisiana's Coonasses."

3. Le Menestrel, "Créolisation, imaginaire racial et marché musical franco-louisianais," in *Parallaxes transatlantiques*, 103; Le Menestrel et al., *Des vies*, 270.

4. Bruce Springsteen is quoted in the exhibit brochure (2007): "I have a love of all these different roots sounds. They can conjure up a world with just a few notes and a few words. These sounds, in all their variety and beauty, are America." Exhibit supported by the Smithsonian and the Federation of State Humanities Councils.

5. Allen, *Gone to the Country*, 248.

6. Liiza Malkki, "National Geographic: The Rooting of Peoples and the Territorialization of National Identity among Scholars and Refugees," *Cultural Anthropology* 7, no. 1 (Space, Identity, and the Politics of Difference, 1992): 29.

7. David Thier, "The Cajun Fire of Feufollet," *Garden & Gun* (April/May 2012), gardenandgun.com/article/cajun-fire-feufollet (accessed May 17, 2012).

8. Arjun Appadurai, "Putting Hierarchy in Its Place," *Cultural Anthropology* 3, No. 1 (Place and Voice in Anthropological Theory, 1988): 36–49.

9. Ann Laura Stoler, Ed., *Haunted By Empire: Geographies of Intimacy in North American History* (Durham and London: Duke University Press, 2006); about this notion, see also in same volume Linda Gordon, "Internal Colonialism and Gender," 427–51.

10. Akhil Gupta and James Ferguson, "Beyond 'Culture': Space, Identity, and the Politics of Difference," *Cultural Anthropology* 7, no. 1 (Feb. 1992): 14.

11. Ibid., 16.

Sources

INTERVIEWS (CONDUCTED BY AUTHOR)

Andrea Rubinstein, June 24, 2008, Lafayette.
Arnold Depass Jr., November 22, 2004, Port Barre.
Billy McGee, February 1, 2005, Eunice.
Chas Justus, June 17, 2008, Lafayette.
Corey Porche, April 12, 2001, Lafayette.
David Greely, January 14, 2003; January 4, 2005, Breaux Bridge.
David Chretien and James Caillier, March 8, 2003, Lafayette.
Dennis Paul Williams, March 21, 2003, St. Martinville.
Don Brasseaux, April 16, 2001, Breaux Bridge.
Don Cravins, April 4, 2001, Lafayette.
Elsebeth Krogh, April 30, 2008, Lafayette.
Etienne, Deborah, Moïse, and Alida Viator, May 11, 2001, Tasso.
Frances Haymark, March 3, 2001, Lafayette.
Fred Charlie, May 1, 2001, Ville Platte.
Gil Lejeune, December 8, 2004, New Iberia.
Herman Fuselier, April 2002.
Hadley Castille, November 16, 2004, Leonville.
Herman James Sr., January 7, 2005, New Iberia.
Horace Trahan, April 30, 2001, Scott.
Joe Hall, November 12, 2004, Carencro.
Joel Savoy, October 29, 2010, Black Pot Festival, Lafayette.
John Broussard, March 7, 2003, Lafayette.
John Potier, January 11, 2005, Parks.
Joyce Menard, Lou Louvière, and Helen Hebert, January 7, 2005, New Iberia.
Linda Castle, June 11, 2008, Hidden Hills.
Lisa Bourque and Joel Breaux, February 11, 2008, Loreauville.
Lori Henderson, March 12, 2008, Lafayette.
Luderin Darbone, January 16, 2005, Sulphur.
Mark Falgout, August 2008, Blue Moon, Lafayette.
Melva Patton and Zenobia Verdun, February 2, 2005, Grand Marais.
Mike Doucet and Mitch Reed, DBCCHW, April 24, 2008, Lagniappe session, twin fiddle workshop.
Michael Seider, April 2, 2001, Breaux Bridge.

Milly Ortego, January 31, 2003, Opelousas.
Missy Maloney, April 28, 2008, Arnaudville.
Mitch Reed, December 6, 2004; March 17, 2003, Carencro.
Orres Leblanc, January 7, 2005, New Iberia.
Ray Baudoin, May 16, 2001, Indian Bayou.
Robin Boudreaux, November 19, 2005, Lafayette.
Terry Angelle, May 18, 2001, Henderson.
Todd Mouton, LEDA, March 29, 2001, Lafayette.
William Hamilton, April 20, 2001, Lafayette.
Zydeco Joe, May 18, 2001, Lafayette.

BOOKS AND ARTICLES

Abrahams, Roger D., with Nick Spitzer, John F. Szwed, and Robert Farris Thompson. *Blues for New Orleans: Mardi Gras and America's Creole Soul*. Philadelphia: University of Pennsylvania Press, 2006.

"AE Forum: Locating or Liberating Creolization," *American Ethnologist* 33, no. 4 (November 2006): 549–88.

Allan, Johnnie. *Memories: A Pictorial History of South Louisiana Music, 1910–1990's, South Louisiana and East Texas Musicians*. Vols. I and II. Lafayette: Johnnie Allan/Jadfel Publishing.

Allen, Ray. *Gone to the Country: The New Lost City Ramblers and the Folk Music Revival*. Urbana, Chicago, and Springfield: University of Illinois Press, 2010.

Ancelet, Barry Jean. "Cajun Music." In *Accordions, Two Step, Fiddles and Swing: A Cajun Music Reader*, edited by R. Brasseaux and K. Fontenot, 197–228. Lafayette: Center for Louisiana Studies, University of Louisiana at Lafayette, 2006.

———. "The Cajun Music Festival: Genesis and Legacy," in *Accordions, Two Step, Fiddles and Swing: A Cajun Music Reader*, edited by R. Brasseaux and K. Fontenot, 301–20. Lafayette: Center for Louisiana Studies, University of Louisiana at Lafayette, 2006.

———. *Cajun Music: Its Origins and Development*. Louisiana Life Series, No. 2. Lafayette: Center for Louisiana Studies, University of Southwestern Louisiana, 1989.

——— "The Limits and Directions of Creolization: From Mercier's L'Habitation St. Ybars to the Eunice Mardi Gras." *Louisiana Folklore Miscellany* 14 (1999): 15–26.

———. "The Theory and Practice of Activist Folklore: From Fieldwork to Programming." In *Working the Field*, ed. J. Henry and S. Le Menestrel, 55–76. Jackson: University Press of Mississippi, 2009 [2003].

———. "Zydeco/Zarico: The Term and the Tradition." In *Creoles of Color in the Gulf South*, ed. James Dormon. Knoxville: University of Tennessee Press, 1996, 126–43.

Ancelet, Barry, and Elemore Morgan. *Cajun and Creole Music-Makers: Musiciens cadiens et créoles*, 2nd ed. Jackson: University Press of Mississippi, 1999.

Ancelet, Barry, and Philip Gould, with Benny Graeff and David Simpson. *One Generation at a Time: Biography of a Cajun and Creole Music Festival*. Lafayette: Center for Louisiana Studies, University of Southwestern Louisiana, 2007.

Anthony, Arthe Agnes. "The Negro Creole Community in New Orleans, 1880–1920: An Oral History." Diss., University of California, Irvine, 1978.

Appadurai, Arjun. "Putting Hierarchy in Its Place." *Cultural Anthropology* 3, no. 1 (Place and Voice in Anthropological Theory, 1988): 36–49.

Argyriadis, Kali. "Les batá deux fois sacrés." *Civilisations* 53 (2006): 45–74.

Argyriadis, Kali, et al. *Religions transnationales des Suds*. Louvain: Harmattan-Academia, 2012.

Argyriadis, Kali, and Sara Le Menestrel. *Vivre la guinguette*. Paris: Presses Universitaires de France, 2004.

Augé, Marc. *Génie du Paganisme*. Paris: Gallimard, 1982.

Baron, Robert, and Ana Cara. "Introduction: Creolization and Folklore—Cultural Creativity in Process." *Journal of American Folklore* 116, no. 459 (Winter 2003): 5.

Bendix, Regina. *In Search of Authenticity: The Formation of Folklore Studies*. Madison: University of Wisconsin Press, 1997.

Bernabé, Jean, Patrick Chamoiseau, and Raphaël Confiant. *Eloge de la créolité*. Paris: Gallimard, 1993 [1989].

Bernard, Shane. *The Cajuns: Americanization of a People*. Jackson: University Press of Mississippi, 2003.

———. "J. D. Miller and Floyd Soileau: A Comparison of Two Small Town Recordmen of Acadiana." *Louisiana Folklife Journal* 15 (December 1991).

———. *Swamp Pop: Cajun and Creole Rhythm and Blues*. Jackson: University Press of Mississippi, 1996.

Blu, Karen I. "'Where Do You Stay At?' Home Place and Community among the Lumbee." In *Senses of Place*, ed. Steven Feld and Keith Basso. Sante Fe: School of American Research Press, 1996, 197–227.

Bourdieu, Pierre. "L'identité et la représentation. Eléments pour une réflexion critique sur l'idée de région." *Actes de la recherche en sciences sociales* 35 (1980): 65n17.

Boyer, Véronique, and Sara Le Menestrel. "Introduction." Special issue "Race, ethnie, communauté," *Journal de la société des américanistes* 95, no. 1 (2009): 113–16.

Brasseaux, Carl. *Acadian to Cajun: Transformation of a People, 1803–1877*. Jackson: University Press of Mississippi, 1992.

———. *The Founding of New Acadia: The Beginnings of Acadian Life in Louisiana 1765–1803*. Baton Rouge: Louisiana State University Press, 1987.

———. *French, Cajun, Creole, Houma: A Primer on Francophone Louisiana*. Baton Rouge: Louisiana State University Press, 2005.

———. *In Search of Evangeline: Birth and Evolution of the Evangeline Myth*. Thibodaux: Blue Heron Press, 1989.

Brasseaux, Ryan A. *Cajun Breakdown: An American-made Music*. New York: Oxford University Press, 2009.

———. "Fabricating Authenticity: The Cajun Renaissance and Steve Riley and The Mamou Playboys." In *Accordions, Two Step, Fiddles and Swing: A Cajun Music Reader*, ed. R. Brasseaux and K. Fontenot, 487–494. Lafayette: Center for Louisiana Studies, University of Louisiana at Lafayette, 2006.

Brasseaux, Ryan A., and Kevin Fontenot. *Accordions, Two Step, Fiddles and Swing. A Cajun Music Reader*. Lafayette: Center for Louisiana Studies, University of Louisiana at Lafayette, 2006.

———. "Saving Culture with A Song: Cajun Music and the Twenty-First Century." In *Accordions, Two Step, Fiddles and Swing. A Cajun Music Reader*, ed. R. Brasseaux and K. Fontenot, 501–6. Lafayette: Center for Louisiana Studies, University of Louisiana at Lafayette, 2006.

Broven, John. *South to Louisiana: The Music of the Cajun Bayous*. Gretna: Pelican, 1983.

Brubaker, Rogers. *Ethnicity Without Groups*. Cambridge and London: Harvard University Press, 2004.

Capone, Stefania. "Conexiones diaspóricas: redes artísticas y construcción de un patrimonio cultural afro." In *Circulaciones culturales. Lo afrocaribeño entre Cartagena, Veracruz y La Habana*, ed. Freddy Avila Domínguez, Ricardo Pérez Monfort, y Christian Rinaudo. México D.F.: CIESAS/IRD/ANR/Universidad de Cartagena/El Colegio de Michoacán, 2012, 269–96.

Cefaï, Daniel. "Introduction." In *L'engagement ethnographique*, ed. Daniel Cefaï. Paris: Editions de l'Ecole des hautes etudes en sciences sociales, 2010, 7–21.

Cohen, Robin, and Paola Toninato. "The Creolization Debate: Analyzing Mixed Identities and Cultures." In *The Creolization Reader*, ed. R. Cohen and P. Toninato, 1–22. London and New York: Routledge Student Reader, 2010.

Cohen, Sara. "Identity, Place and the 'Liverpool Sound.'" In *Ethnicity, Identity and Music*, ed. Martin Stokes. Oxford and New York: Berg, 1997.

Comeaux, Malcom. "Introduction and Use of Accordions in Cajun Music." *Louisiana Folklore Miscellany* 14 (1999): 27–40.

Conrad, Glenn. "Potpourri français: Varieties of French Settlers in Louisiana." *Revue de la Louisiane* X, no. 1 (Summer 1981): 1.

Creagh, Ronald. *Nos cousins d'Amérique*. Paris: Payot, 1988.

Creswell, Tim. *Place: A Short Introduction*. London: Wiley-Blackwell, 2004.

Crutcher, Michael Eugene. *Tremé: Race and Place in a New Orleans Neighborhood*. Athens: University of Georgia Press, 2012.

Cunin, Elisabeth. "Introduction: L'ethnicité revisitée par la globalisation." *Autrepart* 38, no. 2 (2006): 3–13.

Daigle, Pierre V. *Tears, Love and Laughter: The Story of the Cajuns and Their Music*. Ville Platte: Swallow, 1987 [1972].

Darensbourg, Joe. *Telling It Like It Is*, ed. Peter Vacher. Houndmills, Basingstoke: Macmillan Popular Music Series, 1987.

DeWitt, Mark F. *Cajun and Zydeco Dance Music in Northern California: Modern Pleasures in a Postmodern World*. Jackson: University Press of Mississippi, 2008.

———. "The Diatonic Button Accordion in Ethnic Context: Idiom and Style in Cajun Dance Music." *Popular Music and Society* 26, no. 3 (2003): 305–30.

———. "Heritage, Tradition, and Travel: Louisiana French Culture." *The World of Music* 41, no. 3 (1999): 57–83.

D'Jalma Garnier, in collaboration with Robert Willey. *Louisiana Creole Fiddle Method: The Music and Technique for Fiddlers and Guitarists*. Pacific, MO: Mel Bay, 2010.

Dôle, Gérard. *Histoire musicale des Acadiens. De La Nouvelle France à la Louisiane 1604–1804*. Paris: L'Harmattan, 1995.

Dominguez, Virginia. *White by Definition: Social Classification in Creole Louisiana*. New Brunswick, NJ: Rutgers University Press, 1986.

Dormon, James H. *Creoles of Color in the Gulf South*. Knoxville: University of Tennessee Press, 1996.

———. "Ethnicity and Identity: Creoles of Color in Louisiana." In *Creoles of Color in the Gulf South*, ed. James Dormon. Knoxville: University of Tennessee Press, 1996, 166–79.

———. *The People Called Cajuns: An Introduction to an Ethnohistory*. Lafayette: Center for Louisiana Studies, University of Southwestern Louisiana, 1983.

Dronet, Curney J. *A Century of Acadian Culture: The Development of a Cajun Community: Erath (1899–1999)*. Gretna: Pelican, 2001.

Dyson, Michael Eric. "The Culture of Hip-Hop." In *That's the Joint! The Hip-Hop Studies Reader*, ed. M. Forman and M. A. Neal. New York and London: Routledge, 2004, 61–68.

Elliot, John Gary. "The partnership of Amédé Ardoin and Denis McGee." Masters thesis, University of Louisiana at Lafayette, 1992.

Fairclough, Adam. *Race and Democracy: The Civil Rights Struggle in Louisiana, 1915–1972*. Athens: University of Georgia Press, 1995.

Feld, Steven, and Keith Basso, eds. *Senses of Place*. Sante Fe: School of American Research Press, 1996.

Filene, Benjamin. *Romancing the Folk: Public Memory and American Roots Music*. Chapel Hill and London: University of North Carolina Press, 2000.

Fontenot, Kevin. "Foreword." In *When Fiddle Was King: Early Country Music from The North and West Regions of Louisiana*, ed. Ron Yule. Natchitoches: Northwestern State University Press, 2007.

———. "People Buy the Feel: Cajun Fiddle Master Rufus Thibodeaux." In *Accordions, Two Step, Fiddles and Swing: A Cajun Music Reader*, ed. R. Brasseaux and K. Fontenot. Lafayette: Center for Louisiana Studies, University of Louisiana at Lafayette, 2006, 439–42.

Francois, Raymond E. *Ye Yaille Chere: Traditional Cajun Dance Music*. Ville Plate: Swallow, 1990.

Frith, Simon. "The Discourse of World Music." In *Western Music and Its Others: Difference, Representation, and Appropriation in Music*, ed. Georgina Born and David Hesmondhalgh. Berkeley, Los Angeles, and London: University of California Press, 2000, 305–22.

Ghasarian, Christian. "Vivre dans un monde de 'Possibilities'. Une version New Age d'un mythe américain." In *Parallaxes transtlantiques. Vers une anthropologie réciproque*, ed. Anne Raulin and Susan C. Rogers. Paris: Editions du CNRS, 2012, 239–59.

Glevarec, Hervé. "La fin du modèle classique de la légitimité culturelle." In *Penser les médiacultures. Nouvelles pratiques et nouvelles approches de la representation du monde*, ed. Eric Maigret and Eric Macet. Paris: Armand Colin, 2005, 92–93.

Goffin, Robert. *La Nouvelle-Orléans, capitale du jazz*. New York: Éditions de la Maison Française, 1946.

Gordon, Linda. "Internal Colonialism and Gender." In *Haunted by Empire: Geographies of Intimacy in North American History*, ed. Ann Laura Stoler. Durham and London: Duke University Press, 2006, 427–51.

Grassy, Elsa. "'Tradition Can Be a Verb': Covering Songs in the Post-Katrina Era." *Revue française d'études américaines* 120 (2009): 10–22.

Grignon, Claude, and Jean-Claude Passeron. *Le Savant et le Populaire. Misérabilisme et populisme en sociologie et en littérature*. Paris: Gallimard/Seuil, 1989.

Gupta, Akhil, and James Ferguson. "Beyond 'Culture': Space, Identity and the Politics of Difference." *Critical Anthropology* 7, no. 1 (1992): 6–23.

Hamilton, Marybeth. "Sexuality, Authenticity and the Making of the Blues Tradition." *Past and Present* 169 (2000): 132–60.

Havard, Gilles, and Cécile Vidal. *Histoire de l'Amérique française*, 2nd ed. Paris: Champs Flammarion, 2006.

Hebert, Denise. "The Hebert Family and the Music of Acadiana." *Attakapas Gazette* 23, no. 3 (Fall 1988): 99–110.

Heinich, Nathalie. *Ce que l'art fait à la sociologie*. Paris: Editions de Minuit, 1998.

Henry, Jacques. "The Louisiana French Movement: Actors and Actions in Social Change." In *French and Creole in Louisiana*, ed. Albert Valdman. New York: Plenum, 1997, 183–213.

———. "Le Mouvement Louisianais de Renouveau Francophone. Vers une nouvelle identité cadjine?" Diss., Université Paris, René Descartes, 1982.

———. "Pourquoi les Cadiens disparaissent et les Créoles restent invisibles." In *La Louisiane*, ed. Guy Clermont. Limoges: Presses Universitaires de Limoges, 2006, 179–95.

Henry, Jacques, and Carl Bankston III. *Blue Collar Bayou: Louisiana Cajuns in the New Economy of Ethnicity*. Westport and London: Praeger, 2002.

Henry, Jacques, and Sara Le Menestrel, eds. *Working the Field: Accounts from French Louisiana*. Jackson: University Press of Mississippi, 2009.

Hirsh, Arnold R., and Joseph Logsdon, eds. *Creole New Orleans: Race and Americanization*. Baton Rouge: Louisiana State University Press, 1992.

Hodson, Christopher. *The Acadian Diaspora: An Eighteenth Century History*. Oxford and New York: Oxford University Press, 2012.

Hoffmann, Odile. "Introduction." Paper presented at the international conference Racialisation et ethnicisation: contexts socio-historiques et enjeux sociaux contemporains, Afrodesc and Eurescl, URMIS, Paris: Université Paris 7-Diderot, November 24–26, 2009.

———. "Renaissance des études afromexicaines et production de nouvelles identités ethniques." *Journal de la société des américanistes* 91, no. 2 (2005): 123–52.

Holt, Fabian. *Genre in Popular Music*. Chicago: University of Chicago Press, 2007.

Jewett, Laura M. *A Delicate Dance: Autoethnography, Curriculum and the Semblance of Intimacy*. New York: Peter Lang, 2008.

Jordan, Rosan A., and Franck De Caro. "In this Folk-Lore Land: Race Class, Identity and Folklore Studies in Louisiana." *Journal of America Folklore* 109, no. 431 (Winter 1996): 31–59.
Joseph, Miranda. *Against the Romance of Community*. Minneapolis and London: University of Arizona Press, 2002.
Kein, Sybil, ed. *Creole: The History and Legacy of Louisiana's Free People of Color*. Baton Rouge: Louisiana State University Press, 2000.
Kennedy, Al. *Chord Changes on the Chalkboard: How Public School Teachers Shaped Jazz and Music in New Orleans*. Lanham, MD, and Oxford: Scarecrow Press, 2002.
Khan, Aisha. "Creolization Moments." In *Creolization*, ed. C. Stewart. Walnut Creek: Left Coast Press, 2007, 237–53.
———. "Feats of Engineering: Theory, Ethnography, and Other Problems of Model Building in the Social Sciences." *American Ethnologist* 33, no. 4 (November 2006): 569.
Koenig, Karl. "Musical History of Donaldsonville and Claiborne Williams 1868–1952: Gentleman Musician of Donaldsonville, La.: Leader, St. Joseph Brass and String Band." Abita Springs: Basin Street Press, 1996.
Krogh, Elsebeth, and Karen Vinding. *CAJUN, en kultur-og musikhistorisk rejse gennem Cajunland i Louisiana, USA* [A cultural and music historical journey through Cajun Country in Louisiana]. Åbyhøj, DK: Lyren, 1993.
Lahire, Bernard. *La culture des individus. Dissonance culturelle et distinction de soi*. Paris: La Découverte, 2004.
———. "The Individual and the Mixing of Genres: Cultural Dissonance and Self-distinction." *Poetics* 36 (2008): 166–88, 10.1016/j.poetic.2008.02.001.
Le Menestrel, Sara. "Créolisation, imaginaire racial et marché musical dans la musique franco-louisianaise." In *Parallaxe transatlatiques. Vers une anthropologie réciproque*, ed. Anne Raulin and Susan C. Rogers. Paris: Editions du CNRS, 2012, 79–108.
———. "From Commemorating to Healing: Coping with the Scars of a Katrina." Paper presented at the annual meeting of the American Anthropological Association, session "Traces of Tragedy: Reshaping Differences, Reinventing Communities and Retracing Social Ties at the Scene of Disaster," Montreal, November 16–20, 2011.
———. "'I can't leave New Orleans more than it can leave me': Place Attachment, Displacement, and Musical Practices in Post-Katrina New Orleans. Direction for Research." Paper presented at the international conference "Saint-Louis du Sénégal et La Nouvelle-Orléans: Histoire comparée et croisée de deux cités portuaires de part et d'autre de l'Atlantique du XVIIe au XXe siècle," St. Louis du Sénégal, June 5–7, 2012.
———. "Introduction." Special issue "Musiques 'populaires', catégorisations, et usages sociaux." *Civilisations* LIII, nos. 1–2 (2006): 7–22. See civilisations.revues.org/index513.html.
———. *La voie des Cadiens. Tourisme et identité en Louisiane*. Paris: Belin, 1999.
———. "Memory Lives in New Orleans: The Process and Politics of Commemoration." In *From American Sodom to American Phoenix: The Destruction and Rebirth of New Orleans*. Baton Rouge: Louisiana State University Press, forthcoming.

———. "Tourist and 'Cajun from France.'" in *Working the Field: Accounts from French Louisiana*, ed. J. Henry and S. Le Menestrel. Jackson: University Press of Mississippi, 2009, 98–117.

Le Menestrel, Sara, Christophe Apprill, Kali Argyriadis, Julien Mallet, Guillaume Samson, Gabriel Segré, and Nicolas Puig. *Des vies en musique. Parcours d'artistes, mobilités, transformations*. Paris: Hermann, 2012.

Le Menestrel, Sara, and Jacques Henry. "Figure du *survivor*: usages de la mémoire et gestion de la catastrophe en Louisiane après les ouragans Katrina et Rita." *Ethnologie française* 3 (2010): 493–506.

———. "Sing Us Back Home: Music, Place and the Production of Locality." *Popular Music and Society* 33, no. 2 (2010): 179–202.

Levine, Lawrence. *Highbrow/Lowbrow: The Emergence of Cultural Hierarchy in America*. Harvard: Harvard University Press, 1988.

Louveau de La Guigneraye, Christine. "Ma Louisiane: Ces Français qui interprètent la musique Cajun." Diss., Presses universitaires du Septentrion, 1996.

Magnani, José Guilherme Cantor. "O circuito neo esoterico na cidade de Sao Paulo." In *A Nova Era do Mercosul*, ed. M. J. Carozzi. Petrópolis: Editorial Vozes, 1999, 27–46.

Malkki, Liiza. "National Geographic: The Rooting of Peoples and the Territorialization of National Identity among Scholars and Refugees." *Cultural Anthropology* 7, no. 1 (Space, Identity, and the Politics of Difference, 1992): 29.

Malone, Bill C. "Nashville Sound." In *Grove Music Online*. Oxford Music Online, www.oxfordmusiconline.com/subscriber/article/grove/music/19589 (accessed February 1, 2012).

Martel, Frédérique. *De la culture en Amérique*. Paris: Gallimard, 2006.

Martin, Michael S. *Historic Lafayette: An Illustrated History of Lafayette and Lafayette Parish*. Historical Publishing, 2007.

Mattern, Mark. *Acting in Concert: Music, Community, and Political Action*. New Brunswick, NJ, and London: Rutgers University Press, 1998.

———. "Let the Good Times Unroll: Music and Race Relations in Southwest Louisiana." In *Accordions, Two Step*, ed. Ryan A. Brasseaux and Kevin Fontenot. Lafayette: Center for Louisiana Studies, University of Louisiana at Lafayette, 2006, 97–106.

Mazor, Barry. *Meeting Jimmie Rodgers: How America's Original Roots Music Hero Changed the Pop Sounds of a Century*. Oxford: Oxford University Press, 2009.

Miller, Karl Hagstrom. *Segregating Sound: Inventing Folk and Pop Music in the Age of Jim Crow*. Durham: Duke University Press, 2010. Kindle edition, emplacement 143.

Mills, Gary B. *The Forgotten People: Cane River's Creoles of Color*. Baton Rouge: Louisiana State University Press, 1977.

Minton, John. "Creole Community and 'Mass' Communication: Houston Zydeco as a Mediated Tradition." *Journal of Folklore Research* 32 (1995): 1–19.

———. "Houston Creoles and Zydeco: The Emergence of an African-American Urban Popular Style." *American Music* 14, no. 4 (Winter 1996).

New Grove Dictionary of Jazz, 2nd ed. Vol. 1, 2003.

Olivier, Rick, and Ben Sandmel. *Zydeco!* Jackson: University Press of Mississippi, 1999.

Oster, Harry. "Acculturation in Cajun Folk Music." In *Accordions, Two Step, Fiddles and Swing: A Cajun Music Reader*, ed. R. Brasseaux and K. Fontenot. Lafayette: Center for Louisiana Studies, University of Louisiana at Lafayette, 2006, 47–54.

Palmié, Stephan. "Creolization and Its Discontent." In *The Creolization Reader*, ed. R. Cohen and P. Toninato. London and New York: Routledge Student Reader, 2010, 49–67.

Peterson, Richard A. *Creating Country Music: Fabricating Authenticity*. Chicago: University Press of Chicago, 1997.

———. "Understanding Audience Segmentation: From Elite and Mass to Omnivore and Univore." *Poetics* 21 (1992): 243–58.

Piveteau, Jean-Luc. "Lieu et territoire: une consanguinité dialectique? Entretien avec Aline Brochot et Martin de La Soudière." *Communications* 2, no. 87 (2010): 149–59.

Post, Lauren. "Joseph C. Falcon, Accordion Player and Singer: A Biographical Sketch." In *Accordions, Two Step, Fiddles and Swing: A Cajun Music Reader*, ed. R. Brasseaux and K. Fontenot. Lafayette: Center for Louisiana Studies, University of Louisiana at Lafayette, 2006, 321–37.

Radano, Ronald. *Lying Up a Nation: Race and Black Music*. Chicago: University of Chicago Press, 2003.

Radano, Ronald M., and Philip V. Bohlman, eds. *Music and the Racial Imagination*. Chicago and London: Chicago University Press, 2000.

Raeburn, Bruce Boyd. "Faith, Hip Hop, and Charity: Brass Band Morphology in Post-Katrina New Orleans." Paper presented at the international conference From American Sodom to American Phoenix: The Destruction and Rebirth of New Orleans, Tulane University, New Orleans, October 21–22, 2010, and Paris, EHESS, April 1–2, 2011.

———. "Stars of David and Sons of Sicily: Constellations Beyond the Canon in Early New Orleans Jazz." *Jazz Perspectives* 3:2 (2009): 146.

Redhead, Steve, and John Street. "Have I the Right? Legitimacy, Authenticity and Community in Folk's Politics." *Popular Music* 8, no. 2 (1989): 177–84.

Rinaudo, Christian. "Métissage et africanité élective dans la musique populaire de Veracruz, Mexique." Paper presented at the international colloquium Anthropologie de la musique et de la danse: une approche des mondes contemporains, Paris, EHESS, ANR Musmond, June 8, 2010.

Roediger, David R. *Colored White: Transcending the Racial Past*. Berkeley, Los Angeles, and London: University Press of California, 2002.

———. *Towards the Abolition of Whiteness: Essays on Race, Politics, and Working Class History*. London and New York: Verso, 1994.

Rose, Al, and Edmond Souchon. *New Orleans Jazz: A Family Album*. Baton Rouge: Louisiana State University Press, 1984 [1967].

Rosenberg, Neil V., ed. *Transforming Tradition: Folk Music Revivals Examined*. Urbana and Chicago: University Press of Illinois, 1993.

Sakakeeny, Matt. *Roll with It: Brass Bands in the Streets of New Orleans*. Durham: Duke University Press, 2013.

Sandmel, Ben. "The Hackberry Ramblers." In *Accordions, Two Step, Fiddles, and Swing: A Cajun Music Reader*, ed. R. Brasseaux and K. Fontenot. Lafayette: Center for Louisiana Studies, University of Louisiana at Lafayette, 2006, 389–98.

Sansone, Livio. "The Localization of Global Funk in Bahia and Rio." In *Brazilian Popular Music and Globalization*, ed. Christopher Dunn and Charles A. Perrone. London: Taylor and Francis, 2001, 136–60.

Santelli, Robert, Holly George-Warren, and Jim Brown, eds. *American Roots Music*. New York: Harry N. Abrams, 2001.

Savoy, Ann. *Cajun Music: A Reflection of a People*. Eunice: Bluebird Press, 1984.

Segré, Gabriel. "Comments to Lahire." Paper presented at the international colloquium "Anthropologie de la musique et et de la danse: une approche des mondes contemporains," coordinated by Sara Le Menestrel and the ANR Musmond, EHESS, Maison Suger, Paris, June 8, 2010.

Sexton, Rocky L. "Cajun Mardi Gras? Cultural Objectification and Symbolic Appropriation in a French Tradition." *Ethnology* 38, no. 4 (1999): 299–313.

———. "Cajun or Coonass? Exploring Ethnic Labels in French Louisiana Regional Discourse." *Ethnology* 48, no. 4 (Fall 2009): 269–94.

———. "Cajuns, Germans, and Les Americains." Diss., University of Iowa, 1996.

———. "Too Loud, Too Wild? Negotiating Cajun Cultural Representations." *Ethnology* 50, no. 2 (Spring 2011): 117–34.

———. "Zydeco Music and Race Relations in French Louisiana." In *Multiculturalism in the United States*, ed. P. Kivisto and G. Rundblad. Thousand Oaks, CA: Pine Forge Press, 2000, 175–84.

Sexton, Rocky L., and John Guidry. "You Might Be a Cajun If . . . : The Tenacity of Place in a Changing World." In *Worldview Flux: Perplexed Values among Postmodern Peoples*, ed. Jim Norwine and Jonathan M. Smith. Lanham, MD, New York, and Oxford: Lexington, 2000.

Sirinelli, Jean-François, and Jean-Pierre Rioux, eds. *La Culture de masse en France de la Belle Époque à nos jours*. Paris: Fayard, 2002.

Smith, Suzanne E. *Dancing in the Street: Motown and the Cultural Politics of Detroit*. Cambridge: Harvard University Press, 1999.

Sonnier, Austin, Jr. *Second Linin': Jazzmen of Southwest Louisiana, 1900–1950*. Louisiana Life Series no. 3. Lafayette: Center for Louisiana Studies, University of Southwestern Louisiana, 1989.

———. *Willie Geary "Bunk" Johnson: The New Iberia Years*. New Orleans: Crescendo, 1977.

"Special Issue: Creolization." Issue editors: Robert Baron and Ana Cara. *Journal of American Folklore* 116, no. 459 (Winter 2003).

Spitzer, Nicholas C. "Monde Créole: The Cultural World of French Louisiana Creoles and the Creolization of World Cultures." *Journal of American Folklore* 116, no. 459 (Winter 2003): 57–72.

———. "Zydeco and Mardi Gras: Creole Identity and Performance Genres in Rural French Louisiana." Diss., University of Texas at Austin, 1986.

Starr, Larry, and Christopher Waterman. *American Popular Music: From Minstrelsy to MTV*. New York and Oxford: Oxford University Press, 2003.

Starr, S. Frederick. *Inventing New Orleans: Writings of Lafcadio Hearn.* Jackson: University Press of Mississippi, 2001.

Stewart, Charles, ed. *Creolization: History, Ethnography, Theory.* Walnut Creek, CA: West Coast Press, 2007.

———. "Syncretism and Its Synonyms: Reflections on Cultural Mixture." *Diacritics* 29, no. 3 (Autumn 1999): 40–62.

Stewart, Jack. "The Mexican Band Legend. Part I." *Jazz Archivist* 6, no. 2 (December 1991): 1–11.

———. "The Mexican Band Legend. Part II." *Jazz Archivist* 9, no. 1 (May 1994): 1–17.

———. "The Mexican Band Legend. Part III." *Jazz Archivist* 20 (2007): 1–10.

Stivale, Charles. *Disenchanting the Good Times: Identity and Authenticity in Cajun Music and Dance.* Durham and London: Duke University Press, 2003.

Stoichita, Victor A. "Entre prouesse et derision." *Ateliers d'anthropologie* 35 (2011), ateliers.revues.org/8793 (accessed January 12, 2012).

Stoler, Ann Laura, ed. *Haunted by Empire: Geographies of Intimacy in North American History.* Durham and London: Duke University Press, 2006.

Stouck, Jordan. "Identities in Crisis: Alice Dunbar-Nelson's New Orleans Fiction." *Canadian Review of American Studies* 34, no. 3 (2004): 269–89.

Strachwitz, Chris. "Cajun Country." In *The American Folk Music Occasional,* Vol. 1, ed. Chris Strachwitz and Pete Welding. New York: Oak, 1970.

———. "Zydeco Music i.e. French Blues." In *The American Folk Music Occasional,* Vol. 1, ed. Chris Strachwitz and Pete Welding. New York: Oak, 1970, 22–24.

Swenson, John. *New Atlantis: Musicians Battle for the Survival of New Orleans.* New York: Oxford University Press, 2011.

Tate, Paul. "The Cajuns of Louisiana." In *The American Folk Music Occasional,* Vol. 1, ed. Chris Strachwitz and Pete Welding. New York: Oak, 1970, 8–12.

Taylor, Timothy. *Global Pop: World Music, World Markets.* London: Routledge, 1997.

Tichi, Cecelia. *High Lonesome: The American Culture of Country Music.* Chapel Hill: University of North Carolina Press, 1994.

Tisserand, Michael. *The Kingdom of Zydeco.* New York: Spike/Avon, 1998.

Toynbee, Jayson. *Making Popular Music: Musicians, Creativity and Institutions.* London and New York: Bloomsbury, 2000.

Trépanier, Cécyle. "The Cajunization of Louisiana: Forging a Regional Identity." *Geographical Journal* 157, no. 2 (July 1991): 161–71.

Tucker, Stephen R. "Louisiana Folk and Regional Popular Music Traditions on Records and the Radio: An Historical Overview with Suggestions for Future Research." In *Accordions, Two Step, Fiddles, and Swing: A Cajun Music Reader,* ed. R. Brasseaux and K. Fontenot. Lafayette: Center for Louisiana Studies, University of Louisiana at Lafayette, 2006, 229–50.

Turino, Thomas. *Music as Social Life: The Politics of Participation.* Chicago: University of Chicago Press, 2008.

Wacquant, Loïc. "For an Analytic of Racial Domination." *Political Power and Social Theory* 11 (1997): 221–34.

Wade, Peter. "La mercantilización de la musica 'negra' en Colombia en el siglo XX." In *Circulaciones culturales. Lo afrocaribeño entre Cartagena, Veracruz y La Habana,*

México, ed. F. Avila Domínguez, R. Pérez Monfort, y Ch. Rinaudo. México D.F.: Ediciones de la Casa Chata, CIESAS/IRD/ANR/Universidad de Cartagena/El Colegio de Michoacán, 2012, 147–64.

———. *Music, Race, and Nation: Musica tropical in Colombia*. Chicago: University of Chicago Press, 2000.

———. "Rethinking *Mestisaje*: Ideology and Lived Experience." *Journal of Latin American Studies* 37 (2005): 255.

Walton, Shana. "Louisiana's Coonasses: Choosing Race and Class over Ethnicity." In *Signifying Serpents and Mardi Gras Runners: Representing Identity in Selected Souths*, ed. C. Ray and L. E. Lassiter. Athens and London: University of Georgia Press, 2003, 38–48.

Wood, Roger. "Southeast Texas: Hot House of Zydeco." *Journal of Texas Music History* 2 (2001): 23–45.

Wood, Roger, and James Fraher. *Texas Zydeco*. Austin: University of Texas Press, 2006.

Woods, Frances J. *Marginality and Identity: A Colored Creole Family Through Ten Generations*. Baton Rouge: Louisiana State University Press, 1989.

Yule, Ron. *When Fiddle Was King: Early Country Music from the North and West Regions of Louisiana*. Natchitoches: Northwestern State University Press, 2007.

NEWSPAPERS AND MAGAZINES

Berman, Leslie. "Savoy Fare: The Real Family Values of Marc and Ann Savoy." *Sing Out!* 47, no. 3 (Fall 2003): 22–33.

Bradshaw, Jim. "Readers recall clubs where they danced to Louisiana music." *Daily Advertiser* (December 29, 1998), www.carencrohighschool.org/LA_Studies/Parish Series/FrenchMusic/AcadianaDanceClubs.htm (accessed October 20, 2011).

Caffery, Josh C. "Courir de Mardi Gras." *Artworks* (February-March 2001): 20.

———. "Lost and Found." *Independent* (December 1, 2004): 14.

Cross, Dominick. "Jolie Blon Steps Aside for Mammoth Waltz." *Independent Weekly* (April 18, 2012).

Dewan, Shaila. "Louisiana's Zydeco Trail." *New York Times* (April 22, 2011), www.ny times.com/2011/04/24/travel/24zydeco.html?pagewanted=alland_moc.semityn .www.&_r=0.

Fuller, R. Reese. "Marc of Distinction." *Times of Acadiana* (April 4, 2001): 23.

———. "A Sense of Place." *Independent Weekly* (June 2005), www.theind.com/cover -story/183.

Fuselier, Herman. "A Different Place." *Daily Advertiser* (February 17, 2006).

———. "He's Chubby and Gets Little Respect." *Times of Acadiana* (April 6, 2001): 24–27.

Himes, Geoffrey. "The Boys' Life." *Offbeat* 19, no. 10 (October 26, 2006): 26.

———. "Cajun String Bands: The Next Big Thing?" NPR, May 5, 2011.

———. "What Is Truth?" Offbeat.com (February 1, 2009) offbeat.com/artman/publish/ article_3509.shtml.

House, Silas. "Dirk Powell: Family Traditions." *No Depression* 51 (May–June 2004), ar chives.nodepression.com/2004/05/family-traditions/ (accessed July 10, 2012).

Legg, Dege. "Indie Cajun." *Gambit Weekly* (February 1, 2011): 13.

———. "Steppin Out the Box." *Independent Weekly*)January 26, 2011), www.theind.com/cover-story/7663-stepping-out-the-box (accessed March 2012).

"Life of 'Jazz Age' Ruins Girl's Health." *Opelousas News* (November 1, 1928).

Miller, Matt. "Bounce: Rap Music and Cultural Survival in New Orleans." *HypheNation* 1(1): 28.

Mouton, Todd. "Louisiana Crossroads." *Artworks* (February-March 2001): 5–6.

Patoski, Joe Nick. "Huey P. Meaux: The Crazy Cajun: Sex, Drugs, and Rock and Roll." *Texas Monthly* 24, no. 5 (May 1996): 116.

Sandmel, Ben. "Bon Ton Roula: Clarence Garlow." *Oxford American* (Southern Music Issue 2012): 92.

Schwartz, Peter. "Canray Fontenot and Bois Sec Ardoin." *Routes to Roots*, vol. 1 (2001): 11.

Thier, David. "The Cajun Fire of Feufollet." *Garden & Gun* (April/May 2012), gardenandgun.com/article/cajun-fire-feufollet (accessed May 17, 2012).

Willging, Dan. "Ann Savoy: Cajun Music's Cultural Ambassador." *Offbeat* (April 2002), www.offbeat.com/2002/04/01/ann-savoy-cajun-musics-cultural-ambassador/ (accessed May 24, 2012).

———. "[Review] Keith Frank: Follow the Leader/Boot Up." *Offbeat*, www.offbeat.com/2012/07/01/keith-frank-follow-the-leader-boot-up-soulwood-records/.

ARCHIVAL COLLECTIONS

Archive of Cajun and Creole Folklore, Center for Cultural and Eco-Tourism, Edith Garland Dupré Library, University of Louisiana at Lafayette: Ancelet collection; Rinzler Collection; Bernard Collection; John and Alan Lomax recordings, number 8.

Greely, David. "400 Years of Cajun Music." Lecture, Ville Platte, March 1, 2008.

Hogan Jazz Archive, Tulane University, New Orleans: Oral History Collection; Vertical Files.

Louisiana Music Collection 230, Amistad Center, Tulane University, New Orleans.

Newspapers, Microfilms, Edith Garland Dupré Library, University of Louisiana at Lafayette: *Clarion Progress*, 1928; *Clarion News*, 1929–30; *Opelousas News*, June 1927–December 1928; *Daily Clarion-Progress*, 1923; *Daily Advertiser*, 1915–18, 1929–31; *Crowley Signal*, 1925–27; *Weekly Iberian*, 1937–38; *Weekly Messenger*, 1932–36.

Quoi YA, hosted by Corey Porche, KRVS, 2007–08.

WEBSITES, BLOGS, AND PODCASTS

"Blacks, Whites, Blues and Country: Charley Pride and Charlie Musselwhite." *American Routes* Public radio program, October 5, 2005, produced by Nick Spitzer, Tulane University's School of Liberal Arts, New Orleans.

Bodin, Stacy. "The Spirit of Erath Articles." 10, www.vrml.k12.la.us/vpkids/vp/Erath/erathhistory/ErathSchools/erathschoolsystem.htm (accessed September 2012).

bonsoircatin.com/about-us.html (accessed February 10, 2012).
Broussard, Sam. "Ryan Brasseaux: Fabricating Content." November 3, 2008, www.sambroussard.com/writing/rant19.html.
cajunzydeco.net/CajunGuitar/SBroussard.htm (accessed January 11, 2011).
cedricwatson.com
davidgreely.com/?page_id=4 (accessed July 13, 2012).
dirkpowell.org/Bio.
dirtycajuns.com.
gerarddole.free.fr/ (accessed July 9, 2012).
harmony.org.uk/book/pop_and_rock_music_blues_modal_progressions.htm (accessed July 26, 2011).
keithfrank.com
lafayetterhythmdevils.com/lrd_band.html.
lostbayouramblers.com (accessed August 15, 2010).
lsue.edu/acadgate/music/musicmain.htm (discontinued)
lsue.edu/acadgate/music/zydecokingpins.htm.
martelfamily.com.
npr.org/blogs/ablogsupreme/2011/05/07/1360252 (accessed May 9, 2012).
nubreeds.com.
officialchrisardoin.com
"Oui on peut—Yes we can! Obama Zydeco from Louisiana 2008, www.youtube.com/watch?v=FLvgwHGlpdQ (accessed January 2, 2009).
pineleafboys.com (accessed August 15, 2010).
sfbayou.com/.
Valcour Records website. www.valcourrecords.com/artist-of-the-month/artist-of-the-month-2010/ (accessed November 2010).
"The Wisdom of Wilson Savoy," Valcour Records, Podcast, 26 min., August 2008.
thewhirlybird.com/The_Whirlybird.html.
tipitinasfoundation.org/.
zacharyrichard.com/francais/parolesetpoesie.html (accessed July 8, 2012).
zydecoqueen.com/ (accessed March 28, 2011): 11–13.

OFFICIAL DOCUMENTS

2010 New Orleans Cultural Economy Snapshot, Mayor's Office of Cultural Economy.
Baxter, Chery L. "Fiscal and Economic Impact Analysis of Louisiana's Entertainment Incentives." In conjunction with the Louisiana Economic Development Office of Entertainment Industry Development and the Legislative Fiscal Office in accordance with the LA Motion Picture Incentive Act, 4/18/2011.
Louisiana Cultural Economy Foundation. *Our First Five Years*. December 2010.
Louisiana: Culture Is Business. Prepared by Mt. Auburn Associates, July 31, 2005, funded by the National Endowment for the Arts and the State of Louisiana, Office of the Lt. Governor, DCRT, Office of Cultural Development, Louisiana Division of the Arts.

Louisiana Motion Pictures, Sound Recording and Digital Media Industry. Economics Research Associates, prepared for Louisiana Economic Development, February 2009.

Markusen, Ann, and Ann Gadwa, eds. *Creative Placemaking.* Markusen Economic Research Services and Metris Arts Consulting for The Mayors' Institute on City Design, National Endowment for the Arts with the United States Conference of Mayors and American Architectural Foundation, 2010, 3–6.

Office of Entertainment Industry Development. *Building a Permanent Entertainment Economy.* Report prepared by Louisiana Entertainment, April 2010, 18.

VIDEOS AND FILMS

Al Berard Teaches . . . Cajun Fiddle Basics: Learn to Play Lead Fiddle and Seconding While You Watch and Play Along. The Acadian 2-step and Eunice waltz, 50 min., 2002, produced by Tom Gath and Susi Mills.

Blank, Les. *Hot Pepper.* El Cerrito, CA: Flower Films, 54 min., 1973.

———. *Dry Wood.* El Cerrito, CA: Flower Films, 1973, 37 min.

Blank, Les, Chris Strachwitz, and Maureen Gosling. *J'ai été au bal (I went to the dance): The Cajun and Zydeco Music from Louisiana.* El Cerrito, CA: Brazos Films, 1989 and 2002. Narrated by Michael Doucet and Barry Ancelet, 84 min., DVD.

Bruneau, Jean-Pierre, *Dedans le Sud de la Louisiane.* Cinq Planètes, 2007 (1974).

The Corey Ledet Instructional Triple Accordion DVD for Beginner and Intermediate. Almena Pictures, 2006.

Doucet, Michael. *Learn How to Play Cajun Fiddle.* Homespun Video, 90 min., VHS, 1993.

———. *Learn to Play Real Cajun Fiddle.* 6 CDs, 40-page book. Homespun Tapes, 1987, 2004.

Down to the Roots: The Gospel Accordion to Marc, vols. I and II. 2001, presented by Wilson Savoy, Schlagzeug Studios.

Gladu, André. *Zarico.* 57 min., 1986, produced by National Film Board of Canada. Book compiled, transcribed, and copied by Niles Hokkanen for Homespun Tapes.

The Mamou Playboys Rockumentary. Lafayette: Almena Pictures, 2003.

Mugge, Robert. *The Kingdom of Zydeco.* 70 min., BMG Video, 1994.

Pitre, Glen, and Michelle Benoit. *American Creole: New Orleans Reunion.* Co-produced by M. Vappie, A Côte Blanche, Louisiana Public Broadcasting and Vappielle Production, 2006.

Powell, Dirk. *Learn to Play Cajun Accordion.* DVD 1 Homespun Video, 1998, directed by Happy Traum.

———. *Learn to Play Cajun Accordion Intermediate and Advanced.* DVD 2, Homespun Video, 75 min., 2005, directed by Happy Traum.

Reed, Mitch. *Fiddle from Scratch.* 2000, CD, produced by Mitch Reed and Eddie Curnan.

———. *How to Play Cajun and Creole Fiddle.* Vols. 1 and 2. Fruge Records, 2011 and 2012.

Savoy, Wilson, and Bennet Rhodes. *Horace Trahan: Hard Pressed But Never Crushed.* Lafayette: Almena Pictures, BackPorch series.

Spitzer, Nick. *Zydeco: Creole Music and Culture in Rural Louisiana.* El Cerrito, CA: Flower Films, 56 min., 1984.

The Steve Riley Instructional Cajun Accordion DVD, Intermediate. Almena Pictures.

DISCOGRAPHY (ONLY RECORDINGS CITED ARE LISTED HERE)

Anthology of American Folk Music. Edited by Harry Smith. Smithsonian Folkways 40090, 1997 (1952).

Ardoin, Bois Sec, with Balfa Toujours. *Allons Danser.* Rounder Records 6081, 2009.

Ardoin, Chris. *V.I.P.* Maison de Soul 1090, 2010.

Ardoin, Chris, and Double Clutchin'. *Lick It Up.* Maison de Soul 1058, 1995.

———. *Thats Da Lick.* Maison de Soul 1051-2, 1994.

Ardoin, Chris, and NuStep. *M.V.P.* Maison de Soul 1086, 2007.

———. *Sweat.* Maison de Soul 1094, 2011.

Balfa Toujours. *La Pointe.* Rounder 6086, 1998.

BeauSoleil. *Bayou Cadillac.* Rounder, 1989.

———. *Cajunization.* Rhino, 1999.

Bergeron, Jamie. *Traditionally Untraditional.* 2000.

Blind Uncle Gaspard, Delma Lachney, John Bertrand: Early American Cajun Music. Classic recordings from the '20s. Yazoo 2042, 2000.

Broussard, Sam. *Geeks.* Surface to Air 001, 2000.

———. *Veins.* Songs for Adults, 2010.

Cajun and Creole Music 1934–1937. Alan and John A. Lomax: The Classic Louisiana Recordings. Produced by B. J. Ancelet. Rounder 11661-1842-2 and -3, 1999.

Cajun Fiddle, Old and New with Dewey Balfa. Recorded and annotated by Tracy Schwartz. Smithsonian Institution, Folkways Records FM 8362, 1977.

Cajun Honky-Tonk: The Khoury Recordings. Arhoolie 427, 1995.

A Cajun Music Anthology: The Historic Victor-Bluebird Sessions, 1928–1941, vols. 1–3. Charlie Seeman, ed. Country Music Foundation, 1990–93.

Chavis, Boozoo. *Zydeco Trail Ride.* Maison de Soul 1034-2, 1990.

Chenier, Clifton, King of the Bayous. "I'm Coming Home." Arhoolie Records, 1993.

Choates, Harry. *The Fiddle King of Cajun Swing.* Arhoolie 380, 1982.

Clark, Octa, and Hector Duhon. *The Dixie Ramblers: Ensemble Encore.* Barry Ancelet and Nick Spitzer, liner notes. Rounder Records 6011, 1982.

Conner, Varise. *Louisiana Folk Masters: Varise Conner.* Recorded by Barry J. Ancelet 1975–77. Louisiana Crossroads Records 2001, 2004.

Delafose, Geno, and French Rockin' Boogie. *Le Creole Cowboy.* Time Square Records 9063, 2007.

Doucet, Michael. *From Now On.* Smithsonian Folkways 40177, 2008.

Feufollet. *Cow Island Hop.* Valcour Records 0005, 2007.

———. *En Couleurs.* Feufollet Records, 2010.

Folksongs of the Acadians. Recorded by Harry Oster 1956–59. Arhoolie 359, 1994.
Fontenot, Canray. *Louisiana Hot Sauce: Creole Style*. Arhoolie 381, 1992.
Frank, Keith, and the Soileau Zydeco Band. *Follow the Leader/Boots Up*. Soulwood Records, 2012.
———. *Loved, Feared, Respected*. Soulwood Records, 2009.
———. *Undisputed*, 2008.
Greely, David. *Sud du Sud*. Give and Go Records, 2009.
Hall, Joe, and Mitch Reed. *Joe Hall and Mitch Reed*. Self-released, 2003.
Hebert, "Cap," and His Louisianians. *Remember When . . . Those Were the Good Old Days*. Mil Records 101, unknown date.
Landry, Drew. *BP Blues*. Warner Bros. Records, 2010.
Landry, Yvette. *Should Have Known*. Self-released, 2010.
Ledet, Rosie. *It's a Groove Thing*. Maison de Soul 1075, 2000.
———. *Zesty Zydeco*. Maison de Soul 1056, 1995.
Lége, Jesse, Joel Savoy, and the Cajun Country Revival. *The Right Combination*. Valcour Records 18–15, 2012.
Lil' Brian and the Zydeco Travelers. *Funky Nation*. Tomorrow Recording, 2000.
———. *Worldwide*. Freh' Toi Records, 2007.
———. *Z-Funk*, 1997.
The Lost Bayou Ramblers. *Bastille*. Bayou Perdu Records, 2011.
———. *Mammoth Waltz*. Bayou Perdu Records 2012.
Louisiana Cajun Music: The First Recordings, vols. 1–4. Produced by Chris Strachwitz. Old Timey Records, OT 108–111, 1970.
Matte, Travis. *Booty Zydeco*. Mhat Productions, 2006.
———. *Hip Hop Zyderock*. Mhat Productions, 2008.
———. *Zydeco Train*. 2005.
McGee, Dennis. *The Complete Recordings of Dennis McGee, 1929–1930, with Ernest Frugé and Sady Courville*. Early American Cajun Classics. Liner notes Will Spires, Ann Savoy; produced by Richard Nevins and Ann Savoy. Yazoo 2012, 1994.
———. *Himself*. Recorded by Gerard Dole. Valcour Records 0011, 2010.
Paul, J., Jr., and the Zydeco Newbreeds. *Stronger*. Self-released, 2009.
———. *Who Do You Love?* Louisiana Red Hot Records, 2001.
Pine Leaf Boys. *Back Home*. Valcour Records 12, 2010.
Riley, Steve, and the Mamou Playboys. *Bayou Ruler*. Rounder Records, 1998.
———. *Grand Isle*. Self-released, 2011.
Romero, Roddie, and the Hub City All Stars. *La Louisianne Sessions*. Octavia Records, 2007.
Taylor, Curley, and Zydeco Trouble. *Free Your Mind/Close to Midnight*. Louisiana Soul, 2006.
Toups, Wayne, and Zydecajun. *Little Wooden Box*. Shanachie Records, 2000.
Traditional Cajun Fiddle: Instruction by Dewey Balfa and Tracy Schwartz. Smithsonian Institution, Folkways Records FM 8361, 1976.
Trahan, Horace, and the New Ossun Express. *Get On Board*. 1999.

———. *That Butt Thing.* Maison de Soul, 2003.
Trahan, Horace, and the Ossun Express. *Keep Walking.* Self-released, 2010.
Watson, Cedric. *Cedric Watson.* Valcour Records 0004, 2008.
———. *Creole Moon: Live from the Blue Moon Saloon.* Valcour 0014, 2010.
Young, Linzay, and Joel Savoy. *Linzay Young and Joel Savoy.* Valcour Records 0008, 2008.
Zydeco. Putamayo 160, 2000.
Zydeco: Allons danser! Creole Accordions Dance. Rough Guides, 2005.
Zydeco: The Early Years (1961–1962). Recorded by Chris Strachwitz. Arhoolie 307, 1989.

Index

Acadiana Arts Council, 142
Acadiana Center for the Arts, 6, 17, 139, 144
Acadiana Symphony Conservatory of Music, 144, 277
Accordiana Band, 51
Accordion: chromatic or piano, 226, 234; decline of, 57–58; diatonic, 50, 159–60, 181, 225, 233–34; introduction of, 50; revitalization, 113; and role of Mexicans, 52–53
"Adam 3-Step," 128
Adams, J. B., 177
Adaptation: to Louisiana lifestyle, 278, 287; musical, 53, 81, 87, 198–99; notion, 87
Adcock, Eric, 242
Adieu False Heart, 274
"Adieu Rosa," 232
Africa: heritage, 14, 25, 156–57, 196, 199, 318; influences, 156–57, 159, 163, 177
"After the Ball," 41
Allan, Johnnie, 36
"Allons à Lafayette," 55, 252, 254
"Allons à Tepate," 254
Allons Danser, 276, 296
American Federation of Musicians, 221
Ancelet, Barry, 25, 75, 77, 85, 87–88, 91, 119–20, 155, 157, 160, 234
Ann Savoy and Her Sleepless Knights, 88, 273
Anthology of American Folk Music, 151
Arceneaux's Hall (Carencro), 54
Archive of Folk Songs (Library of Congress), 79

Archives of Cajun and Creole Folklore, 25, 32, 120, 144, 152, 254, 262
Ardoin, Amédé, 55–56, 156, 192
Ardoin, "Bois Sec," 53, 121, 172, 230, 276
Ardoin, Chris, 115, 117, 121, 128, 131, 194, 217, 222
Ardoin, Dexter, 128, 178
Armstrong, Louis, 45, 47, 59
Arodin, Sidney, 40
Artmosphere (Lafayette), 257
Atchafalaya (Henderson), 206
Attakappa Night Club (New Iberia), 71
authenticity: claims of, 24, 104; and dance, 295–98; and music, 77–79, 84, 90, 92, 97, 99, 102, 119, 124, 145, 150, 238; power struggles, 21, 33, 76; and sexuality, 196; vs. commercial, 83–84, 89–90, 95, 97, 145; vs. mainstream, 97. *See also* tradition

"Baby Please Don't Go," 56
Back Home, 113
Balfa, Christine, 75, 139, 179, 242, 249, 297–98, 308, 311
Balfa, Dewey, 82–84, 93, 125, 171, 247, 255, 270, 274–75, 311
Balfa Brothers, 75, 83, 92–93, 110, 180, 269, 271
Balfa Toujours, 75, 171, 236, 292
banjo, 90, 99
Banner Band, 45–46, 49, 65–67, 68, 70
"Barres de la Prison," 181
bass, 123, 174
"Bastille," 259
Bayou Ruler, 100

Beachland Ballroom (Cleveland), 276
Beau Jocque, 4, 101, 112, 116, 122–23, 172
Beau Jocque and the Highrollers, 123
BeauSoleil, 11, 108, 117, 133, 307
Bellard, Douglas, 56, 121
Berard, Al, 107, 246, 305
Bergeron, Jamie, 99, 103, 105–6, 128
"Bernadette," 174
Bernard, Rod, 91, 192
Bigard, Alex, 48
Bijou Creole, 113, 132
Bijou Dance Hall (Erath), 70
"Bird in a Gilded Cage," 41
Black Eagle Band, 46
black music, 56, 150, 156, 161–62, 180, 192, 199–200, 221, 226
blackness: culture of, 176; and eroticism, 192, 196, 198–99, 309; and flirt, 190–91
Blind Uncle Gaspard, 151, 162
Blind Uncle Gaspard, Delma Lachney, John Bertrand, 272
Blue Moon Saloon (Lafayette), 4, 120, 143–44, 176–77, 206, 240, 242, 289, 294, 306
"Blue Runner," 5, 174
Bluerunners, 114, 131, 145
Blues, 107, 171–72, 180–86; style, 156; tunes, 181; waltz, 181–82
"Blues à bébé," 4, 174
Bocage, Peter, 50
Bola de Nieve, 53
Bonsoir Catin, 118, 238
"Bonsoir Moreau," 174
Boo Boo's (Lafayette), 117
Booty Zydeco, 122, 195
Bouboul Valentin, 51
Boudreaux, Robin, 256–57
Boutte, John, 258
"BP Blues," 258
Bradford's, 47
Brand New Old Time Cajun Band, 229
Breaux, Cleoma, 54, 58–59

Breaux Brothers, 55, 151
Broussard, Sam, 112–13, 118, 120, 181–82, 231–32, 235
Brown, Les, 47
Buckwheat Zydeco, 98, 105, 112, 122, 129–30, 134, 224
Buddy Bolden, 45, 51
Burgess, Anya Shoenegge, 275, 313

Caffery, Josh, 96, 113, 227, 235
Cailler, J.J. , 222
Cajun du Nord, 271
Cajun French Music Association, 104, 147
Cajun Honky-Tonk, 58
Cajuns: adaptability of, 86; and Appalachian old-time music, 206, 245; bands, 113–14, 117, 127, 146, 197, 263, 274; "cajunization," 73; as category of identification, 11–12, 17, 19, 82, 154; change of status, 93–94; commercial recordings, 54, 58, 60; as coonass, 106–7; country, 12, 17, 80, 126, 154; and country music, 85, 90–91, 151, 185; dance, 186, 197, 295–97, 300; as distinct from Creole style, 167–77; as French blues, 183, 186; as music category, 13, 36; renewal of music scene, 114–16, 209, 238–39; and segregation, 3; swing, 57, 88; and upward mobility, 41, 81–82; as white music, 151, 199
Calloway, Cab, 47
"Canray's Breakdown," 56
Cap Hebert and His Louisianians, 49
Carriere, Bébé, 4, 56, 168–69, 174
Carriere, Calvin, 179, 243
Celestin's Tuxedo Orchestra, 71
"Chanson de Limonade," 60
Charles, Hypolite, 49, 63, 66, 215
Charlie, Fred, 179, 186, 255
"Chatterbox," 115
Chavis, Boozoo, 5, 61, 122–23, 129, 193, 211, 224–25, 228–29

Chenier, Clifton C., 14, 86, 112, 166–67, 205, 218, 221, 253–54
"Chère Joues Roses," 5
Choates, Harry, 57, 87, 125, 219, 233
circuit, notion of, 293, 313–14. *See also* festival; music camps
"Cisco Kid," 116
Cité des Arts (Lafayette), 142, 292
civil rights movement, 8, 153, 166
clarinet, 35, 50, 57, 79
Close to Midnight, 194
clothing, 4–5, 69, 131, 189, 207–9, 222, 257
CODOFIL (Council for the Development of French in Louisiana), 12, 94–95, 120, 154, 271
Coffee Break (Breaux Bridge), 240, 241
color line, 25, 63, 148–49, 156, 185, 196, 198
connectedness, 19, 201, 253–54, 311, 313, 319
Conner, Varise, 54, 87, 124
Cookie and the Cupcakes, 192
Coolick, Daniel, 5, 275
Cormier, Sheryl, 271
cornet, 52
Coteau, 117
Cotton, James, 276
Count Basie, 47
courtship, 189–91, 217
Cow Island Hop, 114, 237
creativity, 16, 113, 118–20, 125–26, 157, 162, 259
Creole Bred, 175, 273
CREOLE Inc., 155
Creole Moon, 176
Creoles: bands, 21; and benevolent societies, 62–63, 215; as category of identification, 7–9, 19, 129, 164–67, 298; of color, 48, 179; as distinct from Cajun style, 167–77; and French blues, 183, 186; and French music, 177–79; as LaLa, 13, 157, 180; as music category, 13; sound, 156; style, 33, 84, 97, 117, 157, 168–78, 199, 217, 281, 310

creolization, 21–27, 81, 86, 148, 155, 157, 162, 191–92, 318. *See also* hybridity; métissage
cultural economy, 136–46

"Dambala," 4
Dance: classes, 188, 297; codification, 250, 297–98; fans of, 278, 282, 293–304; and fun, 250–51, 298, 300; and immersion, 298; stylistic distinctions, 294–302
dance styles: Cajun jitterbug, 197, 294–97, 299–300; East Coast swing, 279, 299; old time, 68, 78; two step, 78, 93, 294, 296–97, 299–300; waltz, 78, 101, 166, 296, 300–301; West Coast swing, 279, 299; Whiskey River, 299–301
dance teachers, 134, 197, 206, 298–302
Darbone, Luderin, 56, 59, 92
Darensbourg, Joe, 38, 41, 47, 60
David, Thomas, 4
"Dear Mr. President," 153
Dedans le Sud de la Louisiane, 270
Delafose, Geno, 116, 207, 211–12, 215, 223, 294
Delafose, John, 5, 115, 184, 189, 193, 211–12
Deluxe Harmony Orchestra, 39
Department of Culture, Recreation and Tourism, 134–35
DePass, Arnold "Pap," Jr., 47, 62–63, 65, 67, 184, 213
Dewey Balfa Cajun and Creole Heritage Week (DBCCHW), 29, 243–47, 297
Dirty Dozen Brass Band, 98, 258
Disasters: BP oil spill, 6, 258; hurricane Katrina, 26, 29, 136–38, 256–58, 263; hurricane Rita, 29, 136–38, 261
discrimination, 8, 18, 102, 148, 157, 165, 212, 216, 268, 318
distinctiveness: musical, 79, 111, 124, 129, 133, 231; regional, 103, 132, 252–53, 263
Dodds, Johnny, 57
"Dog Hill," 5, 228, 254

Domengeaux, Jimmy, 94–95
domination, 8, 20–21, 263, 321
Doucet, Michael, 36, 56, 108–9, 111, 116–17, 180, 232, 244, 247–48, 321
"Dreamer of Dreams," 40
drum, 47, 97–98, 115
Duhé, Lawrence, 45

"Easy Come, Easy Go," 6
El Sid O's (Lafayette), 130–31, 188, 206, 208
Eldorado Ballroom (Houston), 221
Elk's Club (Opelousas), 38
Ellington, Duke, 47
"Elton 2-step," 231
emotion, 97, 99, 180, 186–87, 196, 227
En Couleurs, 88, 115, 127, 239
"Eunice Two-Step," 122, 254
Evangeline Band, 79
Evangeline Made, 273
exoticism, 134, 161, 176, 198, 263, 309

Falcon, Joe, 54–55, 58–59, 126, 160
"Fallen Star, A," 91
Fans: circle of, 282, 291, 308–9; network of, 34, 267
festivals: Blackpot Festival (Lafayette), 5, 6, 246, 287, 312–13; Bunk Johnson Festival (New Iberia), 46; Cajun and Zydeco Festival (Branson, Missouri), 105, 282; Crawfish Festival (Breaux Bridge), 279; Festival International de Louisiane (Lafayette), 140, 282; Festivals Acadiens et Créoles (Lafayette), 119, 178, 271, 277, 282; National Folk Festival (Dallas), 69, 80; Newport Folk Festival, 82, 247, 271; Nuits Cajun et Zydeco de Saulieu (France), 270; Oberlin Folk Festival, 27; Smithsonian National Folklife Festival (Washington, D.C.), 83, 274; Step-N-Strut, 221; Texas Centennial National Folk Festival, 69; Tribute to Cajun Music, 85, 94, 271; University of Chicago Folk Festival, 247
Feufollet, 88, 103, 114, 127, 132, 141, 237, 239, 320
fiddle, 49–50, 108, 113, 174–75, 232–34, 249, 275
"Fi-Do," 56
Films: *Belizaire the Cajun*, 272; *Cold Mountain*, 274; *The Divine Secrets of the Ya-Ya Sisterhood*, 273; *Hot Pepper*, 205; *J'ai été au bal*, 205, 232, 269; *Southern Comfort*, 244; *Spend It All*, 269
Fitzgerald, Ella, 40, 47
Foghorn Stringband, 114, 237, 313
Folk artist, 84, 205
Folk Arts Apprenticeship, 85
Folk dancers, 197, 278, 307
Folk music, 31, 77, 79–83, 89, 97, 151, 162
Folk revival, 82, 83, 127, 288
Follow the Leader, 128
Fontenette, Gustave, 44
Fontenette, Mercedes, 65–67
Fontenot, Canray, 53, 56, 84, 97, 120, 156, 174, 180, 232
Four Aces, 58, 70
Frank, Carlton, 172, 243
Frank, Keith, 106, 116, 123, 128–29, 207, 212, 215, 217
Frank, Preston, 171
Frederick L'Ecole des Arts (Arnaudville), 142
free people of color, 8–9, 62, 167
Free Your Mind, 194
French language. *See* Louisiana regional French
French Louisiana music: as French blues, 179–86; institutionalization, 144; as music category, 16; national recognition, 84–85; record labels, 60–61, 132, 139, 151–52, 219; revival of, 82–85, 103; scholarship, 69, 73, 86, 155, 162; way of life, 210, 245

French music: commercial recording of, 35, 53–57; labeled as Cajun or Creole, 33, 168–69; music category, 13, 16, 18, 153, 177–79, 185; as regional music category, 177–79; stigmatization, 67–68, 71–72
French Renaissance, 82, 85, 88, 135, 154, 271
Front Room (Lafayette), 243, 246
frottoir (washboard), 4–5, 97, 112, 157
Fruge, Columbus, 151
Funky Nation, 225

Gale, Daniel, 275, 308
"Galop à Wade Frugé," 173
Garnier, D'Jalma, 56, 174, 250, 310
Geeks, 118
Get On Board, 148
Girouard, Leo, 48
"Give Him Cornbread," 116
Gonzales, Filo, 53, 70
Good Hope Hall (Lafayette), 63–64
"Grand Gosier," 259
Grand Isle, 115, 237, 239
"Grand Isle," 260
Grand Ole Opry, 91
Grant Street (Lafayette), 145, 206
Greely, David, 100, 109, 117, 121, 132, 180, 184, 230, 235, 255, 260, 295, 307
"Gue Gue Solingail," 205
Guidry, Doc, 61, 92
guitar, 113, 231–32, 235
"Gumbo Waltz," 305

Hackberry Ramblers, 56, 58, 61, 92, 160, 254, 268
Hall, Joe, 120, 168–69
Hamilton's Place (Lafayette), 98, 188, 190, 206–7
"Happy One Step," 173
harmonica, 50, 58
Harris, Charles K., 41
"Haterz," 217

Hawker, Ginny, 6, 308
Hebert, Didier, 151
Hebert, Noah, 48
Hebert, Sidney "Cap," 48
Hebert, Wilson, 48, 64
"High Society," 57
hillbilly music, 36, 54, 56–59, 61, 150–51, 204, 214
Himself, 152
hip hop: aesthetics, 209; rap, 116, 123, 129–30, 216–19, 223–24; style, 116, 131
Hogan Jazz Archive (New Orleans), 32, 35
home, 253–54, 259, 262, 266–67, 280, 313
Horace Trahan and the Ossun Express, 113, 254
Hot 8 Brass Band, 98, 217
humor, 107, 118, 179, 244–45, 289, 312, 321
hybridity, 24, 73, 124. *See also* creolization; *métissage*

"I Just Wanna Be Your Lovin' Man," 4
Identification: ethnic, 17, 148–49, 198, 201, 211, 215, 318; musical, 20, 110, 117, 255, 318; racial, 15, 152, 154, 157, 161, 185, 199–200; regional, 16, 107, 130, 133, 178, 198, 224, 244, 261, 293, 319–21
"I'm Coming Home," 253–54
"I'm Going Back to Grand Mamou," 205
instrumentation, 50–51, 58, 99, 158–59, 185, 221, 257

J. Paul and the Zydeco Nubreedz, 131
Jack, Brian, 223
jam. *See* technique (musical)
James, Harry, 47
James, Herman, 47, 68, 71
Jay's Lounge (Cankton), 270
Jazz: commercial recordings, 49; ensemble, 33, 41, 48, 51, 54; instrumentation, 51; as rural, 35
"Je va t'aimer quand même," 58
Jefferson Theater (Lafayette), 38

Jelly Roll Morton, 45
"Johnny Can't Dance," 128
Johnson, Willie Geary "Bunk," 32, 45–47, 52
Joie de Vivre Café (Breaux Bridge), 240
"Jolie Blonde," 57, 60, 87, 174, 198, 220, 233
Jones, Kelli, 275
Joseph "Zydeco Jo" Mouton, 216
"June Night," 40
jurés, 156, 160
Justus, Chas, 93, 113, 118, 182, 245

Keep Walking, 5, 115, 148, 178
"Kentucky Waltz," 56
Kerr, Clyde, 39, 71
Kershaw, Doug, 91, 236
Kevin Naquin and the Ossun Playboys, 226
Kouyate, Morikeba, 176
Krazy Kajun, 270

"La Cucaracha," 53
"La Danse de la Misère," 174
La Louisianne Sessions, 133
"La Malheureuse," 232
"La misère m'a fait brailler," 185
La Pointe, 236
La Poussière (Henderson), 157, 206, 251, 294, 297
"La Valse de Grand Basile," 254
"La Valse de Grand Bois," 254
"La valse de la prison," 59
"La Valse de l'Anse au Paille," 254
"Lacassine Special," 254
Lâche Pas, 306
"Lache Pas la Patate," 91, 96
Lachney, Delma, 151, 162
Lacoste, Warren, 40
Lafayette Economic Development Authority (LEDA), 139
Lafayette Rhythm Devils, 118, 238, 254
"Lake Arthur Stomp," 124, 173, 254, 305
Lakeview Park (Eunice), 206, 312

Lamour, Ricardo, 259
Landry, Drew, 258, 261
Landry, Viola Hebert, 48
"Lawtell 2-step," 58
"Lazy River," 40
Lazy Six, 216
Le Cowboy Creole, 211, 223
Leblanc, Leroy "Happy Fats," 59
Ledet, Corey, 121–22, 245
Ledet, Rosie, 194
Lége, Jesse, 178, 305, 313
Legitimacy: musical, 19–21, 125, 275; notion, 20. *See also* tradition
LeJeune, Iry, 59, 61, 147, 183, 219
"Les Barres de la Prison," 160, 228
Les Malfecteurs, 5, 113
"Les Tete Fille Lafayette," 58
"Les Zaricots Sont Pas Salés," 14, 97, 270
Levert Gym (St. Martinville), 39, 71, 78
Lewis, Delilah Lee, 269
Lewis, George, 45–46
Lick It Up, 194
Lightnin' Hopkins, 86, 220
Lil' Brian and the Zydeco Travelers, 130, 225
Lil Nate (Nathan Williams Jr.), 106, 128, 223
"Little Rendezvous with Honolulu, A," 57
Little Wooden Box, 127
Lomax, Alan, 79, 81, 127, 156, 267
Lost Bayou Ramblers, 126, 227, 259, 260
Louisiana Blues and Zydeco, 268
Louisiana Crossroads, 139, 311
Louisiana Cultural Economy Foundation, 138
Louisiana Division of the Arts, 142, 243
Louisiana Folk Roots (Lafayette), 139, 171, 178, 240, 243
Louisiana Folklore Society, 80, 89
Louisiana regional French, 168, 271
Louisiana Six, 48–49, 54
Louisiana State Arts Council, 243
"Love Has a Way," 40
Loved. Feared. Respected., 128, 217

"Mama Rosin," 53
Mammoth Waltz, 126, 132, 239, 260
Mamou Prairie Band, 107
"Mamou two-step," 297
mandolin, 58, 108, 265
Manetta, Manuel, 47–48
Maple Leaf Band, 63, 215
"Marée noire," 260
marginalization, 198, 204, 262
Martel Orchestra, 47
Martin Dance Hall (Scott), 47–48, 71
Matte, Travis, 99, 105, 112, 121, 148, 195, 255
McCauley-Reed-Vidrine, 109
McGee, Dennis, 55–56, 85, 102, 162, 169, 230, 232
McKeon, Rocky, 259
Melody Girls, 70
"Memory Lane," 40
métissage (mestisaje), 23–24, 191, 197, 199. *See also* creolization; hybridity
Michot, Louis, 126, 175, 227
Miller, Blake, 5
Miller, Glenn, 47, 49
Millinder, Lucky, 47
Mobility: circulatory movement, 221, 267, 320; geographic, 60, 73, 219–20, 268, 309; social, 82, 319–20; upward, 69, 145, 185, 224, 226, 314
mobilization, 82, 153, 155, 200, 259
morality: judgment, 95, 145; norms, 196
Morvant's (Youngsville), 240
Mulate's (Breaux Bridge), 108, 230, 296
music camps: Appalachian String Band Music Festival (Clifftop), 308; Ashokan Fiddle and Dance (New York State), 308–9, 311; Augusta Heritage Festival (Davis and Elkins College, Virginia), 275–76, 308–9; Dewey Balfa Camp (DBCCHW) (Chicot State Park), 108, 111–12, 139, 171, 178, 180, 231–32, 243, 249, 305, 308–9, 311; Festival of American Fiddle Tunes (Port Townsend, Washington State), 308
music industry, 90, 130, 134, 137–38, 141–42, 149, 211
music market, 98, 106, 129–30, 133, 200, 314
music producers. *See* recording industry
musical dynasties, 21, 128, 145, 253
musical ownership, 24, 123, 159–61, 164, 298
musical technique. *See* technique (musical)
Musselwhite, Charlie, 185

National Endowment for the Arts, 84, 142, 269
National Heritage Fellowship, 84, 133
networks: of Cajun and Creole musicians and Appalachian old-time musicians, 311–15; connections of different circles, 272, 289–93; of dancers, 277, 307; of fans, 267; of Louisiana Cajuns and Nova Scotia Acadians, 103; of transplants, 284–89; websites, 278, 292. *See also* connectedness
New Birth Brass Band, 216
New Drug Store (Opelousas), 40, 65, 69
New Lost City Ramblers, 83–84, 247
New Orleans Jazz Orchestra, 257
Newman, Jimmy C., 91
non-natives: as fans, 273; and legitimacy, 82; as teachers, 299. *See also* fans; transplants
Nunu's Arts and Culture Collective (Arnaudville), 142

Oberlin Playboys, 276
Office of Cultural Development, 243
Old Folks Band, 41
Oliver, Joe "King," 45
Olympia Brass Band, 62
"One step de Mamou," 124, 254
"Opelousas Sostan," 94

Opera label (Texas), 219
Original Toots Johnson, 39
Origins: African, 14, 163, 199, 318; European, 157; rhetoric of, 24–25, 162, 199, 201, 317
Ortego, Adner, 53, 109
Ossun Blues, 147
"Ossun Breakdown," 254
Other Planets, 257
"Oui on peut!," 292
Outlaws (Lafayette), 206
"Over the Waves," 52
Owens, Jack, 310

Palao, Jimmy, 50
Papa Celestin and his Tuxedo Band, 39, 215
"Paper in My Shoe," 61, 211
Pat and Bob Decuir's Louisiana Ramblers, 39
Paul, J., Jr., 217, 222, 224
Paul D. Barnes Orchestra, 39
"Pelican," 259
performances: participatory, 93–94, 101–2; presentational, 93; seated concert, 93, 265, 307
"Perrodin Two-Step," 254
Peyton, Henry, 51
phonograph. *See* recording industry
piano, 47, 57–58, 65, 115
Picou, Alphonse, 51
Pine Leaf Boys, 6, 96, 126, 176, 219, 226–27
Piron, A. J., 50
place: concept, 252; sense of, 29, 203–4, 254, 315; and space, 84, 267. *See also* home
"Pop's Waltz," 173
"Port Arthur Blues," 254
Potier, Harold, 65, 68
Poullard, Danny, 305, 308
Poullard, Ed, 148, 178, 231
Powell, Dirk, 111, 174, 179, 205–6, 228, 246, 248, 274–76, 311

Prejean, Jermaine, 4
"Prenez Courage," 86
Preservation Hall, 217
Pride, Charley, 185
"Put On Your Old Gray Bonnet," 41

"Quand les Fleurs Fleurissent," 305

racial imaginary, 24, 33, 148–49, 175, 198, 318
radio shows: Lagniappe (KRVS), 260, 306; *A Prairie Home Companion*, 133, 311; "Quoi Y A," 107; *Rendez-Vous des Cajuns*, 25
Ramos, Florencio, 52
Ramsey, Frederic, Jr., 45
Randol's (Lafayette), 186–87, 251
rap: bounce, 217; pop rap, 217. *See also* hip hop
Rayne-Bo Ramblers, 59
Reach Out and Touch a Hand, 148
Rebirth Brass Band, 98
recognition: Cajun and Zydeco Grammy Award, 129, 176; and commercial aspirations, 98–99, 106; international, 135, 226, 263–64; local, 137, 145, 290; national, 133–35, 226, 263, 273
record labels: Acrobat (England), 272; Arhoolie Records, 14, 35, 56–58, 86, 268, 273; Asterios Productions, 272; Bear Family (Germany), 272; Bluebird, 57, 152; Cash Money Records, 130; Cinq Planètes (France), 270, 272; Columbia, 45, 54–55; Decca, 58; Excello, 61; Expression Spontanée (France), 272; Folkways Records, 151, 247; Freh' Toi Records, 225; Frémeaux and Associés (France), 272; Gold Star label, 57, 220–21; Goldband Records, 61; Jin label, 152; Khoury, 58; Label Bluebird, 57, 152; Maison de Soul, 152; OKeh label, 54, 69, 205; Opera, 219; Rounder, 141, 276; Sugar Hill, 220;

Swallow, 152; Tomorrow Recordings, 225; Valcour Records, 132, 141, 152, 176, 236–37, 253; Vanguard Records, 273; Yazoo label, 272
record producers: C. C. Adcock, 115, 237; T Bone Burnett, 273–74; Fred Charlie, 179, 186, 255; Ted Fox, 98; Christopher King, 272; Ivan Klisanin, 272; Philippe Krümm, 115; Mack McCormick, 220; J. D. "Jay" Miller, 60; Eddie Shuler, 60; Floyd Soileau, 60, 151; Chris Strachwitz, 56, 85, 91, 98, 160, 180, 205, 268
recording industry: commercial recordings, 54, 124, 220, 268; phonographs, 40–41
Red Stick Ramblers, 5, 88, 124, 126, 227, 246, 291, 311, 313
Reed, Mitch, 102, 107, 152, 174, 232, 242–43, 245, 247, 289
"Reel de Berzas," 305
"Reel de Cajun," 305
"Reel de Coquin," 305
"Reel de Frugé," 305
"Reel de joie," 173, 305
regionalism, 263, 321
respectability: and cowboy figure, 212; and music taste, 211–12; values, 212–15, 223–24
rhythm and blues, 86, 161
Richard, Belton, 122, 125, 255
Richard, Zachary, 94–95, 242, 259
Richard's (Lawtell), 188, 206
Rideau, Step, 130, 221, 223
Riley, Steve, 243
Rinzler, Ralph, 55, 82, 112, 160, 267
River Oaks Club (Abbeville), 53
Robichaux, John, 50
Rockin' Sidney Simien, 193
Rodgers, Jimmie, 59, 280
Roger, Aldus, 115, 255
Romero, Roddie, 133
roots music, 96, 131–33, 143, 144–46, 274, 288, 306, 313

Royal Theater, 38
rural aesthetics, 103, 105–7, 208–9
rural heritage, 33, 203, 216, 225–26
rural imagery, 205, 209
Russell, William, 45

"Saint Martin, A," 254
"Sally," 40
San Diego Cajun Playboys, 229
Sandmel, Ben, 14, 57, 92, 97, 124, 161, 220, 228
Savoy, Ann, 88, 175, 238, 244, 269, 273–74
Savoy, Joel, 96, 132, 236, 313
Savoy, Marc, 95, 109
Savoy, Wilson, 113, 121, 148, 176, 227
saxophone, 5, 41, 64, 66, 100, 113, 187, 257
Schwartz, Tracy, 6, 83, 174, 247, 311
Sean Ardoin + R.O.G.K., 218
Segregation: of music, 149–50, 155, 157; of music clubs, 187–88; racial, 8, 15, 153, 165
sexuality: perception of, 193, 194; risqué songs, 122, 194, 198; sexual themes, 191, 193, 196, 198, 229
"Shine On Harvest Moon," 41
"Shoo, Black," 56
Should Have Known, 118
Simien, Terrence, 101, 129, 276
Slim's Y-Ki-Ki (Lawtell), 188
Smith, Bessie, 6, 56
Smith, Charles E., 45
Smithsonian Institution, 247, 319
Soileau, Leo, 55, 57–59, 170
Sonnier, Austin, 35, 67, 162
Soul Rebels Brass Band, 98, 217
Southern Folk Revival Project (Atlanta), 84
Spires, Will, 269
Spitzer, Nick, 14, 26, 117, 157–58, 215, 218
Stafford, Chris, 4, 113, 118
Steve Riley and the Mamou Playboys, 100, 113, 115–16, 119, 181, 260, 275–76
"Stronger," 217

Sud du Sud, 132
"Sugar Pie, Honey Bunch," 116
survivor, 10–11, 186, 261
swamp pop, 36, 61, 87, 91–92, 158, 192
"Sweet Soul Music," 116

tambourine, 4
taste: and dancers, 100–102; music, 20–21, 62, 103–7, 150, 211, 212, 307; shift from Cajun to zydeco, 309–10; shift from dance to music, 304–9
Taylor, Curley, 194
teaching methods: band lab, 246; codification, 250, 297–99; formal education, 64, 205; fun, 34, 104, 249–51, 298; group lessons, 243; imitation, 161, 247–49; immersion, 103, 114, 132, 243, 298, 308; individual lessons, 246, 307; jam, 142, 239–46; records, 247, 249; storytelling, 244; videos, 33, 108, 111–12, 174, 228, 248–49, 295–96
Teche Club (New Iberia), 53
technique (musical): animal imitation, 228–29; bowing, 113, 169, 175, 232, 249; choppiness, 168, 170; crookedness, 168, 229–32, 310; dissonance, 228, 310; harshness, 227–28; key modulations, 233; limitations, 162, 234; Nashville number system, 235; as simple, 33, 204, 227, 231; smoothness, 55, 91, 93, 99, 113, 168–69, 171, 250, 297; tuning, 112–13, 172, 184, 234
Terry, Al, 40, 61
Terry, Brian, 128, 130, 224–25
"Tes Parents Ne Veulent Plus Me Voir," 174
Texas: in early 20th century musical landscape, 45, 58; and zydeco, 219–21, 224–26
Thats Da Lick, 194
Thibodeaux, Rufus, 91
Thierry, Huey "Cookie," 192
"This Should Go On Forever," 192
Thomas, Evan, 46, 63

Thompson, Suzy, 6, 269
'tit fer (triangle), 51, 101, 127, 265, 306
tourism, 82, 135–37, 141, 154–55, 164, 188, 262, 271, 277, 286, 314
tradition: as creative, 16, 77, 126–27, 145; and instrument, 112; and legitimacy, 78; and lineage, 125, 128; and music style, 77, 83, 85, 128, 177; notion, 33, 146; as pure, 79, 89, 148, 225; vs. commercial, 84. *See also* authenticity
Traditionally Untraditional, 128
Trahan, Horace, 5, 115, 147–48, 178, 193–94, 198
Transplant: and adaptation, 278, 287; circle of, 278, 287, 289, 306; as dancers, 299, 302, 309; as former fans, 303; as musicians, 270, 289–91, 293, 302, 304–7; as permanent resident, 295; and personal development, 287–88; and power struggle, 299, 306; and reconfiguration of French Louisiana music, 267, 314; and roots music, 288, 306, 311; and status, 288, 299, 302, 304, 306–7, 309, 314–15. *See also* connectedness; networks
Treasury of Field Recordings, A, 220
Treme Brass Band, 98
trombone, 51, 79
trumpet, 32, 46–47, 62, 66
"Two-step de Bouki," 4
"Two-step de Grand Marais," 254
"Two-step de Ville Platte," 254

"Under the Double Eagle," 41
Undisputed, 128
Ungar, Jay, 312–13
urban culture: blacks in, 34, 199, 215, 219, 226, 261; centers in Texas, 219–21; music style, 90, 123, 128; negative stereotype, 215–16

"Valse à Reno," 254
"Valse Criminelle, The," 182
"Valse de Balfa," 181, 183

"Veuves de la Coulee," 58
"Vibrator," 96, 195
Victor's Orchestra, 39
Vidrine, Randy, 110
"Ville Platte Two Step," 174
vulnerability, 262–63, 288, 321

Walker, Lawrence, 256
"Waltz That Carried Me to My Grave, The," 55
"Washington and Lee," 40
Watson, Cedric, 4, 120, 176–77, 207–8, 218–19
Wayne Toups and Zydecajun, 126
"Went Out Last Night," 123
western swing, 55, 57–58, 73, 91, 110, 151, 170
"Westphalia Waltz, The," 41
"What's His Name," 116
"Where Is My Sweetie Hiding," 40
Whirlybird, 143, 291–92, 311
Whiskey River Landing (Henderson), 105–6, 203, 206, 212, 294
White Eagle Club, 62
white music, 159, 177, 185, 211
whiteness: and Creoles, 215; and respectability, 214–15; white ethnics, 215
Williams, Clarence, 40
Williams, Dennis Paul, 164, 204
Wills, Bob, 55, 59, 185
Wimmer, Kevin, 170–73, 233
Worldwide, 225

"Y en a des 'Tites Brunes," 5
"Yesterday," 123
"You Belong to Me," 58
Young, Linzay, 5, 110, 236, 259, 313

Z-Funk, 225
"Zolo Go," 220
Zydeco: as black dance, 156, 191, 197, 201; as black music, 199–200, 204; club, 98, 130–31, 144, 187–89, 191, 206, 213, 251, 286; commercial recordings, 220, 268; as dance music, 309; as music category, 13–14, 220; "new," 34, 98, 148, 176, 199, 215, 217–18, 224; stigmatization, 167, 204, 218; success across Louisiana, 197; trail rides, 221–23
"Zydeco Hee-Haw," 229
Zydeco Kingpins, 122
"Zydeco Obama," 292

www.ingramcontent.com/pod-product-compliance
Lightning Source LLC
Chambersburg PA
CBHW052042220426
43663CB00012B/2414